Treason and Rebellion in the British Atlantic, 1685–1800

Treason and Rebellion in the British Atlantic, 1685–1800

Legal Responses to Threatening the State

Peter Rushton and Gwenda Morgan

BLOOMSBURY ACADEMIC
LONDON • NEW YORK • OXFORD • NEW DELHI • SYDNEY

BLOOMSBURY ACADEMIC
Bloomsbury Publishing Plc
50 Bedford Square, London, WC1B 3DP, UK
1385 Broadway, New York, NY 10018, USA
29 Earlsfort Terrace, Dublin 2, Ireland

BLOOMSBURY, BLOOMSBURY ACADEMIC and the Diana logo
are trademarks of Bloomsbury Publishing Plc

First published in Great Britain 2020
This paperback edition published in 2022

Copyright © Peter Rushton and Gwenda Morgan, 2020

Peter Rushton and Gwenda Morgan have asserted his right under the Copyright,
Designs and Patents Act, 1988, to be identified as Author of this work.

For legal purposes the Acknowledgements on p. viii constitute
an extension of this copyright page.

Cover design: Terry Woodley
Cover image: Detail from The Lord Russels Farewel
who was Beheaded for High Treason, in Lincoln Inn Fields, 1683
(Reproduced by permission of the National Library of Scotland)

All rights reserved. No part of this publication may be reproduced or transmitted
in any form or by any means, electronic or mechanical, including photocopying,
recording, or any information storage or retrieval system, without
prior permission in writing from the publishers.

Bloomsbury Publishing Plc does not have any control over, or responsibility for,
any third-party websites referred to or in this book. All internet addresses given
in this book were correct at the time of going to press. The author and publisher
regret any inconvenience caused if addresses have changed or sites have
ceased to exist, but can accept no responsibility for any such changes.

Every effort has been made to trace copyright holders and to obtain their permissions
for the use of copyright material. The publisher apologizes for any errors or omissions
and would be grateful if notified of any corrections that should be incorporated
in future reprints or editions of this book.

A catalogue record for this book is available from the British Library.

A catalogue record for this book is available from the Library of Congress.

Library of Congress Cataloging-in-Publication Data

Names: Rushton, Peter, author. | Morgan, Gwenda, author.
Title: Treason and rebellion in the British Atlantic, 1685–1800: legal
responses to threatening the state/Peter Rushton and Gwenda Morgan.
Description: London; New York: Bloomsbury Academic, 2020. |
Includes bibliographical references and index. | Identifiers: LCCN 2020009669 (print) |
LCCN 2020009670 (ebook) | ISBN 9781350005310 (hardback) | ISBN 9781350005303 (ebook) |
ISBN 9781350005327 (epub)
Subjects: LCSH: Political crimes and offenses–Great Britain–History–18th century. |
Political crimes and offenses–Great Britain–Colonies–History–18th century. | Political crimes and
offenses–North America–History–18th century. | Political crimes and offenses–West Indies,
British–History–18th century. | Great Britain–Colonies–America–History–18th century.
Classification: LCC KD8020.R87 2020 (print) | LCC KD8020 (ebook) | DDC 345.41/023109033–dc23
LC record available at https://lccn.loc.gov/2020009669
LC ebook record available at https://lccn.loc.gov/2020009670

ISBN: HB: 978-1-3500-0531-0
PB: 978-1-3501-9282-9
ePDF: 978-1-3500-0530-3
eBook: 978-1-3500-0532-7

Typeset by Integra Software Services Pvt. Ltd.

To find out more about our authors and books visit www.bloomsbury.com
and sign up for our newsletters.

Contents

Preface   vi
Acknowledgements   viii

Part 1   Law, Empire and Treason

1   Treason, Rebellion and the Rule of Law   3
2   British Laws, Colonial Laws   19

Part 2   Rebellion to Revolution

3   Speaking Words, Writing Sedition   47
4   Domestic Rebellions: From Sedgemoor to Culloden   91
5   Before the American Revolution – The Crisis in Imperial Law: Arson, Treason and Plot   125
6   War, Kidnapped Americans and Treason   149
7   Loyalism and Patriotism   175
8   After the Revolutions: Sedition, 'Revolution', Rebellion and Slavery   199

References   220
Index   246

Preface

This book represents the culmination of many years of archival and library digging, and puzzling over the relationship between the political structure and the legal processes in the early modern British state. We began with mundane crimes in one region, northeast England, even though some, like forging coins or attacking the local militia records, were defined as forms of treason. These crimes led many British criminals to the colonies, where their labour was in high demand, and naturally we built on this work to examine the colonies' ambivalent reactions to their presence among their populations. The study of criminal transportation naturally led to the study of other methods of banishment to the colonies, encompassing ethnic minorities and the poor, religious dissidents and political rebels. We also developed an interest in the ethnic cleansing that occurred under British rule, from Catholic Irish to Acadians to maroons. These were regarded as treacherous peoples. It was by this route we arrived at treason and sedition as focuses, in effect a mixture of deeds and words: these were both seen as 'threatening the state', the subtitle of this book. While some of the topics of this book have been touched on elsewhere, particularly in our book *Banishment in the Early Atlantic World: Convicts, Rebels and Slaves* (London: Bloomsbury, 2013), we have returned to them here with a different agenda.

We speedily discovered that we needed to range into the realm of contemporary ideas, as well as more modern theories, of the state and sovereignty, or war and the rules of war, of loyalty, legitimacy and law. These were all dilemmas as treason, violent conflict and rebellion pervaded the early modern British Empire. A brief word is required, then, as to our general approach. We have generally avoided the list of well-known individual cases, unless a particular example illustrates the method of operation of a regime, domestic or colonial, at a particular time. It may be that one case provides all we need to know about the prosecution of this most political crime. We have tended by contrast to concentrate on the big batches of prosecutions, or attempted prosecutions, where they have coincided with genuine threats to the British state – Jacobites, revolutionary Americans, colonial rebels from the Caribbean in the 1790s and those who rejected and threatened the new United States before and during the War for Independence. We have also explored the limits to freedom evinced by the record of *unfree* speech in both Britain and the colonies, particularly in revolutionary times. Speech as an indication of dangerous disaffection remains at the heart of our anti-terrorist laws, though, and, as developed in the eighteenth-century concern over an uncontrolled print culture, we are more concerned today about such words being published and available to the susceptible, than about everyday exchanges between individuals. That personal side – defamation in the early modern period, hate speech today – has always been a focus of local if not national anxiety, and mechanisms are continually being invented to deal with what is generally regarded as a little local difficulty. In terms of people's determination to sustain their identities and their reputations, however, these verbal attacks have always had immense personal, if not political, significance.

We have tried to keep sufficient background context in each of our major case studies to provide framework for the cases we have taken, but our focus is on the legal procedures, strategies and limitations of the law in practice, rather than the legal doctrines or theoretical frameworks. Many of these limitations were practical, in that the law of treason had much stricter rules as to witnesses, for example, than did laws about ordinary crimes. Other difficulties were essentially political: in an age when appeals against death sentences were to politicians as individuals or committees, there were always doubts about how much severity could be *publicly* justified. The state was not a machine but an adaptive process, and mercy as much as severity was part of the role of those who made it up, as Douglas Hay suggested many years ago. Because treason was often seen as precursor to something worse, the authorities were always anxious. Yet the nature of that 'something worse' over the period had taken here, because the threat changed from *rebellion* to *revolution*. If the British state understood rebellion, to some extent, revolution posed a threat to entire political and social systems, from private property to slavery (which were the same thing in many cases). This became an ideological war as much as one for control in the years after the French Revolution.

Acknowledgements

As always, we have incurred many debts in the process of what turned out to be a much longer project than we had intended. Naturally, the superb service of the National Archives and the British Library and the supporting facilities of the Institute of Historical Research have been at the core of our work. The British Academy Small Grant Scheme helped us in the early phase of our work up to 2008, and this enabled us to make significant progress in exploring the resources of the United States. So, we also must thank, for their hospitality and helpfulness, the Massachusetts Historical Society, the Massachusetts State Archives, the Library Company of Philadelphia, the South Carolina Historical Society, the Charleston Library Society, the Omohundro Institute for Early American History and Culture (OIEAHC) and the Earl Gregg Swem Library of the College of William and Mary in Williamsburg. In the north of England, our neighbouring libraries of the University of Durham, and the University of Newcastle, provided service, resources and access which were much appreciated. The county record offices of County Durham Northumberland and Tyne Wear Archive Services have also been invaluable. Finally, our own library of the University of Sunderland deserves our thanks.

We have given papers, which have led to this book, on various aspects of this project, at the OIEAHC conference in Halifax 2014, at a couple of the biannual conferences of the European Society for Social-Science History, in Ghent and Valencia, and other specialist gatherings such as the British group for Early American History. Our thanks to commentators we have met, notably Krista Kesselring, Matthew Ward, Simon Newman, Tom Rogers. Peter would particularly like to thank the late Chris Brooks (Professor of Legal History, Durham University) for his helpful advice.

Chapter 5 is based on our article 'Arson, Treason and Plot: Britain, America and the Law, 1770–1777', *History*, 100 (341) (2015), 374–91, and is drawn upon here with the kind permission of the editor, Dr Becky Taylor, and John Wiley, with thanks.

Finally, our thanks to our anonymous reader for their sympathetic review, highlighting some of the significant omissions, and to the Bloomsbury Academic team for their support, particularly Maddie Holder and Abigail Lane.

Part One

Law, Empire and Treason

1

Treason, Rebellion and the Rule of Law

This is a study of treason and rebellion in the British Atlantic, an area which consisted of a diverse collection of jurisdictions and territories, different kinds of societies and political systems, with each unit posing difficulties of consistency in law and administration. Moreover, the territory under British control was continually expanding, often rather haphazardly, a process that repeatedly produced difficulties in relations between natives and European settlers. With British authority, it might be thought, went a single body of law and administrative policies: but, as Lauren Benton has pointed out, something as apparently simple as a law of treason, which focussed on actions of disloyalty and threats to the state, proved impossible to render consistently in so many different contexts. Geographic expansion undermined every such attempt at imperial standardization in many European empires, but particularly that of the British. Treason 'far from kings' proved an adaptable but slightly unpredictable strategy for authorities in far-flung colonies.[1] In this study we attempt to focus on the deployment of law in times of rebellion, ranging from the 'home' countries of England and Scotland to the colonies, each with their own legislative bodies and often unique configurations of classes and structures of domination. Nevertheless, there was a somewhat makeshift common framework of law, some aspects of it much clearer than others. On the one hand there were the rules of war: on the other, the rule of law. Of the two, the laws passed by individual states usually had the benefit of being clear and detailed. The laws of war, by contrast, were only gradually being developed in the seventeenth and eighteenth centuries, more as a collection of agreed procedures adopted if possible by European armies in conflicts with one another. They were more like a gentlemen's agreement than a strict code, and

---

[1] L. Benton, *A Search for Sovereignty: Law and Geography in European Empires, 1400–1900* (Cambridge University Press, 2002), pp. 4 and 59.

entirely without any procedures of enforcement. Laws of treason, on the other hand, had a long history in each state. In civil wars and rebellions, both were in danger of becoming blurred. Britain experienced at least five civil wars between 1642 and 1800 – in Britain and Ireland in the 1640s and 1650s; in Scotland and Ireland in 1688–90; in Scotland and England in 1715–16, and again in 1745–6; and in North America in 1776–83. If the Irish rising of 1798 is included, war and rebellion, and various forms of treasonable actions against the British State, were almost an accustomed experience of rule in the first empire. As Barbara Donegan has shown, the civil wars of the 1640s and 1650s were only to some extent governed by the rudimentary laws of war. The rivals viewed each other with hostility, and proclaimed very different loyalties, to King or Parliament. For the Royalists, opponents of the king were generally regarded, but rarely prosecuted, as traitors. Parliamentarians inflicted civil and economic penalties on Royalists, attacking their estates and other economic assets, but little more. With prisoners on both sides, paroles of various kinds in force and exchanges continually being agreed, the protagonists generally conducted the war as though it was between foreign powers. There were terrible exceptions, and the record in the 'age of atrocity' is poor in both Britain and Ireland – most famously, the massacre by Cromwell at the end of the siege of Drogheda in 1649. Yet in the subsequent 100 years both the laws of war and treason were refined and clarified, the latter in both legislation and practice. The beginning of Britain's sequence of wars, initially against the Dutch and then against the French, entrenched a gentlemanly common culture of courtesy and agreement in the matter of prisoners, paroles and exchanges. The law of treason, however, was radically reformed by the two parliamentary acts enshrining rights in statute law for the first time: Habeas Corpus in 1679 and the Treason Act of 1696. While, as we shall see, there were doubts about whether these operated in the colonies, they shaped the policies of the colonial authorities and the assertiveness of those they ruled. This book is therefore concerned with those incidents where rebellion and treason law converged, rather than with rebellions as such. In many ways, the question arises as to why the British state characteristically resorted to legal strategies at all. Rebels had few rights in any political philosophy of the time, and in other empires, such as that of the Turks (the Ottoman Empire), or the ancient Roman Empire, rebels were annihilated militarily and their noncombatant dependants enslaved. Going to court would not have occurred to the rulers of such imperial states. The legal details will be examined in the next chapter, but the characteristic of the British Empire at least was that it was defined by its ruling circles, as an empire of law.

Early modern kingdoms in Europe were riven by divisions, and continually threatened by plots and rebellions. The law of treason figured largely in the murderous political plotting of the royal courts such as that of England in the sixteenth century, but it was also a means of handling the many protests, uprisings and rebellions that the early modern states were prone to. As religious turmoil was often accompanied by dynastic squabbles, and many riotous protests by ordinary people were directed at defending their traditional rights, customs and institutions, there were plenty of opportunities for the state to refine the application of different kinds of law for suppressing disorder. Among the weapons available to the state authorities was the law of treason. Treason as a crime was defined and redefined in many ways in the period between the civil wars and the nineteenth century, but the core was a carefully framed law, the 35 Edward III c. 2 (1352), which was seen by later commentators as a limitation on arbitrary prosecution: its introductory paragraph pointed to the 'divers opinions' that had existed up to that point as to the definition of treason. This is not the place to reiterate the lengthy history of this law, but it is worth noticing that the parallel development of crimes of sedition and seditious words provided an alternative to the potentially deadly charge of treason. In fact, some historians such as Holdsworth point to the development of broader and more all-catching definitions in the eighteenth century, not least of what constituted the 'state': 'we can see the growth of offences cognate to treason' but these were essentially minor or lesser than treason itself. The key to this undergrowth was seditious libel, in spoken or written words, which were deemed to presage or induce a threat to the state. The retention of the complete opposite to sedition, namely oaths of loyalty, was therefore widespread throughout the British world, and among the movements opposing British rule. Loyalty was in some ways *performed* in this period, in the same way that intention and action were generally required for someone to be seen to be treacherous. One theme of this study will therefore be the analysis of *words*, particularly when spoken in public, and how they were judged to be safe or dangerous. Blackstone was cautious in this regard, saying that words spoken in heat, or written in private, could hardly be defined as treasonable, but if the writing was published, that would be another matter. It may be significant (see Chapter 3) that prosecutions for sedition increasingly concentrated on published writings – and their publishers – after the seventeenth century, which by contrast had chosen spoken words to prosecute. It was widely recognized that the definition of treason needed constraint, or, as Blackstone put it, drawing upon the ideas of Montesquieu, 'if the crime of high treason be indeterminate, this alone ... is sufficient to make any government degenerate into arbitrary power'. Thus legislation was needed to limit the latitude given to judges to decide on the crime, or judges would invent treason where none had existed before – what came to be called 'constructive treasons', something that returned to dominate much of the legal debates of the 1790s when gatherings of radicals were interpreted as being an attempt to usurp Parliament with a French-style National Assembly, and were treason because they implied the destruction of the existing government system and the death of the king.[2]

In the fourteenth century, treason was defined as an attempt or plan ('compassing' or 'imagining') to kill the monarch, his spouse, heir or senior ministers including judges of the assizes, adhering to the king's enemies, making war on the king and counterfeiting the coinage. Thus protection was offered to the king and the key ministers of the state, and by implication, members of parliament. Less certain was whether local magistrates were included, though they in some places had powers similar to those of assize judges. Whereas planning the deaths was sufficient proof of treason, far more was needed to prove treason by levying war: later commentators such as Edward Coke thought that just planning to levy war (i.e. conspiracy) was not treason. Similarly, aiding the king's enemies when in rebellion at home was treason, thought Blackstone, but helping or giving relief to a rebel 'fled out of the kingdom' was not, because they were not at that point in actual rebellion.[3] Attempts to extend these concepts under Henry VIII were repealed by subsequent regimes, and the broader ideas of 'constructive treason' were concentrated on what 'levying war' on the king might mean. Words, written or spoken, could be proof of intending treason, though most legal theorists were uncertain whether a follow-up action was needed. The cases that stood as a ringing injustice, memorialized as creating martyrs of Lord William Russell and particularly that of Algernon Sidney in 1683, in part hinged on the revelation of unpublished papers. This explains in part Blackstone's insistence on *publication* of the words as a proof of a treasonable intention.[4] The

---

[2] W. Blackstone, *Commentaries on the Laws of England*, 4 vols (Oxford: Clarendon Press, 1770), vol. 4, p. 75. For constructive treason, imagining: John Barrell, *Imagining the King's Death: Figurative Treason, Fantasies of Regicide, 1993–1796* (Oxford University Press, 2000).

[3] Blackstone, *Commentaries*, vol. 4, p. 83 on the difference between enemies and rebels.

[4] Lisa Steffen, *Defining a British State: Treason and National Identity, 1608–1820* (Houndmills, Basingstoke: Palgrave Macmillan, 2001), pp. 11–13, 17; W. Holdsworth, *A History of English Law* (London: Methuen), 16 vols, vol. 8, p. 322; Blackstone, *Commentaries*, vol. 4, pp. 80–1 on treasonable words.

aftermath of the Glorious Revolution was a political regime that sought to make a self-conscious break with the abuses, as they were seen, of James II's reign, and the new direction was embodied in the 1696 Treason Act. This enshrined in law the rights of defendants to counsel, knowledge of the charges, the names of the juries and certain safeguards such as an expiry date after which prosecutions could not be brought. Because Sidney had been prosecuted for private writings from years before, the new law insisted on prosecutions being brought within three years of the alleged treasonable action. The Act of Union of 1707 allowed the Scots to keep all their existing legislation – except the treason law, which was replaced by the 1696 Act, though where the trials could be held was left to later legislation during the Jacobite risings (see Chapter 4).[5]

The law of treason was therefore always to some extent in continual evolution in the early modern period rather than existing as a completely fixed set of legal concepts and practices: while its general definition remained unaltered in English law, and where adopted in the colonies, derived from that of Edward III, the 1696 Act was designed, as the preamble said, to 'regulate' the conduct of treason trials. In the dilemmas of governments after 1688 in facing revolts and rebellions, however, some very old solutions were occasionally deployed with a much broader sense of what a legitimate government might do. Some strategies involved martial law in specified areas of disorder, since this permitted the use of a proclamation demanding a return to order and the use of extreme military force to achieve it. This was, at best, summary justice through courts martial, though the formalities were rarely gone through in the face of popular insurgencies.[6] The practice was exported to the colonies, and one study notes that it was in Bacon's Rebellion in Virginia in 1676–7 that the largest number of civilians under English laws was tried and executed by martial law before the 1685 Monmouth Rebellion in the west of England, exceeding most recorded examples from England before that.[7] This example suggests that martial law was a way of avoiding the difficulties of the common law when it might fail to achieve the desired political ends. Martial law on the British side was often the first resort of the authorities in the face of colonial resistance in the eighteenth century – Lord Dunmore, for example, declared martial law in Virginia in response to Patrick Henry's famous speech. Thomas Gage in

---

[5] P.D. Halliday, *Habeas Corpus: From England to Empire* (Cambridge, MA: The Belknap Press of Harvard University Press, 2010); Steffen, *Defining a British State*, p. 57.
[6] John M. Collins, *Martial Law and English Laws, c. 1500–1700* (Cambridge University Press, 2017).
[7] Collins, *Martial Law,* p. 220.

Massachusetts also adopted it, as Boston was placed under military occupation, 'as if an enemy country'. In repeated proclamations, governors or military commanders used threats based on martial law. The rules of disorder inside Britain, in areas prone to industrial disputes, riots or food protests, were also subject to military intervention, albeit as an aid to the civil powers, and at their request.[8] On the other side, coercion and force were deployed against loyalist Americans: rules of exclusion and compulsory oaths of loyalty were imposed by the newly constituted state legislatures, as colonies declared themselves states in the American Revolution. The use of martial law or, indeed, any kind of force without formal judicial processes, reflected a crisis in political power, and a failure of legitimate procedures (see Chapter 7).

An even more directly political process was for the legislature to pass an act of attainder: this, by law, named and condemned people for their treasonable actions, and ordered their arrest and punishment. No further consideration of the evidence was required, as the only question that arose was whether those arrested were in fact those named in the act. The only defence was to challenge that identification, and bring evidence that they were in fact someone else entirely. This procedure was unusual after the Glorious Revolution, though it did occur in the colonies, and in Virginia after the Declaration of Independence. To be 'attainted' involved many subsequent disabilities, particularly confiscation of property.[9] An explicitly political strategy, it reduced the proceedings against alleged traitors to a personal attack. In other types of offence, too, the legislature could act as prosecutor and judge in its own case. Publisher and printer William Owen was prosecuted by Attorney-General Dudley Ryder in 1752 for publishing a critique of both electoral and parliamentary procedure. The action which provoked the pamphlet attack arose when an unsuccessful candidate in an election criticized the electoral procedure adopted. Parliament judged this to be seditious – speaking against the government and its system such as to bring it under threat – and ordered the man to be summoned to the bar of the House of Commons, where he was sentenced to a large fine and imprisonment. Owen's printing of an account of this was deemed to be seditious libel also, and his

---

[8] Patrick Henry, *American Revolution: Primary Sources*, ed. Linda Schmittorth, Lawrence W. Baker and Stacy A. Maconnell (Detroit, MI: Gale, 2000), p. 216; R. Archer, *As If an Enemy Country: The British Occupation of Boston and the Origins of Revolution* (New York: Oxford University Press, 2010).
[9] Steffen, *Defining a British State*, pp. 53 and 59; Blackstone, *Commentaries*, vol. I, p. 165 and, Ch. XV; Raoul Berger, 'Bills of Attainder: A Study of Amendment by the Court', *Cornell University Law Review*, 63 (3) (1978), pp. 355–404.

acquittal caused Ryder extreme annoyance when the jury seemed to acquit in the face of the evidence. This 'jury nullification', as legal historians have called it, that is, acquittal despite the overwhelming evidence of guilt, remained a sore point with the prosecuting officials in sedition cases. The parliamentary intervention was, like attainder, an unusual process, but the powers of political bodies acting as legislatures in the British system remained strong and were exercised now and then in the eighteenth century when parliament felt it had been insulted (see Chapter 3).[10]

Treason as a judicial process, by contrast, was in many ways the opposite of martial law or procedures of attainder: subject to repeated efforts at definition and clarification, the law and, increasingly, the process of prosecution and trial were constrained in more and more specific ways that paradoxically recognized the essentially political character of its construction and the dangers of allowing prosecutions to be politically inspired and managed. What was later described in America as 'due process', in effect the rights of defendants to a fair trial with legal representation, was created most explicitly by treason law in the late seventeenth century, and was one of the great achievements of the reforming legislation after the Glorious Revolution of 1688.[11] The rise of explicit rights with the Treason Act of 1696 did not clarify, though, what to do in the face of large-scale risings and rebellion. It is probable that in the minds of legislators and law enforcers, the authorities, the two actions of treason and rebellion are related and, indeed, identical. Yet the problem is immediately posed by those rebellions which reject the legitimacy of the entire political system. Whereas treason might be defined as actions against the current ruler or regime, but not against the system, a rebellion by a national or ethnic group against the forces and systems that rule them has the implication of the overthrow of the entire system. Thus, when it was suggested by Lord Hailsham (Quintin Hogg, then Lord Chancellor in charge of the English and Welsh legal system) in the 1970s that the British state prosecute the members of the Provisional Irish Republican Army in Northern Ireland for treason under the 1352 Treason Act, the absurdity of accusing them of betraying a state they did not wish to be part of became immediately apparent. The then prime minister, Edward Heath, ignored the suggestion, which Hailsham repeatedly discussed in press conferences in the 1974 election, and in later debates in the House of

---

[10] T.H. Green, *Verdict According to Conscience: Perspectives on the English Trial Jury* (Chicago: University of Chicago Press, 1985), pp. 323–4.
[11] J.H. Langbein, *The Origins of the Adversary Criminal Trial* (Oxford: Oxford University Press, 2003); Halliday, *Habeas Corpus*.

Lords. One inventive idea came from Lord Ruthven of Freeland, in debate on 12 December 1974: 'I wonder whether, if the IRA regard themselves as an army, why they could not be tried by court-martial and shot? It is perfectly normal to do that in war, and these people are at war with us.'[12] A parallel can be found in slave risings from the seventeenth to the nineteenth centuries aimed at the overthrow of the slave system: yet slaves were usually never treated as traitors, because this would imply that they were citizens or subjects with rights to be guarded by the state to which they owed loyalty. Such a loyalty would override the ownership of the slaves by their masters. Only the free people involved in slave revolts might be prosecuted as traitors, as happened during Fédon's rising in Grenada in 1795–6 (see Chapter 8). [13] Thus, a war of national liberation (as we might call it today) might be seen as less treacherous than an internal insurgency aimed at overthrow and replacement of a particular regime.

Throughout the period the ideas about loyalty and the state, and the relationship of the state to the individual, were undergoing major transformations. The concept of divine authority was being replaced with more contractual models of the relationship between ruled and rulers. The origins of that authority were removed from divine origin and placed more firmly in a secular origin of natural law. Thus, the constitution of a state and its rights to command the loyalty of those within its borders were rendered highly problematic. The key concept was sovereignty, and Emer de Vattel is often credited with the shift in the debate to place that notion in the hands of political theorists of the Enlightenment. Vattel supposed that matters of war, and its justification, depended on the judgements of a sovereign state, and it was through these moral decisions, based on natural law, that the classifications of enemies, traitors and rebels were rightly created. Carl Schmitt naturally regarded this as an important shift in Western thinking, but neither he nor Vattel's contemporaries were clear about the definition of that sovereign state whose authority had to be acknowledged. As Lisa Steffen has remarked, though, 'if defining sovereignty is what preoccupies historians, defining allegiance was what concerned contemporaries'. The 'what' that loyalty was to, was less important than the allegiance to principled forms or units. The

---

[12] Reported in *The Guardian*, 15 January 2003: he felt that IRA members could be legitimately shot because they were guilty of treason; *The Guardian*, 19 October 2014. House of Lords Debate, 11 December 1984, vol. 458, cc120-2, for Lord Denning's assertion of the applicability of the 1352 Act. David Butler and Dennis Kavanagh, *The British Election of October, 1974* (Houndmills, Basingstoke: Palgrave Macmillan, 1975), p. 133. Lord Ruthven, 'These Terrorists Are Certainly Treasonable to Her Majesty the Queen, So Why Could Not We Try Them, by Court-Martial and Have Them Shot by a Firing Squad? That Is My Only Suggestion' (HoL, vol. 355, col. 855).

[13] See Fédon rebellion bill of attainder list discussed in Chapter 8.

crown, the republic, all were vaguely defined at any time, but allegiance was not.[14] A collection significantly called *Justifying Revolution* is an important exploration of this aspect of eighteenth-century thinking in the context of the American Revolution. In the potential chaos of the revolutionary process, new forms of sovereignty – rather, new sovereign units – were created and their authority proclaimed. In some legal proceedings, notably in Pennsylvania, there was serious debate about the precise dates of this creation, since, it was argued, only when such authority was properly established could it demand loyalty from those under it. This came up for decision in the prosecutions for treason supervised by Thomas McKean where he was concerned that the actions of the accused might have been committed when the state of Pennsylvania had been neither a properly instituted legislature nor had the appropriate legislation. Though his reputation among loyalists was low – they feared being 'McKeaned', this showed unusual legal nicety in dealing with alleged enemies of the new United States.[15]

Eliga Gould conceives of the Atlantic world of the British Empire as consisting of 'zones of violence', where rules were few, and consideration of these legal niceties was rare. Such places – and peoples – might define themselves as outside the rules of war, Vattel's *nation féroce*, who did not follow these rules and thus deserved not to have them applied to themselves, or the territories were deemed lawless in every way. In the face of rebellious peoples, whether at home or abroad, the British state did develop forms of legal justification for violence in these zones. For example, in the face of rioters, the 1715 Riot Act created a procedure of intimidation in which the Act was read in the face of a public assembly which had then an hour to disperse before force could be legally used. In the same way, the use of royal proclamations and, in the eighteenth century, those of his agents in the colonies, declared that oaths of loyalty were required and, moreover, those who were subsequently found in arms would be deemed rebels and traitors. This was adopted most clearly in the Jacobite rebellion of 1745–6, and later in the American colonies during the War of Independence.[16]

---

[14] Lisa Steffen, *Defining the British State: Treason and National Identity, 1608–1820* (Macmillan, 2001), p. 18; Emer de Vattel, *Le Droit des Gens*, 1757, the English edition published in 1759; Carl Schmitt, Tracy B. Strong and Georg Schwab, eds, *Political Theology: Four Chapters on the Concept of Sovereignty* (University of Chicago Press, 2006); see David Dyzenhaus, 'Schmitt V. Dicey: Are States of Emergency inside or outside the Legal Order?', *Cardozo Law Review*, 27 (5) (2008), pp. 2006–40.

[15] Glenn A. Moots and Phillip Hamilton, eds, *Justifying Revolution: Law, Virtue, and Violence in the American War of Independence* (Political Violence in North America) (Norman, Oklahoma: University of Oklahoma Press, 2018); see Ch. 7 on McKean and the Pennsylvania trials.

[16] Eliga H. Gould, 'Zones of Law, Zones of Violence: The Legal Geography of the British Atlantic, circa 1772', *The William and Mary Quarterly*, 60 (3) (July, 2003), pp. 471–510.

Rebellions always provoked a military reaction, but, while war broke out, it was never officially declared, as it might have been through the diplomatic niceties with another sovereign state, rebellions constituting an internal matter. Thus, in the midst of rebellions that produced prolonged military conflict, it was inevitable that the laws of treason and the conventional rules of war overlapped and, at times, contradicted each other in the face of organized warfare. Emer de Vattel, the most influential mid-eighteenth-century theorist of the 'laws of nations' (*Le Droit des Gens*, 1757, the English edition published in 1759), argued that rebels had, in theory, no rights to be treated properly, as they had forfeited all such rights on instigating the rebellion. Yet, he also reasoned, it behoved states to behave with humanity towards such opponents, in effect treating them as an honourable enemy, as they too understood the rules of proper treatment. In this way, the state established its credentials as a civilized and principled authority, and rebels might be persuaded of its legitimacy. Only peoples with no understanding of the concept of proper treatment, *les nations féroces* (not savages since the French word *sauvage* signifies just a primitive state, but *féroce* indicated one without morality), were undeserving of such treatment, a principle that white settlers fully embraced in many different colonial contexts. These ideas – not entirely originated, but certainly made famous by Vattel – were well known throughout Europe and among the educated in the American colonies. Indeed, George Washington and others took an interest in this framework which defined both the sovereignty of the state and the manner in which it should conduct itself in peace and war with other states. It seems that Benjamin Franklin was a key figure in acquiring copies of Vattel's works in 1775 for the Philadelphia Library. His work became important as the newly independent states discussed the ratification of the 1787 constitution.[17]

The basic principle of civilized warfare was first and above all, that enemy troops had to be well treated once they had surrendered and been captured. A second principle was also one of care, more broadly for civilians who had passed into military control and had become their responsibility. If a local population was in effect both rebellious and supporting an armed opposition force, their mode of treatment became more problematic. This arose for the British state in a number of key contexts in the eighteenth century, both in the Jacobite risings

---

[17] W. Ossipow and D. Gerber, 'The Reception of Vattel's *Law of Nations* in the American Colonies: From James Otis and John Adams to the Declaration of Independence', *American Journal of Legal History*, 57 (4) (2017), pp. 521–55, on the role of the ideas in the Declaration of Independence.

in 1715 and 1745, and in the American Revolution. In the two Scottish settings, things were confused by the presence of a number of enemy captives in French uniforms and under officers commissioned by the French state. Irrespective of whether they were Irish or Scottish in origin, these were treated in 1746, after the defeat of Bonnie Prince Charlie's forces, as enemy troops, being paroled and then exchanged. This process was probably aided by the contemporary general war (of the Austrian Succession, 1743–8), in which these forms of negotiation were being constantly undertaken. A different problem arose with the general mass of Jacobite prisoners who had taken part in the rising. Uniforms were few and, as in the Americas, many had weapons of all kinds. The distinction between civilian and combatant was therefore always blurred.

How should rebels be treated or, in terms of everyday aspects of the fighting, how should dealings with rebels be conducted? Pragmatic considerations suggested, as Vattel had to a degree, that rebels should be treated as honourable enemies, or, at least, people with whom business had to be conducted. Courtesies such as lending surgeons to deal with opponents' battle casualties, or paroling prisoners, were common in both the Jacobite risings and the American revolution. Yet the British government was distinctly uneasy in the first case: officers who had given their word and oath to the rebels, and been paroled, were criticized and hastily sent back to England. This was discovered as the British government forces extended their control into Lowland Scotland in 1746. Their offence had been to offer their oaths to rebels. Similar issues arose thirty years later in the war against the American revolution. Loyalists (to Britain) captured in arms by the American patriot forces were at times treated as traitors rather than enemies, and tried or summarily executed rather than being held as prisoners of war. This caused some unease and protests despite the bitter and vengeful fighting in place such as the Carolinas. Yet other states handled things more carefully, perhaps because there were relatively low-level local patterns of retaliation. Connecticut, for example, kept both the correct military etiquette and prosecutions for treason in mind:

> Resolved by this Assembly, That Richmond Berry, Philip Buck, Thomas Silk, Edward Hicks, Edward Hix junr, John Young, Jacob Bowman, Adam Bowman junr Jacob Brenner, John Henry Short, Henry Hover, John Hover, Nicholas Philips, Nicholas Philips jun', John Phillips, Jacob Anguish, George Kentner, and Frederick Frank, who were lately taken in arms against the inhabitants of the United States by the militia of Westmoreland and sent to the deputy commissary general of prisoners in this State, as prisoners, ought to be received by said commissary and treated as prisoners of war: Provided, that nothing in this

resolve shall be understood to excuse them or any of them from any treasonable or other offences against the laws of any particular State, or from being dealt with accordingly.[18]

This was not the sentiment on the other side of the Atlantic, where rebels were strongly regarded as having no rights. Yet, as Edmund Burke pointed out early in 1777, the British government were already negotiating matters such as prisoner exchanges as though the American United States were already a foreign power on a par with France or Spain.[19]

If governments were successful in suppressing a rebellion, there arose the problem of how to dispose of the prisoners. As Vattel had pointed out, excessive brutality would undermine the public reputation and, perhaps, the legitimacy of the authorities. While individuals after the 1715 and the 1745 risings who were considered the leaders were tried for treason, the mass of prisoners were transported to the colonies. This was not entirely an arbitrary process, as there were efforts to compile sufficient evidence (and two witnesses) to put them on trial. For the majority, who were thought to have been 'forced out' into rebellion by the feudal landlords of the Scottish Highlands among others, transportation was judged to be a sufficient penalty. This was conditional, though, on their acknowledging their offence and accepting, in writing, the lawful authority of the King. Some refused to do this, but this was an indication of the desire of the authorities to force rebels back into subordination to the established sovereignty of the Hanoverian regime (see Chapter 4). In these ways, the British government attempted to establish different levels of responsibility, with appropriate degrees of severity and mercy.

It is worth noting that many armies were a mixture of what we today would call professional and the irregular forces: in the Jacobite rebellions, there were some elements of the French army (often Irish and Scots) mixed in with the Highland levies, as we have noted, and these were carefully distinguished and treated differently when they became prisoners of war. In the American War of Independence, it was the British troops which sometimes displayed such diversity. Along with British regiments, there were Loyalist regiments,

---

[18] TNA SP 54/27 Account of the capture of the British officers paroled by the Jacobites and sent to Leith; *The Public Records of the State of Connecticut, from October, 1776, to February, 1778, Inclusive*, ed. Charles J. Hoadly (Hartford, CT: Press of The Case, Lockwood and Brainard, 1894), p. 538.

[19] J. Piecuch, *Three Peoples, One King: Loyalists, Indians, and Slaves in the American Revolutionary South, 1775–1782* (Columbia, SC: University of South Carolina Press, 2008); E. Burke, 'A Letter to John Farr and John Harris, Sheriffs of the City of Bristol on the Affairs in America' (1777), in *The Works of the Right Honourable Edmund Burke* (London: Abel, Daldy, 1864), vol. 2, pp. 5–6.

uniformed and in a sense 'proper' soldiers, but there were also Loyalist militia, with a variety of equipment and dress, and, above all, Native Americans under their own leaders. This last group was a particular object of fear and contempt among the American patriots, and remained a political scandal in Britain, where their deployment was continually criticized by the government's opponents such as Edmund Burke. In the 1777 Saratoga campaign, pro-British Indians were responsible for the infamous murder of Jane McCrae, an incident which was treated as the epitome of British cruelty, and so movingly portrayed in a much-reproduced painting by John Vanderlyn in 1804. American forces were also a mixture of the regular regiments of the Continental Line and militias, and in some areas such as the Carolinas in 1780 and 1781, commanders such as Francis Marion led forces of irregular volunteers who more resembled the forces of classic guerrilla armies. One of the contentious elements in this southern campaign was the treatment by both sides of those captives who had allegedly changed their allegiances, and were judged (though rarely judicially) as traitors. Both Loyalist and patriot drew upon people of uncertain and fluctuating allegiances, and the resort to punitive violence against defectors and waverers was in contradiction to the more gentlemanly rules of war.[20]

A further complicated element in the mix of troops in the American Revolution was the use of runaway slaves by the British, who incorporated some into formal military units, as well as using them in transporting supplies and building fortifications. After Lord Dunmore's declaration at the start of the war in Virginia giving freedom to slaves who ran away to British hands, a major threat to the stability of the southern colonies was the enticement of British promises of freedom to the slaves. Many British commanders, however, were sceptical about their quality as soldiers, and reluctant to recruit too many into the fighting forces, but for their white American opponents, this was seen as a major threat. When slaves ran away to, or were captured, by the British, there was some uncertainty as to how to view them. Piecuch points out that there were no official instructions on the matter, and so slaves could be treated as allies in a common cause, or as captured property, as the occasion seems to dictate. Some British officers had great sympathy for the situation of the slaves, and could understand their reasons for running away, but senior commanders did not regard them as reliable. White Americans in the south were therefore always

---

[20] Piecuch, *Three Peoples*; for the Jane McCrae case, see Gwenda Morgan, *The Debate on the American Revolution* (Manchester: Manchester University Press, 2007), pp. 221, 258 and *A State of the Expedition from Canada as Laid before the House of Commons, by Lieutenant-General Burgoyne*, 2nd ed. (London: 1780, reprinted 1969), pp. 65–7.

afraid of internal subversion from their own slaves, and their flight to the British. They were unlikely to treat them as prisoners of war when they fell into their hands, and there are examples of captured black British forces being summarily executed. Francis Marion's troops in South Carolina in 1781 often clashed with the Black Dragoons, and Governor Matthews replied to his queries about their treatment by requiring them to be tried by 'negro', that is, slave law: 'and if found guilty, executed'.[21] The case in Virginia of a debate on whether to prosecute one black sailor recaptured from the British navy is instructive – there were dangers, clearly recognized by Governor Thomas Jefferson, of treating slaves as citizens with loyalty to the state rather than as property of their owners. In the Caribbean, the British authorities were initially reluctant to follow the French example of creating black regiments, but the experience of the military fiasco in the fighting in Haiti 1790s, where disease destroyed many white troops, forced their hand. Black forces were deployed successfully in the Second Carib War in St. Vincent, for example (see Chapter 8). Unlike the Muslim states of Africa, Christian slave societies were reluctant to create slave armies for their defence, though British efforts had to be made after risings in the Caribbean in the 1790s, partly because the slaves owned by convicted traitors fell into government hands. When white southern slave owners in America made a comment on their black opponents during the War for Independence, they described them as 'treacherous', meaning treasonable to themselves. There had been a longstanding opposition in Virginia to the growth of a free black population, through constraint on manumission, mainly because whites did not want to share citizenship rights with any black population. As Jack Greene has pointed out, in a study significantly called *Exclusionary Empire* the colonial societies were continually drawing and redrawing the lines of inclusion and exclusion, of access to, and denial of, rights.[22]

Despite doubts about precisely where the margins of civilized society lay, and who deserved decent treatment, there was a common legalism, a commitment to lawful action, throughout the British Atlantic world. Whether in war or rebellion, faced with conspirators or spies, the commitment to acting lawfully tended to dominate, and desire to claim legitimacy for the actions taken was part

---

[21] For Dunmore, see Piecuch, *Three Peoples*, Kindle Loc. 2106-7 and for Marion Loc. 8273-81.
[22] Piecuch quotation; for the issue of a Virginia slave in British uniform, see C. Anderson, 'Old Subjects, New Subjects and Non-Subjects: Silences and Subjecthood in Fédon's Rebellion, Grenada, 1795-96', in R. Bessel and N. Guyatt (eds), *War, Empire and Slavery, 1770-1830* (Houndmills, Basingstoke: Palgrave Macmillan, 2010), pp. 201-17; Jack P. Greene, ed., *Exclusionary Empire: English Liberty Overseas, 1600-1900* (Cambridge University Press, 2010). See K. Kesselring, '"Negroes of the Crown": The Management of Slaves Forfeited by Grenadian Rebels, 1796-1831', *Journal of the Canadian Historical Association*, 22 (2) (2011), pp. 1-29.

of the self-proclaimed identities of most leaders. Even when the legitimacy of the actor was denied by their opponents, as occurred in the American Revolution, there was painstaking attention to the gentlemanly proprieties on battlefields, and afterwards (sending surgeons to help the other side with the wounded, for example), even if treatment of prisoners might leave much to be desired. The overwhelming impression is of a ruling culture of legality, however contentious it might be in detail, in which law and legal processes were in part a claim for, and a confirmation of, legitimate government. Justice replaced religion in the eighteenth century.

The book therefore has to start with the laws and their variety, in the second chapter: the issues of local legislation in the context of intermittent imperial interference sit side by side with the way that local conditions often provoked a perceived need for special laws, particularly with regard to natives and slaves. The parallel histories of the prosecution of sedition and seditious words, where the struggle for free speech at home and in the colonies was central, then follows in Chapter 3. Because both sides of the Atlantic are considered together in this analysis, this forms the largest chapter. Thereafter, starting with the 'home' countries, rebellions or threats of it, where the treason law was deployed, are considered, beginning with the Anglo-Scottish experiences from Monmouth's rebellion in 1685 to the two Jacobite risings of 1715 and 1745. A brief contrast is made with the Irish experience from the Glorious Revolution of 1688–90 to the rise of revolutionary politics in the 1790s. Then we switch to the colonial experiences of the North American colonies (Chapters 5 and 6), particularly in the run-up to the revolution itself, which is then considered in terms of the American, rather than the British, use of treason law to defend their new nation (Chapter 7). Finally, the revolutionary period following the 1789 French Revolution and the 1791 Haitian rebellion forms the end of a story which began in rebellion and ended in, at least potentially, revolution. The parallel experiences of military and legal suppression in the Caribbean and Ireland are particularly striking at this time. The story could be wider and longer, of course: the United States went through very similar legal paroxysms in the 1790s culminating in the 1798 Aliens and Sedition Acts, but we have had to curb the scope of this project. Nineteenth-century prosecutions for sedition in Britain, briefly touched on in Chapter 3, would make a study in themselves.

2

British Laws, Colonial Laws

Varieties of treason

This study is one of 'high treason' which was judged to be a threat to the state and its monarch, 'against king and government' as Blackstone put it, but it is worth noting some parallels with the lesser forms of treason, 'petit' or petty treason, which in English law were also severely punished. This was conceived to arise from 'the same principle of treachery, but in private life', 'being breaches of the lower allegiance' to a superior to whom loyalty is owed, that is, a servant killing his master, a wife killing her husband, or a clergyman in holy orders, killing his superior such as a bishop. He was clear that these horrific crimes deserved a punishment that was 'very solemn and terrible'.[1] It is interesting to note how these forms made the transition to the Atlantic colonies to be modified and expanded there. Though petit treasons in England encompassed servants who killed their masters, the latter might be female, in the cases of a widow inheriting a trade business with permission of the guild, or a woman owning a farm employing servants in husbandry. These crimes could, to a degree, be described as rebellions against a natural order of things: when Blackstone discusses marriage and servanthood in his first volume, he was clearly assuming these were fundamental, natural institutions.[2] For these crimes, as it were against the natural order, the punishments involved the destruction of the body and the denial of a Christian burial. Murderous wives, until nearly the end of the eighteenth century, were sentenced to be burnt alive at the stake, though with a noose around their necks fastened to it. Contrary to the precise requirements of the sentence, women were supposed to be strangled before the fire was lit, but this did not necessarily happen successfully. There is evidence,

---

[1] W. Blackstone, *Commentaries on the Laws of England* (Oxford: Clarendon Press, 1765–9), Book 4, pp. 74–5 (quotations; 92–3 and 203–4).
[2] Blackstone, *Commentaries*, Book 1, pp. 410–33.

according to Matthew Lockwood, that there were attempts, particularly by juries, to avoid this sentence by reducing the charge's seriousness.[3] In the American colonies, there were instances of precisely this legal sentence, as in Newcastle (Delaware) in 1731, where servant Peter Murphy and Catherine Bevan were executed for murdering her husband Henry. Though Murphy tried to retract his statement accusing her, Catherine Bevan was executed in the usual way, but the fire burnt through the rope too soon, and she burnt alive, and was seen to 'struggle'.[4] Servants guilty of murdering their masters were also subject to bodily destruction as for high treason but it seems that simple hanging was common, often followed by gibbeting, their bodies left to rot in the open. As in the cases of women, the full details of the sentence (hanging and drawing) were rarely carried out. In one northeast English case in 1739 the accused wife was declared insane, though her servant was executed and gibbeted.[5] Thus, like the gruesome execution by hanging, drawing and quartering for crimes of high treason, those guilty of the lesser forms of rebellion suffered the destruction of their bodies. There are parallels with the punishment of rebellious slaves in the colonies, shown in the savage reprisals taken through court proceedings under the slave laws. In Antigua in 1736–7, slaves found guilty of conspiracy were burnt alive, 'racked to death' by being broken on the wheel, and others gibbeted (also alive). Similar punishments, particularly burning alive, were inflicted on Africans involved in the 1741 conspiracy in New York. One was broken on the wheel, though of the twenty-seven liable to be executed, six committed suicide (which would also deprive them of a Christian burial). Thus the newly formed slave laws in the colonies built upon the petty treason framework of the old English laws, and extended them to slaves who challenged what slaveowners and their authorities regarded as the natural order.[6] At the same time, the colonies created specific servants laws which were of much greater severity than those

---

[3] Matthew Lockwood, 'From Treason to Homicide: Changing Conceptions of the Law of Petty Treason in Early Modern England', *Journal of Legal History*, 34 (1) (2013), pp. 31–49; Ruth Campbell, 'Sentence of Death by Burning for Women', *Journal of Legal History*, 5 (1), pp. 44–59; Simon Devereaux, 'The Abolition of the Burning of Women in England Reconsidered', *Crime, Histoire & Sociétés/Crime, History & Societies* [online], 9 (2) (2005), online since 26 February 2009, URL: http://journals.openedition.org/chs/293, DOI: 10.4000/chs.293 (accessed 11 December 2019).
[4] *Pennsylvania Gazette*, 23 September 1731.
[5] G. Morgan and P. Rushton, *Rogues, Thieves and the Rule of Law: The Problem of Law Enforcement in North-East England, 1718–1800* (London: UCL Press, 1998), Michael Curry, pp. 144 and 149.
[6] G. Morgan and P. Rushton, *The British and French in the Atlantic: Comparisons and Contrasts* (London: Routledge, 2019), pp. 85–8; D. Horsmanden, *The New York Conspiracy, or a History of the Negro Plot, with the Journal of the Proceedings against the Conspirators at New-York in the Years 1741–1742* (originally 1744; New York: Southwick and Pelsue, 1810); J. Lepore, *New York Burning: Liberty, Slavery, and Conspiracy in Eighteenth-Century Manhattan* (New York: Alfred A. Knopf, 2005).

in England under the 1563 Statute of Artificers. Runaways could be severely whipped and have their time of service extended, as could female servants becoming pregnant (the extra time compensating the employer for the time lost during pregnancy and childbirth). Though not as savage as the laws affecting slaves, it is clear that the domestic regime imposed on servants in the colonies was much more severe than in England. Servants served for longer on a single contract, from three or four years or upwards, and their masters had the right to whip them, something that had become impossible or unacceptable in English households by the end of the seventeenth century (though young apprentices were an exception). Unlike slaves, however, servants could turn to the law under duress, with magistrates everywhere hearing complaints about ill treatment. In England, many of these complaints were successful.[7] The activities punished so terribly do fall under the category of rebellion, but were in a sense rebellion against the patriarchal household, the 'natural' order of domestic authority. What was under challenge were the fundamentals of the social structure rather than the state, and as such have reluctantly to be neglected in this study, though the events in the Caribbean in the 1790s reflect the engagement of slaves as well as free in revolutionary activities (see Chapter 8). The state was eager to punish this kind of challenge to domestic society, but these insurrections were not in themselves threats to the state itself.

A recurrent threat to white colonial society was that from the Native Americans or Indians. These were allies and enemies at different times and places, and as in all situations of fluctuating loyalties, issues of rebellion and betrayal surfaced occasionally. Some natives were prosecuted, or at least tried, in the terrible violence of King Philip's War in New England in 1675–6. Even if they were not formally tried, they were certainly judged and sentenced. As Benton has noted, 'The different status of Indian groups at the start of the war influenced the way they were characterized as combatants. Philip and the Wampanoags were rebels who had committed "high treason," while Indians in the north country who had not formally submitted to colonial rule were "enemies"'.[8] How these different groups were treated depended on the way that they came into white hands – coming over willingly, surrendering after conflict or being captured in

---

[7] D. Hay, and P. Craven, eds, *Masters, Servants, and Magistrates in Britain and the Empire* (Chapel Hill, NC: University of North Carolina Press, 2004); C. Daniels, '"Liberty to Complain": Servant Petitions in Maryland, 1652–1797', in C.L. Tomlins and B.H. Mann (eds), *The Many Legalities of Early America* (Chapel Hill, NC: University of North Carolina Press/Omohundro Institute of Early American History and Culture, 2001), pp. 219–49.

[8] Lauren Benton, *A Search for Sovereignty: Law and Geography in European Empires* (New York: Cambridge University Press, 2010), pp. 94 and 100.

war. Four men were tried and executed in Rhode Island, where the authorities seem to have been under great pressure from a vengeful public. In Providence one seems to have been summarily executed:

> Memorandum the on the 25 of August 1676: so called there came into this Towne One Chuff an Jndian so called in time of peace, because of his Surlines against the English He could Scarce come in being wounded Some few dayes before by Providence Men His wounds were corrupted & stanck & because he had bene a Ringleader all the War to most of the Mischiefs to our Howses & Cattell, & what English he could: The Inhabitants of the Towne crjed out for Justice against him threatning themselues to kill him if the Authoritie did not: For with Reason the. Cap: Roger Williams Caused the Drum to be beat, the Toun Councell & Councll of War called, all cried for Justice & Execution, the Councell of War gave sentence & he was shot to Death, to the great satisfaction of the Towne.

This seems more like a lynching, but it is significant that no charge is mentioned, and treason could not be tried by military court martial.[9] The most important aspect, though, of the treatment of natives in this war was that their capture led to their being reduced to servants or slaves. New Plymouth decided that all those who did not come in voluntarily and claim the promised indemnity would be disposed of 'to the colony's use'. Indians had not been regarded as subjects in the same way as whites, and this move created a population of unfree natives in white households, though others were sold outside New England. Despite legal bans on having native slaves, it was common to sell captives into slavery. Though this is beyond the scope of this study, it worth noting that slaves, their seizure and sale, were a major concern of many of the Indian wars up until the early eighteenth century. Selling troublesome slaves and exporting them from the colony were also a part of the colonial repertoire of repression, as happened to the Nanziatticos of Virginia.[10] In the mid-eighteenth century, in the Seven Years' War (the French and Indian War, to the Americans), the Delaware Indians

---

[9] *The Early Records of the Town of Providence*, ed. H. Rogers and G. Fields, vol. 15 (Provience, RI: Snow and Farnham, City Printers, 1899), p. 152; also J.R. Bartlett, ed., *Records of the Colony of Rhode Island and Providence Plantations in New England* (Providence, RI: Crawford Greene and Brother, State Printers, 1857), vol. 2, p. 586.

[10] N.D. Shurtleff, ed., *Records of the Colony of New Plymouth in New England*, vol. 5, Court Orders, 1666-78 (Boston: William White, 1856), p. 209; Linford D. Fisher, '"Why Shall Wee Have Peace to Bee Made Slaves": Indian Surrenderers during and after King Philip's War', *Ethnohistory*, 64 (1) (2017), pp. 91–114; G. Morgan, 'Sold into slavery in retribution against the Nanziattico Indians', *Virginia Cavalcade*, 33 (4) (1984), pp. 168–73; A.Gallay, *The Rise of the English Empire in the American South, 1670-1717* (New Haven CT: Yale University Press, 2002); A.W. Lauber, *Slavery in Colonial Times within the Present Limits of the United States* (New York: Columbia University/ Longmans Green and Co., 1913).

were designated as traitors by Pennsylvania, but no record survives of any prosecution. Yet there was some debate about the suitability of the treason law in these circumstances. As Carlton F.W. Larson has pointed out, if the British made Indians subjects, they could be tried for treason, but this was regarded by the great leader of, and mediator with, the Indians, Sir William Johnson, as 'an impossible outcome'. 'The Seven Years' War eventually concluded with these questions entirely avoided. No individual, either European or Indian, was prosecuted by Pennsylvania for treason'.[11] *High* treason, therefore, was not the way that insurgent Indians were handled, and the resort to servitude of one sort of another reduced them to the unfree statuses where special servant and slave laws applied. They could, though, be tried for *petit* treason, though it seems that this has not been noted frequently in court records.

Britain's legal empires

This introductory diversion already shows the complexity of the laws in the British Atlantic, as new legislatures invented or adapted English law to new situations and types of society. At the start of the seventeenth century, the authorities in London only had three separate legal systems to work with – those of England and Wales (since 1547, making up a unified system of law if not a single pattern of courts), Scotland and Ireland. These did not share a common ancestry: Scotland in particular retained a separate parliament until 1707, and a strong sense of a distinct legal tradition thereafter.[12] By 1700, though, legal systems and law codes had proliferated throughout the Atlantic, and there were even likely outposts in India and elsewhere. The growth of empire was reflected in the numbers of laws and legal jurisdictions, and the desire to keep some kind of order in this diversity had led to only imperfect procedures of monitoring and supervision. There was little desire to follow the French with their standardized slave laws, the *Code Noire*, even if there had been the bureaucratic organizations to carry out such a project. Just as English counties and their magistrates administered the criminal law, welfare system and procedures of tax collection and economic regulation, with almost no interference from central authority, so the individual colonies set out to administer their own affairs, forming legislative bodies of various

---

[11] Carlton F.W. Larson, *The Trials of Allegiance: Treason, Juries and the American Revolution* (New York: Oxford University Press, 2019), pp. 19–20.
[12] Lindsay Farmer, *Criminal Law, Tradition and Legal Order: Crime, and the Genius of Scots Law, 1747 to the Present* (Cambridge University Press, 1997).

kinds and passing their own laws, albeit with governors appointed by London. Hulsebosch regards New York as almost like an English county, complete with its assumption of being validated by antiquity. However, unlike counties, each colony had powers to create its own legislation. Colonists in this respect did not see themselves as 'provincial' in a dismissive sense, but bearers of old traditions of local initiative.[13]

Yet between the two kingdoms of England and Scotland, there had initially been very different treason laws at the beginning of the joint monarchy in 1603, but a degree of uniformity was fixed through the impositions following the Act of Union of 1707. From the start of the shared monarchy, the separation of jurisdictions had been legally troublesome. Bilder notes that even in Britain, rights across borders were unclear before *Calvin's Case*, which centred on the inheritance rights of someone of Scots origin, born after James VI had become James I of England, to a property in England. If loyalty was to king, then all had equal rights: if to the laws, then Scots could not claim English rights in England (and *vice versa*). Essentially, *Calvin* defended the idea of birthright under the sovereignty of the king, even if someone was born in another jurisdiction ruled by him, as well as the powers of the king to command loyalty from all the people in every type of territory over which he ruled. In this way, Scots would not be defined as aliens, and pose the problem of naturalization, in English law. This became almost the foundational case for a colonial empire of many jurisdictions.[14] The problem of sovereignty and loyalty remained, though, in the case of treason.

> Unlike the English treason law, the law of treason in Scotland held that subjects owed allegiance to both the estates of the realm and the king. The offence of treason in Scotland aimed to destroy the representative body of the kingdom *or* the person of the king ....The Act *7 Annae, c. 21* transformed the English treason law into a British treason law. Subjects in Scotland and England now suffered the same penalties for treasonable transgressions against their shared monarch.[15]

Exactly where Scots could be tried for their treasons was left rather vague, but had to be decided in haste when, in both the 1715 and the 1745 Jacobite risings, a large number of prisoners were seized in, or taken to, England. As a result, a

---

[13] D.J. Hulsebosch, *Constituting Empire: New York and the Transformation of Constitutionalism in the Atlantic World, 1664–1830* (Chapel Hill, SC: University of South Carolina Press, 2005), pp. 43, 51.

[14] Mary Sarah Bilder, *The Transatlantic Constitution: Colonial Legal Culture and the Empire* (Cambridge, MA: Harvard University Press, 2004), pp. 35ff; Lisa Steffen, *Defining the British State: Treason and National Identity, 1608–1820* (Houndmills, Basingstoke: Macmillan, 2001), pp. 20–1.

[15] Steffen, *Defining the British State*, p. 75

treason trial could in effect be held anywhere the government wished, something that was contested by accused Jacobites and, later, by rebellious Americans (see Chapters 4 and 5). The precise nature of the treason law in Scotland, though, was challenged in 1794, as lawyers argued about whether there was a concept of sedition in Scotland, debates about **lèse-majesté** in 1794 trials (see later Chapter 8). The Scottish example, together with that of Ireland (which retained its own parliament throughout the eighteenth century), showed the awkward nature of the British forms of governance. Uniformity proved too difficult in many areas of law, and only with regard to loyalty and treason were there efforts to produce, out of the three kingdoms, one specifically *British* law.

This kind of imposition was not attempted with regard to the colonies, though a kind of ideal legal framework for treason and its attendant crimes such as counterfeiting the great seal and the currency did emerge in the early eighteenth century, but this was a piecemeal process that varied between individual colonies. The concepts that have been applied by historians to colonial North America – the 'many legalities' of the American colonies or the 'multiple constitutions of empire' – should in fact be the keynote to the initial analysis of law in the British Atlantic.[16] Some scholars such as Lauren Benton and her colleagues have argued that legal *pluralism* was a common feature of many empires between the sixteenth and the nineteenth centuries, in part because there were several types of proprietors, corporations and other bodies sponsoring their expansion, and each resulting colony might have a unique charter under royal authority. Another factor was the creation of plural legal orders *within* colonial territories, a factor that is most obvious where colonies had laws aimed at slaves which were largely distinct from those affecting white settlers.[17] There has been detailed scholarly work on the legal frameworks developed in the British colonies, based mostly on a case-by-case method of analysing individual colonies, their founding charters, and the subsequent debates and conflicts between the colonial authorities and those in London. 'Conflict' sounds too grand a word, since few of these at time fraught interchanges threatened the essential unity of the empire. Much of the scholarly debate has been about the 'reception' of English law in the colonies, though it is clear that in many cases the law was not handed out in the original

---

[16] C.L. Tomlins and B.H. Mann, eds, *The Many Legalities of Early America* (Chapel Hill, NC: University of North Carolina Press/Omohundro Institute of Early American History and Culture, 2001).
[17] See the collection, Lauren Benton and Richard J. Ross, eds, *Legal Pluralism and Empires, 1500–1850* (New York University Press, 2013), particularly Philip J. Stern, '"Bundles of Hyphens": Corporations as Legal Communities in the Early Modern British Empire', pp. 21–47, and Lauren Benton and Lisa Ford, 'Magistrates in Empire: Convicts, Slaves, and the Remaking of the Plural Order in the British Empire', pp. 173–97, the discussion of protections for slaves notably, pp. 175–6.

charter or later, but on the contrary, English laws were adopted or co-opted as colonies asserted their rights to the same laws and safeguards as other English subjects. Most of the studies suggested that early charters and colonists *assumed* the right to English laws and procedures, but that by 1700 central monitoring and control over colonial laws increased. 'On the basis of the evidence, one may infer that English control over colonial legal systems, and by further inference, the influence of the common law, increased perceptibly very near the year 1700', comments one analysis of the reception of English common law. The colonies themselves thereafter made great efforts to have printed editions of their laws, and make explicit the procedures and rules of legal processes.[18]

Some studies have examined the broader common framework of assumptions about law and rights, particularly stressing the development in the seventeenth century of a shared devotion to Magna Carta and the judicial rights framed there and invented in its spirit, most importantly the 1679 Habeas Corpus Act. English liberty and the common law were in effect taken for granted without much detailed thought.[19] This culture underlay much of the legal and constitutional discourse pervading the British Atlantic. In this regard there was a common legal culture across the Atlantic among Britain and its colonies. Bilder has called this an 'Atlantic constitution' defined as a loose framework of common values within a context where the British authorities acknowledged the rights of local assemblies and legislative bodies to invent new forms of law to meet the needs of new types of settlement and landholding, and new forms of social relationships, particularly the new forms of exploitative labour relations such as slavery. The degree of local autonomy available to the colonies was not clearly defined, and at times the empire resembled a loose alliance of imperfectly coordinated units. There were also significant interactions and relations *between* the colonies themselves – there was much innovation, in which acknowledged pioneering by some was then followed by much copying, certainly with regard to slave and servant laws, as printed collections of laws of individual colonies became available. Other aspects of law seem to have been proclaimed as being conducted under the laws of England, but this was sometimes done in a deliberately vague phrasing that could induce criticism from the legal scrutineers in London. Coke's judgement placed restrictions on the powers of the king in the case of

---

[18] William B. Stoebuck, 'Reception of English Common Law in the American Colonies', *William and Mary Law Review*, 10 (1968), pp. 393–426, 410.

[19] Hulsebosch, *Constituting Empire*, p. 57; C.W. Brooks, *Law, Politics and Society in Early Modern England* (Cambridge University Press, 2008); P.D. Halliday, *Habeas Corpus: From England to Empire* (Cambridge, MA: The Belknap Press of Harvard University Press, 2010).

conquered territories, if Christian, where parliament had to give permission for laws and rights. Yet *Blankard's Case* in the 1690s before John Holt replaced Coke's distinction between settled and unsettled territories with the notion that, with regard to uninhabited territories, the settlers took English laws with them. It was unclear whether this included all subsequent laws passed in England, or those passed at the time of settlement. Consequently it has been well said that 'for colonial attorneys and crown officers, the relationship between English law and the colonies was an evolving set of arguments, not a simple rule'.[20] Nevertheless, a kind of adoption by stealth – adoption without specific statutes – therefore spread rights created since the foundation of the colonies to those territories outside Britain. The rule of law in the colonies, however, was characterized in the seventeenth century, by a shortage of educational and training institutions, in effect unprofessional, which occasioned some snobbery among colonial governors (the absence of trained barristers was one feature). For Bilder, the myth of the seventeenth-century colonies as places of 'law without lawyers' has maintained a powerful hold on historians' imaginations. They had attorneys – now solicitors – who were able to plead cases, but these were not academically trained like counsel/barristers (as in England, they were in effect trained through joining a practice). 'The precise role of English law in colonial attorneys' legal practice was unclear'. Yet a modern scholarly review of proceedings in, for example, Virginia courts in the late seventeenth century provides a corrective to this image, concluding from evidence of the records that there was a high degree of legal knowledge and a punctilious attention to proper procedures. In the eighteenth century, by contrast, there seems to have been a rise in professional lawyers in almost all the colonies. Throughout, the law and the rights underpinned by it was of central concern to many of the colonists as well as their leaders and legislators. Even without formal legal training, many took a very legalistic view of their own affairs.[21]

As a result, historians no longer see the British Empire as a *legal system* in the sense of a centrally controlled organization, with identical constitutional and legal features everywhere. Richard Archer puts it very neatly:

Despite occasional ministerial stabs at bringing administrative oversight and coherent policy, the colonies, for the most part, ran as local enterprises. The

---

[20] Bilder, *The Transatlantic Constitution*, p. 37, see pp. 37–9.
[21] Bilder, *Transatlantic Constitution*, pp. 15, 31; John Ruston Pagan, 'English Statutes in Virginia, 1660–1714', in Warren M. Billings & Brent Tarter (eds), *'Esteemed Bookes of Lawe' and the Legal Culture of Early Virginia* (Charlottesville, VA: University of Virginia Press, 2017), pp. 58–94.

Crown appointed governors, lieutenant governors, and sometimes councils, but popularly elected assemblies who paid the officials' salaries and raised revenue for government operations checked the mother country's power. Diverted by warfare, the empire, by default, was more a federation of affiliated states than a centrally organised institution.[22]

An efficient local system of law operated in the colonies, like a grand and almost supervised version of the semi-independence of magistrates in the English counties. At least, in the latter, judges came out from London to impose some consistency on the trials of major criminals, but this was only developed with regard to the colonies where local people could not be found of sufficient quality to be appointed, in early nineteenth-century Australia for example, but there were few such direct judicial appointments in the North American colonies. Britain's 'first empire' was a great deal less centralized than its second.[23]

Laws had to be made locally for various reasons: one was the requirement for new land law and the local regulation of ownership, leases and rents. A second lay in the new forms of exploitation in the colonies including relations with slaves and indentured servants. New forms of inequality required new laws, with little to draw on in pre-existing English laws. The laws of servants may resemble the 1563 Statute of Artificers in some of the terms, but the lengths of service, and the rigorous disciplinary regime available (no master could whip their servants in England, though young apprentices, like young people in general, were another matter), marked out colonial social relations as very different.[24] Yet the passing of new laws, or even the adoption of new laws passed in England, was under intermittent scrutiny from the London authorities. Bilder regards the criterion of *repugnancy* as providing the justification for central intervention, allowing the colonial supervisors in London to strike down or refuse the local laws on the grounds that they were repugnant to the laws of England. As the Board of Trade put it in the 1730s, 'All these colonies … by their several constitutions, have the power of making laws for their better government and support, provided they be not repugnant to the laws of Great Britain, nor detrimental to the Mother Country'. They recognized that colonial laws had to differ from place to place, because of variations in local conditions

---

[22] R. Archer, *As if an Enemy's Country: The British Occupation of Boston and the Origins of the American Revolution* (New York: Oxford University Press, 2010), p. 3.
[23] B. Kerchner, 'Perish or Prosper: The Law and Convict Transportation in the British Empire, 1700–1850', *Law and History Review*, 21 (3) (2003), pp. 527–84, for the increasingly tight control by London over convict and servant law in Australia.
[24] See Morgan and Rushton, *The British and French in the Atlantic*, pp. 46–58.

which meant that the 'conversation between English law and local concerns played out differently in different places', even though the Privy Council tried to standardize and maintain some consistency. Between them, colonies and central authorities created the 'distinctiveness of transatlantic legal culture'. One problem was that colonial laws were being created at the same time as English laws were being changed or enhanced, and in the eighteenth century there was almost a binge on law-making in certain parliaments. Thus there was a moving feast of laws which provided the 'baseline' against which colonial laws were judged to be repugnant or acceptable. In the example of Rhode Island, at least, Bilder concludes that 'the transatlantic constitution cast a shadow across this country's constitutional founding and early national period'.[25] This study in effect views the 'Atlantic constitution' as a *process* not a fixed construction of common laws and judicial structures: it was as much about shared values and rights as about specific laws and their provisions, and took the form of continual interplay between the colonies and the 'mother country'.

Repugnancy should have acted as a kind of Ockham's razor: divergence alone, however, did not indicate repugnance if there was a good underlying reason for it, nor did entirely new inventions such as slave laws. A certain amount of subterfuge seems to have been adopted by several colonies, Rhode Island among them, in that laws were amended in the colonies, and the full piece of changed legislation was not made available to London, or at least, not in an easily intelligible way. Sometimes a law was changed in practice before the rule was embodied in legislation, such as the three-witness rule for valid wills, which had been introduced in England in 1677, and was eventually embodied in a Rhode Island law in 1719, though it is clear that this had been in force for some years before that. 'This strategy of transatlantic accommodation' was Rhode Island's way of ensuring that, while their laws conformed to those of England, the colony retained its charter and independent paths of law where appropriate. Originally, only the royal colonies of Virginia, Jamaica, Barbados and the Leeward Isles had to send their laws to England, but the laws of Massachusetts, the earliest to print theirs, and then Jamaica, were examined in the 1680s, Massachusetts because their charter was up for renewal. By the foundation of new colonies in South Carolina and Georgia, it was assumed by London that printed copies of their laws would regularly be sent to London for inspection.[26]

---

[25] Bilder, *Transatlantic Constitution*, pp. 2–4, 9–10, quotations pp. 2, 4 and 10.
[26] Bilder, *Transatlantic Constitution,* pp. 52, 54–5, 58–9.

New York had a particularly difficult and fraught relationship with the London regimes of the Catholic James II and the new Whig ascendancy after the Glorious Revolution of 1688. Along with tensions between English and Dutch, the city of New York's factional politics produced serious cases of treason in 1688–91 in the attempted coup by, and prosecution and execution of, Jacob Leisler, and in 1702, the trial of Colonel Nicholas Bayard. The latter was 'tried under a New York statute which provided that it was treason to disturb "by force of arms, or other ways, … the peace, good, and quiet of this their majesties' government, as it is now established"'. This, it has been noted, 'is the only pre-Revolutionary case of which we have an extensive record. Though the issues centered on the interpretation of the New York act, which was not couched in familiar English statutory terms, the defense resorted to Coke and the principal English statutes to evolve a theory of restrictive construction of treason legislation.' The 1691 law under which this trial was conducted had to be replaced, and Bayard, unlike Leisler, was saved from execution by the arrival of a new governor. It may be significant that his trial entered the semi-official collection of state trials. In 1704, New York produced a new treason law, more acceptable than their 1691 celebration of the fall of James II, which London, seizing on the phrase just quoted, thought that to describe a threat to 'the peace good and quiet of this their Majestyes Government as it is now Established' as treason was too 'objectionably broad and vague', and instructions were sent to the governor to procure its repeal. It was, hence, replaced.[27]

The eighteenth-century experience followed this pattern of more careful scrutiny of laws, and also some more relaxed, enabling provisions for areas such as habeas corpus. The difficulty for the historian lies in the way this was done colony by colony rather than consistently and simultaneously across all of them. Thinking of the example of New York, Johnson observes:

> One of the major problems facing historians of early American law is the determination of the extent to which English law applied in any given province at a particular time. While the requirement that the colonies have laws not repugnant to the common law of England provided some conformity throughout the colonial period, there was substantial variation in the seventeenth century,

---

[27] Jabez W. Loane, 'Treason and Aiding the Enemy', *Military Law Review*, 30 (1965), pp. 43–81, 48; Willard Hurst, 'Treason in the United States: I. Treason Down to the Constitution', *Harvard Law Review*, 58 (1944), pp. 226–72, 233–4; 'Trial of Colonel Nicholas Bayard', T. Howell *State Trials*, 14, 471–3 (1702). For the 1691 law, see *Colonial Laws of New York*, vol. 1 (Lincoln, 1894), p. 223, 1691, 'An Act for the Quieting and Setling [*sic*] the Disorders That Have Lately Happened within This Province and for the Establishing and Securing Their Majesties Present Government against the Like Disorders for the Future', 6 May 1691.

not only between the colonies and the mother country, but also among the colonies themselves. With the increasing availability of English statutes and case reports during the eighteenth century, and the growing sophistication of the bar, there was a pronounced tendency to adhere to English norms.

The New York case, he argues, suggests that 'American colonial law was closest to the law of England in the years immediately before the outbreak of the American Revolution'. 'Throughout the eighteenth century and particularly in the decade immediately preceding the War for Independence, New York lawyers, legislators and judges were actively engaged in the extension of English law to the colony.' Thus what had been assumed and accomplished 'by usage' in the seventeenth century was made explicit in the laws, judicial rules and decisions in the eighteenth century. As Johnson himself points out, assertions that English laws operated in the colony were not sufficient, and pieces of legislation such as that of the New York General Assembly, 24 December 1767, that 'it being conducive to the commonWeal, as well as agreeable to his Majesty's most gracious Intentions: that the Laws of this Colony should conform as nearly as possible to the Laws of England', were in fact disallowed by the Privy Council on the grounds that it was too general. Individual laws had to be passed, and not assumed or adopted in their entirety. Yet there are many pieces of evidence suggesting that English laws and legal rules were being adopted in the eighteenth century by usage if not by specific statute.[28] Daniel J. Hulsebosch points out that this was a pattern across all the British colonies, where 'misinterpretations, wilful appropriations, and adamant rejections were not confined to the continental colonies. Colonies in the British Caribbean experienced much the same from their founding to the American Revolution'.[29]

While the initial charters of most colonies contained a clause guaranteeing that the emigrants would enjoy the liberties, privileges and immunities of English subjects, this was not entirely to transplant wholesale the structures of courts and specific laws from England. In fact, it rapidly became clear, as emphasized earlier, that there would need to have new laws for new circumstances, particularly with regard to new social relations such as indentured servitude and slavery. This has rightly been described as a process of local innovation accompanied by 'imperial

---

[28] Herbert Alan Johnson, 'English Statutes in Colonial New York', *New York History*, 58 (3) (1977), pp. 277–96, 277–8 and 287–8 (quotations), and 295.
[29] Daniel J. Hulsebosch, 'English Liberties outside England: Floors, Doors, Windows and Ceilings in the Legal Architecture of Empire', *New York University Public Law and Legal Working Papers*, no. 571 (2016), p. 26, also Ch. 38 of Lorna Hutson, ed., *Oxford Handbook of English Law and Literature, 1500–1700* (OUP); Hulsebosch, *Constituting Empire*, pp. 49–54.

borrowing' by one colony to another.³⁰ Yet the proclamation that emigrants were still English subjects had great significance at the outset of colony foundation, because it guaranteed their rights should they *return* to England. They were not, therefore, becoming some other kind of subject of the king by leaving England. The language of liberties, though, was not static, and in the seventeenth century in particular took on many different meanings that became difficult for the London authorities to constrain. The idea of freedom of worship, for example, was alien to English law before the Toleration Act of 1690, and this was inimical to the exclusionary practices of Massachusetts' Congregationalists who became notorious in England in the 1660s for their mistreatment of Quakers. The developing English notion of freedom of worship seemed a threat to the very foundation of the colony. As Hulsebosch puts it:

> It could be called the problem of imperial subjecthood: What package of legal rights and liberties did royal subjects enjoy across the royal dominions and colonies outside England? This problem was not theorized coherently or regulated by the imperial parliament until the early twentieth century, a generation before the empire disintegrated. Even then the status was not as clear and uniform as some metropolitan officials had hoped it would be.

In some grants it was made explicit, as in Humphrey Gilbert's 1578 grant for Newfoundland, where it was clear that 'emigrant settlers and their heirs would remain English subjects wherever born and no matter in which royal territory they lived'. The disputed laws and lists of rights were the focus of conflict because there was a fundamental difference in worldviews between the managers of the colonies, the ruling classes of slave societies and merchants, and the London authorities concerning them: 'from the metropole, these liberties were grants, while on the west side of the Atlantic they were rights', observes Hulsebosch acutely.³¹

For the Restoration Privy Council, in Hulsebosch's view, these rights were a ceiling, a maximum so to speak, that set limits to colonial rights that could not be exceeded if the colonies tried. In Jamaica, the 1675 Bill of Privileges was disallowed, which provoked the response from the Governor's Council that 'the King may seem to have a greater power here than in England', but the Assembly noted that 'His Majesty had given us here the same privileges as his subjects

---

[30] Bruce P. Smith, 'Imperial Borrowing': A Review of D. Hay and P. Craven, eds, *Masters, Servants and Magistrates in Britain and the Empire, 1562-1955* (Chapel Hill, NC: University of North Carolina Press, 2004), in *Comparative Labour Law and Policy*, 25 (2004), pp. 447-62.
[31] Hulsebosch, 'English Liberties outside England', pp. 5, 18, and 30-1.

in England'. Eventually a bill was signed by the governor guaranteeing 'all the liberties immunities and privileges', such as fair trial by jury and consent to taxation. For two generations, Jamaica's assembly passed statutes appropriating domestic English liberties and privileges, and the Privy Council repeatedly disallowed them. The colonial societies were undoubtedly British, but their legal rights were subject to cautious approval and slow accretion. In part this hinged on what settlers brought with them, especially when the territories were already occupied (with some exceptions such as Barbados, which seems never to have had any natives when the English arrived). The notion of settlement in empty territories – *terra nullius* – allowed full transportation of right, but the government and its judges in the eighteenth century never accepted this:

> The Privy Council did not accept it; Sir William Blackstone did not accept it; Lord Mansfield did not accept it; even imperial liberals like Edmund Burke did not accept it. But in 1774 the First Continental Congress could confidently proclaim the theory of settlement.

The intractable problem remained until the last, particularly in the American colonies, that the local elites made claims to rights that their metropolitan masters would not accept in full. The contradiction was noted by Matthew Hale in the 1650s that 'the English planters carry along with them those English liberties that are incident to their persons': yet 'denial of the colonists' inherited rights as Englishmen would be tantamount to a denial of their status as subjects of the English king'. A common culture lay behind much of the political debate, even if the detailed law books provided the models. Rhetoric about tradition played a major part in the empire of rights, particularly the common heritage of Magna Carta.

> Throughout the eighteenth and nineteenth centuries Magna Carta was invoked extensively across Great Britain and its empire. Building on the foundations laid in the seventeenth century it had become a document of international scope and influence vigorously debated by radicals in Westminster as by lawyers in Bengal or rebels in Massachusetts.[32]

Colonies, though, followed what might be described as English legal fashions as laws changed and developed from the middle of the seventeenth century, in

---

[32] Hulsebosch, 'English Liberties outside England', pp. 30–1, and 33; Agnes M. Whitson, *The Constitutional Development of Jamaica, 1660–1729* (University of Manchester Press, 1929); Pagan, 'English Statutes in Virginia, 1660–1714', p. 60; Alexander Lock, 'Reform, Radicalism and Revolution: Magna Carta in Eighteenth-Century and Nineteenth-Century Britain', in Lawrence Goldman (ed.), *Magna Carta: History, Context and Influence* (London: Institute of Historical Research, 2018), pp. 101–116, 101.

areas such as crime and religious law. Moral laws such as those against bigamy and the freedom of worship of Quakers were adopted in Virginia, and later the rights of Quakers to affirm (rather than take an oath) were placed in law in 1705. Maryland in 1729 deliberately copied the English statutes removing benefit of clergy from thefts from shops, warehouses and storehouses, and later tobacco houses, and stealing to the value of five shillings, copying almost word for word the English laws. As John Beattie pointed out with regard to the original English reforms, the development of specialist storage buildings and commercial premises, separate from their dwelling houses (already covered and protected by laws against breaking and entering and, at night, burglary), led to the proliferation of special amendments covering them. Shops were no longer in the houses of their owners, and warehouses were unoccupied at night, so the severe laws against breaking and entering a 'dwelling house' could not be extended to the new commercial premises. London businesses had petitioned Parliament in the 1690s for more severe laws, and the response was the Shoplifting Act of 1699 making thefts from shops and warehouses hanging offences. The acquisition of printed English statutes books from the 1660s provided some guidance and inspiration for colonial legislators: the results were a sophisticated legal culture, which produced what William Berkeley called 'the best Lawes in the World for the security of the subject'. Some colonial borrowing was therefore inevitable.[33]

The empire of treason

Most early charters and collections of included references to treason and rebellion, often conflated, backed up with the powers of martial law. This allowed the seventeenth-century niceties of procedure to be avoided in what were judged to be emergency responses to rebellions and treasonable plots. Yet the ancient English law of treason, 25 Edward III, was assumed and at times clearly referred to as the basis for colonial law. Accusations of treason were rare, but were inevitable in the 1640s as conflict between King and Parliament drifted to open warfare. Royal governors found themselves with colonists whose loyalties and religious sympathies were against Charles I, and accusations and trials were inevitable. On some occasions, in a few localities such as the

---

[33] Pagan, 'English Statutes in Virginia', pp. 68–9 and 79; *Abridgement of the Laws*, 1759, p. 141; also for breaking into a tobacco house, 1737, p. 211; J.M. Beatttie, *Policing and Prosecution in London: Urban Crime and the Limits of Terror* (Oxford: Oxford University Press, 2001), pp. 31, 37 and 39.

Caribbean, the civil war at home was almost replicated among the colonists. At the same time, the successful parliamentary regime was the first to take a keen interest in transatlantic affairs, culminating in the 1655 takeover of Jamaica. Religious sympathies shared by Oliver Cromwell and the New England colonists did not extend, however, to many of them being persuaded to go to Jamaica to found a virtuous Puritan society. Pestana has noted the game of musical chairs often played as governors tried to control their colonies in the interests of King or Parliament, and their patterns of flight and return reflected the ebb and flow of the civil wars. For example, in Maryland, Richard Ingle's rebellion, 1645–6 was more or less a flight and return after Charles I had sent orders for his arrest in 1645. While the king's execution caused angst among his loyal followers such as William Berkeley in Virginia, yet the Cromwellian takeover of the colony was not so repressive.[34] Similar conflicting loyalties occurred before and after the Glorious Revolution of 1688, with rival loyalties leading to conflicting ideas of treason. Similar problems arose around the time of the 1688 Glorious Revolution, as the Leisler affair in New York was bound up with this same kind of confusion of loyalties and legitimacies (Leisler could be described as a 'premature Whig', in much the same way as leftwing anti-Nazis found themselves described in the McCarthyite era as 'premature anti-fascists', though Leisler received a posthumous pardon and rehabilitation).[35] Loyalty in times of civil war and regime change was therefore never easy, and affairs in Britain were mirrored by events in the colonies.

The colonies certainly possessed the legal weapons to deal with treachery. Laws of treason, or the assumption of the English law, were commonly recorded in the printed collections of colonial statutes. On one side were the unique rules of the New Haven Colony, derived from Biblical sources such as Numbers and Samuel, but the core of the offence was still 'invasion, insurrection or publick rebellion against this jurisdiction', and seizing any plantation, town or guns. On the other, it is significant that from the start the Plymouth colony in 1636 had included under capital offences, 'treason or rebellion against the person of the King, State or Commonwealth, either of England or these Colonies'.[36] In the

---

[34] Carla Gardina Pestana, *The English Atlantic in an Age of Revolution, 1640-1661* (Cambridge, MA: Harvard University Press, 2004), pp. 35 – Maryland; p. 45, Charles I orders arrest, 1645; pp. 89 and 92, Berkeley's reaction to the execution of Charles I as treason; p. 119 Jamaica.
[35] D.S. Lovejoy, *The Glorious Revolution in America* (New York: Harper and Row, 1972).
[36] Hurst, 'Treason in the United States: I', pp. 226-7 and 277-8; New Plymouth 1671, *General Laws of Connecticut, Laws of Massachusetts Bay*, 1677.

Caribbean, with an anarchic pattern of seafaring and plunder, there was a legal connection made between piracy and treason, as it was assumed that ('British') pirates would work for the other side during a war. Thus Barbados decreed in 1684 that trials for 'treasons, piracies or other offences upon the seas' should be tried in front of five commissioners (drawn from the legislative assembly), but the full Habeas Corpus Act was passed in 1698, 'for the better securing the liberty of His Majesty's subjects with this Island, and for Preventing long imprisonment' (1698). Jamaica had similar laws: the 1682 law against piracy specifically included those who in America served *against* the King's allies, rather than on behalf of his enemies, and all 'treasons on the high seas' were tried by a Judge of the Admiralty and a commission appointed by the governor. This was probably the outcome of the recent experiences in the Anglo-Dutch wars, when buccaneers preferred to continue their depredations against the Spanish (at peace with the British) rather than attack the largely unprofitable Dutch ships.[37]

Jamaica also passed in 1682 a specific law making counterfeiting the great seal treason, to be punished by death 'as ordained by the Laws of England'. This was something of an obsession among the London authorities, as Hurst pointed out: Massachusetts' legislation of 1692 was criticized because it contained no such provision, and the Privy Council disallowed it. In the eighteenth-century forging the great seal and also the currency of the realm were often required offences if omitted from colonial law codes. Georgia, for example, specifically added a clause to that effect, protecting the Great Seal, in 1755.[38] The absence of a specific treason statute does not seem to have inhibited the Maryland authorities from prosecuting Richard Clarke of Ann-Arundel county in 1707 for treason. The earlier law of treason, from the 1640s, seems to have lapsed, but Clarke was still charged with a 'wicked and treasonable conspiracy to seize upon the magazine and Governor, and overturn Her Majesty's Government, and bring the Heathen Indians, together with the Conspirators, to cut off and extirpate the Inhabitants of this Province'. He was outlawed, and given twenty days following the end of the session, to surrender himself. Kilty notes that the trial was conducted under the rules of the 1696 Treason Act, with the

---

[37] *The Laws of Barbados Collected by William Rawlin of the Middle Temple, London Esq., and Now Clerk to the Assembly of the Said Island* (London: William Rawlin, 1699), pp. 152–3; *An Abridgement of the Laws in Force and Use in Her Majesty's Plantations, viz., of Virginia, Jamaica, Barbadoes, Maryland, New-England, New-York, Carolina* (London: John Nicholson, 1704), pp. 124–5; on buccaneers as reluctant patriots, see Gwenda Morgan and Peter Rushton, *The British and French in the Atlantic*, pp. 63–4.

[38] *An Abridgement of the Laws of Virginia*, p. 174; Hurst, 'Treason in the United States: I', p. 232; *Digest of the Laws of Georgia, 1755–1798* (1800), p. 46.

prisoner being provided with a copy of the indictment and a list of the jurors, and he seems to have waived some of the processes concerning witnesses. There was a specific 'Act for the Outlawing of Richard Clarke' in 1705, and by 1707 'having obstinately refused to surrender himself to Justice', he was charged with 'various seditious Practices and Intentions, forging of Dollars etc. The said Richard Clarke is therefore hereby convicted and attainted of High Treason, shall suffer Death etc.' In 1716 they signalled their loyalty by passing an Act for the better security and safety of His Lordship's Government and the Protestant Interest, against those who had 'openly in Treasonable Manner taken upon them to give the pretended Prince of Wales the Title of King of Great-Britain' – the Old Pretender, in the year after the '15 Rising. Although the law had not been specifically passed, the practical safeguards of 1696 had been introduced for this case, and in this way English liberties had been co-opted by stealth.[39] Other colonies specified the 1696 Act in their laws such as Pennsylvania in 1718 and South Carolina in 1731. North Carolina in 1749 passed a law to put into force the 'several Statutes of the Kingdom of England, or South-Britain', which included the treason laws of Edward III and William III: at the same time, writs for habeas corpus were recorded.[40] Some specific measures were rejected by London, as New York had discovered: Pennsylvania's attempt in 1700 to protect the governor and proprietor with a special treason provision was firmly rejected six years later, the existing laws being deemed sufficient.[41]

Thus another issue of potential conflict with London was how colonies might acquire the provisions under both habeas corpus and the 1696 Treason Act. It seems that while the London authorities frowned on specific inclusion of habeas corpus provisions in colonial acts, they assumed that the common law writ to free people from unjustified and lengthy imprisonment without trial would be

---

[39] Thomas Bacon, *Laws of Maryland at Large* (Annapolis, MD: Jonas Green, 1765), unpaginated, 1705, c. 5, 1707 c. 1, 1716 c. 5; Chancellor W. Kilty, *A Report of All Such English Statutes as Existed at the Time of the First Emigration of the People of Maryland and Which by Experience Have Been Found Applicable to the Local and Other Circumstances* (Annapolis, MD: J. Chandler, 1811), pp. 217–20.

[40] *Statutes at Large, Pennsylvania* vol. 3, pp. 200–1, 1718 Advancement of Justice; South Carolina 1731, J.F. Grimké, *Public Laws of the State of South-Carolina* (Philadelphia: R. Aitken, 1790), p. 90. 'Regulating of Trials in Cases of Treasons and Misprision of Treasons', in *A Complete Revisal of All the Acts of the Assembly of North Carolina* (NC: James Davis, 1774), pp. 40, 49, 250 and 253 for references to habeas corpus.

[41] *Statutes at Large of Pennsylvania*, vol. 2, 52–3). See also Alison Reppy, 'The Spectre of Attainder in New York, Part 1', *St. John's Law Review*, 23 (1) (2013), pp. 12 and 15. Apart from that of Bayard, the only major trial for treason under colonial rule was that of William Prendergast in 1766; William Pencak, Matthew Dennis, and Simon P. Newman, eds, *Riot and Revelry in Early America* (University Park, PA: Pennsylvania State University, 2002).

admissible at the courts of oyer and terminer, which they stipulated should be held at least twice a year. There are such writs in the Georgia records (see below). Governors, however, according to the collection of instructions given to them, were given the power to authorize the habeas corpus law, it seems. This may not have satisfied all in the colonies for a specific piece of legislation: as Halliday observes,

> Habeas corpus went to new imperial dominions by common law. But the colonial subjects in such dominions generally clamoured for a habeas corpus act of their own. One of the 1679 act's most important consequences was to inspire the idea that only a statute would make the writ effective. In the Caribbean and North American, one colonial legislation after another passed an act in imitation.[42]

The 1696 Treason Act provoked little or no objections, by contrast, and was widely adopted as procedure in colonial treason cases. Connecticut, for example, asserted in its 1702 collection that the procedures for treason trials should follow those of 1696, and in general laid down that no one should be put to death without the evidence of at least two witnesses. Yet this was far from the first time that the colony had been disturbed by matters of sedition and treason: there were several recorded cases in the 1660s and 1670s of sedition and rebellion, and 'usurping the authority of the king', among them the case of John Scott of Ashford, Long Island, charged with 'heinous crimes and practises seditious'.[43]

Delaware was clearly aware that some colonial legislation had run into trouble with the Privy Council and its lawyers, and chose in 1719 to be very specific when it came to treason:

> Whereas the common law is justly esteemed to be the birth-right of English subjects, and ought to be regarded in this government as the safest rule of our conduct; and whereas acts of Parliament have been judged not to extend to the plantations, except where they are particularly named in the body of such acts; and forasmuch as some persons have been encouraged to transgress certain statutes against capital crimes, and other enormities, because those statutes have not been hitherto fully extended to this government; and also, that his Majesty's good subjects, the inhabitants thereof, have not yet been so happy as to obtain the royal confirmation of any law for the better establishment of their constitution

---

[42] L.W. Labaree, *Royal Instructions to British Colonial Governors 1670–1776* (New Haven CT: Yale University Press, 1897), vol. 1, pp. 292–3 and 334–5, items 463 and 464; A.H. Carpenter, 'Habeas Corpus in the Colonies', *The American Historical Review*, 8 (1) (October, 1902), 18–27. Halliday, *Habeas Corpus*, p. 256.
[43] *Acts and Laws of His Majesties Colony of Connecticut* (1702, reprint, 1901), pp. 13–14, 117 and 244; *Public Records of the Colony of Connecticut … 1665*, pp. 421–2; *1675 to 1679*, p. 16 ftn, same man 1664.

and government; For the preventing therefore any failure in the future, in that behalf, may it please the Governor that it may be enacted ...

That all inquests and trials of high treason, shall be according to due order and course of common law, observing the directions of the statute-laws of Great Britain relating to the trials, proceedings, and judgements in such cases.

Later, in 1741, they enacted that

every person or persons, who shall be guilty of any petty treason, misprision or treason, murder, manslaughter, homicide, bestiality, incest or bigamy, shall be tried in the like manner as other felons by the said act are directed to be tried, and punished in the like manner as persons guilty of the like crimes and offences are punishable by the laws and statutes of that part of Great Britain called England.[44]

Alexander Spotswood had issued proclamation in 1710 claiming the Habeas Corpus Act for Virginia, following royal instructions: these had left things to governors. Georgia is assumed to have 'received' both the common law habeas corpus and the 1679 Act in 1733, Writs to that effect were allowed under common law in Georgia in 1743, and it is said by Wilkes that the common law writ, preceding the 1679 Act, was available in that and all the other colonies.[45]

Forgery of the currency, by counterfeiting the coins and copying the paper money, were all varieties of petit treason, but they also posed serious problems for the colonial authorities. It was at first unclear whether the paper scrip issued by individual colonies constituted currency 'of the realm', and another problem shared with the authorities in Britain, moreover, was that much of the hard currency was in foreign coinage, with dollars and Portuguese gold being favourites. These were not new problems, as Elizabethan England had had to face the problem of counterfeiting Spanish and Portuguese gold coins and had passed laws including this in the hanging offence of 'coining': this legislation was easily adopted by colonies such as Virginia, but paper currency was new on both sides of the Atlantic at the end of the seventeenth century. The result was that, around 1700, both home country and colonies had to respond to both the physical threat to the metal currency and the increasing danger to the printed notes. Virginia had traded through values in weights of tobacco, or in Portuguese and Spanish coinage. The latter (1710) were protected by the punishments of the 1570s laws of Elizabeth I, and

---

[44] *Laws of the State of Delaware*, 1797, C.XXIIa, pp. 65–6 and 226 15 Geo.II.
[45] Labaree, *Royal Instructions*, vol. 1, p. 334; Donald E. Wilkes Jr., 'From Oglethorpe to the Overthrow of the Confederacy: Habeas Corpus in Georgia, 1733-1865', *Georgia Law Review*, 45 (2011), pp. 1015–72, 1021 and 1027.

then in 1714 British coin was added to the currency, to be protected after 1727 by a law making 'the counterfeiting of the current silver and copper coin a treasonable offence'. The problems of paper, though, went on throughout the colonial period, and forging American notes was a feature of the British economic warfare in the War for Independence. Because forgery of other written or printed documents was unclearly covered by specific legislation, there were efforts in places such as South Carolina to criminalize it severely. When the state tried to repeal benefit of clergy for counterfeiting, there were doubts about whether a colony could by those means *increase* the penalty for crimes such as counterfeiting.[46]

Far more than in England, treason in the colonies might involve fraternizing, communicating or collaborating with enemies, which, as in the Clarke case, might involve association with the Indians or, equally, their allies the French. This arose in the first and second wars involving the colonies of North America and the Caribbean, King William's War 1688–97 (the Nine Years' War) and Queen Anne's Wars (War of the Spanish Succession, 1702–13). The result was a legislative response through many laws making 'traitorous correspondence' with either a form of high treason. Massachusetts passed legislation to prevent 'all traiterous [*sic*] correspondence with the French king, or his subjects, or the Indian enemy or rebels, and supplying them with warlike or other stores'. The accused were guaranteed the rights of the 1696 Treason Act. This law followed the Deerfield raid of 1704 when dozens of captives were taken, and the alliance between the French and the Native Americans had taken hold of the fearful minds of New Englanders along with the dread of captivity among the Indians. Yet the carefully specific phrase about warlike stores disguised a pattern of normal trade with the 'enemy' territories throughout the colonial period, much of it illegal by the Navigation and other Acts passed by the British parliament, and continuing despite the frequent imperial conflicts.[47] There were prosecutions in several

---

[46] Kenneth Scott, 'Counterfeiting in Colonial Virginia', *VMHB*, 61 (1) (1953), pp. 3–33, 4. NB The Coin Acts 1572 and 1575 (5 Eliz.I c. 11, and 18 Eliz.I c. 1) made clipping coins punishable by death, and 1575 extended it to foreign coins. The year 1575 made it treason to diminish or falsify or lighten the Queen's coinage – hanging for men, burning for women: see S. Deng, *Coinage and State Formation in Early Modern England* (New York: Palgrave Macmillan, 2011), p. 107; Malcolm Gaskill, *Crime and Mentalities in Early Modern England* (Cambridge University Press, 2000), pp. 126–7; colonial examples, Rex v Mellichamp, 1736, in Cooper, *Statutes at Large in South Carolina*, vol. 2, p.738, forgery of writings in 1736-7 act against forgery – these are various Acts of Parliament also accepted, and Herbert A. Johnson, 'The Rule of Law in the Realm and the Province of New York: Prelude to the American Revolution', *History*, 91 (1) (301) (2006), pp. 3–23, 13–14.

[47] Massachusetts, *Acts* 1, p. 595; L. Colley, *Captives: Britain, Empire and the World* (New Haven, CT: Yale University Press, 2002), p. 153; T. Vaughan and E.W. Clark, *Puritans among the Indians: Accounts of Captivity and Redemption, 1676-1724* (Cambridge, MA: Belknap Press 1981), p. 79; Thomas S. Truxes, *Defying Empire: Trading with the Enemy in Colonial New York* (New Haven, CT: 2008).

northern colonies for trade in wartime with the French possessions or territories, but the reference to warlike stores was essential to the charges. In New York, says Thomas S. Truxes, the trade was not of treasonable intent, but 'rather, the naked manifestation of a powerful commercial impulse synonymous with the great metropolis'. It might also be said to be an inevitable fact of geography, with a significant market in the north which happened to be either Indian or French. The situation was even worse where, as among the neighbouring islands of the Caribbean, food supplies were needed for sugar-producing islands, and the suppliers were often across the divides of any particular war. The Massachusetts legislation exempted the supplies to British forces, or to French prisoners of war and, more mysteriously, 'secret services made, or done, at all times, by the direction of the governor with the advice of the council'. New Hampshire had similar legislation in 1744. Uniquely, in Virginia in 1684, following some disturbances and protests, pulling up or destroying tobacco plants was judged to be treason, to be tried only in the twelve months after the offence.[48]

Words of loyalty – A note on oaths

In theory, treason required more than words of intention or even conspiracy yet loyalty and treachery were also often acted through words, with rival oaths of loyalty and rejection. It was not uncommon for there to be exercises in mass oath-taking as a means of enforcing performances of loyalty. The last in England seems to have been in 1723, and the records of oaths in the County of Devon reflect an interesting mix of men and women taking the oath of loyalty: the latter were more than a quarter of the oath-takers, and only a minority were married to the men on the lists. It seems that many independent women were included.[49] In this performative culture, oaths were both a form of abjuration of any alternative allegiance and the affirmation of loyalty to the current

---

[48] Truxes, *Defying Empire*, p. 1; Massachusetts *Acts*, vol. 1, p. 596; New Hampshire, Bachellor, *Laws*, vol. 2, p. 743; *Abridgement of the Laws of Virginia* (1720), p. 14.

[49] Miles Ogborn, 'Orality, Oaths and Evidence in the British Atlantic World, 1650–1800', *Trans.Proc. Inst.Brit.Geographers*, NS 36 (1) (2011), pp. 109–25; Edward Vallance, 'Women, Politics, and the 1723 Oaths of Allegiance to George I', *Historical Journal*, 59 (4) (2016), pp. 975–99. on the last occasion of mass oath-taking in England which derives from the Devon oaths project and his *Revolutionary England and the National Covenant: State Oaths, Protestantism and the Political Nation, 1553–1682* (Woodbridge: Boydell Press, 2005); E. Vallance, *The 1723 Oath Rolls in England: An Electronic Finding List* (2014, University of Roehampton online); John Walter, *Covenanting Citizens: The Protestation Oath and Popular Political Culture in the English Revolution* (Oxford University Press, 2016); David Martin Jones, *Conscience and Allegiance in Seventeenth-Century England: The Political Significance of Oaths and Engagements* (Rochester, NY: University of Rochester Press, 1999).

regime, or monarch. Whereas public rejection of Catholic doctrine – such as that of transubstantiation – had been a clear indication of commitment to Protestantism in the early seventeenth century, the forms of oaths after the 1688 Glorious Revolution in Britain concentrated on repudiation of the claims of James II and his heirs, and the proclamation of legitimacy and loyalty to William III and Mary and their successors. In Scotland, before formal union in 1707, the Oath of Allegiance had been imposed at the Glorious Revolution, and the Oath of Abjuration 'sent Catholics, Episcopalians and Non-Jurors into exile. Many fled acts of attainder and the consequent forfeiture of their lands'. Loyalty to the Hanoverian Georges meant, for Presbyterian Scots, accepting an Anglican monarch and his bishops.[50]

The American colonies were familiar with this kind of oaths of loyalty. Charles Evans notes their frequency from the earliest period of settlement. The Virginia Company demanded that settlers take the oaths of Allegiance and Supremacy, reflecting the practice since Henry VIII's time, but other colonies such as Massachusetts opted out of the oath of Supremacy – or managed to avoid enforcing it, because it required obedience to the Church of England as well as the monarch's headship of it. Yet Governors and their deputies in Massachusetts had to take both oaths, under Charles I's 1629 charter. No attempt was made to enforce this on others in the colony at this time. Opt-out clauses were not unknown: when, after the Nova Scotian territory of Acadia was ceded to Britain under the 1713 Treaty of Utrecht, the Acadians refused to take the full Oath of Allegiance, they were permitted to take a less committed, conditional oath. They swore allegiance to King George, as long as they remained in Acadia, but did not have to forswear the supremacy of the Pope in religion. Thus, the double purpose of the traditional oaths, of loyalty to both the monarchs and their role as head of the Church of England was avoided, and there was no public renunciation of their Catholic faith. This was similar to the oath taken by 'recusants' – those refusing to conform to the Church of England – in England and elsewhere.[51] An unusual late example of the practice of mass oath-taking seems to have been ordered in 1766 in South Carolina, perhaps significantly a period of tension between Britain and her American colonies:

---

[50] Victoria Henshaw, *Scotland and the British Army, 1700-1750: Defending the Union* (London: Bloomsbury, 2014), p. 34; see Andrew Hadfield, *Lying in Early Modern English Culture: From the Oath of Supremacy to the Oath of Allegiance* (Oxford University Press, 2017); Parliamentary Guide to *The Parliamentary Oath* (Houses of Parliament, 2016).

[51] Charles Evans, 'Oaths of Allegiance in Colonial New England', *Proceedings of the American Antiquarian Society*, 31 (2) (1922), pp. 377–438, 378–80; *The Charters of the British Colonies in America* (London: J. Almon, 1774), pp. 15, 28, 29, 93 and 100.

A PROCLAMATION.
WHERE AS in and by an act of parliament passed in the sixth year of his present Majesty's reign, instituted, '*an act for altering the of abjuration and the assurance, and for amending so much of an act of the for seventh year of her late Majesty; Queen Anne*, intituled, *an act for the improvement of the union of the two kingdoms, at after the time limited, requirement the delivery of certain lists therein mentioned to prisons indicted of high treason or misprision of treason*'.
IT IS RECITED, That whereas, by the death of the person who pretended to be Prince of Wales during the life of the late King James and since his decease took upon himself the strike and title of king of England by the name of James the third, or of Scotland by the name of James Eighth, or the stile and title of King of some alteration in the oath of abjuration and assurance enacted to be taken in an act of parliament passed in the first year of the reign of his Majesty king George the first, to be administrated and taken in such manner and form as is there in sat down and prescribed: It is thereof enacted, that all and every person and persons who are enjoined and required to administer, take and subscribe the oath of abjuration.

Oaths were therefore for some people a reflection of divided or contradictory loyalties.[52] The Acadians were loyal to their land and the community they had created with little assistance from the French government. As Jeremy Smith observes, 'colonial communities had social ballast of their own and the cultures they generated acted as another pole of loyalty for the most pre-eminent political and economic classes'. If the colonial authorities depended on the loyalties of property holders, from large planters to smallholders, their insurgent opponents would have to do likewise. In the context of revolutionary America, an oath of loyalty was also possessed of this double purpose, representing both an oath of renunciation of all previous, that is, British allegiances and an expression of loyalty to the new state and United States. Many of the states, following the Declaration of Independence, followed Congress's advice to pass new, more suitable, treason laws, and also to be specific about the form of the oaths of loyalty that would indicate adherence to the new polities. These oaths were both for affirmation among the loyalty and, in effect, a means for those who were accused of disaffection to become reconciled to the new order, a rite of passage of readmission that needed to be certified and thus recorded by legal authorities (see Chapter 7). At the same time, as places changed hands between the protagonists, it was widely understood that many would be forced to swear

---

[52] *South Carolina Gazette*, 15 December 1766.

an oath to the opposing side, as a temporary expedient.[53] Thus testing and proving loyalty went on being essential to definitions of nationality, subjecthood or citizenship. The revolutionary implications of oaths were well understood by the more classically minded Americans, and it was no accident that in 1785 Jacques-Louis David made his famous painting, *Oath of the Horatii*, or that the Tennis-Court Oath played such a part in beginning the French Revolution. Yet oaths to royalty, thought Benjamin Rush, were the only way that they could impose their authority. Oaths of loyalty, however, remained a crucial means of naturalization, the transition from stranger or immigrant to subject or citizen, and still do in modern states today.[54]

---

[53] Jeremy Smith, *Europe and the Americas: State Formation, Capitalism and Civilizations in Atlantic Modernity* (Leiden and Boston: Brill, 2006), p. 218. J.B. Stein and S.G. Donabed, *Religion and the State: Europe and North America in the Seventeenth and Eighteenth Centuries* (Lanham, MD: Lexington Books, 2012), Ch. 8 Tara Thompson Stauch, 'Oaths and Christian Belief in the New Nation, 1776–1789', 127–41, and her 'Taking Oaths and Giving Thanks: Ritual and Religion in Revolutionary America', (Unpublished Ph.D., University of South Carolina, 2013).

[54] Harold Melvin Hyman, *To Try Men's Souls: Loyalty Tests in American History* (Berkeley, CA: University of California Press, 1959); Nellie Protsman Waldenmaier, *Some of the Earliest Oaths of Allegiance to the United States of America* (Lancaster PA: Lancaster Press, 1944); John Michael Huffman, 'Americans on Paper: Identity and Identification in the American Revolution', (Unpublished Ph.D., Harvard University, 2013); Gordon S. Wood, 'Classical Republicanism and the American Revolution', *Chicago-Kent Law Review*, 66 (1990), pp. 13–38, 18 and 31.

Part Two

Rebellion to Revolution

3

Speaking Words, Writing Sedition

Though the main focus of this study is high treason, it is necessary to recognize that the British state in all its forms directed a great deal of its energy in suppressing what might be described as the precursors of treason – the speaking and writing of words that might encourage or even incite treasonable actions. While it was generally accepted that words were not sufficient alone to constitute 'treason', they could be prosecuted under a broader category of offence, namely sedition. This offence, linked to criminal forms of *libel* such as obscene libel, constituted the traducing of the state or its personnel in ways that might undermine their credibility and encourage its overthrow. It is worth noting that during the seventeenth and most of the eighteenth century, this was not an offence in Scottish law, but was inventively imposed on Scotland during the revolutionary period of the 1790s (see Chapter 8).[1] The history of the law of sedition has therefore tended to be written from a very England-centred viewpoint, with little attempt made to examine the impact of the law and legal doctrines outside England in, for example, the colonies. Yet the colonial laws remain in force in India and Malaysia in the twenty-first century and have been re-examined in Australia as part of the reconsideration of post–9/11 anti-terrorism legislation. Even in the period before 1800, its history has been fragmented by period and geography, and crimes of speech have often been neglected for concentration on crimes of print culture, stressing the struggle over freedom of the press, thus separating the history of sedition into one of spoken words and social control on the one hand, and of censorship and its opponents on the other.

---

[1] Lindsay Farmer, '"Subverting the Settled Order of Things": The Crime of Sedition in Scotland, 1793–1849', online at https://www.academia.edu/35867037/_Subverting_the_Settled_Order_of_Things_The_Crime_of_Sedition_in_Scotland_1793-1849?auto=download (accessed 4 December 2019), also in M.T. Davis, E. MacLeod and G. Pentland, eds, *Political Trials in the Age of Revolution: Britain and the North Atlantic, 1793–1848* (Houndmills, Basingstoke: Palgrave Macmillan, 2019), pp. 19–46.

The aim here is to try and bring these back together in an overview which takes into account the parallel and interacting jurisdictions of the British Atlantic, the repression of speech as well as writing and the conflicts over the law in and out of court. Significant similarities united the two sides of the Atlantic in the law of seditious spoken words and in role of the legislature in initiating complaints and legal procedures against print culture and those responsible for writing and producing material deemed offensive. Everywhere under the common law, there seems to have been a decline in court prosecutions of the spoken word after 1700. This overview confirms the impression given by earlier histories of the rising conflict over the liberty of the press as political and legal authorities after the early 1700s concentrated on the printed expressions of criticism, satire and opposition which they saw as 'sedition'. There is a parallel history of personal defamation and its presence in many different kinds of courts between the sixteenth and the nineteenth centuries, which needs to be kept in mind. In the intensity of local social relations in face-to-face communities, insults and name-calling often broke out between old and new protagonists, and these often involved political as well as personal denigration. The dividing line between the personal and the political is at all times difficult to draw in writing the history of insulting words: more importantly, as we shall see, it was similarly difficult for judicial authorities in the past. That talk could be politically dangerous, and was treated as such by the law courts, is almost a staple of early modern English history. Its importance lies in part because so many women were among the accused, as Sharon Jansen has established for the Tudor period.[2]

Free speech, a free people and the law

British law took a momentous step in 2009: after more than 800 years, the common law offence of seditious libel was abolished, along with its close companions, obscene and blasphemous libel. The measure was placed as an

---

[2] Sharon L. Jansen, *Dangerous Talk and Strange Behaviour: Women and Popular Resistance to the Reforms of Henry VIII* (Houndmills, Basingstoke: Macmillan, 1996); see also Dermot Cavanagh and Tim Kirk, eds, *Subversion and Scurrility: Popular Discourse in Europe from 1500 to the Present* (Aldershot, 2000), Debora Shuger, *Censorship and Cultural Sensibility: The Regulation of Language in Tudor-Stuart England* (University of Pennsylvania Press, 2006), and M. Lindsay Kaplan, *The Culture of Slander in Early Modern England* (Cambridge: Cambridge University Press, 1997).

appendix to a bill about coroners' courts, and was widely welcomed.³ The law of sedition, however, was never as simple as its ending, and historians of law and popular politics, of literate culture and political criticism, have struggled with the changes in both the statutory framework and established legal precedents during the early modern period. The problems of integrating evidence on both written and spoken words, of prosecutions at all levels and even of cases heard before Parliament and colonial legislatures have proved almost insurmountable.⁴ The slippery nature of the crime in any period, the variability in the content of what was prosecuted and the changing legal frameworks in English and colonial laws all combine to make the topic difficult to grasp comprehensively and systematically. As a result, there are contrasting histories of the struggle for the rights of free speech and writing, and their embodiment in English and Anglo-American law. There are different emphases and interpretations of the historical and legal evidence, and people working on different historical periods or types of cases often neglect other times and problems.⁵

There have essentially been three established and occasionally overlapping histories of sedition, concentrating on popular cultures of opposition, the development of the free press and the legal history of the crime itself. Firstly, the analysis of popular culture has mined the substance of court cases for indications of the nature of insult and criticism of the powerful, the networks of opposition and the character of rumour and fantasy, as well as for the political and religious scepticism of ordinary people. In the sixteenth and seventeenth centuries, every religious twist and turn, and every change of regime, attracted

---

3   *The Observer*, 22 February 2009, p. 13; Office of Public Sector Information, at Coroners and Justice Act 2009 (c. 25), under section 73 entitled 'Abolition of common law libel offences etc.', listing them as sedition, seditious libel, defamatory and obscene libel; see Neil Parpworth, 'The Abolition of the Blasphemy Laws', *Justice of the Peace*, 172 (15 March 2005), pp. 164-7. The last prosecution for blasphemous libel In England was of *Gay News* in 1979; see Francesca Klug, Keir Starmer and Stuart Weir, *Three Pillars of Liberty* (London: Routledge, 1996); Ian Bryan, 'Unpalatable in Word or Deed: Hostility, Difference and Free Expression', *Crimes and Misdemeanours*, 1 (2007), pp. 126-53, on the Racial and Religious Hatred Act, 2006 and its predecessors; Russell Sandberg and Norman Doe, 'The Strange Death of Blasphemy', *The Modern Law Review*, 71 (2008), pp. 971-86; abolition under the Criminal Justice and Immigration Act, 2008.
4   Donald Thomas, *A Long Time Burning: The History of Literary Censorship in England* (London: Routledge Kegan Paul, 1969); Leonard W. Levy, *Freedom of Speech and Press in Early American History: Legacy of Suppression*, 2nd ed. (New York: Harper and Row Torchbook, 1963); David Cressy, *Dangerous Talk: Scandalous, Seditious and Treasonable Speech in Pre-Modern England* (Oxford: Oxford University Press, 2010); Adam Fox, 'Rumour, News and Popular Political Opinion in Elizabethan and Early Stuart England', *The Historical Journal*, 40 (1997), pp. 597-620; Alastair Bellany, 'Singing Libel in Early Stuart England: The Case of the Staines Fiddlers, 1627', *Huntington Library Quarterly*, 69 (2006), pp. 177-93.
5   See the most recent attempt, by David Cressy, *Dangerous Talk*, who tends to neglect the changes in the law after 1700, and much of the repression of print culture, in what is the best overview available.

responses which the authorities found hard to control and suppress successfully. By the eighteenth century, print culture and greater literacy encouraged an even greater proliferation of seditious techniques: people stuck rude posters on the king's statue, wrote things on walls and sang subversive songs in the dark streets of London. A similar range of targets and forms of expression has been found in the North American colonies in the seventeenth century and in print in the eighteenth. What governments everywhere called sedition was, in fact, a part of a diverse and constantly changing disrespect of the powerful.[6]

Secondly, there has been a focus on the long struggle for freedom of speech and writing, which in American historical narratives has formed the constitutional basis for the freedom of the press. In British history, too, the long march to freedom, with all its difficulties, has had its place, described by A.C. Grayling as a 'tale of a long, tough, ultimately (but perhaps only temporarily?) successful struggle or interrelated series of struggles'. This can be a history of heroes and villains, victories and defeats.[7] In Britain, freedom of speech and publication, though, was not easily won: there were trials for sedition in the 1926 miners' strike, state censorship of stage plays until the 1960s and a trial for blasphemous libel as late as 1979.[8] For some historians of early America, the constitutional right to free speech has, like the right to bear arms, attracted some critical re-interpretations of the original intent of the founders and their ideas of freedom: much of this has been inspired, in various ways, by the sceptical work of Leonard W. Levy.[9] Histories of British and American traditions of free speech divide into optimists and pessimists about the freedoms won, and *when* they were won,

---

[6] See, among others, Cressy, *Dangerous Talk*; Fox, 'Rumour, News and Popular Political Opinion'; and useful chapters in Tim Harris, ed., *The Politics of the Excluded, c. 1500–1850* (Houndsmills, Basingstoke: Palgrave, 2001), E.H. Shagan, 'Rumours and Popular Politics in the Reign of Henry VIII', in Tim Harris (ed.), *The Politics of the Excluded, c. 1500–1850* (Houndmills, Basingstoke: Palgrave Macmillan, 2001), pp. 30–66; A. Bellany, 'Libels in Action: Ritual, Subversion and the English Literary Underground, 1603–42', in Tim Harris (ed.), *The Politics of the Excluded, c. 1500–1850* (Houndmills, Basingstoke: Palgrave, 2001), pp. 99–125. Bellany and Nicholas Rogers, 'Crowds and Political Festival in Georgian England', pp. 233–64; also Alastair Bellany, 'Railing Rhymes Revisited: Libels, Scandals, and Early Stuart Politics', *History Compass*, 5 (4) (2007), pp. 1136–79. For America, the classic and comprehensive study for the seventeenth century is by Larry D. Eldridge, *A Distant Heritage: The Growth of Free Speech in Early America* (New York: New York University Press, 1994), and Levy, *Freedom of Speech*.

[7] A.C. Grayling, *Towards the Light: The Story of the Struggles for Liberty and Rights That Made the Modern World* (London: Bloomsbury, 2007), p. 7; Ben Wilson, *The Laughter of Triumph: William Hone and the Fight for the Free Press* (London: Faber and Faber, 2005).

[8] David Hencke and Francis Beckett, *Marching to the Fault Line: The 1984 Miners Strike and the Death of Industrial Britain* (London: Constable and Robinson, 2009); for the earlier miners' strikes of the 1920s, see Isaac Kramnick and Barry Sheerman, *Harold Laski: A Life on the Left* (London: Allen Lane, 1993), pp. 125–6, on the government's use of sedition charges; Donald Thomas, *Freedom's Frontier: Censorship in Modern Britain* (London: John Murray, 2007), and *A Long Time Burning*.

[9] Levy, *Freedom of Speech*.

with the Americans mostly more optimistic about their current rights. With regard to Britain, at least one author has moved from optimism to pessimism in successive publications, though there is also an anxiety in the United States about the return of something like the crime of sedition in early twenty-first-century counter-terrorism laws.[10]

The third type of history has concentrated on the law and the twists and turns of legal statutes, court decisions and precedents, and the struggle over the independence of juries. The debates concentrate over exactly how and when the legal definition of seditious libel arose, and was fully developed. Less prominent have been comparisons of different jurisdictions and attempts at explaining the direction – or directions – of change. The problem is typical of the difficulties in writing histories of a crime which has largely been defined by common law practices rather than by statute. At no time, moreover, was any working definition free from challenge or contention.[11] The development of a broader Anglo-American tradition has been neglected by legal historians of English law, unlike their American colleagues, though the New York case of John Peter Zenger 1735 was not only repeatedly published in London in the 1730s, but was rapidly granted the important status of being published in the series of English *State Trials*. Similarly, the tribulations of radical John Wilkes in the 1760s were watched with great interest in the American colonies, and English legal precedents carefully studied. There was a crucial worldwide – almost global – aspect to the development of the common law and statutes before 1776. The

---

[10] Ben Wilson, *The Laughter of Triumph*, and his more gloomy *What Price Liberty? How Freedom Was Won and Is Being Lost* (London: Faber and Faber, 2009); as Michael Harris has pointed out, there have been many false dawns in the history of freedom of the press, Michael Harris, *London Newspapers in the Age of Walpole: A Study of the Origins of the Modern English Press* (London and Toronto: Associated University Presses, 1987), p. 153. For the Australian debate on the current situation, see Australian Law Reform Commission, *Fighting Words: A Review of Sedition Laws in Australia* (Commonwealth of Australia: 2006); Sarah Sorial, 'Sedition and the Question of Freedom of Speech', *Current Issues in Criminal Justice*, 18 (2007), pp. 431–48; L.W. Maher, '"Modernising" the Crime of Sedition?', *Labour History*, 90 (2006), pp. 201–9, online at http://historycooperative.org/journals/lab/90/maher.html (accessed 14 June 2010). For the United States, see Ronald J. Krotoszynski and Clint A, Carpenter, 'The Return of Seditious Libel', *UCLA Law Review*, 55 (2008), pp. 1239–319 and Ronald J. Krotoszynski, *The First Amendment in Cross-Cultural Perspective: A Comparative Analysis of Freedom of Speech* (New York: New York University Press, 2006).

[11] Cressy, *Dangerous Talk*, p. 41; William Holdsworth, *History of English Law* (London: Methuen, 1945), pp. 4, 511–12; Brian Manning, 'The Origins of the Doctrine of Sedition', *Albion*, 12 (1980), pp. 99–121, may have been the first to exonerate the Star Chamber, but the more comprehensive analysis of the late seventeenth- and early eighteenth-century legal decisions is in Philip Hamburger, 'The Development of the Law of Seditious Libel and the Control of the Press', *Stanford Law Review*, 37 (1985), pp. 661–762, followed largely by James Oldham, *English Common Law in the Age of Mansfield* (Chapel Hill: University of North Carolina Press, 2004), pp. 209–35.

parallel histories of juries' refusal to convict in some cases have established a debate about 'jury nullification' – that is, acquittal in the face of overwhelming evidence of guilt – that resonates down to the present day.[12]

This suggests that a broader perspective is needed, one that sees the British state and its varied legislative constituencies, for want of a better word, as operating in an increasingly wide world of interacting, and perhaps imperfectly coordinated, legal actions. The complex interactions of a burgeoning empire embracing many different forms of law and legal system make this at first glance a daunting task. At the least, the analysis should adopt an Atlantic perspective incorporating recent reconceptualizations by scholars such as Benton, Bilder, Hulsebosch and Konig (see Chapter 2).[13] The law of sedition was not a fixed item in a code to be exported to the colonies, but one that was under development and redevelopment in England in the seventeenth and eighteenth centuries, a process occurring simultaneously in different circumstances in different places. Rather than a simple relationship in which English statutes dominated and were imposed on the colonies, law was being created simultaneously on both sides of the Atlantic. The aim was to draw a line between acceptable and unacceptable politics, one that naturally varied according to local circumstances. Everywhere, as one recent study has suggested, the empire was thus inherently 'exclusionary'.[14] New forms of social relations required new laws, and this was also true of the new structures of political order. Just as slavery and indentured servitude had to be reinvented or re-framed in the contexts of the colonies, so the boundaries

---

[12] Note that both Levy, *Freedom of Speech*, and Eldridge, *A Distant Heritage*, explored the English legal framework, and Levy in particular shows some of the interaction between English and colonial law; on juries, see Alan Scheflin and Jon Van Dyke, 'Jury Nullification: The Contours of a Controversy', *Law and Contemporary Problems*, 43 (1980), pp. 51–115, particularly their historical summary 56–9; T.H. Green, *Verdict According to Conscience: Perspectives on the English Trial Jury, 1200–1800* (Chicago: University of Chicago Press, 1985), pp. 28–63 and 319–55; J. Hostettler, *The Criminal Jury Old and New: Jury Power from Early Times to the Present Day* (Winchester: Waterside Press, 2004).

[13] Many of the most recent advances in interpretation have broadened the perspective on England to include its wider connections to the 'four countries' of Britain and the colonies, and the understanding of the colonies has moved in the opposite direction to incorporate an Atlantic perspective: see, among others, Mary Sarah Bilder, *The Transatlantic Constitution: Colonial Legal Culture and the Empire* (Cambridge, MA: Harvard University Press, 2004); Daniel Joseph Hulsebosch, *Constituting Empire: New York and the Transformation of Constitutionalism in the Atlantic World, 1664–1830* (Chapel Hill: University of North Carolina Press, 2005); Lauren Benton *Law and Colonial Cultures: Legal Regimes in World History, 1400–1900* (New York and Cambridge: Cambridge University Press, 2002); Eliga H. Gould, 'Entangled Atlantic Histories: A Response from the Anglo-American Periphery', *American History Review*, 112 (2007), pp. 764–86.

[14] Jack P. Greene, *Exclusionary Empire: English Liberty Overseas, 1600–1900* (Cambridge: Cambridge University Press, 2009), p. 54.

of political discourse had to be set anew.[15] This perspective goes to the heart of the problem of understanding the legal formations of the state at the local level in the British empire, addressing the extent of diversification of the law, and the way it was adapted to local social and political relations. Treason laws in the colonies drew upon the core elements of the legislation, but sedition remained largely a contextual offence, to be flexibly applied to a wide range of sayings and writings deemed unacceptable to local authorities. How this mixture of common tradition and local invention developed before 1776 is the key focus of what follows.

In order to develop interpretative categories for comparison, clear criteria are needed for establishing similarities and differences in the use of 'sedition' in both England and her colonies. Without assuming that 'sedition' meant the same thing in different places in the Anglo-American world, there are common problems in analysing the many practices and their differences in this broader perspective. In that regard, the key questions are, firstly, to examine sources of the law, that is, the legislative and common law framework on which prosecutions drew. Secondly, it is important to establish the judicial or political forces or bodies applying the law and in what kinds of judicial processes cases appeared. A third requirement is an examination of the kinds of offences and offenders pursued – in effect, a survey of the kinds of people and words, whether spoken or printed, targeted for prosecution. Finally, the overall aim is to track and explain the trajectory – or many trajectories – of change in the period up to the American Revolution, for the diverse legal contexts of the early British Empire. In this last, it is clear that the materials for a total survey do not yet exist, so it is hoped that a selection of contexts both from around England and from the two 'great hearths' of American law, the Chesapeake and New England, will provide sufficient scope for interpretation.[16]

---

[15] On convicts and servants, Gwenda Morgan and Peter Rushton, *Eighteenth-Century Criminal Transportation: The Formation of the Criminal Atlantic* (Houndmills, Basingstoke: Palgrave Macmillan, 2004), Ch. 6; Douglas Hay and Paul Craven, eds, *Masters, Servants and Magistrates in Britain and the Empire, 1562–1955* (Chapel Hill, NC: University of North Carolina Press, 2004); on slavery, see particularly Bradley J. Nicholson, 'Legal Borrowing and the Origins of Slave Law in the British Colonies', *The American Journal of Legal History*, 39 (1994), pp. 38–53; Benton *Law and Colonial Cultures*; Gould, 'Entangled Atlantic Histories'; Bilder, *Transatlantic Constitution*.

[16] David T. Konig, 'Regionalism in Early American Law', in Michael Grossberg and Christopher L. Tomlins (eds), *The Cambridge History of Law in America* (Cambridge: Cambridge University Press, 2008), p. 145.

The development of the English law: The sources of the law of sedition

The history of sedition in English law in the early modern period was, at least up to the mid-eighteenth century, one of fluctuation (perhaps oscillation) between reliance on specific statutes on the one hand and judicial activism in the highest courts on the other. Moreover, there were many cases in the local courts before county magistrates which were subject to variable interpretation by local authorities managing intense local social relations rather than implementing a simple policy of political repression. In the first mode, in the sixteenth century time-limited laws specified subjects which could not be discussed or sentiments which could not be expressed, and included an increasingly wide range of media which could be prosecuted. For the Tudors, many subjects were legally unmentionable – Henry VIII's marriages, Elizabeth I's parentage and the identity of her likely successor. When these statutes lapsed, precedents were established by prosecutions in court extending moral and legal condemnation to a wider and wider range of activities, even those apparently entirely private, which could be regarded as sedition. Before the 1640s, the court responsible was the Star Chamber. For most of the Restoration, without this court, the Licensing Acts, supported in part by the provisions about speech in Charles II's treason law, could be used to suppress sedition. The repeated enactment of licensing acts from 1662 onwards allowed many printed threats to be prosecuted simply as illegal publications, and this remained the key method of control over printers until the legislation lapsed in 1695.[17] From the 1680s onwards, however, the role of 'custos morum' was adopted by the King's Bench, a role which was greatly enlarged in dealing with sedition in the 1690s and the early eighteenth century. Thus a repeated cycle of alternating legislation and adjudication dominated the development of the English law of sedition from the mid-sixteenth to the mid-eighteenth centuries. In short, legislative initiatives alternated with judicial activism.

The appearance of change and fluctuation, however, was deceptive, as the established precedents and embodied concepts of sedition found by the Star Chamber were little changed through the revolutionary upheavals of the mid- to late seventeenth century, and appear almost unchanged to govern legal

---

[17] Hamburger, 'The Development of the Law of Seditious Libel', pp. 679–80, 714 and particularly, Lois G. Schwoerer, *The Ingenious Mr Henry Care, Restoration Publicist* (Baltimore, MD: The Johns Hopkins University Press, 2001), pp. 7, 12–13 and 18 on the effects, and the political problems of renewal, of the law.

proceedings in the eighteenth century. There are parallels with the laws of blasphemy which (in England) drifted from the severity of the punishments for heresy in the early seventeenth century, to more moderate forms of sanction for blasphemy by the 1690s. The judicial initiative enshrined in Lord Chief Justice Sir Matthew Hale's judgement in *R. v. Taylor* (1676) in the King's Bench was a key shift in this process, but was rather overtaken by the 1698 Blasphemy Act criminalizing apostasy by most Christians.[18]

Exploring this process in more detail, it is worth emphasizing that at the beginning of the early modern period, Tudor legislation in the reigns of Philip and Mary, and Elizabeth I, set the framework for quite specific prohibitions, but did so in part by reiterating earlier laws and establishing their continued validity.[19] At the same time, they also introduced new ideas of intent and content. As Holdsworth put it, the 'statutes of 1554 and 1558 had made it a misdemeanour to speak or write with a malicious intent false and slanderous words of the king and queen'. Later in her reign, anxiety about Elizabeth's health and the uncertainty about the identity of her successor led to additional legislation which made it illegal to discuss the queen's parentage, prophesize her successor or speculate about the changes which would occur when she died.[20] With regard to treasonable words in all this legislation, two witnesses were required for a conviction, and later this would be remembered when it came to expressions of sedition. At the Restoration, Norfolk justice of the peace Robert Doughty briefed the court in a charge to the Grand Jury, that 'two witnesses must accuse in treason, petty treason, misprision of treason and for the words', and cited the legislation from the reigns of Edward VI and Elizabeth. Nothing was comparably clear in cases of sedition, but in the face of one allegation Doughty noted that there was only one witness, and therefore could not proceed unless he could be sure that the words were fully treasonable.[21]

---

[18] Except for Unitarians, whose rejection of the Trinity was accepted; see Elliott Visconsi, 'The Invention of Criminal Blasphemy: Rex v. Taylor (1676)', *Representations*, 103 (2008), pp. 30–52, who argues that there were no prosecutions under the Act; David Nash, *Blasphemy in Modern Britain: 1789 to the Present* (Aldershot: Ashgate, 1999) and *Blasphemy in the Christian World* (Oxford University Press, 2007).

[19] John G. Bellamy, *The Tudor Law of Treason* (London: Routledge Kegan Paul, 1979), pp. 45–6.

[20] Holdsworth, *History of English Law*, vol. 4, pp. 511–12; 2 Philip and Mary, c. 3; 1 Eliz c. 6; 23 Eliz c. 2, which Holdsworth says supplanted all previous legislation in her reign.

[21] Bellamy, *Tudor Law of Treason*, p. 46; Sir John Baker, *The Oxford History of the Laws of England, Vol. 6, 1483–1558* (Oxford: Oxford University Press, 2003), pp. 518–19; *The Notebook of Robert Doughty, 1662–1665*, ed. James M. Rosenheim, Norfolk Record Society. vol. 54 (1989, printed Aberystwyth, 1991), pp. 84 and 95, June–July 1662, citing 1 Edwd VI c. 12; also cites 5 & 6 Edwd VI c. 11, and 13 Eliz 1, c. 1. See L.M. Hill, 'The Two-Witness Rule in English Treason Trials: Some Comments on the Emergence of Procedural Law', *The American Journal of Legal History*, 12 (1968), pp. 95–111, 106 for the 1571 Act's longlasting citation.

As some elements of Tudor legislation died with Elizabeth, the courts – particularly the Star Chamber – in Holdsworth's words, 'had assumed the power to deal with defamation in general on the ground that it disturbed the security of the peace of the state', and the court's decisions did not rely on those earlier statutes.[22] Amidst all this litigation, involving many personal libels (part of a much larger takeover of this business from the church courts), were many libels against the powerful, political and the government, including the monarch, deemed seditious because of the threat to the state itself.[23] Essential principles were established that lasted nearly 200 years. For example, the right of government to be free from criticism was fundamental to the developing idea of seditious libel. Unlike treasonable words, such libel might have the effect of undermining the government, while showing no *intent* to overthrow it. The idea was that because even a very private speech or writing might produce disruption of social peace and ordered government, it had the potential to be a public offence. By the end of the sixteenth century, the sneaky character of whispered or printed allegations was also highlighted: as Edward Coke put it, 'in a settled state of Government the party grieved ought to complain for every injury done him in an ordinary course of law, and not by any means to revenge himself, either by the odious course of libelling or otherwise'. Furthermore, the fact that a statement was true might make it more likely to result in a breach of the peace: 'for as the woman said she would never grieve to have been told of her red nose if she had not one indeed'.[24] It was this shift from treasonable words to seditious libel that marked the innovations of the cases before the Star Chamber, and the punishments inflicted followed the previous legal statute of Elizabeth.[25]

In the subsequent cases before the civil wars, the basic principle was established, that words, even words of truth, could be dangerous for social order and political peace. Moreover, certain institutions, offices and their holders, particularly those embodying or representing royal authority, were inherently deserving of legal protection against words. In a major departure from the customs of civil law of personal libel, the object of seditious libel did not have to be alive, nor did the libel have to be untrue. Publication or promulgation

---

[22] Holdsworth, *History of English Law*, vol. 5: 208–9.
[23] Adam Fox, 'Ballads, Libels and Popular Ridicule in Jacobean England', *Past and Present*, 145 (1994), pp. 47–83, for enterprising use of Star Chamber cases. For New England verse libels mocking two men a 'Sir Thomas' and 'Lord Heywood', see Roger Thompson, '"Holy Watchfulness" and Communal Conformism: The Functions of Defamation in Early New England Communities', *The New England Quarterly*, 56 (1983), pp. 504–22, 513–16.
[24] Holdsworth, *History of English Law*, vol. 5, p. 210; Coke, *De Libellis Famosis*, 1605, section 4 online at the Online Library of Liberty, online at http://oll.libertyfund.org/title/911/106331 (accessed 10 August 2010).
[25] Bellamy, *Tudor Law of Treason*, p. 46.

was defined very flexibly, and could be very private and still be prosecutable. Where statute law was vague or absent, the common law as developed in the Star Chamber provided the essential definitions and practices to deal with dangerous words, by extending the principles of *scandalum magnatum* or libelling of the powerful to a broader range of public servants and officers, and a wider range of means of expression (cartoons, rhymes, songs etc.). This was laid out in the core document, of 1637, *A Decree of the Star Chamber Concerning Printing*.[26] This tacit recognition of the failures of government to control the print industry was also an acknowledgement that both the means of attack and their targets were becoming more diverse. As the legal systems proliferated across the British Atlantic, the nature of sedition came to vary by actors and objects of criticism, and local legislatures, where they thought it appropriate, developed their own forms of law in statute and legal processes. Whereas Tudor legislation tended to specify clearly what could not be said, Star Chamber precedents established the context and focus of what was said in terms of its tendency to produce unstable government.[27] The key case *De Libellis Famosis* of 1605 in which Coke defined many of these principles is rightly famous. Elements were subsequently elaborated: while he spoke of non-written libels such as pictures and 'signs' (perhaps placed on a party's door to inflict ignominy), the 1637 proclamation by the Star Chamber on the press spoke about the need for printers and authors to be clearly named in the prints of books, ballads, 'charts', portraiture 'or any other thing or things whatsoever', safely incorporating the seditious potential of all verbal, printed and visual material. Thus sedition law adapted to the changing technologies of the times.[28]

At the Restoration, new legislation in 1661 affected what could be said about Parliament and the King. It was not permitted to declare that the Parliament which started in 1640 had continued after the death of Charles I, nor accuse his son,

---

[26] John C. Lassiter, 'Defamation of Peers: The Rise and Decline of the Action for *Scandalum Magnatum*, 1497–1773', *The American Journal of Legal History*, 22 (1978), pp. 216–36.

[27] Holdsworth, *History of English Law*, vol. 5, pp. 207–12, and vol. 7: pp. 333–45; Manning, 'The Origins of the Doctrine of Sedition'. Note that the 'bad tendency' test runs through twentieth-century American history, and became the centre of debate as things shifted towards a criterion of 'clear and present danger': see, among many others, Louis B. Boudin, '"Seditious Doctrines" and the "Clear and Present Danger" Rule: Part I', *Virginia Law Review*, 38 (1952), pp. 143–86; Bernard Schwartz, 'Holmes versus Hand: Clear and Present Danger or Advocacy of Unlawful Action?', *The Supreme Court Review* (1994), pp. 209–45; Krotoszynski and Carpenter, 'The Return of Seditious Libel'.

[28] *De Libellis Famosis*, section 4; *A Decree of the Star Chamber Concerning Printing* (originally London, Robert Barker, 1637, reprinted The Grolier Club, 1884), section 8, 44: charts probably meant telling people's fortunes by astrological charts, in this context.

now Charles II, of being a Catholic and trying to introduce the Catholic religion into England. Also, it was not allowed to assert the 'Opinion that both Houses of Parliament or either of them have a Legislative Power without the King'. More generally, people who 'maliciously and advisedly by writing printing preaching or other speaking expresse publish utter or declare any Words Sentences or other thing or things to incite or stir up the people to hatred or dislike of the Person of His Majestie or the established Government' were specified.[29]

In some ways, though, as Hamburger and Oldham point out, this kind of measure was scarcely needed as long as printers, under the licensing laws, needed a prior licence to publish, and could be prosecuted if they went ahead with something the government disapprove of: there was little need for large-scale judicial effort in prosecuting printers and authors for the content of their publications. This may explain why most sedition prosecutions in the period are concentrated in lower courts at the county level, both assizes and quarter sessions, and focus on the spoken, rather than the written word (see below). This may not have caught the attention of earlier generations of historians, but it seems that court prosecutions for spoken sedition peaked in the later years of Charles II's, and throughout James II's, reigns, and thereafter declined steeply, reviving only in occasional periods of panic such as the two Jacobite rebellions and the revolutionary fervour of the 1790s.[30]

The 1696 Treason Trials Act, passed the year after the licensing laws had lapsed, made some crucial alterations to the statute law, enshrining the defendant's pre-trial legal rights to lawyers, to a precise notification of the charge, to the names of the witnesses and jurymen, and some sight of the evidence. It also narrowed the scope of the definition of 'treason' from that before 1688 which (in the case of Lord Russell, for example) was thought to have been widened dangerously and loosely. Although some of these rights had been widely granted in practice, this was the first statute which guaranteed them.[31] For a treason charge, words were not sufficient, because some kind of realistic action was needed to confirm the intent. This meant that there was

---

[29] 1661, 'An Act for Safety and Preservation of His Majesties Person and Government against Treasonable and Seditious practices and attempts', in John Raithby (ed.), *Statutes of the Realm* (1819), vol. 5: 304–6, clauses 2 and 3, from British History Online, http://www.british-history.ac.uk/source.aspx?pubid=351 (accessed 2 June 2012); Lois G. Schwoerer, 'Liberty of the Press and Public Opinion, 1660–1695', in J.R. Jones (ed.), *Liberty Secured? Britain after 1688* (Stanford, CA: Stanford University Press, 1992).

[30] Cressy is the key study for England, *Dangerous Talk*, see P. Rushton, 'The Rise and Fall of Seditious Words, 1650–1750', *Northern History*, 52 (1) (2015), pp. 68–84.

[31] Schwoerer, 'Liberty of the Press', p. 200; John H. Langbein, *The Origins of the Adversary Criminal Trial* (Oxford: Oxford University Press, 2003), pp. 85 and the whole of 68–105 (Ch. 2); he elevates this Act to a central place in the origins of 'due process'.

still the question of what constituted sedition. Lord Chief Justice Sir John Holt, perhaps picking up where Hale had left off, gave key judgements in the 1690s and early 1700s. As James Oldham puts it, 'Holt was able to transform the law of seditious libel while maintaining the appearance of continuity.'[32] Subsequent developments built on his legacy. The extension of 'sedition' to include many areas of immorality, obscenity, satire and mockery marks the early eighteenth century as another period of inventive prosecution, which picked up many of the features pioneered by the Star Chamber a century before.

What characterizes this period of moral 'entrepreneurship' (to use the concept created by sociologists of deviance) by the King's Bench is the screaming silences when it comes to precedents, because so many of the principles had been established by the now-discredited Star Chamber or later prosecutions under both Charles II and James II.[33] These cases became the unmentionable forces behind the late Stuart and early Hanoverian prosecutions. In prosecuting Richard Francklin of *The Craftsman* in 1731, for example, the Attorney-General was desperate to reassure the jury that the 'law of false news' preceded the Star Chamber, deriving from thirteenth-century law (3 Edward I, 1275, a law against reporting slanderous news). He went on:

> that court of the Star-Chamber punished without juries; but though juries were taken away, yet the law remained the same as to libels and crimes: So I hope it appears to you to be very plain, that the liberty of the press is limited and governed by law; and that the law sets limits both to the king, and his subjects.

This was unusually explicit, and formed a half-hearted justification of the innovative prosecution of 'news'.[34] In Beare's case before Holt in 1698, more than thirty years earlier, the King's Bench has established that seditious material did not have to be printed, intended to be printed or even given to someone else. 'Publication' meant simply being potentially available:

> That the transcribing and collecting this libellous matter was highly criminal, without publishing it, and that it was of dangerous consequence to the Government for tho' the writer or collector never published these libels, yet his having them ready for that purpose, if any occasion should happen, is highly

---

[32] Oldham, *English Common Law in the Age of Mansfield*, p. 216.
[33] Howard Becker, *The Outsiders: Studies in the Sociology of Deviance* (New York: Free Press, 1963), distinguishes between rule creators and rule enforcers.
[34] T.B. Howell, *A Complete Collection of State Trials and Proceedings for High Treason and Other Crime and Misdemenors ... Vol. 17, 12 George I to 17 George I, 1726–1743* (London: for Longman etc, 1816), pp. 670–1; see pamphlet account *The Tryal of Richard Francklin for a Misdemeanor ...* (Edinburgh: Gavin Hamilton and Company, 1731).

criminal; and tho' he might design to keep them private, yet after his Death they might fall into such hands as might be injurious to the Government; therefore men ought not to be allowed to have such evil Instruments in their keeping.

Seditious words, like explosives, were dangerous if left lying about for people to find. Moreover, the writing was a threat to the 'safety of all civil society', an echo of the blasphemy trial of the Muggletonian sceptic John Taylor in 1676.[35] The precedent that could *not* be mentioned was that of Algernon Sidney, whose manuscript writings seized from his desk formed the key evidence against him (though there was potentially far more convincing proof of his involvement in several plots and conspiracies had the authorities bothered to look more deeply). This was the trial where Lord Chief Justice Jeffreys laid down the principle, 'scribere est agere': to write is to act. Yet this precedent, derived from the trial of a Whig martyr before a demonized judge, could not serve as the precedent for *R. v. Beare* only fifteen years later. New grounds had to be established.[36]

Limited references to cases under the Stuarts before 1688 could be made, therefore, and only when they were safely non-political. Legalistic amnesia did not prevent continuity through adoption of Star Chamber principles, as Oldham has pointed out, but the specific cases used as precedents could not be listed. In the prosecution of Edmund Curll in 1727, for publishing obscene books (at least one of which had been licensed under Charles II), reference was made to prosecution for shocking and lewd behaviour in the 1660s. It was part of a much larger argument by the prosecution establishing that moral offences were a perfectly proper focus of the secular courts. The case was designed to recoup the failure of the 1708 prosecution of Read for publishing *The Fifteen Plagues of a Maidenhead*, in which Sir John Holt agreed with the defence that there were church courts for that sort of thing, in the absence of precedents elsewhere.

In prosecuting Curll, the Attorney-General rejected a similar argument from the defence, and justified a King's Bench prosecution by asserting, 'it is a libel, if it reflects upon religion, that great basis of civil government and liberty, and it may be both a spiritual and temporal offence'. He went on, 'as to morality. Destroying the peace of the government; for government is no more than public order, which

---

[35] *A Report of All the Case Determined by Sir John Holt, Kt., from 1688 to 1710, Which Time He Was Lord Chief Justice of England* (London: E. and R. Nutt and R. Gosling, 1738), pp. 423–4; Oldham, *English Common Law in the Age of Mansfield*, p. 215, regards the rule about civil society as new, and 'extreme' (p. 216) – he derives the phrase from Hamburger p. 732: it is not in the 1738 report.

[36] For *R. v. Taylor*, see Visconsi, 'The Invention of Criminal Blasphemy', p. 31, quoting Hale, 'to say religion is a cheat, is to dissolve those obligations whereby the civil societies are preserved'; Jonathan Scott, *Algernon Sidney and the Restoration Crisis, 1677–1683* (Cambridge University Press, 1991), pp. 268–9.

is morality'. He continued: 'My Lord Chief Justice Holt used to say, Christianity is part of the law. And why not morality too? I do not say that every immoral act is indictable, such as telling a lie, or the like. But if it [is] destructive of morality in general; if it does, or may, affect the King's subjects, it is then an offence of a public nature.'[37] He cited the case of Sir Charles Sedley, prosecuted in 1663 for lewd behaviour and showing his naked body to crowds in Covent Garden. In that case, 'it was said, this court is the *custos morum* [moral guardian] of the king's subjects', and numerous, mostly unsuccessful, prosecutions of 'players for obscene plays' had followed it. He argued that the court could deal with pornography and Curll's breach of public morality despite the absence of any specific statute law, since there was no evidence of presentation of any similar case involving written or printed material in a church court.[38] Ironically, Curll generally was not one of the usual Tory pro-Jacobites who formed the main object of prosecution at this time, for he tended to support the Whig government, as his earlier attack on Nathaniel Mist, in the guise of 'Britannus', shows.[39] Edmund Curll was convicted, and despite an appeal on the grounds that libels had to have a person or the state as their object, was put in the pillory, but by a trick won the crowd over on his side:

> This Edmund Curll stood in the pillory at Charing Cross, but was not pelted, or used ill; for being an artful, cunning (though wicked) fellow, he had contrived to have printed papers dispersed all about Charing Cross, telling the people, he stood there for vindicating the memory of Queen Anne; which had such an effect on the mob, that it would have [been] dangerous even to have spoken against him: and when he was taken down out of the pillory, the mob carried him off, as it were in triumph, to a neighbouring tavern.[40]

The other official success of this period was to establish the applicability of sedition to printed satire and other documents criticizing government or individual politicians by 'innuendos' – the latter sparking off a serious debate in

---

[37] Howell, *State Trials*, vol. 17, p. 155; Oldham, *English Common Law in the Age of Mansfield*, p. 216; Thomas, *A Long Time Burning*, p. 22; John, Lord Fortescue, *Reports of Select Cases of All the Courts of Westminster-Hall* ... (London: Henry Lintot, 1738), pp. 98–100; one problem was the lack of reference to pornography in Coke.

[38] Howell, *State Trials*, 17: 156–7, and detailed footnote on Sedley, 155.

[39] *An Answer to Mr. Mist's Journal of the Twenty-Eighth of January, No. 93*, by 'Britannus' (London: N. Blandford, 1727). Curll was also involved defending a case brought by Alexander Pope which decisively established that the author of letters owned the copyright: see Mark Rose, 'The Author in Court: Pope v. Curll (1741)', *Cultural Critique*, 21 (Spring 1992), pp. 197–217.

[40] Howell, *State Trials*, vol. 17, pp. 153 and 160. For the general context of Curll and the pornography trade in London, see Julie Peakman, *Mighty Lewd Books: The Development of Pornography in Eighteenth-Century England* (Houndsmills, Basingstoke: Palgrave Macmillan, 2003), pp. 41–2; for the case's role in Anglo-American law, see Geoffrey R. Stone, 'Sex, Violence and the First Amendment', *University of Chicago Law Review*, 74 (2007), pp. 1857–71, 1861–2.

legal circles. The point was established in the case of *Mist's Journal*, that it was not necessary to name persons specifically, but the prosecution could be based on a common understanding of who was meant by the pseudonyms adopted, a doctrine that was important a few years later in the cases against both Richard Francklin of *The Craftsman* and, in the American colonies, Zenger of the *New York Weekly Journal*.[41] The case against Nathaniel Mist's paper had to be brought against his subordinates, and this mimicked the old statutory hierarchy of the Elizabethan laws, which punished those who repeated libels, as well as those who created them, albeit with milder penalties. The printer, compositor, apprentices and servants, as well as the 'mercuries' – women paper sellers and dealers – were all in court as defendants and witnesses. The pressman John Clarke, compositor Robert Knell, apprentice Joseph Carter and maid Amy Walker were severely punished for printing but not publishing the libel, the apprentice by having to tour the courts with a paper on his head announcing his crime and serve a month with hard labour. But the maid was sentenced to be whipped and serve six months in Bridewell. This strategy was adopted because Mist himself had fled the country.[42] The same process was undertaken with regard to Francklin in 1731 and the distributors were rounded up as well as the producers: 'on Saturday night Mrs. Nutt, Mrs. Dodd, and Mrs. Pearce, 3 Mercuries, were taken into custody of one of his Majesty's Messengers, for publishing the *Craftsman* of the same day'. In a subsequent story Mrs Dodd is called 'the Publisher', perhaps because of her vital role in the large-scale distribution of newspapers. In this case the final prosecution was confined to the publisher alone, Richard Francklin, who was successfully convicted and imprisoned.[43]

The government successes of the 1730s derived from the Juries Act of 1730, in part, but this can be over-emphasized. The rule that the judge decided whether something was seditious, while the jury decided if the defendant had spoken or published it, meant that there was less scope in these trials than in ordinary criminal prosecutions for juries to decide on which law applied (see below). In 1707 there were several targets successfully prosecuted at government behest, without

---

[41] A point noted by Alison Olson, 'The Zenger Case Revisited: Satire, Sedition and Political Debate in Eighteenth-Century America', *Early American Literature*, 35 (2000), pp. 223–45. On innuendos, see *The Doctrine of Innuendo's Discussed or the Liberty of the Press Maintain'd* anon, sometimes attributed to Nicholas Amhurst (London: 1731), a reply to John Hervey's criticism of *The Craftsman*.

[42] *London Journal*, 24 May 1729; Howell, *State Trials*, vol. 17, pp. 667–8, footnote, omits the servantmaid; Harris, *London Newspapers in the Age of Walpole*, p. 148, on Mist's flight; Bellamy *Tudor Law of Treason*, p. 46 for gradations of punishment under Elizabethan law.

[43] *Grub-street Journal*, 14 January 1731 and 21 January 1731 for bailing of all. Harris, *London Newspapers in the Age of Walpole*, p. 39 for the scale of Mrs Nutt and Mrs Dodd's operations; Howell, *State Trials*, vol. 17, p. 676. See *The Doctrine of Innuendo's Discussed* for the beginning of a critical reflection on these cases.

apparent difficulties. Nevertheless, it usually took a great deal of intimidatory pressure on the printers and distributors, and several attempts at prosecution, for the government to achieve its end in the 1720s and 1730s.[44] In terms of legal innovation, there were few entirely new principles or interpretations established between the 1690s and the 1730s by King's Bench cases, apart from the inclusion of pornography and satire. What had been achieved, however, was a collection of precedents which could safely be cited without reference to the politically discredited courts before 1688 or, more seriously, before the civil wars. The case against Francklin, for example, depended on the successful prosecution of satire in *Mist's Journal*. Earlier attempts such as against novelist Mary Delarivier Manley in 1709 for satirizing the Whig government had failed, partly because the insulted government fell from power while she lay in jail awaiting trial.[45] Like a group of self-referential authors who only cite their own or each other's previous works, the judges in subsequent cases, like Mansfield, could rely on a series of successful precedents, largely in King's Bench since 1688, to demonstrate the principles which had in fact been in existence in various forms for nearly 200 years. They could avoid mentioning politically sensitive cases under the earlier Stuarts. The debate would hinge upon the freedom of both of the press to print whatever they wanted, and juries to decide if it was seditious.[46]

The extension of sedition law to the empire

The law of sedition, it needs to be repeated, was not there simply to be inherited: on the contrary, it was there to be invented wherever authority felt threatened

---

[44] Thomas, *A Long Time Burning*, pp. 55 and 58; see 1707 list of prosecutions, 'the government thinking fit to check the licentiousness of the press', in N. Tindall, *The Continuation of Mr Rapin's History of England from the Revolution to the Present Times*, vol. 14 (4th of the Continuation) 6th ed. (London: Mr. Knapton, 1758), pp. 383–6, five men, among them two doctors and one minister; G.C. Gibbs, 'Press and Public Opinion: Prospective', in Jones, *Liberty Secured?*, pp. 231–64, 239, 244–5.

[45] See Howell, *State Trials*, vol. 17, p. 666, specifically cited by the prosecution as establishing the principle that anonymous satire could be seditious; see also Pat Rogers, 'Nathaniel Mist, Daniel Defoe and the Perils of Publishing', *The Library*, 10 (2009), pp. 298–313, on the probable relation between Defoe and Mist over *Captain Singleton*. For Manley, see Thomas, *A Long Time Burning*, p. 59; Rachel Carnell, *A Political Biography of Delarivier Manley* (London: Pickering and Chatto, 2008), pp. 180–2; Susan Sage Heinzelman, *Riding the Black Ram: Law, Literature and Gender* (Stanford, CA: Stanford Law Books, 2010), pp. 61–9; her name was printed often as 'de la Rivière'; she was arrested for *The New Atalanta*, though she was never brought to trial, saved by the election of a Tory administration; *The London Post-Boy*, 9–11 August, 29 October–1 November, and 5–8 November 1709, records her arrest; the novel is available online in ECCO.

[46] See, particularly, Oldham's study of Mansfield and his references to previous cases in his own judgements, *English Common Law in the Age of Mansfield*, pp. 217ff. Laski, 'Procedure', p. 1034, makes the point that contempt of court, with cases brought and tried by the judge offended by the criticism, was also a creation of this period, passing insensibly into the law by the 1760s.

in the British empire. Given the legal pluralism that characterized the imperial territories, and the absence of a single statute defining sedition, the law in practice was always likely to be highly variable. Yet as a common law offence, sedition – or seditious libel – was part of the common heritage that colonists claimed. As Konig and Nelson have pointed out, colonial laws frequently departed from English models, particularly in the concepts and procedures of civil law. But criminal law was also drastically altered in the colonies: early efforts at codifying the laws in Massachusetts reduced the number of crimes deserving the death sentence (from 100 to 12, Cahn suggests). The colony also shared with the others the failure to develop adequate mid-range punishments which could serve between simple corporal penalties such as whipping and the severity of the execution, so that the English pattern of developing the transportation of ordinary criminals abroad or imprisonment at home was not adopted. Codification took the form of attempts to print all the existing laws, a practice which made it increasingly easy for English commentators and imperial inspectors to examine the differences developing in North America. Such clarification could reveal precise details of the level of 'repugnancy' to English law to those British administrators taking an interest, or, perhaps, hearing appeals from colonial litigants.[47]

If the colonies refused to copy blindly from England, it is possible that some colonial innovation travelled the other way, and fed back into English laws. It is not surprising that one of Charles II's responses to New England's repression of Quakers was to endorse the 'sharpe laws' that had proved necessary on both sides of the Atlantic: but the Massachusetts proclamations in 1658 were the first to establish the association of Quaker meetings with 'sedition' and specify the punishment of banishment ('on pain of death'). Quaker practices and beliefs were deemed destructive of good government, that is, of the government of the governor, assembly and congregational church. This had been of longstanding, as the colony had always reacted against criticism both religious and secular. For example in 1631, 'It is ordered that Phillip Ratliffe shall be whipped have his eares cutt of fyned 40s & banished out of [th]e lymitts of this Jurisdiccon, for uttering

---

[47] Mark D. Cahn, 'Punishment, Discretion, and the Codification of Prescribed Penalties in Colonial Massachusetts', *American Journal of Legal History*, 33 (1989), pp. 107–33, n.73, 107 and 119; Kathryn Preyer, 'Penal Measures in the American Colonies: An Overview', *The American Journal of Legal History*, 26 (1982), pp. 326–53; it was hard to avoid the consequences of English transportation as 50,000 convicts arrived across the Atlantic – see Morgan and Rushton, *Eighteenth-Century Criminal Transportation*; see Bilder, *Transatlantic Constitution*, p. 65, on Rhode Island, whose authorities delayed the printing of their laws, as Connecticut's printed statutes were used as evidence against her in 1705–6. On the state of collections of laws, and British response, see Erwin C. Surrency, 'Revision of Colonial Laws', *The American Journal of Legal History*, 9 (3) (1965), pp. 189–202.

mallitious & scandalous speeches against the gov't & the church of Salem'. This event provoked critical attention in England, and John Winthrop received an account of 'diverse complaints against the severitie of your Gouernment' about cutting off the ears of 'the Lunatick'. By contrast, another man the same year was only whipped and banished 'for writing into England falsely and mallitiously against the government and execution of Justice here'. Insulting ministers, many of whom were also magistrates, was always a dangerous game in Massachusetts. Offences against magistrates, in particular, were generally severely punished. As George Lee Haskins noted in his classic study, 'freedom of speech and debate were subject to many limitations in Massachusetts, and the colonial authorities, like their English counterparts, were quick to punish what they deemed to be malice, presumptuousness or sedition, in public utterances'.[48]

The threat to good government became the core of allegations against Quakers, and it was here that England copied the colonies. In Maryland in the late 1650s, the refusal of Quakers to swear to take the 'Engagement' to promise to assist Lord Baltimore's regime led to accusations that their 'principles tended to the destruction of all government'.[49] This was echoed in England only in part because the Parliamentary authorities concentrated on suspicions of heresy and blasphemy, despite Oliver Cromwell's personal commitment to liberty of conscience. The theme of sedition, however, was taken up after the Restoration in 1660, and accusations of sedition and the punishment of banishment became the hallmark of English laws in the subsequent decade, though unlike in Massachusetts, the death penalty was avoided. When Virginia passed its own

---

[48] *Records of the Court of Assistants of the Colony of the Massachusetts Bay, 1630–1692*, printed for J. Noble (Boston: Suffolk County, 1904), 3 vols, vol. 2, pp. 16 and 19; on English complaints about the Ratcliffe case, see Cahn, 'Punishment, Discretion and Codification', pp. 119 and 122–3; George Lee Haskins, *Law and Authority in Early Massachusetts: A Study in Tradition and Design*, 2nd ed. (Lanham MD: University Press of America, 1985), p. 196. For threats to constables, magistrates, and 'authority', see *The Records and Files of the Quarterly Courts of Essex County Massachusetts, Vol. 1, 1636–1656* (Salem, MA: Essex Institute, 1911), p. 69; vol. 2, 1656–1662 (Salem, MA: 1912), pp. 95, 310. New England Quakers had sent an account of their sufferings with George Burrough, *A Declaration of the Sad and Great Persecution and Martyrdom of the People of God called Quakers, in New England for the Worshipping of God* (Boston and London, 1661), online at http://digitalcommons.unl.edu/etas/23 (accessed 12 June 2018), ed. by Paul Royster (2007), who notes that Charles II's initial order had been to cease capital and corporal punishment of Quakers, p. 35.

[49] *The Colonial Laws of Massachusetts, Reprinted from the Edition of 1672, with the supplements through 1686*, ed. William H. Whitmore (Boston, Rockwell and Churchill, 1890), pp. 61–2 for the revised general laws of 1658; Charles II in *Records of the Governor and Colony of the Massachusetts Bay in New England, Vol. 4 1664–1674*, part I (Boston: William White, 1854), pp. 164–6, 'sharpe', 166; Kenneth L. Carroll, 'Persecution and Persecutors of Maryland Quakers, 1658–1661', *Quaker History*, 99 (2010), p. 18. On New England, see the work of Carla Gardina Pestana, 'The Quaker Executions as Myth and History', *The Journal of American History*, 80 (1993), pp. 441–69, and 'The City upon a Hill under Siege: The Puritan Perception of the Quaker Threat to Massachusetts Bay', *The New England Quarterly*, 56 (1983), pp. 323–53.

legislation against Quakers in 1663, it was modelled largely on that of Charles II's England the year before, rather than on the proclamations of New England, and it made careful reference to legislation from Elizabeth I's reign designed to maintain the supremacy of the Anglican Church. This time, the colony copied from England. As in the English laws, banishment was established for a third offence of attending a seditious meeting. The legislation accused several groups of 'separatism' and holding 'sundry dangerous opinions and tenets'. A significant adaptation had to be made as monetary fines were translated into pounds of tobacco. This example points to the workings of 'regionalism' of law in the colonies, within a transatlantic world of circulating texts and legal ideas, the different religious establishments of the two colonies sharing a common idea of sedition, but contrasting versions of the established religion to be defended. Local legal cultures varied between colonies.[50]

The local context of sedition therefore differed between the colonies: the key was the different concepts of 'government'. Billings notes that 'even though they sprang from common origins, no two groups of colonists saw the problems of law and order in the same light'. In terms of the definition of 'government' that is only partly true – the religious element varied, but the common core of colonial laws lay in the definition of *who* constituted the 'government'.[51] As Sir Thomas Dale's 1611 law put it:

> No manner of person whatsoever, contrarie to the word of God ... shall detract, slaunder, calumniate, murmur, mutenie, resist, disobey, or neglect the commaundments, either of the Lord Governour, and Captaine Generalle, the Lieutenant Generall, the Martiall, the Councell, or any authorised Captaine, Commaunder or publike Officer, upon paine for the first time so offending to be whipt three severall times, and upon his knees to acknowledge his offence, with asking forgivenesse upon the Saboth day in the assembly of the congregation,

---

[50] See Craig W. Horle, *Quakers and the English Legal System, 1660–1668* (Philadelphia: University of Pennsylvania Press, 1988); Joseph Besse, *A Collection of the Sufferings of the People Called Quakers ...*, 3 vols (London: Luke Hindle, 1753), on Cromwell's attitudes, 1: vi–vii; William Waller Hening, *The Statutes at Large, Being a Collection of the Laws of Virginia, from the First Session of the Legislature in the Year 1619, Statutes*, vol. 2, pp. 180–3; Owen Ruffhead, *The Statutes at Large from the Fifth Year of King James the First to the Tenth Year of the Reign of William the Third*, 3 vols (London: Mark Basket, 1763), vol. 3, pp. 217–18, 295–6 on laws; Konig, 'Regionalism'; on 'legal culture' as a concept, see Richard J. Ross, 'The Legal Past of Early New England: Notes for the Study of Law, Legal Culture, and Intellectual History', *The William and Mary Quarterly*, 3rd ser., 50 (1993), pp. 28–41 and 'Puritan Godly Discipline in Comparative Perspective: Legal Pluralism and the Sources of "Intensity"', *American Historical Review*, 113 (2008), pp. 975–1002.

[51] Warren M. Billings, 'The Transfer of English Law to Virginia, 1606–50', in K.R. Andrews, N.P. Canny and P.E.H. Hair (eds), *Westward Enterprise: English Activities in Ireland, the Atlantic, and America, 1480–1650* (Liverpool: Liverpool UP 1978), pp. 215–44, 215.

and for the second time so offending to be condemned to the Gally for three yeares: and for the third time so offending to be punished with death.

This was unusual only in the punishment but not the values, above all the assumption of the need to enforce deference to authority, that lay behind it. As a later Virginia order put it, 'that no person upon the rumour of supposed change and alteration, presume to be disobedient to the present government, nor servants to their private officers, masters or overseers, at their uttermost peril'. The great chain of authority ran from household to royal governors to the king himself, and all needed to be protected. So, though punishments became less, the law was found to be essentially the same: in one case, Daniel Cugley was sentenced to be pilloried 'for scandalous speeches against Governor and Councell', but was 'forgiven'.[52]

By the 1670s, Massachusetts had extended their treason law to include uttering such 'compassing', 'by Printing, Preaching or malitious ... speaking'.[53] In Virginia, following Bacon's Rebellion of 1675, specific laws were passed against *words*, either in sympathy for the rebels or against general contempt of local authority: these were 'seditious and scandalous libels, the usual fore runners of tumult and rebellion'. Consequently, the law stipulated:

> That all and every person and persons that shall from the tyme to come presume to speake and utter mutinous or contemptuous words, or shall by any wayes or meanes abuse the right honourable the governour or any of the councell, justices of the peace or commissionated militia officers, and shall be thereof lawfully convict, shall for his such offence, if against the right honourable the governour, be whipped on the bare back with thirty lashes, or pay eight hundred pounds of tobacco and caske, if against any of the honourable councell, that then he shalbe whipped on the bare back with twenty fowre lashes, or pay six hundred pounds of tobacco and caske, and if against any justice of the peace or comissionate feild officer, then to be whipped on the bare back with twenty lashes, or pay fowre hundred pounds of tobacco and caske.[54]

---

[52] *Colonial Origins of The American Constitution: A Documentary History*, ed. Donald S. Lutz (Indianapolis: Liberty Fund, 1998), online at http://oll.libertyfund.org/EBooks/Misc – American Colonial Docs_0013.pdf, 331; Hening *Statutes at Large*, vol. 1, p. 128 (1624), repeated on p. 198 (1632); Cugley in Hening, *Statutes at Large*, vol. 1, p. 146, 13 July 1630; on the distinctive character of Dale's Laws, see David Thomas Konig, 'Dale's Laws and the Non-Common Law Origins Of Criminal Justice In Virginia', *American Journal of Legal History*, 26 (1982), pp. 354–75.

[53] *Laws of Maryland at Large* ... Thomas Bacon (Annapolis MD: Jonas Green, 1765), no. 22 'An Act for Treasons'; *Colonial Laws of Massachusetts*, p. 263, 1678.

[54] Hening, *Statutes at Large*, vol. 2, pp. 385–6, February 1677; Russell noted that the colony had been in difficulty with the Privy Council over its determination to punish those involved in Bacon's rebellion, and had struck down three laws in the same year as contrary to the royal amnesty, Labaree, *The Review of American Colonial Legislation*, p. 29.

Everywhere, the preservation of respect for authority was the aim of government, but whether signs of *disrespect* were seditious remained a matter of some discretion. There was great overlap in the law of defamation, the use of 'scandalous' or 'opprobrious words' and sedition. The mighty probably thought all insults directed at them seditious, but discretion might lead them to reduce the complaint to defamation. A public apology might be more effective than punishment. Cases could be found in any colony which conflated defamation and sedition, exactly as the English law of libel did at the same period: for example, John Curtis was prosecuted in 1680 in New York 'for having uttered scandalous and seditious words and Expressions ag[ain]st the Gov[erno]r and Gov[ern]nm[en]t'. It seems that everywhere there were 'Seditious Spiritts', particularly after disturbances or political uncertainties – what New Jersey's Governor and Council called the 'Distraction' of the times.[55]

Sedition remained very much a crime shaped by personal and political relations. Thus, when printer William Bradford was prosecuted for printing a 'malitious and seditious paper' in Pennsylvania in 1692, he asked, 'what law is the presentment founded on?', to which the 'attorney for the government' replied, 'it is grounded both on statute and common law'. This was not entirely true with regard to the definition of sedition, and Bradford's request to 'see that statute and common law, else how shall I make my plea?' produced little response except a citation of a Charles II law which repeated the Star Chamber requirements that all authors and printers should print their names on their publications, of whatever kind. Bradford characteristically pointed out that this law had not been followed by the Quakers of the colony in their numerous publications.[56] Some colonies, such as North Carolina, passed their own treason legislation with sedition clauses, thus firmly establishing that the governor was a figure not to be insulted, and thereby making it clear that he represented royal, legitimate authority in the colony. Like Virginia thirty years before, North Carolina, in the aftermath of a rebellion (the Cary rebellion), legislated in 1711 make sedition, and particularly speaking against the governor of the colony, punishable by a fine, imprisonment or the pillory, or as the Justices decreed. As Spindell notes, sedition 'was almost always prosecuted as a crime'. In this measure, the colony enshrined in law the penalties which were inflicted by English assize courts at the time, where the offence was

---

[55] *Documents Relating to the Colonial History of the State of New Jersey*, vol. 1, 1631–1687, ed. William A. Whiteread (Newark, NJ: Daily Journal, 1880), pp. 176, 313 and 320ff.

[56] Isaiah Thomas, *The History of Printing in America, with a Biography of Printers ...*, 2 vols (Worcester, MA: I. Thomas, June 1810), vol. 2, pp. 12 and 16.

under common law. By this time, however, punishments for sedition on both sides of the Atlantic were becoming much milder than those of the early 1600s.[57]

As it became more and more difficult for governors to win over their assemblies and judiciary to assist them in pursuit of seditious writings in the 1760s and 1770s, the British authorities contemplated centralizing the 'Atlantic constitution'. In the face of continued protests against the Stamp and Townsend Acts, legal experts in the British government asserted that rebellious Americans could be tried in England under an ancient of Henry VIII. As they reported in 1768, with reference to activities in Massachusetts: 'upon this we beg leave to observe, that the Statute of the 35th Henry 8th C.2 is the only Act by which Criminals can be tried in England for Offences committed in America. By this Act all Treasons, Misprisions or Treasons, and concealments of Treasons out of the Realm of England, may be determined in his Majesty's Court of King's Bench, or before Commissioners in any County in England'. They concluded, however regretfully, that 'the Provisions of this Act are not extended to Offences of an inferior Degree' and that recent events in the colony did not yet justify its use. More adventurously, recent English legislation also offered possibilities. After the burning of the revenue cutter the *Gaspee* in Rhode Island in 1772, the British minister Lord Hillsborough made urgent inquiries of the Solicitor and Attorney Generals whether the recent 'An Act for the better securing & preserving His Majesty's Dock-Yards, Magazines, Ships, Ammunition & Stores' (passed after a damaging fire in Portsmouth naval dockyard in 1770) could be interpreted as allowing the prosecution of those responsible for arson in royal dockyards or ports to take place in England, irrespective of where the offence had occurred (see Chapter 5).[58] Not surprisingly, complex arguments were developed by New Englanders in particular showing that the doctrine of automatic extension of English laws to their territory could not hold: 'We have already shown that this country was taken possession of by individuals, and by them settled at their own risque and private expense, and not by the nation as a nation.' They were therefore bound by different laws. In England, those who agreed with them would find themselves suspected of sedition.[59]

---

[57] Donna J. Spindell, 'The Law of Words: Verbal Abuse in North Carolina to 1730', *American Journal of Legal History*, 39 (1995), pp. 25–42, 28–30; Cressy, *Dangerous Talk*, p. 66; Eldridge, *Distant Heritage*, p. 117.

[58] The National Archives CO 5/767 132–7 (ff.65v-68), 25 November 1768; CO 5/250 47, 7 August 1772.

[59] 'From the County of Hampshire', *Essex Journal*, 5 April 1775; this was part of a series of articles concerning the laws of nations and the extension of their laws into their colonies; Troy O. Bickham, 'Sympathizing with Sedition? George Washington, the British Press, and British Attitudes during the American War of Independence', *The William and Mary Quarterly*, 3rd ser., 59 (2002), pp. 101–22; *The Public Records of the Colony of Connecticut from May, 1775 to June 1776 ...*, ed. Charles J. Hoadly (Hartford, CT, 1890), pp. 22–3.

The role of Parliament and the colonial legislatures in legal processes

Even without passing specific laws of sedition, legislatures such as the British Parliament played a crucial part in detecting offences, denouncing authors and initiating prosecutions of sedition, particularly where the insults were against themselves or their conduct. This practice of political instigation was common in the colonies too. Cases often began with a denunciation of a particular printed work by legislators, and the summoning of the author or publisher to the bar of the house.[60] Prosecutors often made a point that offenders had already been warned for a previous offence, but generously escaped prosecution. As the court was reminded in the case of John Tutchin in England in 1704: 'It is has been the great indulgence of the government that he has not been prosecuted before. He has been taken notice of by the House of Commons, and been before the Secretary of State; where he has been admonished to take care of what he should write; but he would not take the warning'. Guilty reputations could thus be established prior to prosecution. Both Tutchin and Daniel Defoe were prosecuted because Parliament had in effect ordered the cases to be brought because of their criticisms of its attitudes to religious nonconformists. A similar process occurred with regard to Nathaniel Mist, who was complained of in Parliament by the Bishop of Gloucester, a Whig government loyalist, in response to which the House of Lords in 1720 ordered his prosecution, which led to the warrant for his arrest.[61] Unusually, spoken words were sometimes reported to Parliament and the speakers arrested. In 1719, three men were accused by a 'stole-man', that is, a legal officer of the House of Lords, who had arrested him: one of them, Edward Kelly, had 'used very disrespectful Words of this Honourable House'. The officer reported this, and the House then issued a warrant:

> It is Ordered, by the Lords Spiritual and Temporal in Parliament assembled, That the Gentleman Usher of the Black Rod attending this House, his Deputy

---

[60] The origins of this tactic are unclear, but in the case of the South Sea Bubble scandal, Parliament had acted to summon and try those deemed responsible for the damage: see *Mr. Aislabie's Two Speeches Considered: With His Tryal at Large in Both Houses of Parliament* ... (London: A. Moore, 1721).

[61] Thomas, *A Long Time Burning*, pp. 44–5; Tutchin in Howell, *State Trials*, vol. 14, p. 1105; for Mist, see Rogers, 'Nathaniel Mist, Daniel Defoe and the Perils of Publishing', p. 301; *The Trial of Mr John Tutchin for Writing a Certain Libel Called the Observator* (London: Thomas Spring, 1704); *The Trackers Vindicated or, an Answer to the Whigs' New Black List … and a Word to Mr John Tutchin about his Scandalous Ballad* ... (London: n.d., 1705); *An Account of the Birth, Education, Life and Conversation of That Notorious and Bold Scribbler, the Observator* ... (Licensed, according to order, London, 1705). The case established that attacks on governments without a named target could be actionable.

or Deputies, do forthwith attach the Bodies of the said *Edward* Kelly, *Henry Anderson*, and *Richard Sparrow*, and bring them in safe Custody to the Bar of this House, to answer for their said Offences; and this shall be a sufficient Warrant on that Behalf.

Kelly escaped soon after his arrest, and with Sparrow went into hiding, so fresh orders had to be given to Black Rod to send people to find them again – he was a lawyer, and may not have been too hard to find, and then ' keep them in safe Custody till further Order of this House; and this shall be a sufficient Warrant on that Behalf'. Little seems to have come of this, except perhaps a deterrent impact on those likely to express criticisms of the house of Lords.[62]

It was not unknown, however, for publishers and authors to be cast into Newgate jail and denied any proper trial. The process varied, as did the judicial consequences, since Parliament could act as a court in its own defence against criticism – something which directly contradicted the basic principle of *Bonham's Case* in the early seventeenth century.[63] In the case of disappointed parliamentary candidate Alexander Murray in 1751, whose accusations against his opponent earned him a summons to the bar of the Commons, and imprisonment in Newgate, the libel lay in the pamphlet which gave an account of, and denounced, the process as arbitrary and oppressive. Thus, when its publisher William Owen came to trial in 1752, the Attorney-General Sir Dudley Ryder was able to assert that the publication had *already* been deemed seditious by the Commons: 'the House of Commons has voted this pamphlet a libel', and all the jury needed to do was decide if Owen was the publisher. This they refused to do, which led an infuriated Ryder to persuade the judge to summon the jury back to the court for interrogation. Asked if the evidence had not been sufficient to prove that Owen had printed the pamphlet, 'the foreman appeared a good deal flustered' said 'Yes', but repeated 'Not guilty' twice, and several of the jury interjected 'That is our verdict, my lord, and we abide by it'.[64] Some targets of this kind of process recognized the danger: nearly ten years before his conviction in 1731,

---

[62] *Journal of the House of Lords: Volume 21, 1718–1721* (London, 1767–1830), pp. 96–108 and 185–91.
[63] Dr Bonham's Case, 8 Co. Rep. 107a, 114a C.P. 1610, online at http://press-pubs.uchicago.edu/founders/documents/amendV_due_process (accessed 19 November 2010); the case involved the Royal College of Physicians both prosecuting and judging an unlicensed physician, that is, one who had not registered with them.
[64] The literature on Owen is large: Howell, *State Trials*, vol. 17, 1203–29, quotations from 1225–6 and 1228–9; *The Case of the Honourable Alexander Murray Esq …* (London: C. Pugh, 1751); *London Magazine*, 20 (1751), pp. 364–6, and vol. 21 (1752), pp. 205–6; *Journals of the House of Commons*, vol. 26, pp. 27–8, 31–2, 36, 39, 164, 303, 309–10.

Richard Francklin had been summoned, fined and imprisoned for contempt of Parliament. A committee of inquiry was set up into one of his publications which had alleged corruption in high places, and, when he refused to appear when summoned, it came to the conclusion that he was guilty of 'a notorious contempt of the authority, and a breach of the privilege of this House'. Arrested, he was held in custody, probably for several months.[65] John Wilkes was perhaps a special case, as he was himself sitting in Parliament, but John Reeves, friend to the Pitt government in the 1790s, was the subject of an opposition motion before his prosecution (see below).

The same process of involvement of the legislature and political initiation occurred in many of the colonies. Assemblies and councils could react badly to even implicit criticism. For example, in Virginia in 1658, during a period of dispute over the style of government under the Interregnum, the assembly judged that 'the paper subscribed by name of the inhabitants of Northampton county is scandalous and seditious and hath caused much disturbance in the peace and government of that county', and ordered that 'all the subscribers of the said paper bee disabled from bearing any office in this countrey'. They ordered the punishment of the 'delinquents', though the order was reversed subsequently by an order of the Assembly.[66]

Nearly a century later, in 1752, Captain Joseph Wadsworth managed to offend both houses in the Connecticut assembly by alleging that their legislation contradicted the charter of the colony, in a speech responding to petitions read at the session, that was 'resented as of a seditious nature and tendency'. He was brought to the bar of the assembly, and forced to admit that

> in my discourse yesterday, in the hearing of both Houses when the Assembly was publick (and upon the hearing of a petition), relating to the constitution and power of this Assembly, as to the manner of their passing of acts according to our charter, I had no design to reflect upon or expose the proceedings of the Houses of the said Assembly ... and I am heartily sorry that what I said was of any such tendency as to give offence to this Assembly, for which, as for the charter, I had a great regard and honour.

This was read before both houses when they were in public session.[67]

---

[65] Howell, *State Trials*, vol. 17, p. 627.
[66] Hening, *Statutes at Large*, vol. 1, p. 380.
[67] *The Public Records of the Colony of Connecticut from October, 1706 to October, 1716*, ed. Charles J. Hoadly (Harford, CT: Case, Lockwood and Brainard, 1870), pp. 492-3, May 1752 – the admonition, says the editor, was a 'gentle one', ftn. 493.

In two eighteenth-century instances, legislatures seem to have resented the publication of accounts of their procedures without their specific authorization, and conflated the scandalous with the seditious. Although William Parks is said by a patriot printer in his later history to have got himself into trouble by alleging that a member of the Virginia House of Burgesses had a long-forgotten conviction for theft, the only recorded difficulty occurred in 1749 when he was summoned to the House to explain why he had published a 'malicious and scandalous libel, highly and injuriously reflecting on the Proceedings of the House of Burgesses'. He explained he had done so at the express order of the Council, which suggests that he was the victim of a dispute over privilege between the two bodies. After a short period, the House discharged him out of custody. Thomas Powell, printer of the *South Carolina Gazette*, faced exactly the same accusation by the upper house of the assembly and chief justice of South Carolina in 1773, of publishing an account of their proceedings without their permission (it had been given to him by a member, William Henry Drayton). Found guilty of 'a high breach of the privileges and a contempt of the house', he was committed to the common jail.

Drayton himself dissented during the proceedings, and spoke in his, and Powell's defence, with a carefully judged speech aiming to avoid further offence. He argued that there had been no specific order forbidding publication of the house's proceedings, nor had they in fact been misrepresented in the publication, and the printer, he noted, had 'not even made any Remark', but had only 'published a protest'. He also pointed out that one of the cases cited in debate, the imprisonment of a man called Bingley in England, had been misread: 'Bingley was not committed by the House of Lords, as was erroneously insisted upon, for having printed a Protest; but he was committed by the Court of King's-Bench, for refusing to give Bail to answer Interrogatories upon Oath, upon Charge of having printed a Libel against the said Court.' Perhaps more than in any other case this speech reflects the sense of the American attachment to English precedent.[68] Significantly, as Drayton's protest was being debated in the house a few days after, the door-keeper of the house reported that sympathizers in the lower house had taken out a *habeas corpus*, and effected Powell's discharge.[69] Both Drayton and

---

[68] Thomas, *History of Printing*, vol. 2, pp. 143–6, and (Powell), pp. 161–8; *Journals of the House of Burgesses, of Virginia, 1742–49, 1748–49*, ed. H.R. McIlwaine (Richmond, VA: Virginia State Library, 1904), vol. 7, pp. 402–4. For lengthy accounts of the Powell debates, see *South Carolina Gazette*, 7, 13 and 15 September 1773. This quotation *South Carolina Gazette*, 7 September 1773 (datelined 31 August 1773), italics in the original.

[69] *South Carolina Gazette*, 7 September 1773, on 2 September, Upper House of the Assembly. The news of the habeas corpus was at the same session, and the president of the House diplomatically commented that 'he had not doubt of the Justice of those Magistrates' who had granted it.

Powell's lawyer in subsequent hearings emphasized the threat to civil liberties the house's action represented. Nevertheless, the house pursued Powell and resented the interference by *habeas corpus*, alleging that the justices, in acting as they did, had 'been guilty of the most atrocious Contempt of this House, and by their public Avowal and Declaration made by them, in pronouncing Judgment, that this House is no *Upper House* of Assembly ... have subverted the Constitution of this Government, and have expressly sounded the most dangerous Alarm to the good Subjects of this Province'.[70] Powell was perhaps lucky with his supporters, his lawyer and the political paralysis produced by the squabble between the two houses. Both appealed to London, and the matter seems to have lapsed as Britain's conflict with the colonies grew worse. Isaiah Thomas in his account of the printer, at least, knew of no resolution. Others accused in this way simply avoided coming to the assembly at all, fled the colony and left the money put for their recognizance to be forfeit.[71]

Less direct styles of writing and publishing also attracted the attention of councils and assemblies before the Revolution: here, the problem was the implicit criticisms of government and the connotations of the names and characters mentioned in association with it. James Franklin of the *New England Courant* in 1722 was summoned to the Massachusetts council, которое objected to a critical essay heavily laced with biblical references, and demanded scrutiny of publications before circulation:

> whereas in the Paper called the *New England Courant* printed Weekly by James Franklin, many, passages have been published boldly reflecting on His Majesty's Government and on the Administration of it in this Province, the Ministry, Churches and College; and it very often contains Paragraphs that tend to fill the Readers minds with vanity to the Dishonor of God, and disservice of Good Men.

The House of Representatives concurred, and, in parallel with legal proceedings, banned him from publishing the newspaper. He defied them, and, despite the grand jury failing to indict him for contempt of the order, was hit with severe conditions of sureties for his good behaviour. An account of his troubles was

---

[70] Drayton, on 2 September, in *South Carolina Gazette*, 7 September 1773; before the court-room of the State House, E.R., 'Barrister at Law', *South Carolina Gazette*, 15 September 1773; resolution in the same edition dated 7 September 1773.

[71] Thomas, History of Printing, vol. 2: 166–7, and John Drayton, *Memoirs of the American Revolution from Its Commencement to the Year 1776, Inclusive, as Relating to the State of South Carolina*, 2 vols (Charleston, SC: A.E. Miller, 1821), vol. 1, pp. 100–3; *The Public Records of the Colony of Connecticut from October, 1706 to October, 1716*, ed. Charles J. Hoadly (Harford, CT: Case, Lockwood and Brainard, 1870), pp. 139–40, Daniel Scot of Waterbury, presented before a grand jury as having refused to appear before the assembly, May 1758.

printed in the *American Weekly Mercury* by Andrew Bradford (son of William), who commented that 'the Assembly of the Province of the Massachusetts Bay are made up of Oppressors and Bigots, who make Religion the only engine of Destruction of the People'. He was, though, more conciliatory with his own local authorities in subsequent years.[72]

In the same way, John Peter Zenger in 1735 saw his newspaper, the *New York Weekly Journal*, denounced and sent to be burned by the common hangman for a satirical piece that named no one specifically. An initial attempt at indictment failed before the grand jury, and the council offered rewards for more evidence, and in the meantime ordered the burning of issues 7, 47, 48 and 49, at or near the pillory 'by the hands of the common hangman or whipper … as containing many things tending to sedition and faction'. Significantly, it also ordered the Mayor and magistrates of New York to attend the burning. A reflection of the divisions over the matter is that, after the famous trial, the Mayor and common council of New York city thanked defending counsel Andrew Hamilton, from a 'gratefull sense of the remarkable service done to the Inhabitants of this City and County … by his learned defence of the Rights of Mankind and the Liberty of the Press', and gave him the freedom of the city.[73] The Zenger case became one of the prime sources and inspirations for debates about the liberty of the press, reinforcing one that had already been conducted in the *Craftsman* in London. Indeed, Hamilton's speech was reproduced in it, and this was noted in America in its own debate in the newspapers, provoked by critical responses from two Barbadian writers, 'Anglo-Americanus' and 'Indo-Britannicus'. When John Almon – Boston politicians' favourite London printer of the 1760s and 1770s – reprinted the account of Zenger, he accompanied it with one of William Owen's trial, thus marrying the two triumphant defeats – by juries – of sedition cases on both sides of the Atlantic. This joint pamphlet was

---

[72] Thomas, *History of Printing*, vol. 2, p. 217, and in general pp. 217–23; *American Weekly Mercury*, 26 February 1722/3, quoted in Anna Janney de Armond, 'Andrew Bradford', *Pennsylvania Magazine of History and Biography*, 62 (1938), pp. 463–87, 469.

[73] *The Tryal of John Peter Zenger, of New York, Printer …* (London: J.Wilford, 1738), pp. 2–3; Howell, *State Trials*, vol. 17, pp. 677–9 reproduces this account; *Minutes of the Common Council of the City of New York, 1675–1776*, 8 vols (New York: Dodd, Mead and Company, 1905), vol. 4, pp. 277–8, 9 September 1735, reproduced in the *Boston Evening Post*, 22 March 1738; Livingston Rutherford, *John Peter Zenger: His Press, His Trial and a Bibliography of Zenger Imprints* (New York: Dodd, Mead and Co, 1904); Paul Finkelman, 'The Zenger Case: Prototype of a Political Trial', in Michael R. Belknap (ed.), *American Political Trials* (Westport, CT: Greenwood Press, 1994), pp. 21–42; see also Joseph H. Smith and Leo Hershowitz, 'Courts of Equity in the Province of New York: The Cosby Controversy, 1732–1736', *The American Journal of Legal History*, 16 (1972), pp. 1–50, for the debate about the powers of governors to institute courts of equity.

subsequently advertised in New York a few years later.⁷⁴ The case has rightly been described as part of American 'legal mythology', but it was landmark victory for radicals on both sides of the Atlantic.⁷⁵

The experiences of Alexander McDougall in New York in 1770 and 1771 were more severe and unpleasant, given the time he spent in jail while the governor and assembly together tried to make a case against him. One of the Sons of Liberty, he formed a challenge to the Tory controllers of the colony. His arrest was hailed as a boost to the American cause, and led to a long newspaper war between the two sides.

> Tho' the Imprisonment of Capt M'Dougall fill'd the People at first with a melancholy Distress, yet many now imagine it will conduce greatly to the common Weal, and tend particularly to open the eyes of the Public with respect to the Politics of certain Families, who have been twice concerned in prosecuting for what the Star Chamber Lawyers call Libels.⁷⁶

Another linked the attack on him to the general threat to trial in their own country, as the British authorities quoted a treason law of Henry VIII to justify the policy of removing Americans to England for trial, an issue that had rumbled through the colonial papers over the previous couple of years: 'a libel do they call it– To-morrow it may be called Treason. And who knows but that some men, even in this Country, may have it in their hearts to send our Patriots from Goal here to die as Traitors in England!' (see Chapter 5).⁷⁷ In the meantime, as the prosecution faltered – McDougall was bailed in May 1770, and proceedings staggered on inconclusively until the following year – a series of attacks on him under the heading *The Dougliad* (presumably deliberately echoing Alexander

---

⁷⁴ *Remarks on the Trial of John Peter Zenger, Printer of the New-York Weekly Journal Who Was Lately Tryed and Acquitting for Publishing and Printing Two Libels against the Government of That Province* (London: J. Roberts, 1738); *The Craftsman*, 21 January 1738 (no. 602) and *London Magazine*, January 1738, pp. 27–30 (from *The Craftsman*), with Hamilton's speech; the *Barbados Gazette* essays reprinted in Andrew Keimer, *Caribbeana*, vol. 2, pp. 198–221 (Anglo-Americanus), and pp. 225–41 (Indo-Britannicus); these evoked responses from James Alexander, author of the original account, in the *Pennsylvania Gazette*, 17 and 4 November, 1, 8 and 15 December 1737; *The Trial of John Peter Zenger, of New-York, Printer, … to Which Is Now Added, Being Never Printed before, the Trial of Mr William Owen, Bookseller* (London: J. Almon, 1765); *New York Journal*, 19 April 1770.
⁷⁵ Thomas, *History of Printing*, vol. 2, pp. 234 and 473–5; Hulsebosch, *Constituting Empire*, pp. 59 and 62. There were other targets of elected bodies at this time, such as Thomas Fleet (of the *Boston Evening Post*), denounced in 1741 by the colonial council for publishing a leaflet, though the results are unknown.
⁷⁶ *New York Journal*, 1 March 1770, A.L. writes to 'Mr Printer'; see also the 'eminent counsellor' in *New York Gazette*, 19 March 1770.
⁷⁷ *New Hampshire Gazette*, 9 March 1770, news of the arrest of Captain 'M'Dougall' and imprisonment, one gentleman on hearing made a patriotic speech; see also *Boston Post-Boy*, 24 April 1769, W. Bollan gives a column-and-a-half's advice on the applicability of 35 Hen.VII, c. 2, and *New York Gazette*, 17 July 1769, also discusses 35 Henry VIII, c. 2; see Edmund Burke's reported speech on the subject, *Boston Post-Boy*, 30 July 1770 with a resolution in the House of Commons against its applicability.

Pope's *Dunciad*) was published in twelve editions of the *New York Mercury*, and, while he said it would be deleterious to his defence for him to reply in detail, a widespread debate about the law of libels broke out across the press.[78] The governor was not alone in his attack, as the assembly gave him full backing throughout.[79]

The use of summons to its meetings, however, smacked too much of earlier Star Chamber proceedings, and the newspapers embarked on a long series of articles prompting the appropriate historical memories. As the case became a concern throughout the colonies, the critical articles reminded colonists of the appropriate legal references. In March 1770, 'an eminent counsellor and a Friend to Liberty', and 'Brutus' wrote biting criticisms of the procedures adopted in New York. 'Away with all the Star Chamber nonsense' wrote one, while the other conceded that though 'it is not *prudent* to speak the Truth at all Times; yet what Law in a *free state* has ever made it criminal to speak or write the Truth?', and made reference to the 'infernal doctrine of Despotism that *a Libel is not the less so for being true!*'.[80] Much of the atmosphere of learned disgust was summarized by 'The New-York Satyrist' in April, recommending the reading of the joint account of the Zenger and Owen trials, as well as denouncing the 'rude and malicious writings of *some* of the New York Tories' responsible for the *Dougliad*. As he pointed out too, truth was no defence – 'that is, *Common-Law* will prove it to be white, whilst *Star-Chamber Law* will prove it to be black; or one pulls east while the other west, yet both are striving hard to exist under the *very same Line of Jurisdiction*'. Ironically, that summer saw the trial in London of John Almon and John Woodfall for the publication of the Junius letters, details of which were published in the colonies. In January 1771, the *Boston Gazette* published the first of the Junius letters, the address to judge Lord Mansfield criticizing his conduct of libel cases which was 'another powerful evidence of settled plan to contract the legal power of Juries'.[81] Politically, the New York government cause was lost early the previous year, as

---

[78] *New York Gazette*, 23 April 1770, no. 3 of 'The Dougliad on Liberty', and McDougall's own narrative, 24 December 1770, widely published in, for example, *Pennsylvania Gazette*, 31 December 1770; he says in his narrative that no. 3 was suppressed. See the excellent summary in Levy, *Freedom of Speech*, pp. 79–85.

[79] Levy notes that the assembly voted unanimously to prosecute him: Leonard W. Levy, 'Did the Zenger Case Really Matter? Freedom of the Press in Colonial New York', *William and Mary Quarterly*, 3rd ser., 17 (1960), pp. 35–50, 44–5; *New York Journal*, 20 December 1779, summoning McDougall to the bar of the house, headlined 'from the General Assembly now sitting 13 December'; Thomas, *History of Printing*, 2, pp. 479–83.

[80] *New York Gazette*, 26 February and 12 March 1770 for *The Craftsman*; same 26 February for the extract from the *London Chronicle*, 16 November 1769; *New York Gazette*, 19 and 26 March 1770 (counsellor and 'Brutus' respectively).

[81] *New York Journal*, 19 April 1770; *Virginia Gazette*, 27 September 1770 for front-page report of defence speech on behalf of Woodfall, and *Boston Gazette*, 28 January 1771 for Junius Letter to Mansfield.

Captain McDougall joined John Wilkes among those celebrated by patriotic oaths as having defended the cause of liberty. Not only were New Yorkers drinking to the 'Liberty of the Press', but in more detail for 'a total abolition of the Star-Chamber Doctrine of Libels, as held up in the Trials of Zenger, Mead and Penn'. Legal history was not easily forgotten in such circumstances.[82]

A good example of the difficulties facing the last governors of Massachusetts when they were *unable* to harness the support of the assemblies or senior judiciary is the indignation and general helplessness of Massachusetts Governor Francis Bernard in the face of the publication by the *Boston Gazette* in 1768 of a carefully abstract editorial piece on the effect of bad ministers on good government: it was immediately read by Bernard as a slur on him. The anonymous article pointed out that bad ministers had done 'some Service to the Cause of Liberty', if only because along with some good kings, they had destroyed several bad ones. Moreover they had driven people to insist on their rights, thus producing Magna Carta, the Habeas Corpus Act and the Bill of Rights. Bernard jumped to the conclusion that he was under criticism, saying to the Massachusetts House of Representatives concerning what he called a 'libellous paragraph': 'I have been used to treat the publications in the *Boston Gazette*, with the contempt they deserve; but when they are carried to a length, which, if unnoticed, must endanger the very being of government'. After receiving the offending edition, the House of Representatives responded, rather regretfully, a couple of days later:

> This House, after examination into the nature and importance of the paper referred to, cannot see reason to admit of such conclusion as your Excellency has formed. No particular person, public or private, is named in it. And as it does not appear to the House, that any thing contained in it, can affect the majesty of the King, the dignity of the government, the honor of the General Court, or the true interest of the province, they think they may be fully justified in their determination to take no further notice of it. The liberty of the press, is the great bulwark of the liberty of the people. It is, therefore, the incumbent duty of those who are constituted the guardians of the people's rights, to defend and maintain them.

They probably knew who was meant and agreed with the sentiments.[83]

---

[82] *New York Gazette,* 26 March 1770.
[83] *Boston Gazette,* 29 February 1768; *Speeches of the Governors of Massachusetts, 1765-1775; the Answers of the House of Representatives Thereto,* ed. Alden Bradford (New York: da Capo Press, 1971; unabridged reprint of 1818 (Boston) edition, originally Boston: Russell and Gardner, 1818), pp. 118-19. This echoes the earlier gubernatorial impotence of Jonathan Belcher in New Jersey in the late 1740s, when he was in dispute with 'audacious villains' guilty of 'sedition and rebellion' by making land deals with the Indians: *Documents Relative to the Colonial History of the State of New Jersey, Vol. 7 1746-51,* ed. W.A. Whitehead (Newark, NJ: Daily Advertiser Printing House, 1883), pp. 29-30, 42, 250, and 333.

Challenges to this kind of politically driven process occurred at many levels, in part legalistically, not least on the grounds that the insulted authorities were acting in their own case–something that both William Owen in London and Alexander McDougall in New York made central to their defences. Yet colonial governors and legislative assemblies retained a strong sense of their own dignity, and were highly active until the Revolution in defending it.[84] Another problem occurred at the initiation of the indictment. While the Attorney-General in England could proceed *ex officio*, that is, without a grand jury finding an indictment a true bill, this was more problematic in the colonies after the Zenger affair. Above all, juries at the subsequent trials were also extending the scope of their involvement in the cases, and nullifying the prosecutions by acquittals in the face of the evidence.

The central and the local: The decline of seditious words

There is a powerful contrast between the exercise of full governmental powers, the deployment of King's Messengers, government lawyers and attorney-generals, and the use of senior courts such as the King's Bench on the one hand and the efforts by local authorities to deal with the mutterings and occasional printed reflection of political dissent on the other. In England, the prosecutions at King's Bench fluctuated in the later eighteenth century according to the tense political relations occasioned by the American or the French Revolutions. An overview of the variation was created by officials in the early nineteenth century, as they logged the important cases and monitored their own practices:

Prosecutions for Libels on Information ex Officio from 1760 to 1810			
By Decade:			
1760 - 0	1771 - 0	1781 - 11	1791 - 0
1761 - 1	1772 - 0	1782 - 2	1792 - 19
1762 - 3	1773 - 0	1783 - 1	1793 - 7
1763 - 4	1774 - 2	1784 - 0	1794 - 0
1764 - 3	1775 - 12	1785 - 0	1795 - 5
1765 - 0	1776 - 1	1786 - 3	1796 - 1
1766 - 0	1777 - 0	1787 - 1	1797 - 1
1767 - 0	1778 - 2	1788 - 4	1798 - 6
1768 - 0	1779 - 0	1789 - 5	1799 - 0
1769 - 1	1780 - 0	1790 - 3	1800 - 1
1770 - 15			
27	17	30	40

Source: TNA PRO KB 33/24/2 Returns on Sedition, Anne to William IV, unnumbered piece.

[84] Barry Cahill, 'The Sedition Trial of Timothy Houghton: Repression in a Marginal New England Planter Township during the Revolutionary Years', *Acadiensis*, 24 (1994), pp. 35–58.

This indicates that there were some flashpoint years, such as 1770 and 1775, and then 1781, which perhaps indicate the amount of critical material in print about American affairs. The years 1792–3, the period of the French Revolution when the British government pursued well-known oppositional figures such as Tom Paine, were also a time of heavy suppression. Many of the accusations in the 1790s were 'libels' on the government, parliament as a system and the role of the monarchy. Some sound almost respectable: in 1796 John Reeves was prosecuted for seditious libel in his work *Thoughts on English Government, Addressed to the Quiet Good Sense of the English People in a Series of Letters*. Eastwood remarks that 'the Reeves trial signified a profound political struggle both to define an authentic constitution and to possess the language of constitutionalism. This contested idea of the constitution takes us to the heart of the political and ideological debates of the 1790s'. He had founded loyalist associations to criticize the rival pro-reform and revolutionaries of the Corresponding Societies, yet found himself accused of sedition by a government nervous of the slightest criticism.[85] These cases reflected the way that the political system as a whole came under criticism in the revolutionary period, to an extent not seen since the civil wars of the 1640s. Targets included the monarchy, parliament and the army: radicals had hopes of enticing soldiers to join the revolutionary cause, and at least disobey their orders in repressing protests, for which Francis Ward was prosecuted in 1796 for a leaflet significantly called *Scarlet Devils*. Prosecutions were often instigated in the 1790s by parliament itself, continuing the practices outlined earlier.[86] In the same bundle of retrospective lists, there are many details of the bail conditions imposed on the accused, and the sentences of fines, pillory and imprisonment imposed. Since the convicted also had to find large sums of money for securities after their release, conditional on their good behaviour for

---

[85] Cobbett, *Parliamentary History of England* (London: T. Hansard, 1820), vol. 36, 608–86; D. Eastwood, 'John Reeves and the Contested Idea of Constitution', *Journal for Eighteenth-Century Studies*, 16 (2) (1993), pp. 197–212, 197; A.V. Beedell, 'John Reeves's Prosecution for a Seditious Libel, 1795–6: A Study in Political Cynicism', *Historical Journal* 36 (1993), pp. 790–824, despite his conspicuous loyalism, the House of Commons denounced his pamphlet, *Thoughts on English Government* and in May 1796 he was on trial at the Guildhall for a seditious libel (pp. 790–1). Clive Emsley, 'Repression, "Terror" and the Rule of Law in England during the Decade of the French Revolution', *The English Historical Review*, 100 (397) (1985), pp. 801–25, and 'An Aspect of Pitt's "Terror": Prosecutions for Sedition during the 1790s', *Social History*, 6 (2) (1981), pp. 155–84, 157 and 160.

[86] TNA PRO KB 33/24/2 Returns on Sedition, Anne to William IV (many of the pieces are unnumbered); see also a handwritten order from George Rose, Clerk of Parliament, 23 May 1817, 'that there be laid before this House [Lords] An Account of the Numbers of Recognizances since the year 1640' after which an indictment for Libel had been instituted; a printed source on bail, *An Account of Persons Held to Bail to Answer in the Court of King's Bench for Libels, from 1 Anne to 57 Geo.3 both inclusive* (ordered to be printed 3 March 1818); Mary Thrale, *Selections from the Papers of the London Corresponding Society, 1792–1799* (Cambridge University Press, 1993), pp. 380–1.

up to five years afterwards, the sentence in effect carried on for many years. Some security against conviction was provided by Fox's Libel Act which attempted to underpin in the role of the jury. They were empowered to assess both whether the material was seditious *and* whether it was intentionally so. In effect, proof of publication was no longer sufficient for conviction. In some ways, this brought the scope of jury discretion into line with that in many criminal cases.[87]

From words to print: The eighteenth-century transformation

Enforcement of the law in the English tradition depended on the local forces of ordinary complaints, constables and magistrates. In the absence of centralized organizations, legislation such as that of 1663–4 making meetings of 'sectaries' such as the Quakers (Society of Friends) and Baptists acts of sedition, depended on local prosecutions. It may be the effect of metropolitan influence, but it is probably significant that the prosecutions and sentences of banishment of Quakers in that period were concentrated in London and the surrounding Home Counties. That was where many metropolitan figures retreated from London when they needed to. Ironically, instead of speech, Quaker meetings were already notorious for *silence* in the absence of preachers or ministers. The local bodies watching the ill behaviour of their local population were more interested in speech and action. The possibility of the latter – violent disputes and assaults being a major part of the business of local courts – may have dominated the way they chose their priorities.

So far, the concentration here has been on some of the major cases that established either common or distinct patterns of law and precedent in the Anglo-American world. History from below would require a countervailing analysis of the ordinary and the humble at the local level. Yet such a study seems difficult compared with the repression of the literate in print culture. There is a good reason for this: cases of prosecutions in the local courts in English counties and American colonies decline steeply after the early 1700s. Old Bailey figures suggest that from thirty-eight cases in the last quarter of the seventeenth century, the number of sedition prosecutions declined to twenty-three in the first quarter of the eighteenth: three of them involved Dryden's satire on sedition. After the 1720s, there were few cases of prosecution for sedition or seditious words at the

---

[87] Green, *Verdict According to Conscience*, pp. 330–3; Thomas A. Green, 'The Jury, Seditious Libel and the Criminal Law', in R.H. Helmholtz and Thomas A. Green (eds), *Juries, Libel and Justice: The Role of English Juries in Seventeenth- and Eighteenth-Century Trials for Libel and Slander* (Los Angeles, CA: William Andrews Memorial Library, 1986), pp. 39–91, 41.

Old Bailey – none at all from 1726 to 1750, and only one in the quarter-century thereafter. While the Old Bailey saw a combination of cases which in other places would have been divided between the quarter sessions and the assizes, what evidence there is from lower courts suggests a similar pattern. The 1690s represented the last period of serious persecution of sedition: in Middlesex, with a dozen prosecutions, while in the first decade of the eighteenth century there were three. In the North Riding of Yorkshire, a similar pattern can be seen, with forty-three cases in the last half of the seventeenth century, and only three in the first half of the eighteenth.

Patchy evidence from elsewhere suggests that there were flurries of cases at times of regime change, or challenge, so that in Shropshire there were a few cases in 1688 and 1689, and then none until the aftermath of the Jacobite rising in 1715.[88] The Welsh Great Sessions only saw eleven in the whole of the eighteenth century, five of them concerned with the Dean of St. Asaph and his Wrexham bookseller in 1783.[89] In North Yorkshire, magistrates were more willing to impose fines on those who committed the ordinary offence of defaming their neighbours than on those allegedly producing seditious speeches. As in other areas of local prosecution in the period, the purpose of the cases may have been intimidatory rather punitive, an attempt to prevent any recurrence rather than exact retribution for past actions. In northeast England, there were occasional official panics about drunken words spoken in taverns and inns at times of war or rebellion, and prosecutions seem to have been provoked by the strange character of the words or the speaker. In Newcastle-upon-Tyne in 1746, John Shearer appeared at the Assizes, on the evidence of Sarah and Thomas Brown, innkeeper, who said that Shearer and James Woodburn (a soldier in the King's Scottish regiment) came in to drink a pint of ale, when Shearer said 'it was time King George was gone home and he would have him home for that the Crown of England was the pretended right of all the Stuarts ffamily and the Rebels would face the Duke and then would put such Bitches as this Dep[onent] into the Dog

---

[88] Old Bailey online, http://www.oldbaileyonline.org, electronic search 1 September 2010; *Middlesex, Calendar of Sessions Books, 1689 to 1709*, by W.J. Hardy (Westminster: 1905); *North Riding Quarter Sessions Records*, 9 vols, ed. Rev. J. Atkinson (North Riding Record Society), vol. 5: 1887; vol. 6: 1888; vol. 8: 1889; North Yorkshire Record Office, survey of QSM Minutes Books (MF 98, 99, 100, 101, 102) and QSB indexes, 1661–1733; *Abstract of the Orders Made by the Court of Quarter Sessions for Shropshire*, vol. 1, 1638–1709, ed. R. Lloyd Kenyon (Shropshire: no date), three in 1688-9, then one in 1716.

[89] Welsh Great Sessions, see http://www.llgc.org.uk/sesiwn_fawr/index_s.htm (accessed 3 September 2010); Sharon Howard, 'Crime, Communities and Authority in Early Modern Wales: Denbighshire, 1660–1730' (unpublished Ph.D. thesis, University of Wales, Aberystwyth, 2003), pp. 152 fn. 41 and 153.

wheel and uttered several other Treasonable Expressions'.[90] In the same year, Newcastle man John Warden was reported by a gentleman, William Rawling, as refusing to drink the Duke of Cumberland's health, but proposed to drink to the 'Chevalier's' instead, that is, to the Pretender.[91] Other comments were less predictable: in Hexham in 1748 Henry Elliott denied treasonable expressions (before magistrate John Fenwick), but was accused by three men of saying in conversation, 'God damn the Queen of Hungary and all her allies', and one witness, knowing that he often played on a violin, asked him if the Pretender and the Queen of Hungary were both present, who would he play for, Elliott said the Pretender. After questioning him about who had the better right to the throne, Eliott answered 'King George has no more right to the crown than I have', and of the Pretender, he expressed the hope 'in a short time to see him enjoy it by force of arms and you will all see it and I will do what is in my power for his Interest', and added that all the Stuarts had better right to the throne than King George. Cases of this nature could be found anywhere in times of panic, such as when a foreigner, probably a Venetian, was accused in 1756 in a village near Sunderland and sentenced to the pillory. He had, the accusation went, 'resided at Monkwearmouth Shore c[irca = about] six months ... in a very clandestine manner without any visible way of subsistence and to the terror of the Inhabitants there', and was seen in a tavern swearing an oath to the Young Pretender. The company had been equally drunk, and the case went forward apparently almost by accident, probably at the instigation of one magistrate. The conviction provoked the submission of a 'unanimous petition of the neighbourhood' for a pardon, involving most of the local establishment, which was supported by the judge at the trial, and the prisoner was released.[92]

The increasing concern in England for print culture at the local level paralleled that in the colonies. One anxiety concentrated on new forms of sociality and intercourse, particularly the new coffee houses. In County Durham, for example, these had to be licensed like alehouses, and strict rules imposed: one man, Ralph Middleton of North Bailey, gentleman, licensed to sell coffee and tea in Durham City in 1680, was ordered to allow 'no evill rule or discord to be kept in his house', and to

---

[90] TNA ASSI 45/23/2/101B-F, John Shearer Newcastle Assizes 1746.
[91] TNA ASSI 45/23/2/103C.
[92] TNA ASSI 45/23/4/16B-C, 1748 (Northumberland); ASSI 45/24/4/109 1752 NL warrant to arrest one Radcliffe; case of Timothy Cecilion, TNA SP 36/136/1; f.3 Warrant to Keeper of Gaol to Receive and Keep and to Cons of Monkwearmouth, 10 February 1756; f.4, Petition pro Timothy Cicilian to Earl of Holdernesse; f.30; warrant of discharge 22 April; all abbreviations have been spelled out.

use his utmost endeavours to prevent and hinder all scandalous papers, books and libells concerning the government or the public Ministers thereof from being brought into his house or to be there read perused and divulged and to prevent and hinder all and every person and persons from declaring uttering and divulging in his said house all manner of false and scandalous reports of the government or any of the Ministers thereof and in case any papers books or libells shall be brought into his said house and there openly read perused or divulged or in case such false and scandalous reports shall be there openly declared uttered or divulged if the said Ralph Middleton shall within two days respectively next ensuing give Information thereof to one his Majesty's principall Secretaries of State or to some one of his Majesty's Justices of the Peace and also shall make due payment to his Majesty of all the duties of excise as hereafter shall grow due to his Majesty for selling and retailing of the said liquors then this recognizance present to be void or else to be and remaine in full force and virtue.

Middleton must have lost his licence for some unrecorded reason, and in 1688 was 'readmitted' to keep his coffee house, on his own recognizance.[93] Open circulation of paper caused even more official nervousness. In the town of Leicester in 1738, a shocking scandal was caused by advertisements for a 'treasonable' play, stuck on posts around the town, which provoked the Mayor and Corporation to offer £100 'from his Majesty'. A few years later, Leicester's authorities themselves were the object of a 'false, scandalous, and seditious Libel, against the Mayor of the said Borough', published by George Smith alias Green, who was indicted at the assizes in 1750.[94] Sometimes the distribution of London-derived printed sedition to the provinces caused local clampdowns. In Newcastle reproduction of an edition of *The Craftsman* provoked the arrest of the printer of the *Newcastle Courant*, John White. In Edinburgh the arrival of the pamphlet concerning the sufferings of Alexander Murray (above) led the London authorities to instruct the magistrates of the city to search the printers' premises and seize all copies. Investigation revealed that several were on the point of publishing it, with little idea of who had written it or why. It was reported to London that

---

[93] Durham Record Office, Q/S/OB/6, July 179 (Edward King), July 1680 (Ralph Middleton), January 1680/81 (Samuel Hodgkins of Sunderland gent.); Q/S/OB/7, p. 100; John Barrell, 'Coffee-House Politicians', *Journal of British Studies*, 3 (2) (2004), pp. 206–32. For an interesting twentieth-century comparison, see Khaurudin Aljunied, 'Coffee-Shops in Colonial Singapore: Domains of Contentious Politics', *History Workshop Journal*, LXXVII (2014), pp. 66–85.
[94] *London Evening Press*, 2 and 9 February 1738; *Whitehall Evening Post*, 5 April 1750.

the Magistrates chearfully undertook to do their duty in this particular, and have exerted themselves with zeal, by apprehending one Gideon Crawford a bookseller, who was examined by the L[or]d Provost, he ingeniously acknowledged the delivering it [to] the printer, and the way the copy came to his hands, and gave in the frank and anonymous letter inclosed with the pamphlet directed to him.

The unfortunate Crawford confessed that he had managed to sell only a dozen of the pamphlets before the raid. As in the colonies, printed accounts spread and were difficult to suppress in one place, for almost as quickly they emerged somewhere else. Print culture was increasingly a many-headed hydra, as printers grew in numbers everywhere and professional plagiarism was the essence of their technique for feeding the growing local markets for news. While the attempts at control were, in England, directed by a central government increasingly accustomed to offering legal and technical advice to local authorities trying to suppress protest and disorder, the more devolved and independent character of colonial government, and particularly the isolation of individual governors, prevented any systematic attempts at blocking the reproduction of offending material in other areas.[95]

In the colonies, by the middle of the eighteenth century, occasional prosecutions of Jacobites and other anti-Hanoverians suggest that there may have been intermittent muttering, and official reactions, similar to those in England. But these instances seem remarkably few: indeed, sedition was a rare charge in colonial courts after 1700.[96] In the late seventeenth century, in North Carolina, for example, men like John Philpott in 1694 were discovered saying 'God Damn King William', and 'I'll drink King James health for he is the right king'. In the eighteenth century, too, cases could be found, one person saying in 1728, 'God damn King George our Sovereign Lord the King'. In 1755 there were seditious words from a James Castello, of Chester County Pennsylvania, 'King George has no more right to the crown of Great Britain than I, and if he had his just deserts, he would have his Neck cut off', and he was accused of drinking the health of the French King and the Pretender. He pleaded guilty at quarter

---

[95] Kathleen Wilson, *The Sense of the People: Politics, Culture and Imperialism in England, 1715–1785* (Cambridge: Cambridge University Press, 1998), p. 325; TNA SP 54/41/13A [State papers, Scotland]. The spread of pamphlets from England to Ireland had been a problem in James II's reign in the 1680s, see T.C. Barnard, 'Athlone, 1685: Limerick, 1710: Religious Riots or Charivaris?', *Studia Hibernica*, 27 (1993), pp. 68–9.

[96] It is tempting to agree with Larry Eldridge who has proclaimed we must 'start from scratch. We must go to the original court records', *Distant Heritage*, p. 2.

sessions, and was sentenced to one hour in the pillory.⁹⁷ More explicit were the actions of several Jacobites who, it was reported in Annapolis, Maryland, had only just arrived in the colonies – possibly transported as prisoners of the '45 rebellion:

> the Grand-Jury of the Assize for this County ... found Bills of Indictment against Two of the rebels lately imported, for Drinking the Pretender's Health, and some other treasonable expressions; for which the Court adjudged, (as they were Servants, incapable of paying Fines) that they should be well whipped at the Whipping Post, and stand in the Pillory, which Sentence was immediately put into Execution.

A few years later a recruiting sergeant in the Virginia Regiment was roughed up by a small group of Jacobites damning 'King George's soldiers', and singing 'several disloyal songs' while cheering the 'Tartan Pla[i]d and White Cockade' of the '45 rebellion. These were unusual instances, though local legends of transported Jacobites remain strong in the modern United States.⁹⁸

From the Restoration to the '45, therefore, the substance of much sedition in England and occasionally in the colonies took the form of the sedition of nostalgia – the lost leader, initially Oliver Cromwell in the 1660s and 1670s, or the King over the water, after the exile of James II. Unconnected to those longings were the insults which were directed at government and which may have been common anywhere: but it was increasingly rare for a case to appear in the local courts by the mid-eighteenth century. In the colonial courts there were occasional cases, such as that of Daniel Scott, for 'certain false, opprobrious and scandalous words and expressions in contempt of his Honour the Governor and the General Assembly of this colony' of Connecticut in 1758. Little came of the complaint.⁹⁹ Political criticism became part of everyday

---

⁹⁷ Larry D. Eldridge, 'Before Zenger: Truth and Seditious Speech in Colonial America, 1607–1700', *The American Journal of Legal History*, 39 (3) (1995), pp. 337–58, and his *A Distant Heritage* – a study of more than 1,200 colonial cases before 1702; Eldridge suggests that *scandalum magnatum*, speaking against the government, and false news, dominated these speeches Spindell, 'Law of Words', pp. 25 and 39; *Pennsylvania Gazette*, 5 June 1755, also in *Boston Gazette*, 16 June.

⁹⁸ *New York Gazette Revived in the Weekly Post-Boy*, 28 September 1747, also *Pennsylvania Gazette*, 1 October, *New York Evening Post*, 5 October 1747; *Proceedings of the Council of Maryland, August 10, 1753–March 30, 1761*, ed. William Hand Browne (Baltimore, MD: Maryland Historical Society, 1911), *Archives of Maryland*, vol. 31, pp. 31–3; See career of revolutionary war general Hugh Mercer, *Norwich Packet*, 17 March 1777.

⁹⁹ *The Public Records of the Colony of Connecticut from October, 1706 to October, 1716*, ed. Charles J. Hoadly (Harford, CT: Case, Lockwood and Brainard, 1870), pp. 139–40, Daniel Scot of Waterbury, presented before a grand jury as having refused to appear before the assembly, May 1758.

American politics as the political relations of empire changed. Drinking toasts, as in the official Stamp Act anniversary celebrations, were deployed to indicate the very different sentiments developing in the North American colonies: Americans included seventeenth-century heroes of repressive prosecution such as Algernon Sidney in toasts together with the Zenger jury, John Wilkes, Edmund Burke and the 'total abolition of the Star Chamber doctrine of Libels'. It was this kind of expression and the direct action of the Boston Tea Party that led some local authorities in the colonies, trying to stem the tide, to denounce the movement as 'tending directly to sedition, civil war and rebellion'. In that respect the authorities (from Worcester, Massachusetts, in 1774) were right.[100] Unlike English drinkers, American colonists offered a real threat to the established government. Up to that moment of imperial disintegration, however, there seem to have been two patterns, of declining local prosecutions of spoken words in courts at any level in England and the colonies, and, by contrast, waves of attacks by government on dissident writers and publishers. The former cases contain the largely forgotten victims of repression, while the latter have often produced the legal precedents and heroic cases of the published state trials and the history of radicalism. It was this second history, of the defence of the freedom to print, that England really shared with its North American colonies.

Conclusion

Sedition was everywhere in the British empire, at least in the eyes of its governments. The legal forms and the precise meaning of the crime, however, varied from place to place, depending on who constituted the 'king's government', and how their relations with the ruled developed. As previous studies have suggested, this was affected by culture and politics as well as the particular legal history of a jurisdiction. The diversity of the foundations of the North American colonies meant that proprietors, commissioners and governors joined magistrates and legislators as those who were given protection from criticism. In England, faced with an increasingly diverse range of print culture, governments increasingly concentrated on incorporating into the scope of the law all forms of

---

[100] *New York Gazette,* 26 March 1770, in the midst of the McDougall case (who was also toasted); *Worcester Town Records from 1753 to 1783,* ed. Franklin R. Rice (Worcester, MA: Worcester Society of Antiquity, 1882), p. 232.

potential expression of opposition in satire, novels, pornography and cartoons. At the local level, urban mayors and magistrates assumed that they should be protected from critical assaults. The key developments in English law, however, were in the highest courts, as judicial activism and parliamentary indignation combined to set new precedents in eighteenth-century England remarkably like those of the previous century under the hated Star Chamber. The authorities everywhere were in effect trying to catch up with a rapidly changing political culture of criticism. The most consistent feature of cases against printers and publishers in many contrasting contexts was the essential role of politicians in the legislatures, from British houses of parliament to colonial assemblies, in initiating the cases that came to court. Legislators seemed to have felt free to complain of individual articles or reports, and, as a body, often summoned the offenders to answer the case before any official judicial proceedings had been instigated. Once transferred to the public sphere of a jury trial, though, prosecutions were not always so easy to control and convictions could not be guaranteed wherever, as in London and New York, bloody-minded juries defied the courts. This is one reason why so many of these cases have entered the legal annals as classic examples of jury independence. Thus, the law was everywhere in a continual process of being established, and rejected, and while there was little opposition to the idea of legal protection for governments from 'illegitimate' criticism, it proved difficult to lay down consistent rules about what this meant.

The shift in prosecutions from spoken to printed word was a significant transformation in the direction of political control in the period after 1700, reflecting official anxiety that what was read was more dangerous than what was spoken. Possibly, speech was easier to suppress than print, because it was achievable through local courts, persuadable juries and summary justice: moreover, the penalties were milder. Print culture, however, was increasingly non-local, being circulated and copied by other printers, particularly in the systematic plagiarism essential to early newspapers. This had a transatlantic dimension, as Ian Steele demonstrated: news stories circulated the Atlantic ports.[101] Once in the public domain, printed opinions often could not be contained. As Simon Schama has pointed out, prosecution might actually

---

[101] Ian K. Steele, *The English Atlantic: 1675-1740: An Exploration of Communication and Community* (New York: Oxford University Press, 1986); for examples of news concerning criminals and the politics of crime, see Morgan and Rushton, *Eighteenth-Century Criminal Transportation*.

make both the writer and the writing more popular and widely known. This happened with the prosecution at the House of Lords of Dr Henry Sacheverell for preaching a virulent anti-Whig sermon and printing a huge number of copies of it subsequently. 'The trial was a public-relations fiasco for the government. Henry Sacheverell became a hero of the streets of London'. Riots followed and overtly Protestant targets were attacked by mobs championing the victim of legal persecution. Here, repression backfired.[102] Nevertheless, the authorities' fear of paper sedition produced a disproportionate number of prosecutions of printers and writers in the eighteenth century, and radical elements everywhere played on that fear. This does not mean that criticism vanished from other forms of communication, as print formed but one of the available technologies of criticism. Words and deeds often went together when targeted vandalism became part of street politics. As one London report in 1727 recorded,

> Last Saturday night the fine statue of the King on horse back made by Mr. Nost and set up in Grosvenor Square, was very much defaced by some villainous persons yet unknown, the left leg being torn off at the length and laid upon the pedestal, one rein of the bridle almost cut through, the sword and truncheon wrenched off and carried away, the neck also hacked as if they designed to cut off the head, and a most scandalous libel was left at the place.

There were many different ways of making a point and, in a society where the law was vigilant and repressive, there was a natural role for Edward Thompson's famous 'crime of anonymity' involving unattributable rumour, insult and threat. Official paranoia in the eighteenth century concentrated on what the authorities could trace back to authors, printers and distributors whom they could make accountable to their concept of sedition.[103]

As the focus of prosecution changed, so did the nature of the penalties. In a broader development of punishments in this area from the physical to the financial, the use of the pillory, whipping and mutilation declined before 1700 in England and the colonies. By the mid-eighteenth century, the main deterrent in sedition cases lay in crippling fines for printers and authors, often accompanied by long spells in jail until they could raise the equally punitive amounts of funds

---

[102] S. Shama, *A History of Britain: The British Wars 1603–1776* (London: The Bodley Head, 2009), vol. 2 of The History of Britain, Kindle edition Loc. 5384.
[103] *The Weekly Journal, or The British Gazetteer*, 18 March 1727; for sources on local politics and identity in England, see Wilson, *The Sense of the People*. See Barnard, 'Athlone, 1685: Limerick, 1710' for the folkloric character of many protests; Edward P. Thompson, 'The Crime of Anonymity', in Peter Linebaugh, John G. Rule, E.P. Thompson and Cal Winslow (eds), *Albion's Fatal Tree: Crime and Society in Eighteenth-Century England* (Harmondsworth: Penguin, 1977), pp. 255–344.

for sureties for their good behaviour for several years. Such tactics had their limits in the colonies, and in the end the isolation and impotence of British governors deactivated the law of sedition there in the 1760s and 1770s. Words remained dangerous, at least for those in power, but it became more difficult in America to turn that danger into a crime. There is no scope, however, for a teleological history with a happy ending in press freedom, as the kinds of struggle seen before 1776 were resumed once again in the 1790s, this time in the face of revolutionary rather than rebellious sentiments. If the effects of the 1798 Alien and Sedition Acts in the United States were short-lived, the repression of free expression in politics remained in English and Scottish law for a long time. There were more than a hundred prosecutions in a decade of political conflict before 1821, for example, and people were still being sentenced to criminal transportation to the colonies or, more mildly under Scottish law, to 'banishment' (i.e. from Scotland to anywhere else, including England).[104] In Britain, there was still anxiety about absolute freedom of speech, and only in the twentieth century did governments finally become a legitimate target of criticism.[105] The decline in sedition cases in the criminal courts after 1700 accompanies a parallel decline in the personal defamation cases, and it is possible that people were taking their private grievances elsewhere, to the poorly recorded processes of summary justice conducted by local magistrates. It is worth noting that there was a return to prosecutions for spoken sedition in the revolutionary panic of the 1790s, and again in the early nineteenth century in the decade after the 1815 peace, a time of great agitation, rumoured conspiracies and government reaction.[106]

---

[104] For the United States, see Levy *Freedom of Speech*, pp. 266ff, James Morton Smith, 'The Sedition Law, Free Speech and the American Political Process', *William and Mary Quarterly*, 3rd ser., 9 (1952), pp. 497–511, David Jenkins, 'The Sedition Act of 1798 and the Incorporation of Seditious Libel into First Amendment Jurisprudence', *American Journal of Legal History*, 45 (2001), pp. 154–213, Philip I. Blumberg, *Repressive Jurisprudence in the Early American Republic: The First Amendment and the Legacy of English Law* (Cambridge: Cambridge University Press, 2010); British national data was collected for ten years up to 1821 and eventually published as a Parliamentary report by the House of Commons, 'Political Libel and Seditious Conduct', 5 April 1821, but a simultaneous attempt was made to list the cases since the start of Queen Anne's reign – see TNA KB 33/24/2 Returns on Sedition, Anne to William IV.

[105] See, among many others, Ellen Parker, 'Implementation of the UK Terrorist Act 2006 – The Relationship between Counterterrorism Law, Free Speech, and the Muslim Community in the United Kingdom versus the United States', *Emory International Law Review*, 21 (2007), pp. 711–57.

[106] Michael T. Davis, 'The British Jacobins: Folk Devils in the Age of Counter-Revolution?', in David Lemmings and Claire Walker (eds), *Moral Panics, the Media and the Law in Early Modern England* (Houndmills: Basingstoke, 2009), pp. 221–44; Emsley, 'An Aspect of Pitt's "Terror"', pp. 155–84; and John Barrell, *The Spirit of Despotism: Invasions of Privacy in the 1790s* (Oxford, 2006).

4

Domestic Rebellions: From Sedgemoor to Culloden

The threats of disorder, rebellion and civil war pervaded the European bases of the British state in the period from the end of James II's reign to 1800. Supposedly a powerful imperial state, the British system was dependent on local structures of administration and support, and, where these were absent or disaffected, the power of the centre could be reduced to nil. Even where the loyalty of dominant groups could be guaranteed, as in Ireland among the Protestant landowners, the quiescence of their subordinates could not be guaranteed, as we shall see at the end of this chapter. In Scotland, by contrast, there was at best scepticism about the replacement of the line of James II with another branch of the Stuarts and with the death of Queen Anne, there was little affection for the Hanoverian Georges. Religion and religious differences pervaded these divisions, and the intertwining of state and church, particularly in Ireland, and the sense of insecurity among Scottish Presbyterians who felt threatened by religious diversity, led many to decide whether or not to support the British state. Loyalty therefore was often equivocal and fragile, and the authorities found themselves working with a legal framework much changed in terms of the law of treason. Disloyalty and treason were not so easy to merge into a single crime.

Rebellion and the state: Britain, 1685–1700

The seventeenth century established some legal and political precedents in the way treason and sedition were treated, and there are some continuities in eighteenth-century practices. In other respects, particularly in the area of legal rights, the century also produced new patterns of judicial guarantees. Yet the

1680s came to be remembered for its examples of severity which were explicitly rejected at the Glorious Revolution and were held up as examples of the tyranny that was brought to an end in 1688. English rebels, in both the Interregnum under parliament and later under James II, were not treated kindly, in the sense that traditional treason law was applied to selected numbers of them, complete with the brutality of public executions. There were similar processes in Scotland, applied both to Covenanters and to those who supported Argyll's rising. Yet there was also, in parallel, a growing tradition of trial and transportation, either by direct confessions of the accused or by reprieve by the supreme authority of the king. This had in fact been pioneered under Cromwell, as prisoners from the battle of Dunbar and those prosecuted for minor rebellions were transported to the Caribbean.[1] Thus, as Douglas Hay and Peter Linebaugh have argued, the parallel strategies of severity and mercy went hand in hand, and the state, cruel to some, might be depended on to be more forgiving to others. A selective deployment of carefully applied severity accompanied a parallel policy of mercy. Generally, the majority were treated with relative leniency and the growing practice of transportation to the colonies allowed an outlet for both exile and punishment of these exceptional criminals.[2] The severity of the judicial response to the Monmouth rebellion of 1685, however, set a precedent that could not be fully followed by the successful Whigs after the Glorious Revolution. The state was faced with the largest revolt in England since the 1650s and had to 'process' the largest number of prisoners since battles such as Worcester and Dunbar. In the Somerset and Dorset assizes, the infamous Judge Jeffreys sentenced hundreds to death by the customary method of hanging, drawing and quartering.[3] These events were carefully distributed across the towns of the two counties, as were the pieces of the victims' bodies. In this way the population at the geographic core of the rebellion was subject to demonstrative and intimidatory terrors of the executions, in ways that became part of the Protestant 'martyrology', that integrated this repression with those of previous regimes, the more recent

---

[1] G. Morgan and P. Rushton, *Banishment in the Early Atlantic World: Convicts, Rebels and Slaves* (London: Bloomsbury Academic, 2013), pp. 65–6.
[2] See J.M. Beattie, *Policing and Punishment in London, 1660–1750: Urban Crime and the Limits of Terror* (Oxford: Oxford University Press, 2001), for the growing judicial practice (with a negligible legislative support before 1718) of transportation after the Restoration.
[3] Melinda Zook, "'The Bloody Assizes': Whig Martyrdom and Memory after the Glorious Revolution', *Albion*, 27 (3) (1995), pp. 373–96; John Tutchin, *The Western Martyrology; or Bloody Assizes* (orig. 1795; 5th edition, reprinted, London: James Blackwood, 1883); Peter Earle, *Monmouth's Rebels: The Road to Sedgemoor, 1685* (New York: St. Martin's Press, 1977); H.B. Irving, *The Life of Judge Jeffreys* (New York: Longman, Green and Co, 1898).

martyrs assembled into a coherent narrative of suffering that paralleled those of specific groups such as the Quakers and the Covenanters.[4]

The court records are missing in terms of detailed accounts of processes of sentencing, pardoning or transportation, but from the documents that do survive, largely in the Treasury accounts, there seems to have been grades of forgiveness or leniency. Apart from the condemned, and the acquitted, there were three forms of pardon. Firstly, there were those who had deserted Monmouth's forces and so, under the Royal Proclamation of June 1685, more than two weeks before the battle of Sedgemoor, could receive a confirmatory certificate and pardon. After his defeat, Monmouth had debated seriously with his commanders a flight from the remains of his army, thus enabling the troops to claim this form of pardon.[5] Secondly, there were those convicted whom the court felt deserved a pardon and whose names went forward to the king. It is likely that some of these had been persuaded to give evidence against their fellow prisoners. Thirdly, there are many who were sentenced to transportation. It is unclear whether, as in criminal trials as conducted in this period, the latter two categories were first condemned and then reprieved straightaway by the presiding judge or perhaps after a few days thought (as happened in the eighteenth century in provincial criminal assizes such as those in northeast England). The numbers condemned and executed are therefore uncertain. The treatment of Scottish and northern English rebels in the eighteenth century was markedly different in significant ways. While mixing severity and mercy in the same way, the large-scale deployment of executions and exhibitions was avoided.[6] The scale of the events of 1685 entered an essentially Protestant culture of martyrdom – the 'western martyrology' of John Tutchin, who was on trial himself. The victors, not just of 1685 but of the Glorious Revolution of 1688, have shaped the subsequent views of James II's government and its response to rebellion. Massacre, even if judicially implemented, was defined as martyrdom.

The killing began almost as soon as the battle was over, in extrajudicial executions by army officers. Nearly all these, as far as can be established from the reports, were after Monmouth's men had surrendered and during the early period

---

[4] George Roberts, *The Life, Progresses and Rebellions of James, Duke of Monmouth*, vol. 2 (London: Longman, 1844), pp. 178 and 225 (summary executions and gibbeting at Weston Zoyland; distribution of body parts of the twelve men executed at Weymouth, distinguishing quarters from heads).
[5] Roberts, *The Life, Progresses and Rebellions*, vol. 22, pp. 27–8.
[6] *Calendar of Treasury Books, Volume 8: 1685–1689*, part 1, ed. William A. Shaw (London: HMSO, 1923), pp. 413–26, first transcribed in F.A. Inderwick, *Side-Lights on the Stuarts*, 2nd ed. (London, Sampson Low, Marston, Searle and Rivington 1891), pp. 365–97. Monmouth's Rebellion, Appendix, pp. 398–427, transcription of TNA PRO ASSI/23.

of their custody. As Timmons commented, 'The number of executions that the royal army carried out immediately following Monmouth's rebellion in July 1685 has always puzzled scholars.' He notes, ironically, that the accounts of summary executions following the battle of Sedgemoor are rather better attested – there were orders to erect gibbets in Weston Zoyland and hang twenty of 'the most notorious Rebels, of which four must be hanged in chaynes', and at Bridgwater a gibbet for ten more; and twenty more to hang at Taunton in the marketplace. At least twenty-two were executed in Weston Zoyland, taken from their prison in the parish church the day after the battle.[7] Some were still being carried out away from the battlefield. Militiaman Adam Wheeler recalled that some took place as his regiment marched guarded prisoners through Glastonbury:

> From the Camp in Weston Moore his Honor Coll Windham marched with his Regim[ent] to Glastonbury: Heere at the signe of the White Hart a Duell was fought betweene Captaine Love and Major Talbot. The Major fell, and Captain Love fled for it.
>
> Heare alsoe were six men of the Prisoners that were taken hanged on the Signe Post of that Inne, who after as They hung were stripped naked, and soe left hanging there all night.

This too seems to have been on the day after the battle at Sedgemoor, or the next day, when his regiment were in charge of nearly 300 prisoners, that is, either the 7 or 8 July.[8]

The more formal processing of prisoners through the assize courts of three counties was long remembered but is poorly recorded. The only full account we have of the detailed legal processes was provided by Henry Pitman, Monmouth's surgeon, whose subsequent Caribbean adventures provided the exciting inspiration for Rafael Sabatini's 1922 novel, *Captain Blood*. He recounted the mixture of terror and blackmail applied to the prisoners at the Dorset assizes: it is worth quoting in full.[9]

---

[7] Stephen A. Timmons, 'Executions Following Monmouth's Rebellion: A Missing Link', *Historical Research*, 76 (192) (2003), pp. 286–91; Abstract, p. 286; cites British Library, Additional MS 32000 fols.91–2; Feversham to Col. Percy Kirke of the First Tangiers Regiment or 'Kerk' here, dated 7 July 1685, Sedgemoor p. 287.

[8] 'Adam Wheeler: His Account of 1685', in H.E. Malden (ed.), *Camden Miscellany* 8 (London: 1910), pp. 153–68, p. 165: his report concludes on 9 July, and he noted the Royal Proclamation on the 29 June, p. 161.

[9] Henry Pitman, *A Relation of the Great Suffering and Strange Adventures of Henry Pitman* (London: Andrew Sowle, 1689), pp. 434–6 (edited slightly for punctuation).

Who called us forth, one after another, and told us, that 'the King was very gracious and merciful, and would cause none to be executed but such as had been Officers capital offenders': and therefore if we would render ourselves fit objects of the King's grace and favour, our only way was to give them an account where we went into the Duke's army, and in what capacity we served him, etc. Otherwise we must expect no mercy or favour from the King, who would certainly punish all such wilful and obstinate offenders.

But seeing our former Confessions were sufficient only to find the [True] Bill against us, by the Grand Jury, and not to prove us 'Guilty'; the Petty Jury being obliged to give their verdict according to the evidence in Court: the Lord Chief Justice (fearing lest we should deny what we formerly confessed, and by that means, put them to the trouble of proving it against us) caused about twenty-eight persons at the Assizes at Dorchester, to be chosen from among the rest, against whom he knew he could procure evidence, and brought them first to their trial. Who pleaded 'Not Guilty', but evidence being produced, they were immediately condemned, and a warrant signed for their execution the same afternoon.

The sudden execution of these men so affrightened the rest, that we all, except three or four, pleaded 'Guilty' in hopes to save our lives: but not without large promises of the King's grace and favour. For the Lord Chief Justice told us that 'if we would acknowledge our crimes, by pleading Guilty to our Indictment, the King, who was almost all mercy, would be as ready to forgive us as we were to rebel against him; yea, as ready to pardon us, as we would be to ask it of him'.

And now was that common saying verified, 'Confess, and be hanged!' ... And by his order, there were two hundred and thirty executed; besides a great number hanged immediately after the Fight.

The rest of us were ordered to be transported to the Caribbee Islands. And in order thereunto, my brother and I, with nearly a hundred more, were given to Jeremiah Nepho; and by him, sold to George Penne, a needy Papist.

It was obviously difficult to gather sufficient evidence from two witnesses in many cases, despite some being reprieved for turning King's evidence, and pressure was needed if the high numbers were to be processed through the court in the limited time available to the court. There were other allegations of such persuasive methods: as Wigfield argues, 'to give each rebel-suspect trial with at least two witnesses against him would have been difficult and time-consuming. Those responsible for planning the trials, therefore, agreed to try and get the rebels to plead guilty, thereby obviating the need to procure witnesses'. John

Whiting, Quaker prisoner at Ilchester, reported seeing the county clerk David Timms gave them the causes of their commitment and

> wheedled them to confess how far they were concerned; pretending, if they would confess they would do them all the kindness they could at the assizes; and so drew out of them all they could, in the hopes of favour, and then went in and writ down their examinations; which I was eye-witness of ... It was such a piece of treachery to betray them out of their lives ... Some were terrified into confessing in hopes of pardon, and then hanged, whom otherwise they could have had little against.[10]

The precise numbers executed and transported under this process are still uncertain. Roberts, followed by Macaulay, established the figures that have stood until the mid-twentieth century. There were, he calculated, at least 331 executions, with an additional sixty-one 'executed by martial law'. A total of 849 were transported, and, for the largely verbal offences of seditious or scandalous speeches, thirty-three were fined or whipped, or both. Some the last were particularly severely treated, as Jeffreys ordered that they should be whipped repeatedly, in each of the major towns of the counties. Macaulay, following a pamphlet probably by Daniel Defoe, struck a contrast between this and late practices in the Jacobite rebellions: 'yet all the executions of 1715 and 1745 added together will appear to have been few indeed when compared with those which disgraced the Bloody Assizes', with their 'inhumane Barbaritys'.[11] These figures were based on the lists surviving in the archives and in the books kept by the Treasury. Until the mid-twentieth century, they were accepted: 'The view taken by Macaulay is completely established by the official compilations and licensed publications of the reign of James II.'[12] Yet the publication of a transcription of the Treasury records reveals the difficulties of being certain. About 350 people, nearly all men, are listed as having been sentenced to death, the majority, about 250, from Somerset assizes at Taunton and Wells.[13] More than ninety were sentenced in Dorset and Devon, in the latter a dozen sentenced to be executed at Exeter. Earle commented:

---

[10] W. Macdonald Wigfield, *The Monmouth Rebels, 1685* (Taunton: Somerset Record Society, 1985), pp. vi–viii, quotation pp. vii–viii.

[11] Roberts, *Life, Progresses and Rebellions*, p. 261; T.B. Macaulay, *History of England from the Accession of James II*, 4 vols, Introduction by Douglas Jerrold (London: J.M. Dent and Sons, Everyman Library, 1906), pp. 484, 476–7. Kirke legend and wife's plea, p. 467. *The Proceedings of the Government against the Rebels, Compared with Persecutions of the Late Reigns* (1716, attributed to Daniel Defoe), p. 1; *The Mercy of the Government Vindicated, to Which Are Added Remarks upon a Late Pamphlet Entitled an Argument to Prove the Affections of the People the Best Security of the Government* (London: James Roberts, 1716, also attributed to Defoe) has figures very like those of Roberts a century later, p. 1.

[12] E.S. De Beer, 'Executions Following the "Bloody Assize"', *Bulletin of the Institute of Historical Research*, 4 (1926–7), pp. 36–9, p. 39.

[13] *Treasury Accounts* 8, pt.1, 414–25.

No one knows exactly how many rebels were actually hanged, drawn and quartered as a result of the Bloody Assizes. We can be fairly sure that eighty-six were executed in Devon and Dorset, but it is impossible to get accurate figures for Somerset. Three days after the end of the assizes, Jeffreys signed a warrant for the execution of two hundred and thirty-nine rebels condemned at Taunton and Wells. However, the executions were not carried out on receipt of the warrant. Indeed, they were still going on months later, a fact which meant that they rapidly lost their novelty value and were not always recorded by the news-writers. It is clear, however, that not all the condemned men were executed.

He makes the point that the smallpox epidemic in the jails that summer may have killed many. By contrast, Markus Eder throws doubt that the number of executions in the Western Circuit was much higher than the fifty-two marked for execution in the jail book. The surviving assize records do not add much to the picture, except that they provide long lists of the accused. Some sentences are given, condemnation to death being written against 126 names, but there are no confirmatory indications that the executions were carried out. This has driven one modern historian to conclude that 'the only consistent point of agreement among memoirists and scholars is that England's last popular rebellion ended in a bloody shambles'.[14]

Earle notes that there are surviving local accounts of executions, as at Lyme in Dorset where twelve of the more famous rebel leaders were executed. Even if a substantial proportion of the Somerset condemned were eventually reprieved, there may have been as many as 250 executions.

> If anyone should miss the sight of the actual executions they could hardly avoid the two hundred and fifty pickled heads and the thousand quarters of corpses which were more widely distributed than the executions themselves, being stuck on spears and poles at crossroads, bridges and other prominent places throughout the area. Here they were to stay till the summer of 1686 when the King made his tour of inspection of the West Country. Now he was to see what his subjects had had to see for nearly a whole year and, sick at the sight, he ordered the rotting heads and quarters to be taken down and buried.

---

[14] Earle, *Monmouth's Rebels*, p. 174; Markus Eder, *At the Instigation of the Devil': Capital Punishment and the Assize in Early Modern England* (Hilgertshausen-Tandern, Germany: BookRix GmbH & Co. KG, 2009), pp. 70–1; TNA ASSI 23/3, ff.19–29, lists of rebels from Monmouth's army, divided into 'for treason', 'levying war against the king', 'high treason', amounting to 577 or so; f.36, 5 men, were all 'not guilty'; one on f.50v was whipped; ff.34v-38 seem to have 126 people condemned and executed, with nearly all of them with 'exec' or 'cond and exec' over their names. Timmons, 2003, p. 291. Also, TNA SP 31/2 Monmouth's Rebellion 'Letterbook' – 'Inland Letters relating to the Duke of Monmouth's Rebellion – From June 13th 1685 to July 21st following'.

Certainly the county sheriffs may have made a careful distribution of the heads and body parts, selecting villages of origin of known rebels or those notoriously sympathetic to them. Harris agrees with these basic figures and calculates that about 7 per cent of Monmouth's army was condemned and executed.[15]

In the chaos of overcrowded jails and hasty judgements, it was possible to find a way out. John Coad in Wells jail (possibly the Thomas Coad listed among the condemned there) bribed a guard to let him answer to another man's name on the list for transportation and escaped into bondage. He had been badly wounded and was confined in Ilchester jail for ten or eleven weeks, then Wells assizes. After the sentence, he recalls being visited by his sister:

> For while I was at prayer with many others, in a morning came my sister that attended me, and calling hastily upon me, I went to her; and she told me there was an Officer come into the cloister to call out 200 men for Jamaica she much pressed me to endeavour to get out amongst them, she being much troubled that morning by an information that she had, that my flesh was to be hung up before my dore, at which she swooned away twice that morning: I seeing her in so sorrowful a plight, did go with her to the Officer, and privately told him the circumstances I was under, and offered him a fee to take me into his list, which he refused, but told me that when he called a man that did not answer, I might answer to his name and step in. To deny my name, I was cautious of, and stood by while many others under my circumstance went in, for I judge there was near 30 men saved by so doing.

The idea that his corpse, or part of it, would be displayed at his home is not mentioned elsewhere, but the identification of villages which had produced noted rebels was certainly part of the disposal of the bodies.[16]

The irony is that with regard to 1685, our accounts derive from the survivors of the losing side at the time, who later seized both the moral and political high ground and the monopoly of written history. Even if prone to exaggeration, these authors established in the popular mind the horrors of the Bloody Assizes and their aftermath. The new styles of government introduced at the Glorious Revolution would as a consequence have to be seen to behave in a very different way.

---

[15] Earle, *Monmouth's Rebels*, pp. 175–7. Roberts, *The Life, Progresses and Rebellions*, vol. 2, p. 225, for distribution of body parts of the twelve men executed at Weymouth, distinguishing quarters from heads; Tim Harris, *Revolution: The Great Crisis of the British Monarchy, 1685–1720* (London: Penguin, 2007), pp. 88, 175.

[16] John Coad, *Memorandum of the Wonderful Providences of God to a Poor Unworthy Creature, during the Time of the Duke of Monmouth's Rebellion and to the Revolution in 1688. By John Goad, One of the Sufferers* (London: Longman, Brown, Green, & Longmans, 1849), pp. 12 and 16–17 for quotation.

After the Glorious Revolution

Jacobites after 1688 posed particular difficulties. Many Scots, particularly Catholics, had established a tradition of employment in the armies of other European states, particularly Spain and France. The mixture of rebellion and emigration was in effect already established first by the Irish exiles of the early seventeenth century and subsequently by the Scots. The political closeness of the exiled James II to his cousin Louis XIV of France may not have been emotional, but it was convenient as Louis pursued his long-standing conflict with William of Orange, who ascended the British throne in his place. Thus divided loyalties in effect became the norm for the next twenty years, with Scots, Irish and English serving rival monarchs in different contexts in Europe and in the Atlantic world. Jacobites were scattered, and some, deploying ships gathered from anywhere in the Atlantic, acquired letters of marque in the 1690s from the exiled James II and pursued their war against Anglo-Dutch forces. They were accepted in Britain as legitimate enemy privateers rather than traitors.[17] 'Treason' therefore became a more than usual contentious accusation, and this provides some of the context for both the 1679 Habeas Corpus Act and the 1696 Treason Act. It seemed almost too easy to accuse someone of treason, and there were genuine fears of imprisonment without trial or even banishment. The anxiety in the first piece of legislation seems to have focused on the location of suspects when under arrest without charge, and in the latter, there were efforts to enshrine rights to a defence counsel and the accused's right to advance knowledge of witnesses and jury members. These were not entirely new, but assembled together in a kind of consolidatory legislation for the first time.[18]

The Highland Line as a frontier

The geography of loyalty was distinctive in the case of the Jacobites of the early eighteenth century. This was partly because of widely accepted if not officially acceptable frontiers within Britain. There were frontiers of many kinds in the colonies and territories of the British Empire, between the settled and the

---

[17] J.S. Bromley, *Corsairs and Navies, 1600–1760* (London: The Hambledon Press, 1987).
[18] See Paul D. Halliday. *Habeas Corpus: From England to Empire* (Cambridge, MA: The Belknap Press of Harvard University Press, 2010); Christopher W. Brooks, *Law, Politics and Society in Early Modern England* (Cambridge University Press, 2008).

mobile, the farmers and the hunters, between the 'civilized' and the 'savage'. This was as true of Britain and Ireland as it was of North America. Some borders were drawn in the landscape, while others in cities such as London were embodied in reputations and labels in districts where civilized society was apparently surrounded by threatening zones of deviance and disorder. In the wider framework, it was uncertain, for example, whether the Anglo-Scottish Borders, so violent up to the early seventeenth century as the fringes of the two kingdoms indulged in mutual hostilities, kidnapping, horse theft and cattle rustling, had a century later been reduced to a peaceful respectability.[19] The participation of local gentry from Northumberland in the northeast, and Lancashire in the north-west, in the 1715 particularly, suggested otherwise. Inside Britain, however, the boundary that caused most difficulty in the late seventeenth and early eighteenth centuries was the Highland Line that divided Lowland Scotland from the Highland clans. Like all the other frontiers, this was neither clear nor fixed and formed a straggling porous and moveable zone where travellers sensed a cultural and social difference as they moved across into the clan territories. Although this was never made explicit with regard to Britain and Ireland, crossing from a civilized to a wild territory was, in practice, to forgo the niceties of lawful behaviour to adopt the values and practices of what Gould has called a 'zone of violence'. These zones existed in different ways throughout the British Empire and particularly in the Atlantic world.[20]

Even if the difference was apparent to travellers, Scots themselves had relatives and contacts on both sides of the 'line', and many Lowlanders had Highland ancestry. There was a kind of economic symbiosis: the Highlands depended on Lowland markets for the cattle sales, providing a major source of income. Yet differences could be profound in the face of cultural incompatibilities, Gaelic versus English-speaking, clan versus town and county, Catholic or Episcopalian versus Presbyterian. If Lowland society felt rather threatened by both the English (rather than the Scots) language and by the style of English religiosity, the Highlands were attempting the difficult trick of maintaining social and cultural differences within both the kingdom of Scotland and the United Kingdom. From the point of view of government, control of this alien territory was

---

[19] G. Morgan and P. Rushton, *Rogues, Thieves and the Rule of Law: The Problem of Law Enforcement in North-East England, 1718–1800* (London: UCL Press, 1998).
[20] E.H. Gould, 'Zones of Law, Zones of Violence: The Legal Geography of the British Atlantic, circa 1772', *The William and Mary Quarterly*, 60 (3 July, 2003), pp. 471–510; see also C.J.M. MacLachlan, ed., *Crossing the Highland Line: Cross-Currents in Eighteenth-Century Scottish Writing* (Association for Scottish Literary Studies, 2009; selected papers from the 2005 ASLS Annual Conference).

through leaders who acted also as mediators between the Highlands and the rest of the political system. Like the selected favoured leaders of Native Americans in British North America, certain Highland chiefs were favoured and became the mainstay of British rule, most notably the Clan Campbell, with its chief the Earl of Argyll. It was through these leaders that the central British state hoped the wilder areas of empire would be brought into the boundaries of the controlled territory, tamed and 'civilized'. After the Act of Union in 1707, and the repeated real and rumoured risings of Jacobites, this strategy was supplemented by ideas of cultural and economic policies aimed at transforming the Highlands, one might say, normalizing them. This policy was long-standing by 1700. As Silke Stroh has noted, 'In the early modern period, Scotland's central government authorities increased their efforts to bring the kingdom's geographical and political "fringes" more fully under their control, aiming to align the cultures and societies of the margins with the principles of the emerging capitalist nation-state.' This integrative aim became acute after 1707 as the Highlands became a centre of an oppositional, rebellious politics as well as an obstinately different concept of Scottishness. Gaelic antiquity was deployed in bolstering this identity and at the same time used to defend the culture against what Colin Kidd has called 'charges of barbarism'.[21]

For the British authorities and their Scottish supporters, the reform of the Highlands was to be both cultural and social, with Lowlanders particularly concerned with religious change. Later in the eighteenth century there were plans for economic 'improvement', to provide greater opportunities for work, and increased agricultural productivity, as a solution to the long-standing poverty of the Highlands, but until the 1745 Rising the problem was seen as political and cultural. The Highlands were a society apart and beyond control. The economic contrast, though, was widening, as an increasingly capitalist Lowlands stood self-consciously as part of the joint British future of production and imperial trade. This was no easy process: as Neil Davidson remarks, 'England was the first state to complete the transition from feudal to capitalist agriculture. The second was Scotland': the people, who can be 'usefully described as the Scottish peasantry', were productive of a surplus which was appropriate by their clan landlords, who

---

[21] Silke Stroh, *Gaelic Scotland in the Colonial Imagination: Anglophone Writing from 1600 to 1900* (Evanston, IL: Northwestern University Press, 2017), p. 33: see also her chapter, particularly pp. 55–65, on measures to normalize and assimilate the Highlands; Colin Kidd, 'Gaelic Antiquity and National Identity in Enlightenment Ireland and Scotland', *English Historical Review*, CIX (434) (1994), pp. 1197–214, 1199. For a useful introduction to these issues, see Alexander Murdoch, *British History, 1660–1832: National Identity and Local Culture* (Houndmills: Macmillan Press Ltd., 1998).

could demand, in addition to agricultural produce, military service. This can most properly be described as 'military feudalism'.[22] Plans for altering the social relations and economy of the Highlands, though, came up against the deeply entrenched character of local culture. If the military effort was paid for by the peasantry, who also paid in blood during the conflicts, the masculine character of Highland society produced other obstacles. A widely acknowledged problem was that Highlanders usually carried weapons, including pistols and broadswords (this was partly for defence against each other, though Lowlanders felt they were the predominant target): General Wade, reviewing the situation twelve years after the '15, noted that this was a fundamental part of Highland pride.[23]

One discussion after the 1745 Rising – significantly called 'on civilizing the Highlands', rejecting killing the population or sending them to the 'plantations' – remarked that 'the great difficulty will be to make them industrious, and convince them, that a life of labour is vastly preferable to what they now lead'.[24] The peasants had to be liberated for capitalism, Britishness and integration into being normal subjects of the Hanoverian monarchy. This approach to the Highlands, therefore, was more than just a critique of wilful backwardness: it represented a clash of cultures of values and, above all, loyalty. This did not bode well for the reaction to

---

[22] Neil Davidson, 'The Scottish Path to Capitalist Agriculture 1: From the Crisis of Feudalism to the Origins of Agrarian Transformation (1688–1746)', *Journal of Agrarian Change*, 4 (3) (2004), pp. 227–68, 227; see also Margaret I. Adam, 'Eighteenth-Century Landlords and the Poverty Problem', Part 1, *The Scottish Historical Review*, 19 (73) (1921), pp. 1–20, and Part 2, 19 (75) (1922), pp. 161–79.

[23] General Wade's Second Report, 1727, in J. Allardyce, *Historical Papers Relating to the Jacobite Period, 1699–1750*, 2 vols (Aberdeen: The New Spalding Club, 1895), vol. I, pp. 159–70. There is a large literature on Highland 'improvement'; see *Culloden Papers: Comprising an Extensive and Interesting Correspondence from the Year 1625 to 1746 … from the Originals in the Possession of Duncan George Forbes of Culloden* (London: T. Cadell and W. Davies, 1815), item no 20 (XX), pp. 14–18, 'Memoir of a Plan for Preserving the Peace of the Highlands: written a short time after the Revolution' and both General Wade's reports on the state of the Highlands; pp. 131–48, item XV, 'Report etc. Relating to the Highlands, 1724'; item XVI pp. 150–65, 'Report etc. Relating to the Highlands, 1727'; also item XVII pp. 166–76, 'Memoriall anent the True State of the Highlands … ' undated; TNA SP 54/3/168, which may be the report mentioned earlier at SP54/3/35, letter dated 8 May 1746, 'Mr Morris's Paper for the future Regulation of the Highlands, 8 May 1746'. See also *An Act for the More Effectual Securing the Peace of the Highlands of Scotland* (1716) and the printed report of the commission to establish the schools, in 1724, SP 54/12/229-33, and the parallel activities of the Society for Scotland for Propagating Christian Knowledge, established in 1709 by Royal Proclamation, accompanying it in SP 54/12/234. On legal reforms of 1747, see Lindsay Farmer, *Criminal Law, Tradition and Legal Order: Crime and the Genius of Scots Law, 1747 to the Present* (Cambridge: Cambridge University Press, 1997); Scher, 'Scotland Transformed: The Eighteenth Century', in Jenny Wormald (ed.), Scotland: A History (Oxford University Press, 2005), pp. 150–175, on attacks on the clan system. On similar attitudes to traditional Ireland, see Kerby A. Miller, *Emigrants and Exiles: Ireland and the Irish Exodus to North America* (New York and Oxford: Oxford University Press, 1985), p. 23. Also in 1724, commissioners established by the Act for the more Effectual Peace of the Highlands in Scotland (TNA PRO SP54/12/229) complained that the Highlands were Catholic ('entirely Popish', p. 1), and it was from this area that the rebels came; 150 schools were proposed to effect the conversion (complete with names of possible places).

[24] Anon., *Gentleman's Magazine*, 16 (1746), p. 241.

the 'treason' found there. It was acceptable to regard such peoples as an example of Emer de Vattel's *les nations féroces*, to whom the niceties of the somewhat rudimentary rules of war of the early eighteenth century did not apply because they were not understood in that culture. Highland society was, in the view of the British state, one designed for treason and rebellion: its very social structure seemed treacherous as well as alien. It would be no great exaggeration that the British authorities were prone to regard the Highland clans as both tribal and feudal. The similarity with their view of Native American peoples has been noted by Colin Calloway, who sees in General James Oglethorpe's classification of his armed forces as 'White people, Indians and Highlanders' an almost unconscious refusal to regard Highland Scots as normal white Europeans.[25] This may be an exaggeration, but the view of the Highlanders that the ordinary men were not free, under their feudal obligations to fight for their chiefs, and that therefore they had a plausible explanation that they had been 'forced out' into rebellion, was widespread among the legal administrators trying to sort out the culpabilities of Jacobite prisoners in both the '15 and the '45 Risings. The legalistic problem was distinguishing between the leaders responsible from their coerced followers. Feudalism enabled landowning traitors to command a rebel army comprising their own tenants, and the policies for transforming the Highlands were explicitly aimed at setting these small crofters and other followers 'free', in both the legal and economic sense: they were to be free for capitalism and of any excuse for deviance. They would become subjects of the king, not of their feudal lords.

The legal proceedings of captured rebels reflected these distinctions. In the history of transportation to the colonies the procedures directed at traitors and rebels were decidedly odd: the transportees, before their shipment, had to acknowledge their guilt, the legitimacy of the Hanoverian king – and his mercy towards them. Ordinary criminals did not suffer such impositions, though confession was often a shrewd tactic when pleading for mercy.[26] Thousands of prisoners were seized in both Jacobite rebellions and the task of bringing some to law, and others to court, provided a severe test for the ingenuity of the government lawyers. Sifting according to class was combined with a search for gradations of legal culpability. The powerful could not be let off – 'unless they be gentlemen' was one condition for exclusion for the lottery by which those being sent to trial were selected in 1716–17. The problem of jurisdiction was

---

[25] Colin G. Calloway, *White People, Indians and Highlanders: Tribal Peoples and Colonial Encounters in Scotland and America* (New York: OUP, 2008), p. xi.
[26] G. Morgan and P. Rushton, *Eighteenth-Century Criminal Transportation: The Formation of the Criminal Atlantic* (Houndmills, Basingstoke: Palgrave Macmillan, 2004).

another difficulty, most notably in the trials of the leaders of the '45. Powerful statements were made by their defence counsel that crimes allegedly committed in Scotland could not be tried in England. For those arrested or who surrendered themselves in England (after the defeat at Preston), as most did in 1716, this was not a problem, but in the '45 both the number of state trials and the location raised the legal dilemma. If the rights of Scottish-born subjects had been an issue in the early years of James VI/I's reign (as debated in Calvin's Case), the jurisdictional rights of the two kingdoms, and the ancient idea of trial by your peers in the jurisdiction where the alleged offence had been committed, had been entrenched in various ways since Magna Carta.[27] Even English counties were accustomed to transfer cases, in effect by a kind of extradition, writs of a certiorari, to one another when appropriate, as suspects were caught in distant counties. In 1716, prisoners were grouped into categories of nobles, gentlemen followers, servants, officers in noblemen's regiments, and then the general mass of socially undifferentiated followers – the 'inferiors', distinguished only by degrees of guilt that could be proved in court. These did receive some detailed attention, with religion being one item frequently added besides their names as well as their occupations, nearly always 'labourer'. The concentration of prisoners in north-west England after the battle of Preston necessitated the marching of several parties of prisoners from Edinburgh across the border to Carlisle, on the grounds that 'tis certain that the prisoners who are most likely to be evidence against the rest will be easier to resolve to be so at Carlisle for they will then think their Lives in much more danger than if they were to be tried here'. The prisoners were sent in some haste, it was reported by Lieutenant General Carpenter in the summer of 1716, because 'otherwise some few of them would have right to Liberty by the Habeas Corpus Act'. This was not an easy task, as the countryside possessed few large villages where they could stay be rested overnight. There were also prisoners held in a number of other places in Scotland, such as Stirling and Aberdeen, and who, as 'common prisoners', would have to be let go.[28]

The procedure adopted was to try and identify the required two witnesses for a successful treason prosecution. This was far easier with regard to the titled or landed classes than for the poor. The results were that for most of the ordinary prisoners, at most one witness and, frequently, none at all were available. It was on these that the policy of confession and transportation was mostly directed:

---

[27] Brooks, *Politics and the Law*.
[28] TNA PRO KB 33/14-65; also Margaret Sankey, *Jacobite Prisoners of the 1715 Rebellion: Preventing and Punishing Insurrection in Early Hanoverian Britain* (Burlington: Ashgate, 2005); SP/12/122 [stamped 290], 23 August 1716; also 133 and 152; SP/12/210.

prisoners could petition, acknowledge the authority and legitimacy of the king and be pardoned for transportation. The legal rights granted were in many ways a result of the Hanoverian sense of legal righteousness rather than a formal acknowledgement of the rights of rebels. Francis Douglas, for example, in his 1755 history of the '45, noted the protest of one gentleman towards the end of 1746 against the cavalry grazing their cattle in his parkland, taking the officer responsible to court. But in court

> after stating the facts, it was observed that a mistake in the law runs thro' the whole complaint; inasmuch as the complainer supposes, that as in time of peace, or in the time of open rebellion, rebels must be tried and convicted by the civil courts before either their persons or goods can be touched; but that the law stands directly otherwise: for that in an open rebellion, rebels are to be treated as enemies, and to be proceeded against by the military law, with which, in such cases the King is intrusted; and that the King and his legal officers have a legal power to destroy or seize the persons and effects of rebels without trial or conviction, in the same manner as if they were foreign enemies; with this remarkable difference, that rebels have no privileges allowed to enemies in a lawful war; as they are to be held as enemies, and not subjects, during the subsistence of the war, and after it are subjected to the pains and forfeitures inflicted by the laws of their country.[29]

The rights of the defeated rebels, this implied, were a privilege to be granted, not to be legally asserted. This paralleled (and may have been influenced by) the doctrines being developed at this time by Emer de Vattel (and only published in English in 1760, two years after the French edition published in London) that it reinforced the dignity and legitimacy of a government or sovereign to concede such rights even though they had no legal reason to do so.[30] Yet the Hanoverian government became increasingly, not decreasingly, anxious to be seen to act lawfully by the time of the 1745. Strictly speaking, the laws of war allowed the disposal of enemies and rebels without rights, even through death or slavery, but there were sufficient sceptics and critics among the government's own supporters to guarantee that legal forms were followed, particularly in the proceedings following the defeat of the rebellion in 1746.

---

[29] Francis Douglas, *The History of the Rebellion in 1745 and 1746, Extracted from the Scots Magazine; with an Appendix, Containing an Account of the Trials of the Rebels; the Pretender and His Son's Declarations etc.* (Aberdeen: F. Douglass and W. Murray, 1755), pp. 266–7, Ogilvy of Coul against one Captain Hamilton.
[30] E. De Vattel, *The Law of Nations or the Principles of the Law of Nature*, edited and with an Introduction by Bé´la Kapossy and Richard Whatmore (Indianapolis, IN: Liberty Fund, 2008), pp. 421–5.

Although never made explicit, at least not as a programmatic statement, the legal strategy adopted involved four elements. First, the leaders must be put on trial, and, secondly, the trials, if possible, should be in England not Scotland, wherever the treasonable action was alleged to have occurred. These would be the most obvious targets, well-born and prominent instigators, organizers and leaders of the conflict. With regard to the rest, there was a third element, namely selection by lot of one in twenty of the ordinary sort, with the proviso that there were two witnesses available to give evidence against them: the particulars of the traditional treason law, as well as the rights under the 1696 law, had to be observed. Finally, there was a fourth strand with regard to the ordinary prisoners, against who there might not be sufficient evidence provided two witnesses. For these, transportation would be ordered when they had acknowledged the sovereignty of the King and his government. Voluntary exile, allowed in the proceedings after 1715, when the French or Spanish forces still actively recruited Scots, was less stressed as adoption for the more aristocratic rebels permitted after the '45.

One crucial precedent established in the proceedings after the 1715 Rising was the use of a lottery to decide who should be tried and who offered pardon on condition of transportation (which they had to sign for and agree to): one in twenty were chosen for trial. The role of the judges in choosing who would be tried and who 'lotted' was made explicit in government instructions, and the purpose was to identify the most culpable:

> The most considerable of Note and condition as well as the most criminall of the Inferior Rank, that all such should be distinguished and sett apart and that the lotts should afterwards be drawn amongst the Bulk of the Inferior people but notwithstanding this drawing Lotts Evidence was to be continued to be got against every individual person of any rank or degree and that as well from among officers and soldiers of the Kings Troops as from any of the prisoners themselves.

In this way a minority of the 'inferior', five per cent if possible, were subject to random selection for trial and probable execution, while their superiors, those of 'note', had already been taken out of the pool and scheduled for court proceedings.[31] The 'gentlemen or persons of substance' were not to be transported, partly because this involved servitude and therefore would contradict the traditional social order but also, suggested one official, 'to prevent the public from being deprived of the Forfeitures of such Estates, [and] not to delay delivering to the

---

[31] TNA TS 20/47/2, 26 and 29 December 1715.

Merchants the Prisoners on account of his being an uncertainty in this Matter'. The commission forfeiting the estates did not get going until the end of 1716.[32]

The working notes of the law officers in 1716, summarized in Table 1, suggest that in reviewing more than a thousand cases, they were not going to be able to bring prosecutions against very many. The scale of the problem, and the need for witnesses for each case, proved almost too much. Like the processes in 1685,

Table 1 Particulars and against whom are or are not evidence

Gentlemen agt[against] whom noe particular evidence	131
Inferior ditto	520
	651
Gentlemen agt [against] whom are two particular witnesses	40
Gentlemen agt [against] whom are but one particular witness	40
Inferior agt [against] whom are two or more particular witnesses	383
[then repeats Gent with one witness but puts forty in the column]	40
Inferiors agt [against] whom ditto [one witness]	185
Inferiors agt [against] whom are two or more particular witnesses	383
	605
	1259
Lott men to be tried out of the 383	19
Inferiors appointed for tryall by reason of their degree of guilt	25
Gentlemen agt [against] whom are one or more particular witnesses	40
Prisoners in custody by virtue of warrts of Justices of the peace to be tried because not entitled to draw lotts	30
In all to be tried	114

Source: TNA PRO KB 33/1/5/54

[32] TNA TS 20/47/2, 18 April 1716, to Col Rapin.

Table 2 Prisoners, 1716

Lancaster	222
Wigan	157
Chester	467
Preston	446
Total	1,292

Source: TNA KB 33/1/5/65.

an element of explicit blackmail was deployed in order to induce men to accept the authority of the king and thereby earn transportation, but there was little likelihood of a successful prosecution for treason for most of these.

These figures are to some extent confirmed by the listings held in a document delightfully called the Bag of Secrets, of the numbers in jail at this time (**Table 2**).

The rough notes and this list more or less agree: about one in ten might stand trial, but of the total held the majority were intended for transportation.[33] It was expected that all those who were not prosecutable, together with those not selected for trial by the lottery, would petition for transportation. On a number of occasions, it was reported to the legal officers that the King had expressed his 'hope' that no proceedings would be undertaken against those not selected:

> H[is] M[ajesty] hoped there would be no occasion to proceed to the Trial of any of those who had Escaped the Lotts neither was it HM's Intentions to go any farther than to strike a Terror in Case you should find a Combination among them to stand out agt the terms of Transportation which I expect to hear they have pretty generally submitted to by the return of the Messengers sent to Lancaster and Chester for that purpose but till that is done it will be necessary to keep them under such sort of Tie that thay may not appear as it were in defiance of the Government or think themselves secure as if they had done nothing to deserve Punishment.

If they went to colonies quietly, in other words, there would be no need for any further trials and executions. If the King was expressing the general aim of the government here, the most significant objective was an explicit desire to avoid 'terror', a word that seems to reflect a parallel wish to prevent accusations of cruelty of the kind that dominated accounts of 1685.[34] In fact, there was little chance of a legal conviction against most of these men, and the pressure to make them petition was a kind of sleight of hand, involving bullying and threatening,

---

[33] TNA KB 33/1/5/65.
[34] TNA SP 44/118/190v, copied in TS 20/47/2, 7 February 1716.

whereby those who were never going to be tried were persuaded to plead guilty and petition for pardon. At least 206 are mentioned in one source in 1716 as, in effect, going on strike and refusing to sign a petition for mercy, and it was hoped by officials that the preparation of others for trial and potential execution would 'probably go far in breaking that Combination which seemed to be amongst them'. In any case they were to be transported and, in instructions to the governors of the colonies receiving them, were to be held 'in custody' until they had signed indentures. Then they could be released into colonial bondage. The language of industrial disputes – 'combinations' were becoming part of the London scene, particularly in trades such as the Spitalfields silkweavers – reflects a recognition that government policies might be frustrated by collective action in any sphere. Many of the Jacobites with greater legal knowledge realized the legal weaknesses in this process, particularly where indentures had not been signed, and organized resistance was directed at challenging the legality of the procedures. The result was, as Sankey notes, that just as those on the gallows produced the same forms of self-justifications which challenged the legitimacy of the Hanoverian state and church, so from Lancashire to the Americas, Jacobite petitioners framed their resistance to the transportation orders with remarkable consistency.[35]

Nevertheless, even with little danger of a formal prosecution, a large number of prisoners did petition, even 113 'gentlemen' in custody at Chester. Only one of these – John Rutherford – was also on the lists of those from Chester to be sent to trial at Liverpool, though for one other it was noted that there were two potential witnesses against him. Petitions were also difficult to obtain from prisoners of lesser rank. As noted earlier, 206 were recorded as refusing to sign in the various jails in the northwest, and a further seventy-three were judged too sick to do so.[36] Those sentenced to transportation after their petitions from Preston were not all taken out of the country – there were still appeals to be heard, and several were successful. Two men were able to bring 'particular circumstances' in their favour to the government's notice in May, but it was only in August, as the transports were preparing to sail, that they were taken off the ship and set free. Yet their success also demonstrated the government's wish to display mercy and considerate leniency where appropriate. The rest were to be sent off as willing to

---

[35] Sankey, *Jacobite Prisoners*, p. 69.
[36] 'Gentlemen' TNA KB 33/1/5/19-19v; SP 54/12/19 Rutherford's plea for mercy; Sankey, *Jacobite Prisoners*, pp. 62–3; evidence from ship listings suggests that nearly half of these were in fact transported: fifty-three of the 113, traced in David Dobson, *Directory of Scots Banished to the American Plantations, 1650–1775* (Baltimore, MD: Genealogical Publishing Co, 1984).

work as indentured servants (and like convicts), their indentures signed before departure in the presence of the 'chief magistrate' or mayor, if they were fit and healthy enough to do so.[37]

With the executions set, the transported selected and a few left to be subject to trials in London, the judges left Liverpool with their job done. Some of the condemned had already been executed. In all, thirty-three were executed in various parts of Lancashire: the visible terror was confined to the major towns of Preston, Wigan, Manchester, Lancaster, Garstang and Liverpool itself, carefully calculated to have an effect on the entire region. In this respect, though involving far smaller numbers, the intimidatory strategy resembled that in the West Country in 1685. The executions began a few days after the start of the trials, and continued during them, in a deliberate effort to 'strike a terror' in case there was organized resistance to the conditions of transportation.[38] However, there was one legal difficulty to be overcome. Some of the prominent leaders at Preston, particularly those from Scotland and Northumberland, were sent to London for trial, which was far from the counties where their alleged crimes had been committed. In English law, the accused were to be tried where their crimes occurred or else they had to be removed (by a writ of a certiorari and habeas corpus) to that county. Just as moving Edinburgh prisoners to Carlisle was legally dubious, so was sending some of the Preston prisoners to London. Individuals such as 'General' Thomas Forster M.P. from Northumberland were formally attainted by Parliament to be tried for high treason: he was an English traitor whose treachery was inside English borders. For the others, in order to overcome the transference to London required special legislation after the Liverpool trials had been completed. One London paper noted, 'The King came to the House of Lords with the usual Solemnity, and gave the Royal Assent to the Bill for the more easy and speedy Tryal of Rebels.' The Act 'for the more speedy Trials of such Persons who have levied War against his Majesty' observed that 'as the Law now stands' indictments were to be heard in the countries where the treasonable acts were committed, 'it will be very inconvenient to the public Justice of the Nation that the Judges should remain so long in the said Counties'. Therefore, the law allowed that 'all persons in custody before 23 January 1716

---

[37] Successful plea by Richard Withington and Richard Birches, TNA SP 44/118/255 (17 May 1716) and 287 (2 August 1716); and SP 44/118/204v, order about indentures.
[38] *Newsletter*, 11 February 1716; *Weekly Remarks and Political Reflections*, 18 February 1716; Sankey, *Jacobite Prisoners*, pp. 50–1, the executions began on 28 January, eight days after the trials started; and p. 51, quoting SP 44/118/188 Townsend 2 February 1716; see p. 56, more than half of those executed had been selected by lot; 638 were transported.

may be tried in such Shire as his Majesty shall direct. And no challenge for the Shire shall be allowed'. Thus the decision to try some notable northern English rebels in London acquired legal validity, but for these prisoners, even though they begged to be transported in some instances, transportation was not what the government intended.[39]

Szechi calls the whole process the Hanoverian government's 'grim pageant of justice'. About 1700 prisoners had been seized in Scotland and England, from whom thirty-four 'particular enemies' were selected and tried, and seventeen executed; of the forty-seven chosen by lot, another eighteen were executed, but most of the rest in both batches were convicted, with only seven acquitted. In other words, of the eighty-one tried, seventy-four were convicted and condemned, and thirty-five executed – that is 47.3 per cent of the condemned, on these figures. Of the 1,500 or more left, 'a few dozen … escaped and then went into hiding and exile. What to do with the rest was a serious problem'. The first ships sailed in August 1716 with at least 638 prisoners, while it seems likely that those remaining in the English gaols were eventually released. More than 450 were sent to the North American colonies and about 170 to the Caribbean. The king and his ministers originally expected that they would all be sold in the West Indies, where a seven-year indenture was always likely to prove a death sentence for transportees from the British Isles. In fact, most were sold in their first port of call in the North American colonies, which were desperate for skilled, fit labour that did not come with a proven aptitude for common felony. Lenman may be right that the London government was not 'particularly interested in rounding up humble men who had probably acted throughout under the orders of their social superiors', but this group formed the major problem that they had to deal with. They had little choice but to develop a policy that distinguished the Hanoverian government from the alleged tyranny of James II: to do this, they had to treat the poorer rebels with relative humanity. Transportation was not a death sentence in disguise, a principle developed in 1716 and enshrined in the 1718 Transportation Act.[40] Above all, following this experience, there was no intention of trying anyone in Scotland after the 1745 rebellion.

On the arrival of the 185 men sent to South Carolina, the Governor bought 'as many of them as he could in order to arm them and send them to the

---

[39] *The Postman*, 8 March 1716; *The Statutes at Large from the First Year of the Reign of George the First to the Third Year of the Reign of King George the Second*, 5 vols, vol. 5 (London: Mark Basket, 1763), pp. 74–5.
[40] Morgan and Rushton, *Criminal Transportation*.

frontier to fight the Yammasee Indians, with whom the colony was at war'.[41] In Maryland, the Council logged the arrival of two ships with 135 rebels and were forced to debate the legality of the whole process because of a petition from John Chalmers, one of the fifty-five from the *Good Speed*, who argued that there was no law authorizing their transportation. He went back to medieval law to make his case. This was brushed aside, but the Maryland authorities speedily resolved that while they could not stop anyone buying rebel servants and setting them free, they would have to give surety for their ex-servants' good behaviour for seven years. In Virginia the Governor and his Council faced both legal difficulties and resistance. Most of the difficulty arose from the people on the *Elizabeth and Anne* from Liverpool. Only about a quarter of the passengers, twenty-nine of the 112 on board, had signed indentures before the voyage, though they must have signed a petition for mercy. This refusal caused the authorities some irritation, and a procedure was developed whereby purchasers of rebel servants received a certificate from the Council confirming that it was the king's pleasure that they serve seven years. A second difficulty arose with another petition which cited the same legislation as John Chalmers, and similarly claimed that no British subject could be forced to serve without their consent or the suspension of the laws. There was clearly a consistent argumentative line in challenging their transportation. In addition, they complained of 'divers hardships imposed on them' by the master and owner of the ship. The Captain, Edward Trafford, was sent a copy of the protest and summoned to reply. Despite these delays, they were all sold successfully in the end.[42] Little is known about the subsequent lives of the rebel servants landed in the Chesapeake, but at least one of the '15 rebels brought in that year, on the *Friendship*, did well. William Cumming served in various public offices, including as a member and clerk to the Lower House of the Assembly, and in 1751 executed a deed of trust to his son William transferring all his real and personal property for the benefit of his creditors, including 117 law books, forty slaves, one black and three white servants, and silver plate.[43]

[41] Szechi, *1715*, 206–8; see Sankey, *Jacobite Prisoners*, pp. 70–2; Lenman, *Jacobite Risings*, pp. 158 and 271; there were 639 in all according to the shipping lists in TNA TS 20/47/3, 340 intended for the North American colonies, 173 for the Caribbean, and 126 for either Virginia or Jamaica on the *Friendship*, which went to the Chesapeake.

[42] *Executive Journals of the Council of Colonial Virginia*, ed. H.R. McIlwaine, vol. 3 (Richmond, VA: D. Bottom, 1938), pp. 428–31; petition 430–1, and *Calendar of Virginia State Papers, 1652–1781*, vol. 1, ed. W.P. Palmer (Richmond, VA: R.F. Walker, 1875), pp. 187–8; Geoffrey Plank, *Rebellion and Savagery: The Jacobite Rising of 1745 and the British Empire* (Philadelphia, PA: University of Pennsylvania Press, 2006), p. 95.

[43] *Archives of Maryland*, vol. 25, pp. 347–51, and vol. 426, pp. 245–6; Thomas Scharf, *A History of Maryland*, 3 vols (Baltimore, MD: John B. Piet, 1879), vol. 1, pp. 385–9.

The rebellion might be over, but in the years after 1715, there were patterns of local vigilance and alarms, where suspected participants and their helpers were traced and suppressed, and continued support for the Jacobite cause was identified. There was a local aspect to the risings, therefore, with county authorities in particular being engaged in anxious surveillance during the periods of violent uncertainty and, in aftermath, the pursuit of those who had assisted the rebels. There were recurrent rumours of another Jacobite rising. In Northumberland, which provided notable Jacobite supporters, there were attempts at clearing out the local rebels through the county quarter sessions. The means of detection often involved the verbal expression of sympathies for the Pretender or his son, and in circumstances that required drink and witnesses (see the Chapter 3 on seditious words). This was the bare minimum of rebellion, words without deeds, so to speak. But there were many who had actively participated. Three years after the rebellion was suppressed, the county authorities were still anxious.

> Whereas this court is given to understand that divers persons concerned in the late Rebellion who escaped after being taken and others concerned therein who were not taken conceal themselves in this County and also that severall other persons disaffected with the government and others who harbour or entertain and countenance such persons resort and caball themselves together in divers parts of this County.

The order to the constables, both high and petty, to make a diligent search was signed by all the magistrates.[44] They had some reason to be anxious. Local allegations, often reflecting deep personal differences, turned up for several years. Many accusations were directed at those suspected of having escaped from the fiasco in Lancashire in 1715. For example, as late as 1718 one man appeared before the magistrates, against one man who had sheltered – 'harboured' a rebel in Jesmond (just north of Newcastle-upon-Tyne). Two men Henry Dixon and Edward Humble of Jesmond accused William Ram,

> who was one of the Rebells taken lately att Preston in Lancashire and came after that Rebellion privately to the house of Cuthbert Fenwick of Jesmond aforsd where he was harboured and entertained and has since continued and now is there and is called and goes by the name of William Carr.

As so often, in a face-to-face society like that of the eighteenth century, it was difficult to hide successfully from the eyes of prying neighbours.[45] Accusation

---

[44] Northumberland Record Office (henceforth NRO), QSB 50, Easter 1719/48.
[45] NRO, QSB 48, p. 73, a printed recognizance, Easter 1718.

brought its dangers for the accusers, however: loyalty to the king came at a price. In the autumn of 1719 one John Hunter came to the quarter sessions to complain of threats against him.

> Had the misfortune to be in the late Rebellion and became an Evidence for the King both at Leverpool and London and convicted severall by which he hath incurred the hatred of their freinds and survivors who threaten to Murder your Petitioner as by Information does more at large at appear so that Your Petitioner is afraid of his Life.

He begged the justices to 'take him under your Protection and to order what is in your Prudent consideration would shall think fit for your Petitioners security'. Turning King's evidence was, for many, a kind of treason.[46] These divisions went on for years, as there was little reconciliation between the supporters and opponents of Jacobite claims. Another loyalist found himself in difficulties a year later, when Abraham Bunting applied for the post of bookkeeper of Hexham. There was a letter of recommendation, from Thomas Sisson, clerk to prominent Newcastle lawyer and politician William Coatesworth of Gateshead Park. He was loyal to King George, it was said, and

> was so obnoxious to the Rebbels and the enemies of the Government that when the rebels came into Hexham, he was forced to fly into Newcastle and take sanctuary there under my Lord Scarbrough; this my master knows to be true for he was present when he applyed to his Lordship.[47]

While loyal men were in difficulty, old rebels were still being hunted. In 1723 two men from the county town of Morpeth claimed to have seen Nicholas Cooper in the rebellion 'under arms amongst the Rebels in Morpeth' and one reported that he had seen Cooper several times a prisoner among the rebels 'the first time in Lancaster castle and the other times in West Chester Castle wherein this Deponent left the said Nicholas Cooper a prisoner', which Cooper admitted 'having been in the late Rebellion'. There were no recorded penalties for these actions, but they probably had the effect of keeping the question of loyalty of edgy conflict.[48]

---

[46] NRO, QSB 50, p. 48, Michaelmas sessions 1719 – John Hunter, p. 52 – continues, servant to James Atkinson, accuses the threateners as Thos Hunter of Sheely Hill, Jeffrey Potts of the same, Tallbot Hunter ditto, and Jeffrey Hunter servant to Elizabeth Cooke of Sweethope – orders for warrant (Jn Cotesworth).
[47] NRO, QSB 52, p. 4, January 1720 (new style), 4.
[48] NRO, QSB 60, p. 25, Michaelmas 1723, Michael Thompson of Morpeth cordwainer and Jn Challoner of Morpeth accuse Nicholas Cooper.

The 1745 Rising

In the '45, there was a wider variety of prisoners, some being taken at sa in suspicious vessels leaving from the French coast and far more were captured in Scotland than in northern England. The '45 presented the British government with both a military scare and a legal conundrum. Much of the fighting had been taking place in Scotland, or at least the initial battles, but the army of Bonny Prince Charlie had marched into north-west England, as had happened in 1715, and then south to Manchester and Derby, within 200 miles of London. This was no idle threat. The British state had to import Dutch troops to secure the northeast of England and, given the poor performance of the troops stationed in Scotland in their battles with the rebels, particularly the Highland troops, were nervous of committing an army to direct confrontation with the enemy. In the end, the retreat of the rebel army to Scotland, and the weight of numbers and fire power, brought Bonnie Prince Charlie's army to defeat and slaughter at Culloden in 1746. As in 1715, the problem then arose as to how to dispose of the numerous captives. It is perhaps significant that selected documents from the procedures after the '15 were copied as a guide for the administrators of 1746–7.

The '45 has entered the realm of legendary history, heroic individuals and national failure: in effect a Scottish equivalent of the hagiography directed at the dead and transported of England in 1685. Yet some realism has entered the written histories, as detailed studies of the prisoners and their fates have established the outlines of a sober analysis. The study by Sir Bruce Gordon Seton and Jean Gordon Arnot represents the best attempt to extract the statistical truth from the detailed administrative records kept by government officials on the 'remnants of the broken Jacobite army' captured at Culloden and in the aftermath of the battle. These figures cannot include the hundreds, perhaps thousands who suffered starvation, destruction of property or random killing in the aftermath of the battle, as areas were brought under Government control by terror tactics such as those adopted by Lord Loudon, sent by Cumberland to Badenock in May 1746 'for two or three days to burn and destroy that country which has not yet laid down its arms'. The aim was to force the submission of those still resisting, and he concluded that 'I believe they immediately will', noting that the brutal strategy had worked with regard to the McPhersons who had submitted to these techniques the same month.[49] Seton and Arnot concluded that with reference to the listed 3,463 prisoners,

---

[49] TNA SP 54/31/138 Cumberland to Newcastle, 27 May 1746.

88 died of wounds or illness in prison; 120 were executed (including 40 deserters from the Hanoverian army), 936 transported, 348 banished (including 126 who were allowed to go to America), 1,287 set free (including 387 French and Spanish), and 684 whose fate is unknown, although a large percentage of these must also have died of neglect in the prison hulks to which the prisoners were taken.

Despite Cumberland's idea of transporting whole clans, 'not as slaves, but to form Colonies in the West Indies', transportation was confined to these prisoners and those arrested as rebels subsequently. They were subject to careful filtering and processing, with trials and executions aimed at some and a gradual procedure of pardon and transportation for the majority. The legalistic tactics replicated those adopted after the 1715. Other captives were treated more summarily: when at least thirty-two deserters from the Hanoverian army were found among the Jacobite prisoners in and around Inverness, they were tried by court-martial and 'hanged on the spot'. Eight hundred and sixty six of the prisoners applied for the king's mercy, but only after many of the Scottish had been moved to the Thames and held in forts and ships. Here, a selection by lot was instituted, as in 1716, while others were pre-selected for trial. Of 430 prisoners listed by one Captain Eyre, for example, the lot chose seventeen for trial randomly (slightly less than 5 per cent), while another seventy-five had been 'set apart for Tryal or further Examination, and for Evidence, who have not been lotted'. The English who had joined the Prince's army in Manchester were particularly likely to be subject to trial and denied any opportunity to gain release by lot. These were mostly local Catholics and, unlike the gentry who had been the main focus of prosecutions in the previous rising, of more ordinary social standing. The English recruits to both rebellions, though, seem to have provoked great alarm and a more repressive response from the government. In the documents, the language of class and hierarchy was faithfully produced when summing up the social statuses of the captives. Prisoners were 'common men', 'really gentlemen', 'not properly gentlemen but above the rank of the common men' or of 'a lower degree than the preceding'.[50]

The trials of the famous Jacobite leaders in London (actually in Southwark, across the river in Surrey) produced a number of sustained legal challenges to their legality. Whereas there was no emotional response from the public, as had accompanied the trial and execution of the young Earl of Derwentwater

---

[50] Figures as summarized by Davidson, *Discovering the Scottish Revolution*, p. 258, following *The Prisoners of the '45, edited from the State Papers*, Sir Bruce Gordon Seton and Jean Gordon Arnot, 3 vols, vol. 1 (Edinburgh UP for the Scottish Historical Society, 1929).

in 1716, there was much public interest in the proceedings, as well as relief that the crisis was over. The trials began with the case of Francis Towneley and others of the Manchester regiment, perhaps deliberately chosen as obviously guilty Englishmen whose crimes had been clearly committed in England. When it came to trials of Scots, however, there was more critical questioning of the lawfulness of the process. It was raised

> whether natives of Scotland, resident in Scotland, and taken in Scotland, could, without a breach of the union, be tried in England for acts of treason committed in Scotland?' The court adjourned, and the Attorney-Gen argued for the crown, Mr Gordon and Mr Joddrell for the prisoners, but they were overruled and verdicts of guilty given for Captain. Andrew Wood.

The trials of Scots, though validated by the emergency 1716 legislation, were nevertheless subjected to some debate. In addition to the London trials, there were proceedings against ordinary Jacobites in a number of northern English towns, including York where more than seventy were executed.[51] In the newspapers, there were careful accounts of both the trial arguments and the subsequent executions. It was noted that some who pleaded that they had been forced to join the rebels were acquitted. The executions seem to have been conducted with a view to minimize the horror. Batches of the condemned were executed by standing together on a plank, which was then 'turned off': they were left to hang for about ten minutes, before being cut down, stripped and having their hearts cut out and waved at the crowd with the cry 'Behold the heart of a traitor'. Their limbs were scored with knives but not severed, and the executioner cried 'Behold the quarters of a traitor'. Only two heads were displayed on one of York's medieval gates, Micklegate Bar, and the rest of the bodies were put in coffins. All the dead were then buried behind the Castle (the jail).[52]

Elsewhere, the general policy of pardon and transportation was well underway and steadily reported in the press from early 1747 to 1748: it was reported in March 1747 that 'a pardon has passed the great seal for a great number of rebels to be transported to the American colonies'. By May, '430 rebel prisoners from the goals of Carlisle, Lancaster, Chester, York and Lincoln, were transported this month from Liverpool for the Plantations; 8 of them were drowned by a boat oversetting, not being able to swim, because hand-cuffed. This number with the

---

[51] Douglas, *History of the Rebellion in 1745 and 1746*, pp. 294–5; quotation p. 342; p. 352 (York).
[52] *Newcastle Courant*, 1, 8 and 15 November 1746, with the 8 November giving the fullest description.

rest makes above 1000 transported'. Unusually an open-ended order of pardon and banishment was given more than two years after Culloden to one gentleman and a group of unspecified men – 'a pardon has passed the great seal to Hector M'Kenzie and 36 others, of all treasons, etc. committed on or before April 13, 1748, on condition they immediately depart his majesty's dominions, and never return'.[53] The individual biographies of many Jacobites were collected, almost in the fashion that Quakers and Covenanters had years before, as a record of individual examples illustrating the collective sufferings, by Bishop Robert Forbes and kept in his private papers, until they were eventually published in the nineteenth century, when Jacobitism had been almost rehabilitated within the context of Gaelic nostalgia and clan revival.[54]

Other individual consequences can only be retrieved from the fragmentary references in newspapers. In particular, the fate of many ordinary rebels in the Americas is hard to trace. Some fell foul of the law, as happened to one forger of coins. For example, in 1720, Edward Hunt was executed in Philadelphia for coining (making false coinage). It was reported that he had been a 'bound servant' in Antigua, transported for rebellion at Preston.[55] Others arrived in America and were bought out of their indentured servitude. For the rest, their masters and their sales are recorded in some instances, and it seems that many entered the world of colonial servants along with criminal convicts, mostly sold, though some arrived unindentured, suggesting continuing resistance to the process. Those escaping servitude were few and largely confined to Catholic gentry who found a sympathetic reception in some colonies. Others were promptly recruited to the local militias, as happened in Maryland and the Carolinas in particular, when the frontier wars against the Native Americans were short of fighting men.[56] Rebellion at home had few implications for political relations in America. Most Highlanders, paradoxically, became loyalists and only a handful of known Jacobites became prominent revolutionaries. Hugh Mercer (1726–77) was one soldier-turned physician and then brigadier general in the American

---

[53] *Gentleman's Magazine*, vol. 17, 1747 p. 153 (col. 1), 31 March 1747 p. 246 (col. 1), 31 May 1747; vol. 18, 1748, p. 474, 31 October 1748.
[54] *The Lyon in Mourning, or a Collection of Speeches, Letters, Journals etc. Relative to the Affairs of Prince Charles Edward Stuart*, by the Rev. Robert Forbes, A.M., Bishop of Ross and Caithness, 1745–1775, edited from his Manuscript, with a Preface, by Henry Paton, M.A., 3 vols, vol. 2 (1895; reprinted, Edinburgh: Scottish Academic Press, 1975, The Scottish History Society).
[55] *American Weekly Mercury*, 24 November 1720, datelined Annapolis 8 September.
[56] For the numbers identified, see Dobson, *Directory of Scots Banished*: of the 113 gentlemen given in KB 33/1/5/19-19v 'List of the Gentlemen prisoners at Chester who have petitioned for transportation' in 1716, Dobson can provide some details on forty-five of them.

Revolution, who died as a result of wounds and subsequent mistreatment after the Battle of Princeton: the event was memorialized in painter John Trumbull's *The Death of General Mercer at the Battle of Princeton, January 3, 1777*. He had been at Culloden and fled to America in 1747 and fought alongside Washington in the French and Indian War.[57]

Plank has done much to fill in the details of those transported to places such as Barbados in 1747.[58]

> In 1747 after most of the criminal trials were concluded, hundreds of war captives from Charles Edward's army were boarded on ships and sent across the Atlantic. The merchants and ship captains who took custody of the prisoners were selective in where they brought them. In general, they carried the former Jacobite soldiers to places with a high demand for labour and an established infrastructure for disposing of bound servants in large numbers. Hundreds of men were taken to the British West Indies, where, in ceremonies that might have seemed legally superfluous, they were induced to sign contracts of indenture. None of the prisoners had signed such contracts before their arrival in the Caribbean, and the government officials who had arranged their passage assumed that the men could be sold for lifelong service whether or not they agreed to any terms.

As in the case of the men of the 1715, a handful of the transported got into trouble in America. In Annapolis (Maryland), it was reported in September 1747 that 'the Grand-Jury of the Assize for this County (which ended this Day) found Bills of Indictment against Two of the rebels lately imported, for Drinking the Pretender's Health, and some other treasonable expressions; for which the Court adjudg'd, (as they were Servants, incapable of paying Fines) that they should be well whipped at the Whipping Post, and stand in the Pillory, which Sentence was immediately put into Execution'.[59]

A most cynical view is taken by Calloway who feels that these settlers did not raise the tone of the colonies.[60]

---

[57] See the dramatic nineteenth-century version of his life by John T. Goolrick, *The Life of General Hugh Mercer* (New York: The Neal Publishing Company, 1906).
[58] Plank, *Rebellion and Savagery*, pp. 92–6, 95. See also Eric J. Graham, 'Letters from a Jacobite transported to Virginia after the 1715 Rebellion', *Scottish Local History*, 78 (Spring 2010).
[59] *New York Gazette Revived in the Weekly Post-Boy*, 28 September 1747 and *New York Evening Post*, 5 October 1747, *Pennsylvania Gazette*, 1 October, 1747.
[60] Colin G. Calloway, *The Revolution in Indian Country: Crisis and Diversity in Indian Communities* (New York: Cambridge University Press, 1995), pp. 19–20.

> As the eighteenth century wore on, the Indian people and Indian cultures were being engulfed by an ocean of European and African people ... Five thousand Scots migrated to North Carolina alone in the decade before the Revolution ... Products of cultures of violence and much else that was undesirable besides, they made 'hard neighbours' to the Indians.

Conclusion: Law and internal rebellion in Britain at the mid-eighteenth century

The rebellions that racked Britain between the 1680s and 1740s exposed two features of the early modern British state: its vulnerability and general military weakness, on the one hand, and the reliance on the colonies as the destination for the dangerous, on the other. This second aspect had been initiated during the seventeenth century during the Cromwellian Interregnum of the 1650s and continued for 100 years. It was resumed after American independence, in a limited way, as trials for sedition and treason in Britain, Ireland, and Canada resulting in the transportation to Australia of dozens of critics and opponents of the British state. The military weakness is beyond the scope of this study, though it forms a background to the greatest revolt against British rule, the American War for Independence. The use of the law, however, is a core theme of this study, and the careful mix of severity and mercy, so familiar to historians of British criminal law and punishment, is found even in these examples of major threats to government and dynasty. As with burglars and horse thieves, severity had to be selective rather than universal, and mercy proved the majesty of the state and the beneficence of its ruler. Such a policy kept demonstrative brutality to a minimum, something that perhaps made it all the more striking – and in its effect – for the public.

A note on Ireland – Rebellious without rebellion?

Before the 1790s, when the French Revolution's impact changed everything, Ireland was continually troubled by violence and rural protests, but while it was rebellious, Ireland was not really treacherous. The state was relatively secure in the face of many forms of violent action. The contrast with Scotland, whose Highland ruling class, both Catholic and Episcopalian, had been left intact by the Whig revolution, complete with their traditional economic and ideological clan structures, is very striking. The Irish Catholic gentry had either been replaced or had conformed to the Protestant Church of Ireland in order to retain their land and civil rights. They were not enthusiastic Jacobites, though some retained a residual sentimental loyalty to the cause, with, for example, a certain amount of poetry and verse being produced in support.[61] Violence, though, from the aftermath of the 1688 Glorious Revolution to the end of the eighteenth century, was generally regarded as an Irish characteristic. The level of violence in eighteenth-century Ireland has been evaluated by scholars such as Neal Garnham who challenges its general reputation, both then and now, for being a violent society. Another difficulty lies in the methods of distinguishing and contextualizing the different *purposes* of violent actions. Violence arises in particular relationships, and those actions that had wider implications for either community cohesion or the working of an unequal economy can be seen, like the many forms of slave resistance, as challenging the social and economic structures and, by implication, the political dominance enjoyed by certain groups. Garnham points out that many of the urban disturbances were not untypical of many European cities, and Catholic celebrations of the significant Jacobite dates such as the Pretender's birthday added only a slightly subversive element. Interestingly, Ireland was late to adopt a riot act on the English model, in 1787, having failed in its earlier attempts in 1715 and 1719. Only at this point did 'riot' become a hanging offence.[62] Kathleen S. Murphy makes the point, though, that the context of many Irish violent actions was very different from that in, say, England.

> The history of Ireland, with its centuries of unrest and rebellion, and with its social divisions along lines corresponding to economic and religious differences, precluded English legal traditions from being transplanted without alteration .... The beginning of the eighteenth century was marked by a period of relative peace and stability. However, by the middle of the century, popular protests, like the Whiteboys violence in the 1760s, demanded economic and political change, but seemed to government officials and local gentry to promise only chaos.[63]

---

[61] Murray Pittock, *Poetry and Jacobite Politics in Eighteenth-Century Britain and Ireland* (Cambridge University Press, 1994).

[62] Neal Garnham, 'Police and Public Order and Eighteenth-Century Dublin', *Proceedings of the British Academy*, 107 (2001), pp. 81–91, and *Courts, Crime and the Criminal Law in Ireland, 1692–1760* (Dublin: Irish Academic Press, 1996).

[63] Kathleen S. Murphy, 'Judge, Jury, Magistrate and Soldier: Rethinking Law and Authority in Late Eighteenth-Century Ireland', *American Journal of Legal History*, 44 (2000), pp. 231–56, 251.

Before the revolutionary period of the 1790s (see Chapter 8), the main forms of action in Ireland lay in the resort to violent action by organized bands of rural protestors, called at various times the Whiteboys or Rightboys, Hearts of Oak and Hearts of Steel, from the 1760s to the early 1790s. The threats and acts of violence were largely aimed at intimidating landlords and their agents over issues such as rents and tenancies, or more generally, the enclosure of open lands and aggregation of smaller farms into larger, more efficient units. These attempts by landowners at agricultural 'improvement', common across England and Scotland too, confronted the smaller cottagers and peasants in Ireland with the impact of modernization (though the word did not exist at the time). 'Improvement and civilization must there descend from above; they will not rise spontaneously from the inward workings of the community', remarked George Cornewall Lewis in 1836, reviewing nearly a century of disturbances.[64]

Resistance was inevitable and was treated by the authorities as a serious threat. Rural activism in Ireland could be both violent and highly personal, but derived from a distinctive moral economy in the assertion of tenants' rights and freedom from church impositions. Yet the violence was particularly nasty. The 'houghing' (cutting the Achilles tendon) of animals and people indicated levels of personal viciousness not seen elsewhere in rural protests: there had been an outbreak earlier in the century, and the habit was resorted to recurrently. By the 1770s it was common to cut off or slit the ears of their targets. The secrecy – the deployment of oaths and uniforms – of the Whiteboys and other rural protestors also provided a template for later, wider and more nationalist, movements, as well as grounds for official paranoia. Yet the oaths, the uniforms of white shirts or tunics and the marching on agreed targets reinforced peasant solidarity and communal values against the landlords in particular. It created the mechanisms of a revolutionary and rebellious culture that had a lasting effect on subsequent movements, but until the 1790s neither rebellion nor revolution was the aim. The purposes were to ensure fair treatment for the smaller farmers, both from landlords and the established Church of Ireland which tried to tithe all agriculture produce. This opposition to tithes was shared by both Catholic and Protestant rural protestors.[65] J.S. Donnelly notes that 'eighteen men met at Ballyin near Lismore in January 1762 and decided to form an oath-bound secret

---

[64] George Cornewall Lewis, *On Local Disturbances in Ireland and on the Church of Ireland Question* (London: B. Fellowes, 1836), p. vi.
[65] D.W. Hayton, 'Parliament and the Established Church', in D.W. Hayton, James Kelly and John Bergin (eds), *The Eighteenth-Century Composite State: Representative Institutions in Ireland and Europe, 1689-1800* (Houndmills, Basingstoke: Palgrave Macmillan, 2010), pp. 78-106, 96.

society to combat enclosures and tithe-farmers; they did so, as one of them, Darby Browne, confessed, because "the Levellers or Whiteboys in the county of Tipperary had partly succeeded in redressing some of the grievances they complain". The use of the term 'Leveller', little heard since Cromwellian times, occurred in both Ireland and New York at the same time (see Chapter 5). Few were killed by these agitators, though many animals and farm buildings were destroyed: the authorities responded as fiercely as they could, using the most demonstrative forms of bodily punishments. In 1762, "'the greatest number of examples" ... was made at Waterford, where seven Whiteboys were hanged, five of them under the ancient treason statute of 25 Edward III, even though in burning a house they were far from levying war against the king'.[66]

In addition to the use of the ancient law of treason, the authorities passed special Whiteboy legislation, the 1765 law (known as the Whiteboy Act), creating many new hanging offences, such as 'the imposition of unlawful oaths by violence; woundings or other assaults committed at night by five or more persons; the destruction of property or the digging up of ground by such bands between sunset and sunrise; and the breaking open of gaols or the rescue of felons'. This seems to have been pretty ineffective, as the evidence suggests that few were convicted under its provisions, with more mundane charges being used. A striking feature of the executions is the use of the full hanging, beheading and quartering in cases other than treason, a demonstration of power that sometimes met with opposition and stone-throwing from the crowd at the hangman. The local authorities became more adept at collecting evidence, protecting witnesses and bringing prosecutions: in 1776, an unusually high number of thirty condemnations were achieved.[67]

The pattern of repression in Ireland therefore stands out as extreme in its legal response, adopting the form of treason executions where there are no treason charges. The 1760s seem to represent a kind of watershed in severity, with the use of hanging, beheading and quartering becoming part of the discretionary weaponry allowed to judges in felony executions thereafter. This punishment

---

[66] James S. Donnelly, 'The Whiteboy Movement, 1761–5', *Irish Historical Studies*, 21 (81) (March, 1978), pp. 20–54, 22 and 47. See also Martyn J. Powell, 'Ireland's Urban Houghers: Moral Economy and Popular Protest in the Late Eighteenth Century', in *The Laws and Other Legalities of Ireland, 1689–1850* (Farnham: Ashgate, 2011), pp. 231–300; Timothy D. Watt, *Popular Protest and Policing in Ascendancy Ireland, 1691–1761* (Woodbridge: The Boydell Press, 2018).

[67] J.S. Donnelly, 'Irish Agrarian Rebellion: The Whiteboys of 1769–76', *Proceedings of the Royal Irish Academy: Archaeology, Culture, History, Literature*, vol. 83C (1983), pp. 293–331, 308, 317, 325 and 327.

of the body, as James Kelly has pointed out, was exceptional in the experience of British rule.[68] Precise details about the numbers killed during the Whiteboy actions are hard to establish: Ian McBride suggests that up to 200 may have died, few of them by the hands of the protestors. At least 110 were condemned to death by the courts and 'around 85' hanged. Ironically, despite the almost hysterical official reports of Whiteboy activities, regarded as 'outrages', we still know more about state killing.[69] Ireland shared with other British jurisdictions a policy of inventive extension of the treason law to prosecute actions that seem well beyond a threat to the state or the political system, but was distinctive in that the traditional punishment for treason was applied in cases of more ordinary felonies. These were treated as treasons, therefore, in all but name.

---

[68] James Kelly, 'Punishing the Dead: Execution and the Executed Body in Eighteenth-Century Ireland' in Richard Ward (ed.), *A Global History of Execution and the Criminal Corpse* (Palgrave Macmillan, 2015), pp. 37–70, 52–4.

[69] Ian McBride, *Eighteenth-Century Ireland: The Isle of Slaves* (Dublin: Gill & Macmillan, 2009/2014), Kindle ed., Loc. 8161 and ftn.76.

5

Before the American Revolution – The Crisis in Imperial Law: Arson, Treason and Plot

Treason in the North American colonies, 1688–1766

Though this chapter concentrates on the growing tensions of the 1760s and 1770s, and the role played by the treason laws, it is worth noting that the deployment of those laws in the North American colonies during the previous century had been sparse and ineffective. The exception was their use by Sir William Berkeley in Virginia in Bacon's Rebellion of 1676, where many prosecutions and executions occurred. Thereafter, the New York trials of Jacob Leisler, Nicholas Bayard and William Prendergast were a reflection of the tension-ridden character of local politics in the colony, though land and rents shaped the disturbances that led to Prendergast's trial. The 1670s and 1680s were in fact the high water mark in treason prosecutions in America, as it was at the same time as Bacon's rebellion that Native Americans involved in King Philip's War were tried and executed for treason, or at least treasonable forms of rebellion. By contrast, the disturbances over key issues of land supply, taxes and rent that pervaded Pennsylvania from the movement known as the Paxton Boys in Philadelphia, the protests in New York against landholders and the similar events in North Carolina from the self-styled Regulators in the early 1770s were suppressed by either the threat or the deployment of a Riot Act modelled on the English 1715 legislation. With this procedure, assembled 'rioters' were given an official warning to disperse within an hour or be arrested under the capital offence of illegal assembly – a procedure remembered today in the British phrase of someone 'reading the Riot Act' to another person, despite the replacement of the legislation long ago. In the creation of riot acts, the colonial authorities were deliberating following the English strategy of developing lesser legislation, below the level of treason, which could intimidate oppositional groups and crowds by threatening the death penalty for offenders without the full horror of the treason execution. The exception to this pattern was the trial in 1766 of William Prendergast for treason in leading collective protests and direct actions against the proprietors of land and the practices of civil courts in rent arrears and debt cases.

The shifting pattern from treason to riot was therefore not entirely uniform or clearly planned. The conflicts of the 1760s and early 1770s can be seen against a broader background of organization and mobilization against British policies, and the attempts by the colonial authorities to control them were but a part of a much larger struggle to suppress such grassroots agitation. The Paxton Boys of Pennsylvania echoed the issues of conflict almost a century earlier in Bacon's Rebellion concerning access to Indian land. In 1763 they attacked a peaceful Indian village, initially killing six inhabitants, then returning to kill the rest. The colony passed a Riot Act, copied largely from the English law of 1715. The Paxton boys then marched on Philadelphia itself, and a volunteer militia was formed by the colonial government to meet them. Though this movement was described at the time as an 'insurrection', there seems to have been no effort to treat it as treasonable, partly because of the sheer numbers of protestors involved, and partly because it was not clear that the 1718 treason legislation in the colony could be stretched to cover agitation against the colonial government. At the same time there were protests across the border in Connecticut, and a border dispute between the two colonies, that produced many marches and protests. Treason against Pennsylvania would form an uncertain charge, in law.[1]

The prosecution of William Prendergast in New York in 1766 stands out as an exceptional legal response to these disturbances. As in the case of the Paxton Boys, there were large-scale mobilization and protest, with the targets being the land tenure systems imposed by large-scale proprietors, and their abuse of the law courts. Historical interpretations of these protests include a recognition of the severe conditions of the landholding system, and it was widely thought at the time that 'the plight of the besieged landlords was recognized as being of their own making'. Thomas Gage said they had sowed the seeds of sedition in their own people by opposing government.[2] As in Ireland at the same time – and it may be significant that Prendergast was of Irish origin, there was a strong culture of righteous grievance in these protests, however intimidatory they appeared to the landowners facing assaults on their houses. This could be seen as a culture of 'rough music', as Thomas J. Humphrey has suggested, in which

---

[1] Carlton F.W. Larson, *The Trials of Allegiance: Treason, Juries and the American Revolution* (New York: Oxford University Press, 2019), pp. 21–8, particularly pp. 21–2.

[2] Mary Lou Lustig, *Privilege and Prerogative: New York's Provincial Elite, 1710–1776* (Cranbury, NJ: Associated University Presses, 1995), p. 141.

what the authorities see as violent riot, the protestors see as a form of legitimate expression of wrongs.³ Mary Lou Lustig notes that the authorities believed that the rioters were not just trying to secure their tenancies, but were determined to seize the land and distribute the land equally. Their leader, William Prendergast, found himself on trial before Daniel Horsemanden who had presided over the trials of the black and white rebels in New York City in 1741. Yet he was an opponent of British policy by this time, and Prendergast remarked, 'if opposition to Government was deemed Rebellion, then no member of that court was entitled to set up his tryal'.⁴ Yet the fear of an egalitarian movement was palpable, as the rioters became known (among the authorities, at least), as 'Levellers', a term hardly used since the 1650s in the aftermath of the civil wars. For example, Captain John Montresor, an office in the 28th regiment sent to face the protestors, used the label in his diary:

> 28 July 1766: Advices from the Manor of Livingston that the Levellers there have rose to 500 men, 200 of which have marched to murther the Lord of the Manor and level his house, unless he would sign leases for 'em agreeable to their form, as theirs were now expired and that they would neither pay rent nor taxes etc. nor suffer other Tenants. The Levellers met by Mr Walter Livingston the son who made a sally with 40 armed men – the 200 having only sticks – obliged them to retire, not without their threatening a more respectable visit on the return of Col [Walter] Livingston of the Manor.
>
> 29 July 1766: Seventeen hundred of the Levellers with fire arms are collected at Poughkeepsie. All the gaols broke open through all the countries this side of Alabany along the East side of the River by people headed by Prendergast. 8,000 cartridges sent up to the 28th Reg. 70 people entered the Court of Justice at Wallingford in Connecticut declaring that no writs or processes should be issued for debt [:] the Sheriff and a party were sent after them but suffered much.

At the same time, the Stamp Act protests were in full swing, and Montresor found that the Sons of Liberty used 'scurrilous language' against the soldiers of his regiment. There were also reports in the newspapers that the soldiers were fired upon by the protestors. While some have commented that the death

---

[3] Thomas J. Humphrey, 'Crowd and Court: Rough Music and Popular Justice in Colonial New York', in William Pencak, Matthew Dennis and Simon P. Newman (eds), *Riot and Revelry in Early America* (University Park, PA: University of Pennsylvania Press, 2002), pp. 107–24, and also 'William Prendergast and the Revolution in the Hudson River Valley: "Poor Men Were Always Oppressed by the Rich"', in Nancy L. Roden and Ian K. Steele (eds), *The Human Tradition in the American Revolution* (Wilmington, DE: Scholarly Resources, 2000), pp. 81–98.
[4] Lustig, *Privilege and Prerogative*, p. 140.

sentence was intimidatory rather than seriously intended it is worth noting that there may have been a determination to carry out the full gruesome ceremony of hanging, drawing and quartering: certainly an advertisement for an executioner was placed in the *New York Gazette* in September, but a full royal pardon was obtained, arriving in February the following year.[5]

The North Carolina Regulators of 1771, like the agitators in New York, had grievances concerning security of land tenure, rents and taxes (particularly those going to the Church of England). The London authorities certainly had a low opinion of these backcountry settlers, and appreciated the successful efforts made by Governor William Tryon to suppress the movement:

> I cannot say I envy him his situation. The Back Parts of that Colony where these disturbances began, having been long the Receptacle of Fugitives for debt and felony from the adjoining Provinces, and Runaway Convicts from Virginia and Maryland. It is difficult, My Lord, very difficult to bind People of that kind by any Laws.[6]

Tryon mobilized militia forces from the eastern half of the colony, including a selection of artillery by which the confrontation at Alamance was decided. The 1769 Riot Act was deployed, and an hour was spent while the Regulators taunted the militia, after which the fighting began. After a short confrontation the Regulators were scattered, and many arrested. Shortly after, twelve men were condemned to death but six were immediately reprieved by Tryon – as Governor, he had the authority to reprieve in cases of riot, but not in cases of murder or treason. Thus, his use of the law was carefully chosen to give himself the maximum legal discretion, and it may be significant that one of the first acts he chose to see passed in New York shortly after was one controlling riots. Yet in some ways, as in other rural protests, there was a very dignified and legalistic element to the way the grievances were expressed, and the manipulation of the law courts, distorted allegedly by powerful forces in the eastern part of the colony, was a particular point of objection. As with the Whiteboys and New York's 'Levellers', the Regulators asserted a moral case as much as a political one, with a very different idea of 'moral economy'. The applicability of this idea of E.P. Thompson to these kinds of situation is perhaps to overstress the clash between

---

[5] *The Montresor Journals*, ed. G.D. Scull, John Montrésor, and James Gabriel Montrésor (New York Historical Society, 1881), pp. 375–6 and 382; Humphrey, 'Crowd and Court', p. 117; *Connecticut Courant*, 11 August 1766 (shot soldier), and *New York Gazette*, 1 September 1766 (executioner required) and 19 February 1767 (pardon).
[6] TNA CO 5/1278/53 (Board of Trade 1769–78): to Maryland, 4 August 1771 from Robert Eden, congratulations on the suppression of the Regulators by Governor Tryon.

official and popular cultures, but in this instance it is surely appropriate. Reports (supposedly from London) claimed that the treason law had been contemplated by the authorities, but this came to nothing:

> A letter of the 13th of June, from a Gentleman in London to his Friend in Boston, says 'it is Lord Mansfield's Opinion, that the Authors of the Riots and seditious Pieces in America, should be sent for to England and there tried for Treason; particularly the Writer of a Pamphlet, sometime since published in Boston; ... against which Author there is particular Evidence for his seditious and treasonable Speeches in an American Ass[embl]y'.[7]

Arson, treason and plot

The preceding events suggest, therefore, that successful control depended on the creation and enforcement of an appropriate legal framework in the colonies, matched by sufficient local forces to overawe the protestors. The events of the early 1770s highlighted the dilemmas of the British authorities when these two conditions were absent. The working of the legal systems in the many jurisdictions of the British Empire had usually been devolved to the local authorities. There were no administrative mechanisms for centralizing prosecution, trial and sentencing. Yet the idea that this might be necessary spread in government circles in the 1760s and early 1770s by a double crisis of order arising simultaneously at home and in the colonies. In part, this crisis was of the authorities' own making. Between the end of the Seven Years' War and the start of armed conflict in North America, the British authorities were repeatedly troubled by fears of domestic sabotage by foreign agents, particularly to the naval dockyards. In part this reflected the repeated occurrence of fires in the dockyards themselves, but there was also a fear of attack by subversive, enemy forces. For nearly a century, political anxiety had been directed at the Jacobite threat supported by France, but as this declined the problems of security were redefined. In the official view, threats from abroad were everywhere, in the colonies and in Europe, and from the enemy within. At the same time,

---

[7] This account draws largely on Carole Watterson Troxler, *Farming Dissenters: The Regulator Movement in Piedmont North Carolina* (The North Carolina Office of Archives and History, 2011) and Marjoleine Kars, *Breaking Loose Together: the Regulator Rebellion in Pre-Revolutionary North Carolina* (The University of North Carolina Press Chapel Hill and London, 2002). James G. Carrier, 'Moral Economy: What's in a Name?', *Anthropological Theory*, 18 (1) (2018), pp. 18–35. *Boston Evening Post*, 7 September 1767 (Mansfield).

increasing oppositional agitation in the North American colonies led the British authorities there to cast around for legal forms of suppression, in the end looking to extend some recent legislation to the colonies and coordinate prosecutions for treason. This chapter is concerned with the British government's attempt to find legal solutions to threats to its security in England and America between 1770 and 1777. As we have seen, there were increasingly violent flashpoints between British armed forces and protesting Americans, and the marginalized and isolated governors were increasingly unable to deploy local legal solutions to the problems: neither juries nor judges proved reliably loyal enough. Understanding this complex situation necessarily requires an exploration of British attempts to extend the law across the Atlantic.

Despite the triumphs of the Seven Years' War, the first truly global conflict, a peculiar sense of insecurity, fear and even panic soon followed.[8] Within a few years of the peace of 1763, the British state reacted nervously to rumours of plots and conspiracies, not just of rebellion, but of sabotage and destruction. This was accompanied by increasing official concern about printed criticism of government policies, much of which was about, or actually came from, the North American colonies. The crisis partly derived from the financial problems of public debt and the inability of the government to impose taxes on America.[9] Thus, the 'paranoid style' of British politics was fully revealed in the years after the peace of 1763 on both sides of the Atlantic, as though the authorities felt both beleaguered and unaccustomedly helpless. As Gordon Wood has suggested, a paranoid style had long been characteristic of British (and American) political culture. The century or so following the Restoration was the great era of conspiratorial fears and imagined intrigues. Terror and plot had a long history but their origins and targets changed in this period. In the early part of the eighteenth century, as Julian Hoppit notes, 'there were frequent and vociferous complaints that immorality and irreligion was sweeping the nation: drunks and Dissenters, prostitutes and pamphleteers, actors and activists might all be censured. Anxiety bred censoriousness, uncertainty a vivid paranoia.' He called the period 'an anxious age'. Wood concurs: 'The Augustan Age, said Daniel Defoe, was "an Age of Plot and Deceit, of Contradiction and

---

[8] Daniel A. Baugh, *The Global Seven Years War: Britain and France in a Great Power Contest* (London, 2011).
[9] Jan Eloranta and Jeremy Land, 'Hollow Victory? Britain's Public Debt and the Seven Years' War', *Essays in Economic & Business History*, 29 (2011), pp. 101–18; Charles P. Kindleberger and Robert Z. Aliber, *Manias, Panics, and Crashes: A History of Financial Crises*, 5th ed. (Hoboken, NJ: John Wiley, 2005), p. 59, on both 1763 and 1770 crises.

Paradox". Pretence and hypocrisy were everywhere, and nothing seemed as it really was.[10] These were more like moral panics, perhaps, than worries about national security, though the responses were very similar in seeking, through parliamentary legislation, what David Lemmings calls 'law solutions'. Yet threats to national unity and imperial loyalties were also keenly feared, with good reason, as we have seen in Chapter 4. The legislative reflex accelerated as the century progressed with large numbers of laws of all kinds being passed in George III's reign. Laws were framed in the face of public pressure and political lobbying, as well as newspaper and pamphlet representations, and did not form a coherent or logical body of rules about crimes and their punishments (something which concerned Blackstone and formed the core of Bentham's critique of the criminals laws). Yet the responses were often in the form of new or modified criminal laws (something which continued, and continues today, with new laws passed to deal with a specific anxiety, as in the Victorian garotting panic).[11] Threats seem close to home: the two fires in Portsmouth naval dockyard in 1770 and 1776 were not merely criminal, however, for they struck at the heart of the British Empire's power, the Royal Navy on which British global reach depended.[12] Similarly, the burning of the schooner the *Gaspee* in Rhode Island in 1772 evoked equal alarm. These incidents represent episodes in this growing culture of conspiracy, as rebellion seemed to presage revolution: in the twenty-first century it would be called terrorism. With the exception of the Gunpowder Plot of 1605, this kind of deliberate sabotage by arson was rare. Fire had a particular resonance in the popular imagination as well as the political memory, partly because of the Great Fire of London in 1666: yet it also struck terror, particularly in small towns and the countryside, because it was a typical 'crime of anonymity'.[13] Equally significant,

---

[10] Julian Hoppit, *A Land of Liberty? England, 1689–1727* (Oxford University Press, 2000), pp. 2–5; Gordon S. Wood, 'Conspiracy and the Paranoid Style: Causality and Deceit in the Eighteenth Century', *William and Mary Quarterly*, 39 (3) (1982), p. 407.

[11] David Lemmings and Claire Walker, eds, *Moral Panics, the Media and the Law in Early Modern England* (Basingstoke, 2009), p. 10, note, as does David Lieberman, the increase in laws passed after 1760; David Lieberman, *The Province of Legislation Determined: Legal Theory in Eighteenth-Century Britain* (Cambridge University Press, 1989); Jennifer Davis, 'The London Garotting Panic of 1862: A Moral Panic and the Creation of a Criminal Class in Mid-Victorian England', in V.A.C. Gatrell, B. Lenman and G. Parker (eds), *Crime and the Law: A Social History of Crime in Western Europe Since 1500* (London: Europa Publications, 1980), pp. 190–213.

[12] Daniel Baugh, 'Maritime Strength and Atlantic Commerce: The Uses of "a Grand Maritime Empire"', in Lawrence Stone (ed.), *An Imperial State at War: Britain from 1689 to 1815* (London, 1994), pp. 185–223; Jeremy Black, *Natural and Necessary Enemies: Anglo-French Relations in the Eighteenth Century* (London, 1986).

[13] Peter Borsay, *The Eighteenth-Century Town: A Reader in English Urban History, 1688–1820* (London, 1990) p. 122; E.P. Thompson, 'The Crime of Anonymity', in Douglas Hay, Peter Linebaugh, John G. Rule, E.P. Thompson and Cal Winslow (eds), *Albion's Fatal Tree: Crime and Society in Eighteenth-Century England* (London, 1975), p. 275.

the 1770 fire occurred in a time of peace rather than war, suggesting a state of perpetual and secret hostility to Britain and its source of naval supremacy. In some ways, the ground had been laid by the report a few years earlier that Portsmouth was a likely object of French attack, as a deliberate strike against the country's 'naval strength'.[14] The British state, despite its overwhelming success in the peace of 1763 that ended the Seven Years' War, still felt that it was facing threats on both sides of the Atlantic.

The political response to this menace depended on the laws of treason which had undergone considerable development and procedural elaboration in the eighteenth century, and on the 1772 law making arson in naval dockyards a capital offence. Treason, as we have seen, contained, under the 1352 Treason Act, the element of making war on the monarch; planning, imagining or encompassing their death; working for their enemies; having sexual intercourse with the monarch's consort; or trying to kill, or killing, the ministers of the crown (and justices or judges). Making war was an apparently simple concept, but there were some careful safeguards in the later doctrinal discussions. It was not the case that supplying warmaking materials to a traitor, for example, was itself treason. Intention and action combined were required. Moreover, while there were some statutes that covered arson and damage to economic assets, such as linen frames or hayricks, there was little by way of law to protect the heartland of the state and its military assets.[15] Moreover, outstanding issues remained: in the two Jacobite risings of 1715 and 1745-6, legal precedent had established that trials for treason need not be held in places where the alleged offences had been committed: protests against being tried in England rather than Scotland had been brushed aside in the Southwark trials of Scottish rebels in 1746 (see Chapter 4). Secondly, there were attempts to broaden the concept of treason, primarily to include joining a foreign army but also to include support of a more passive kind for rebellion. 'Making war on the king' had become a rather elastic concept, as a result.[16]

In this context of both heightened political anxiety and tension in Britain and America, a series of events occurred that revealed the weaknesses in the British

---

[14] *Gentleman's Magazine*, 41 (1771), p. 422, 6 and 7 September; *London Evening Post*, 17 September 1771; *Virginia Gazette* (Purdie and Dixon), 21 November 1771.
[15] Lisa Steffen, *Defining the British State: Treason and National Identity, 1608-1820* (Houndmills, Basingstoke: Palgrave Macmillan, 2001), pp. 9, 50-7; Roger B. Manning, 'The Origins of the Doctrine of Sedition', *Albion*, 12 (2) (1980), pp. 99-121; John Barrell, *Imagining the King's Death: Figurative Treason, Fantasies of Regicide, 1793-4* (Oxford University Press, 2000), pp. 382-3; John H. Langbein, *The Origins of the Adversarial Criminal Trial* (Oxford, 2003), pp. 90-100.
[16] M. Forster, *A Report of Some Proceedings on the Commission of Oyer and Terminer and Goal Delivery for the Trial of the Rebels in the Year 1746 in the County of Surry* ... (Oxford, 1762).

state's hegemony. The fire in Portsmouth dockyard in the early hours of 27 July 1770 remained a mystery for some time, though the damage was estimated at an enormous £489,000. Wood's 'conspiratorial modes of explanation' involving 'plots by dissembling men' dominated the first reports. The press immediately concluded that the fire had been so extensive that it was no accident. In Portsmouth, 'French desperadoes' were immediately suspected, perhaps acting in reprisal for the alleged plot by Alexander Gordon and others to burn the French port of Brest the previous year, for which he had been beheaded, and in which Lord Harcourt, the British ambassador to Paris, had been implicated. Gordon was thought by the French to be a British agent, though he vehemently denied it. Certainly his execution made it difficult for Harcourt to recruit new agents in the French ports. This theory provoked newspaper discussion of the rules of the *lex talionis* or law of reprisal.[17] Others thought that the fire was the fault of some 'worthless workmen' rather than the French. Though the fire was widely reported, and a large reward of £1,000 for information offered, with a free pardon for those informing on their co-conspirators, investigations led nowhere.[18] More than a year later, in 1771, however, two men separately confessed to the sabotage, and at the same time made allegations of deep plots. Jonathan Britain (also known as William Unthank) wrote from Reading jail, where he was under arrest for a forgery committed in Bristol: 'he pretends to be have been a principal actor in that dark scene, and insinuates that several persons of the first rank were concerned in it'. Simultaneously, Joshua Dudley, imprisoned for debt in a London prison, gave lengthy testimony of his own supposed involvement (and that of various sinister plotters). Jonathan Britain wrote large numbers of letters alleging plots from his jail cell, and his personal story survives in accounts written at the time of his trial and execution in Bristol in April 1772, when he told his life story to a clergyman visiting him in jail. He denied any knowledge of Joshua Dudley. It is clear that he was interrogated at the outset by two 'under-secretaries of state', suggesting that the authorities were contemplating a charge of treason. In addition to rather vague accounts of the arson, he also confessed to receiving payment in June 1770 (with four others) to shoot 'a great man in Hyde Park', which he would have done if the pistol had

---

[17] Wood, 'Conspiracy', p. 408; *London Evening Post*, 28 July 1770, and 2 August 1770 'no accidental fire'; *London Evening Post*, 30 July and 2 August 1770; Jeremy Black, *British Diplomats and Diplomacy, 1688–1800* (Liverpool University Press, 2001), p. 140 on Gordon.

[18] P. Levot, *Procès d'Alexandre Gordon, Espion Anglais, Décapité a Brest en 1769* (Brest, 1861); his last plea was published, *Middlesex Journal*, 4, January 1770; *Gentleman's Magazine*, 40 (1770), p. 343, 27 July 1770; p. 361 letter from 'Mr Urban', Portsea, 2 August 1770; also p. 387, 28 July and p. 389, 4 August 1770; *Lloyd's Evening Post*, 8 August 1770; *Pennsylvania Gazette*, 1 November 1770.

not misfired. In his final confession, he admitted that the intended victim was the king himself. Originally arrested for the capital crime of forging promissory notes, Britain, like Dudley, sought to make himself an indispensable witness to a crime he did not commit. Having sought to negotiate with the authorities for a full pardon as a prelude to the full disclosure of what he knew, they called his bluff: he was hanged for forgery.[19]

The other confessor, Joshua Dudley, also spun a detailed story, and in many ways his persuasive story-telling was a fundamental aspect of his criminal activity. In the end, his narrative talents led to his conviction for perjury and transportation to America in 1772 for alleging that he had evidence of the plot by French agents, including an Irish captain and a Catholic priest, instigated by the 'Court of France' to destroy the Portsmouth dockyards. He concocted his story while languishing in a debtors' prison, from where the authorities took him to Portsmouth to test his account. As in the case of Britain, his interrogation also involved important people headed by the Lord Mayor of London, two aldermen, the secretaries of both the Earl of Rochford (Secretary of State for the Southern Department) and the Earl of Sandwich (First Lord of the Admiralty), and members of the Board of Admiralty. It seems from the transcripts that daily reports were given to the politicians on the progress of the questioning, and newspapers on both sides of the Atlantic followed the 'parade of examination'.[20] Diplomatic difficulties were caused by both sets of false accusations: the French ambassador was threatened because of the supposed plots, and demanded severe punishments for the slanderous allegations against his country. He had been driven out of London initially, only to complain a few months later about his 'injured honour'.[21]

The whole process was followed in great detail by the press in both Britain and America, with almost weekly instalments during the early months of 1772. There was some scepticism from the beginning about the two men's

---

[19] *London Evening Post*, 17 September 1771; *Exeter Flying Post*, 22 May 1772; letters were published in repeated editions of *The Whisperer*, nos. 86 to 92, between 5 October and 16 November 1771; *The Rev Mr Talbot's Narrative of the Whole of His Proceedings Relative to Jonathan Britain* (Bristol, 1772) and *Some Particulars of the Life and Death of Jonathan Britain Who Was Executed at Bristol for Forgery, by a Gentleman Who Attended Him, with a Preface by the Rev Mr. Rouquet* (Bristol, 1772). See *Home Office Papers (George III): 1770-2* (1881), pp. 70–84, 310–32, 494–505, British History Online, http://www.british-history.ac.uk/report.aspx?compid=62441&strquery=dockyards fire and http://www.british-history.ac.uk/report.aspx?compid=62448&strquery=dockyards 1772 Date (accessed 4 August 2014).

[20] *London Evening Post*, 3 and 7 September 1771; TNA PRO SP/37/17 and TS 11/933 interrogations; *Annual Register 1771*, p. 143; *Pennsylvania Packet*, 16 December 1771, 'parade'.

[21] *New York Gazette*, 28 October 1771 Count de Guigne's hasty departure from London; *New Hampshire Gazette*, 10 January 1772.

'pretended discoveries', which gained no credit 'at the West end of the town' (i.e. in political circles in Westminster). Both men were allegedly interested in escaping legal penalties of different kinds, and making money.[22] Yet the authorities were cautious, taking Dudley to Portsmouth to challenge the details of his story at the place of the fire. Dudley himself left several long accounts of his activities in England, including the lengthy depositions in the legal records on the occasion of his investigation by the Lord Mayor and others, and a pamphlet of memoirs together with numerous newspaper accounts tracking his accusations step by step.[23] In the end, the exciting allegations of Britain, that at least five 'great men' had been concerned in the fire, attracted most attention, and above all, his trial and execution were more titillating. The *Virginia Gazette* followed Britain and Dudley to their ends – noting when Dudley had been shipped out with sixty felons from Newgate.[24] One American paper, most unusually, drew a dramatic conclusion from this stage of the story, to criticize the current administration –

> Your Sovereign's life has been attempted by the hands of J. Britain; Portsmouth dock, with all the stores, have been burned, and plans deep and dark as hell have been laid to destroy the protestant interest, and the Administration charged with having a hand in it; yet no serious enquiry had been made about it, and the King persuaded by his ministers that all is a farce and he in no danger.[25]

Little more was heard from Joshua Dudley until a two-column letter of great emotional content and dramatic force was published in the British press in 1774. This document, apparently sent from Winchester, Frederick County, Virginia, was accepted as a genuine letter from Dudley, correctly identified as the man

---

[22] *Gentleman's Magazine*, 41, p. 424, 30 September 1771; *Annual Register for 1771* (London: 1772), p. 137 and p. 143, 24 and 30 August.

[23] *London Evening Post*, 31 August 1771; *Gentleman's Magazine*, 41 (1771), p. 422, 6 September 1771. *Memoirs of the Life of Joshua Dudley Explaining amongst Other Particulars the Motives of His Pretended Discovery of the Persons Concerned in Setting Fire to the Dock-Yard at Portsmouth in July 1770 Written by Himself* (London, 1772); *The Rev Mr Talbot's Narrative of the Whole of His Proceedings Relative to Jonathan Britain* (Bristol, 1772) and *Some Particulars of the Life and Death of Jonathan Britain Who Was Executed at Bristol for Forgery, by a Gentleman Who Attended Him, with a Preface by the Rev Mr. Rouquet* (Bristol, 1772); TNA SP 37/17, and TS 11/933; Old Bailey Sessions Papers, February 1772 and 3–9 June 1772; *Gentleman's Magazine*, 40, pp. 343, 361–3, July 1770, 41, pp. 422–3 and September 1771, 42, p. 339, July 1772; *London Evening Post*, 31 August, 3, 7, 10, 12 and 17 September 1771.

[24] *New Hampshire Gazette, Connecticut Journal* and *New London Gazette* 28 September 1770; *Boston Gazette*, 1 October 1770; *Providence Gazette*, 6 October 1770; *Boston Post-Boy* and *Boston Evening Post*, 21 October 1771; *Providence Gazette*, 2 November 1771; *Virginia Gazette* (Purdie and Dixon), 21 November 1771 and 24 September 1772.

[25] *Massachusetts Spy*, 30 January 1772; *Boston Evening Post*, 31 August 1772, from London datelined 26 July.

who had been transported in 1772 for perjury concerning the Portsmouth fire. The story he spun at great length was of his virtual adoption by his new mistress in the colonies, who acquired him as an indentured servant from the Matthews brothers of Staunton, Augusta County, Virginia. Hired to educate some young people, he had acquired responsibility for a young woman on the death of her mother, the lady of the house. She in turn died, leaving him everything, and at the time of writing he was living alone with her tomb in the house. He also added some account of the political upheaval in the colony as well as the cruelties of Indian warfare. It is possible that, along with some other convicts, he sought to make peace with the authorities in England at this time. A copy of Dudley's letter appeared six months later in the *Virginia Gazette*, with the ironic comment.

> This very same Joshua Dudley (if the printer is rightly informed) is still with Messrs Sampson and George Matthews, in the capacity of a servant; ergo, the whole account of his good and bad fortune is a most notorious falsity.

Thereafter Dudley vanishes from the printed record.[26]

While the fate of Britain and Dudley still hung in the balance, the government ordered a bill on 23 March 1772 entitled 'An Act for the Better Securing and Preserving his Majesty's Dockyards, Magazines and Stores', prepared by Lord North, chief minister, and the Attorney and Solicitor Generals, and signed by the king on 26 April. This Act reflected the panic and established the death penalty for both burning the royal dockyards and their stores, an offence that remained on the statute books as a capital offence until the second half of the twentieth century. Also, anyone acting to 'cause to be set on fire, or aid, procure, abet or assist in the setting on fire' was as liable for the death penalty as the arsonists. Equally important were the provisions for trial, which could be held anywhere the government wished, either in the place where the offence occurred or elsewhere. Thus, offences committed 'in any place out of this realm' could be tried in England or where they had been committed, a choice which reflected increasing uncertainty about the potential for successful prosecution in some of the colonies.[27] In this way, the 1772 dockyards law incorporated a key

---

[26] *Morning Chronicle and London Advertiser*, 18 October 1774; *Leeds Mercury*, 25 October 1774; *Cumberland Pacquet*, 27 October 1774; *Virginia Gazette* (Purdie), 10 March 1775; letter for Joshua Dudley, Augusta post office, *Virginia Gazette* (Rind), 17 February 1774; Gwenda Morgan and Peter Rushton, *Eighteenth-Century Criminal Transportation: The Formation of the Criminal Atlantic* (Basingstoke, 2004), pp. 109–10.

[27] 'An Act for the better securing and preserving his Majesty's dockyards, magazines, ships and stores', *Journal of the House of Commons*, 33, p. 608; 12 Geo. III. c. 24, *Statutes of the Realm*, Charles Eyre and William Strahan (1786), VIII, p. 170.

legal strategy of the authorities towards treason and rebellion in the eighteenth century, that is, the legal right to try 'rebels' and traitors where the government chose rather than in the places where the alleged acts had actually occurred. In January 1773, the *Boston Evening Post* reported disquiet in Massachusetts concerning the Act in the framing of which their legislature had no share and which struck at

> the greatest of Blessings, personal Security to the Innocent, as it exposes the Lives and Fortunes of the most virtuous, to the low Revenge of any who are vile enough to be guilty of Perjury ... the Accused may be removed for Trial to any County in England where he, by being a Stranger, loses that benefit that would arise from his good reputation was the Trial by a Jury of the Vicinity. – One of the Justest Complaints against the Inquisitorial Court, in Romish Countries.

The problems of jurisdiction and location speedily became acute as conflicts in North America turned violent.[28]

In the summer of 1772, shortly after the dockyards act became law, there came news from Rhode Island of the destruction of the Royal Navy schooner *The Gaspee*. The law and the events in America were unconnected, although David Ramsay in his 1789 history thought they were, and at least one modern historian, J. Philip Reid, regards the act as being designed to frighten the Whig leaders in the colonies. A little over a month after the ship's destruction in June, the first brief reports reached London, with the erroneous news that the captain had been killed.[29] Official discussions centred on the use of a Henry VIII act allowing treasonable actions designed or executed abroad to be tried at 'home', that is, in England. The 1746 Jacobite trials had set a precedent by enabling Scots to be tried in England. Just to be sure, as was mentioned in Chapter 4, special legislation had been passed in the middle of the rebellion.[30] Troublesome Americans, though, were threatened with the much earlier legislation from 1543. Historians have doubted whether this Act had survived subsequent repeals, but the legal advisers to the government in 1768 had no doubts. Certainly the law was well known, being reproduced in law books and, more significantly, listed

---

[28] *Boston Evening Post*, 4 January 1773.
[29] David Ramsay, *The History of the American Revolution*, 2 vols (Philadelphia, 1789), I, p. 137 and J. Phillip Reid, *A Constitutional History of the American Revolution* (Madison, WI: University of Wisconsin Press), I, p. 54; *St James's Chronicle, London Chronicle*, 18 July 1772, *Daily Advertiser*, 20 July 1772, first reports from Admiral Montagu.
[30] See Forster, *A Report of Some Proceedings ... in the Year 1746 in the County of Surry*, p. 1; 19 Geo. II c. 9, 'impowering HM to issue Commissions for Trying the Rebels in any County of the Kingdom, in the same manner as if the Treasons had been committed in that County', and pp. 15, 19–21.

among the extant treason laws which the government ordered published in the aftermath of the '45.[31]

The law had been introduced into political debate in an 'Address to the King' adopted by the House of Lords on 16 December 1768, invoking the statute of 35 Henry VIII as a 'remedy' for the disorders in the American colonies in general and Massachusetts Bay in particular, in the wake of the adoption of the Townshend Duties.[32] Following an examination of the state of affairs in Massachusetts based on papers presented to it by Secretary of State Lord Hillsborough on 28 November and 7 December 1768 'by his Majesty's Command', the Lords adopted a series of resolutions and an address to the King supporting government policy. Nothing was more necessary to maintain royal authority, they argued, than to inflict 'condign punishment' on those responsible for the disorders, and the Massachusetts Governor should

> take the most effectual Methods for procuring the fullest Information that can be obtained, touching all Treasons or Misprisions of Treason committed within his Government since the Thirtieth Day of December last, and to transmit the same, together with the Names of the Persons who were most active in the Commission of such Offences, to One of Your Majesty's Principal Secretaries of State.

The government could then form a special commission and prosecute those identified under the Henry VIII law.[33]

A full debate on the merits of the Resolutions and the Address to the King took place in the House of Commons on 26 January 1769. The opposition attacked various aspects of the proposal, questioning the use of the Henry VIII law in the colonies, whether it was a fit response, and whether it undermined the practice of trial by jury given that it would be impossible to produce a jury of their peers. In addition, it would be difficult if not impossible for the accused to call witnesses in their defence. Above all, they challenged the idea that the disturbances in

---

[31] Geoffrey R. Elton, *The Tudor Constitution: Documents and Commentary*, 2nd ed. (Cambridge, 1982), p. 61; J. Bellamy, *The Tudor Law of Treason: An Introduction* (London, 1979), Ch. 2, note 27, p. 246; William Holdsworth, *History of English Law*, IV pp. 495–6; Coke, *Institutes*, III, pp. 1ff. suggests that some Henrician laws were in place; also see John Raithby, ed., *The Statutes at Large from Magna Carta to the Union of the Kingdoms of Great Britain and Ireland*, 20 vols (London, 1811), III, p. 431; *A Collection of the Several Statutes and Parts of Statutes Now in Force Relating to High Treason and Misprision of High Treason* (Edinburgh, 1746), pp. 14–15; Peter D.G. Thomas, *George III: King and Politicians, 1760–1770* (Manchester, 2002), p. 201.

[32] I.D. Thornley, 'The Treason Legislation of Henry VIII (1531–1534)', *Transactions of the Royal Historical Society*, 3rd ser., 11 (1917), pp. 87–123.

[33] R. Simmons and P.D.G. Thomas, eds, *Proceedings and Debates of the British Parliaments Respecting North America 1754–1783*, 6 vols (White Plains, NY: Kraus International Publications, 1984), III, p. 52.

Massachusetts were really a case of treason. William Dowdeswell, spokesperson for the opposition, denounced the idea of using treason law and specifically addressed the adoption of the statute of 35 Henry VIII. 'We had no colonies at that time', he protested, and therefore the law could not apply to America. The government, in reply, asserted that since it was generally agreed that the colonists had carried with them the Treason Act of 25 Edward III, the same must apply to that of Henry VIII.[34] As Edmund Burke noted, however right their criticisms, opponents of the policy could not win: the opposition might have the speakers, but the government had the numbers. It 'behoved government to take strong, wise measures', but whatever they did in America would backfire. Inroads had already been made on the principle of using juries from the neighbourhood in cases of smuggling and the excise. Now trials for high treason threatened to take away the privilege of a jury. 'I am pleading the cause of our ancient constitution, of our charters, of everything that is dear. There is a serpent creeping in the grass.'[35]

The 1769 debates had the effect of alerting American critics to the danger of this legislation – this 'bugbear law', as the American newspapers came to call it. There were immediate debates and newspaper reports concerning it. In the colonies in 1769 the Virginia Assembly was the first to repudiate the notion that men could be taken to England for trial. All trials for treason, they said

> ought of Right to be had, and conducted in and before his Majesty's courts, held within ... the said Colony ... And sending such Person or Persons to Places beyond the Sea to be tried, is highly derogatory of the Rights of British Subjects as thereby the inestimable Privilege of being tried by a Jury from the Vicinage, as well the Liberty of summoning and producing Witnesses on such Trial, will be taken away from the Party accused.

The same week an almost identical motion was passed by Rhode Island. They pleaded with the king to avert 'those Dangers and Miseries, which will ensue from the seizing, and carrying beyond Sea, any Person residing in America, suspected of any crime whatsoever'. Even in Parliament the critics were blunt about the idea: the government's language showed, said one, that 'the intended object ... was to bring the unhappy Americans to England to be tried, under

---

[34] Simmons and Thomas, *Proceedings and Debates*, III, pp. 64–6, 68–9.
[35] Simmons and Thomas, *Proceedings and Debates*, III, 26 January 1769, pp. 63, 72; Peter D.G. Thomas, *The Townshend Duties Crisis; The Second Phase of the American Revolution* (Oxford, 1967), pp. 114–20; Peter J. Stanlis, 'Edmund Burke's Legal Erudition and Practical Politics: Ireland and the American Revolution', *Political Science Reviewer*, 25 (1) (2006), pp. 82–3; Edmund Burke, *The Works of Edmund Burke* (Boston, MA, 1836), I, pp. 68–9; 91–3, 95, p. 99 quoted, from 'The Letter to the Sheriffs of Bristol'.

the act of Henry VIII, and have them butchered in the King's Bench'. The law became one of the grievances repeatedly referred to, so in January 1775 the Continental Congress specifically mentioned it in a petition to Parliament. By 1776 it was an important point in the Declaration of Independence, in Thomas Jefferson's draft, to denounce the measures 'for transporting us beyond seas to be tried for pretended offences'. At that point, the Henry VIII law was recalled in the American press as one of the 'antiquated' laws threatening America, while in April 1778 the *Pennsylvania Packet* carried a bitter comment, copied from the *Gentleman's Magazine*, that 'murder by form of law again takes root in Britain, by the revival of the bloody tyranny of Henry the Eighth'.[36]

The issue of treason and its prosecution resurfaced with the burning of the ship *Gaspee*, which was deployed against smuggling.[37] On 9 June 1772, the *Gaspee* ran aground on a sandbar some five miles below the town of Providence, Rhode Island, and twelve miles above Newport. Lieutenant Dudingston, its already unpopular commander, waited for a high tide to refloat the schooner but around midnight a number of rowing boats closed in on the vessel. Fighting broke out as men boarded the schooner, overpowering the crew who were bound and put ashore, along with Dudingston who had been seriously wounded. From a distance, they witnessed the burning of the *Gaspee*, an event, according to William Leslie, which began a sequence of incidents that led directly to revolution.[38] Located to the south of Massachusetts, Rhode Island was no ordinary colony. Though small in size, and with a population of only 60,000, it was a corporate colony with greater powers of self-government than other colonies. Under its charter of 1663, it elected all its officials including its governor. George III in conversation with Thomas Hutchinson, former governor of Massachusetts, described it as having 'a strange form of

---

[36] John P. Kennedy, ed., *Journals of the House of Burgesses of Virginia, 1766–69* (Richmond, VA, 1905), XI, pp. 214–16; *Acts and Laws of the English Colony of Rhode-Island ... Made and Passed since the Revision in June 1767* (Newport, RI, 1772), pp. 22–3; *Scots Magazine*, 28 (Edinburgh, 1775), p. 182; 'bugbear law' *Massachusetts Spy*, 22 April 1774; *Essex Gazette*, 26 April 1774; *Connecticut Journal*, 29 April 1774; *Providence Gazette*, 30 April 1774; *Pennsylvania Packet*, 2 May 1774; *Newport Mercury*, 9 May 1774; *New Hampshire Gazette*, 13 May 1774; 'antiquated law'; *New York Journal*, 18 January 1776; *Pennsylvania Packet*, 23 January 1775 Congress petition, reproduced widely in many other papers; *Pennsylvania Packet*, 1 April 1778 thought the statement was signed by George Washington, the editor expressed scepticism about its providence (as have others) but he printed it because he endorsed the sentiment. David Armitage, *The Declaration of Independence: A Global History* (Cambridge, MA: Harvard University Press, 2007), p. 160.

[37] Bradley Chapin, 'The American Revolution as Lese Majesty', *Pennsylvania Magazine of History and Biography*, 79 (3) (1955), pp. 318–21.

[38] William R. Leslie, 'The *Gaspee* Affair: A Study of Its Constitutional Significance', *Mississippi Valley Historical Review*, 39 (1952), p. 233; Neil L. York, 'The Uses of Law and the *Gaspee* Affair', *Rhode Island History*, 50 (1992), pp. 1–22.

government'. Dominated politically and socially by a wealthy merchant class, it had long enjoyed a dubious reputation as a nest of smugglers.[39]

Governor Joseph Wanton and his deputy Darius Sessions moved to keep the investigation into the affair under their control, publishing a proclamation offering a reward of £100 for information. Wanton wrote to the Secretary of State, the Earl of Hillsborough, of his determination to 'detect and bring to justice the perpetrators of this violent outrage' and 'daring insult upon authority', but Whitehall overrode him.[40] After all, the *Gaspee* was a Royal Navy ship employed in the government's reinvigorated effort to enforce the Trade and Navigation Acts. Rhode Island authorities were instructed by Hillsborough to use the recent dockyards act, but the Privy Council, meeting on 20 August 1772, cancelled his orders after they had already been dispatched. Instead, they set up a commission of enquiry which was to investigate the charge of high treason on the basis of the Henry VIII Act. The switch in policy hinged on the receipt of an opinion dated 10 August from the Attorney and Solicitor Generals, Edward Thurlow and Alexander Wedderburn, who both agreed that the attack on the *Gaspee* was an act of high treason, constituting levying war against the king; therefore the offenders could be indicted for high treason in England or in Rhode Island provided the ship was stationed within the boundaries of the colony. But they also judged that the dockyards act might be difficult to implement, as it extended only to 'such ships as are burnt or otherwise destroyed in some Dockyard and not to ships upon active Service'. The *Gaspee* was not precisely in a dockyard either: it was on a sandbank a few miles from harbour. Interestingly, there was no suggestion that the law of piracy might have been applicable.[41]

A high-level inter-colonial commission was appointed consisting of the chief justices of Massachusetts, New Jersey and New York, a justice of the court of vice admiralty in Boston and Governor Wanton.[42] Members of the crew were interviewed, but despite the increase in the size of the reward for information to £500, and the offer of a free pardon to participants in the affair who would name others, the members of the commission failed to uncover any reliable information that would allow a legal case to be brought against the alleged perpetrators. Thus, 'this heinous crime' went unpunished, but its consequences were significant.

---

[39] Peter O. Hutchinson, *Diary and Letters of Thomas Hutchinson* (Boston, 1884), p. 172; Mary Sarah Bilder, *The Transatlantic Constitution: Colonial Legal Culture within the Empire* (Cambridge, MA, 2008), pp. 5–6; York, 'The Uses of Law', pp. 5, 3.
[40] Leslie, 'The *Gaspee* Affair', pp. 236–7.
[41] Thurlow and Wedderburn, 10 August 1772; TNA PRO CO 5/159, fos 26–7.
[42] York, 'The Uses of the Law', p. 9.

According to William Leslie, the appointment of the royal commission and the threat to carry culprits to England for trial led to the formation of a web of inter-colonial committees of correspondence. The *Providence Gazette* and the *Newport Mercury* published the following response. It was copied widely by other colonial newspapers and printed in the London press. The government's strategy was a gift to New England radicals.

> A court of inquisition more horrid than that of Spain and Portugal is established within this colony, to inquire into the circumstance of destroying the Gaspee schooner; and the persons who are the commissioners of this new-fangled court, are vested with most exorbitant and unconstitutional power. They are directed to summon witnesses, apprehend persons not only impeached, but even suspected! ... To deliver them to Admiral Montague, who is ordered to have a ship in readiness to carry them to England, where they are to be tried.[43]

How this episode was perceived by New Englanders is suggested by letters between Hannah Winthrop, the wife of John Winthrop, professor of Mathematics and Natural History at Harvard College, and Mercy Otis Warren, patriot propagandist, wife of James Warren and sister of James Otis. 'One of the most extraordinary political manoeuvres this century has produced', wrote Winthrop to her friend, 'is the Ministerial mandate transporting the Newportonians a thousand leagues for trial'. Events looked quite different, however, to Arthur Lee of Virginia, at that time resident in London. Though initially welcoming the attack on the *Gaspee*, he was horrified by the government's reaction fearing that it would bring matters to a head prematurely. 'An unsuccessful struggle now', he cautioned, 'might perhaps rivet our chains forever'. The northern colonies were pushing matters too far, though he conceded that the New Englanders 'have had more than their proportion of insult and oppression'. The official line, however, was adopted by Thomas Hutchinson, who, writing to Commodore Gambier at the Boston station, welcomed the establishment of the commission of enquiry (despite its failure) on the grounds that 'if there should be another like attempt, some concerned in it may be taken prisoners and carried directly to England. A few punished at Execution Dock would be the only effectual preventive of any further attempts.'[44]

---

[43] 'Americanus', *Providence Gazette*, 26 December 1772, from the *Newport Mercury*, 21 December; *New York Journal*, 7 January 1773; *London Evening Post*, 23 March 1773.

[44] Hannah Winthrop to Mercy Otis Warren, January 1773 cited in Elizabeth F. Ellet, *Revolutionary Women in the War for American Independence* (1848), p. 48; Governor Hutchinson to Commodore Gambier, Boston, 30 June 1770 cited in Mercy Otis Warren, *History of the Rise, Progress and Termination of the American Revolution*, ed. Lester H. Cohen (Indianapolis, IN, 1988 [1805]), note no. XI, pp. 356–67; Arthur Lee to Samuel Adams, 20 July 1772 and to Richard Henry Lee, 14 February 1773 cited in Louis W. Potts, *Arthur Lee: A Virtuous Revolutionary* (Baton Rouge, LA, 1981), p. 102.

The destruction of the *Gaspee* would not be forgotten. It reappeared during the subsequent crisis regarding the burning of the dockyards in Portsmouth and Bristol in 1776 when it too assumed mythic proportions. The attack on its captain and his injuries were described in gruesome detail while 'every man … that opposed the attackers was cruelly butchered'. These details though patently untrue were alleged in the *Hampshire Chronicle* in 1777 when, in reviewing the affair of John the Painter at great length, an anonymous author accused the Americans of always using fire.[45]

Only a few months after the *Gaspee* commission of inquiry was disbanded came the more famous incident of the Boston Tea Party of 16 December 1773 when vast quantities of tea belonging to the East India Company were dumped into Boston Harbour in defiance of the Tea Act. Without a specific crime such as arson, the legal difficulties the British authorities faced were almost identical: seemingly treasonable actions were beyond their power to prosecute successfully. The Earl of Dartmouth, Hillsborough's replacement as Secretary of State, sought the Attorney and Solicitor Generals' opinion on the acts and proceedings which had taken place in Boston. Their reply confirmed that some of the activities did amount to the crime of high treason, namely levying war against His Majesty, but others amounted only to 'High Misdemeanours'. Once again, sworn testimony was lacking. This was, as Neil York has suggested, the ultimate in 'imperial impotence'.[46]

American and domestic threats came together, or apparently so, in 1776, as arson in Portsmouth dockyards once again became a matter of terror and alarm. The well-known case of John the Painter, or James Aitken, as he was also known, executed for arson as an American rebel and spy in 1777 seemed to epitomize the danger facing the British state.[47] In December and January 1776–7, first Portsmouth then Bristol suffered serious fires, the second provoking official alarm. By this time, James Gambier had returned from America to run the Portsmouth dockyard and played an active part in the investigation. Suspicion fell on James Aitken, a native Scot and self-styled American patriot, otherwise known as John the Painter, the subject of a fine study by Jessica Warner. 'During

---

[45] *Hampshire Chronicle*, 21 April 1777.
[46] TNA PRO CO 5/160/fo. 40; Neil L. York, 'Imperial Impotence: Treason in 1774 Massachusetts', *Law and History Review*, 29 (2011), pp. 657–70; Peter D.G. Thomas, *Tea Party to Independence: The Third Phase of the American Revolution 1773–1776* (Oxford, 1991), pp. 48–87; Viola F. Barnes, 'Francis Legge, Governor of Loyalist Nova Scotia 1773–1776', *New England Quarterly*, 4 (3) (1931), pp. 420–47, 1775 disturbances.
[47] Joseph Gurney, *The Trial of James Hill al. James Hinde or James Aitkin (Known Also by the Name of John the Painter) for Feloniously … Setting Fire to the Rope House of HM's Dock-yard … 6 March 17 Geo III, 1777*; Jessica Warner, *John the Painter: The First Modern Terrorist* (London, 2004).

a residence of some years in America he imbibed principles destructive to the interests of this country', claimed the *Newgate Calendar*. Aitkin reportedly received funding from Silas Deane, one of America's commissioners in France. As in the cases of Dudley and Britain in 1771, his initial interrogation was carefully conducted, this time by Sir John Fielding, with representatives of the Board of the Admiralty attending. Aitkin was examined with scrupulous care, being allowed to confront each witness as they presented evidence against him, though he was also foolish enough to be tricked into making damaging admissions to a sympathetic visitor.[48] The final prosecution was not for treason but for arson (under the 1772 Act, probably), a crime without benefit of clergy, and it may have been a careful matter of political calculation that a conviction could be obtained on the less dramatic charge, either for damage to Portsmouth dockyard or for the fires in Bristol. If that tactic did not succeed, there were still numerous thefts and burglaries for which he could be tried. Perhaps executing a Scot for treason at a time when they made up so many of the recruits to the armed forces might have been impolitic. Nevertheless, he was executed in naval style being hauled up on a masthead outside the dockyards where he had started the fire, which was an exceptional way of hanging a civilian.[49]

As in 1770 and 1771, the role of the newspapers and the printing industry in general was highly influential in shaping the image of this affair. As before, suspicions were aroused very early – in Bristol, the *Morning Post* reported, there were some 'violent Americans'. A huge reward of £1,000 was offered in the newspapers for both fires to expedite the investigation. By the end of the first week in February, James Aitken was being interrogated at Bow Street, and witnesses from Portsmouth were brought to give evidence against him.[50] An unprecedented number of pamphlets was published to exploit the drama of his execution on 10 March 1777, many of them claiming to be based on the official shorthand transcript of the trial made by Joseph Gurney, whose more accustomed stamping ground was the Old Bailey. One pamphlet even told in verse the story of Aitken's ghost which appeared to Lord Temple, who had assisted in the investigation, on the night of his execution. Less fancifully, most of the trial accounts record the examination and cross-examinations of the witnesses and the process of the prosecution and defence. His own words were

---

[48] *Newgate Calendar* (London, 1825) III, p. 41; Warner, *John the Painter*, pp. 176, 181; Neil L. York, *Burning the Dockyard: John the Painter and the American Revolution* (Portsmouth, 2001).
[49] Warner, *John the Painter*, p. 183; Howell, *State Trials*, XX, pp. 1317–64, 1365–8; York, *Burning the Dockyard*, p. 11.
[50] *Morning Post*, 21 January 77; *London Gazette*, 25 January 1777; *Morning Chronicle* and *London Advertiser*, 29 January 1777; *Morning Post*, 8 and 18 March 1777 (pamphlets advertised).

supposedly given to a Mr Tomkins for publication after his death, consisting of a strange account of his 'motives' as well as his life story. He explained that Americans (like himself) had to come secretly into the country, because 'our side cannot do things openly and above board, as the Ministry does. Why can they not? Because they are not strong enough.' This kind of statement led Jessica Warner to call him the 'first modern terrorist'.[51]

William Gordon noted in 1788 in his early history of the American Revolution the connection between Aitken's arson and the exceptional legislation of 1777 directed at American privateers and traitors, which suspended habeas corpus for suspected rebels. The Act 'to secure and detain Persons charged with or suspected of, High Treason committed in North America, or on the High Seas, or the Crime of Piracy' meant in effect that prisoners could be held without actually being prosecuted for treason. Though, like previous suspensions of habeas corpus there was actually no mention of the phrase in the title of the bill, the law in fact departed from previous practice in a number of ways, as Paul Halliday has pointed out. It distinguished one group of British subjects from others for the first time (American supporters or activists), and, renewed annually for six years until the end of the war, ran for an unprecedented period. There was no obvious rebellion inside Britain, unlike the brief periods of earlier suspensions during the Jacobite rebellions, but the coincidence of arson and trial of John the Painter provided a usefully emotive context. Opposition to the law in Parliament was fierce.[52] Charles James Fox referred to the 'improbabl[e] story' of John the Painter and remarked that ministers were 'credulous in the extreme', clearly a reference back to the falsehoods of Dudley and Britain. In reply, Lord North rejected the accusation, and argued that conspiracies were best stifled in their earliest stages. The Attorney-General added, expressing a sentiment heard many times since with regard to exceptional 'temporary' measures, 'no innocent man had anything to fear, the guilty man had everything'. That week, perhaps trying to regain the initiative, Burke proposed a motion to inflict

---

[51] *John The Painter's Ghost: How He Appeared on the Night of His Execution to Lord Temple* (London, 1777); *A Short Account of the Motives Which Determined the Man Called John the Painter and Justification of His Conduct, Written by Himself and Sent to His Friend Mr A. Tomkins, with a Request to Publish It after His Execution* (London, 1777), p. 9; *The Trial of James Hill, Alias John the Painter, for Wilfully Setting Fire to the Ropehouse in the King's Yard at Portsmouth* ... (London, 1777); *The Trial of James Aitken, Commonly Called John the Painter, an Incendiary* ... (London: 1777); *The Trial at Large of James Hill Otherwise James Hind, Otherwise James Aitken, Commonly Known by the Name of John the Painter* ... (1777).

[52] See Steffen, *Defining the British State*, p. 95; William Gordon, *The History of the Rise, Progress and Establishment of the Independence of the United States of America*, 3rd ed. (New York, 1801), II, pp. 183–5; Paul D. Halliday, *Habeas Corpus: From England to Empire* (Cambridge, MA, 2010), pp. 250–2.

severe punishment on those who *attempted* arson in the dockyards, the law, he argued, being insufficient for this purpose. The proposal was widely accepted initially, but fell after an initial hearing. In the debate, the suggested law had been extended to include both attempted and successful arson in private docks as well as ships and warehouses. One critic of the death penalty proposal, however, William Meredith, noted that it would have been an ineffective deterrent in the case of James Aitken: 'John the Painter was so far from fearing death, that he courted it', he observed.[53]

James Aitken created his own legend in the various statements published at his death, claiming 'I cannot deny being very active in the riots at Boston, particularly in sinking the tea, and insulting the friends of government, in which I did not escape the notice of many principal persons among the Americans', which has led two modern historians to claim him for membership of the revolutionary Atlantic. There is no record of his participation in the Tea Party, however.[54] Yet there can be no doubt of his desire for martyrdom. 'The people of England may perhaps condemn my action as a very vile one. The Americans will extol it as very noble', he claimed, predicting that he would be hailed as 'a martyr to my country'. Some Americans at least recalled his sacrifice and used him as an example of the threat the individual could pose to the powerful oppressor. 'Great Britain is not without her arsenals, her yards and magazines ... Remember John the Painter', warned one American patriot in 1780, addressing protests to a commander of despised Hessian mercenaries in New Jersey, printed in the *New Jersey Journal* and the *Pennsylvania Packet*: 'he was a poor man, without friends, and unassisted by public council or money'. This writer supposed him to have lost property destroyed at Perth Amboy early in the Revolution, but almost certainly confused him with the portrait painter John Watson (c.1685–1768) whose property, left to his loyalist nephew, was destroyed by patriots during the Revolution.[55]

---

[53] *Derby Mercury*, 14 and 21 March 1777; *Parliamentary Register* (London, 1777), VI, pp. 181, 175–82.

[54] *The Life of James Aitken, Commonly Called John the Painter, and Incendiary ...* (London, 1777), p. 18; more briefly in *The Trial at Large of James Hill ... Commonly Known by the Name of John the Painter ...* 2nd ed. (London, 1777), p. 83; Peter Linebaugh and Marcus Rediker, *The Many-Headed Hydra: Sailors, Slaves, Commoners and the Hidden History of the Revolutionary Atlantic* (London, 2002), p. 221. For the participants in the Tea Party, see Benjamin L. Carp, *Defiance of the Patriots: The Boston Tea Party in the Making of America* (New Haven, 2010).

[55] *A Short Account of the Motives Which Determine the Man Called John the Painter; and Justification of His Conduct, Written by Himself, and Sent to His Friends Mr Tomkins, with a Request to Publish It after His Execution* (London, 1777), p. 13; *Pennsylvania Gazette*, 19 July 1780, also in *Pennsylvania Packet*, 25 July; William A. Whitehead, *Contributions to the Early History of Perth Amboy* (New York, 1856), p. 126; John Hill Morgan, 'John Watson, Painter, Merchant, and Capitalist of New Jersey, 1685–1768', *Proceedings of the American Antiquarian Society*, 50 (1940), pp. 225–317; *The Trial of James Hill Alias John the Painter* (London, 1777), p. 18.

Both the 1770 and the 1776 fires threatened the navy on which British power was based. The *Gaspee*, like the Tea Party, established the limits of British power in the colonies. Equally important, all three incidents were the object of political panic and legal debate, as well as attempts at carefully conducted investigations. Fire and fear drove the three legislative responses between 1770 and 1777, built on converging anxieties about naval supremacy and control of the American colonies. The legality of the political response was a continual concern in government circles: ensuring precise applications of the law was essential to the legitimacy that was proclaimed as fundamental to the Anglo-American world and, moreover, was ingrained in government practices. Arbitrary actions which stretched the legal interpretations too far would undermine that carefully constructed regime. It might have been best, as it was said later, to have seized Americans and brought them over for execution in England (something that was not achievable even in the wartime conditions after 1777), but the concerns of legality and justice – a self-conscious legalism – restrained the government in England in the absence of war. Cautious legalism was one of the surprising responses to threats at this time: as E.P. Thompson put it, 'the essential precondition for the effectiveness of law, in its function as ideology, is that it shall display an independence from gross manipulation and shall seem to be just'.[56] New laws were passed, but proved generally useless in the colonial setting of the 1770s, and the various laws of arson were never consolidated into a coherently defined crime in the eighteenth century.[57] Paranoia took carefully plotted legal routes. In London, Alexander Wedderburn, Solicitor-General, began proceedings against Virginian William Lee, a London tobacco merchant, suspected of a scheme to transport disaffected shipwrights in the naval dockyards to the rebellious colonies, but abandoned it. In addition, there was the failure in 1775 to prosecute a supposed plot to kidnap the king attributed to Stephen Sayre (a well-connected American and former sheriff of London) and to the radical MP John Wilkes. Sayre was locked up in the Tower of London but was released without charge, allegedly because further investigation threatened to expose the existence of government agents embedded in a network of underground activities. Sayre sued the authorities for false imprisonment. Two years later, he left for France.[58]

[56] E.P. Thompson, *Whigs and Hunters: The Origin of the Black Act* (London, 1975), p. 263 and pp. 258–65 more generally.
[57] T.E. Tomlins, ed., *The Law Dictionary, originally complied by Giles Jacobs* (London, 1809) for the details: houses and outhouses were given protection, as were coalmines and mills.
[58] Julie Flavell, 'The Plot to Kidnap George III', *BBC History*, November 2006, pp. 13–16; John Richard Alden, *Stephen Sayre: American Revolutionary Adventurer* (Baton Rouge, 1983), p. 36 and Arthur H. Cash, *John Wilkes: The Scandalous Father of Civil Liberty* (New Haven, 2006), pp. 235, 323–5.

While the government pursued the *conventional* law in England, Massachusetts Governor-General Thomas Gage had declared martial law in Boston in June 1775, following the fighting at Lexington and Concord. Even this step, though, was taken under the Massachusetts charter, but, importantly, before the King declared America in a state of rebellion. Such a tactic was dubious, and the pretext – that because of the 'unnatural rebellion, justice cannot be administered by the common law of the land' – clearly untrue, as all the normal judicial processes were intact.[59] This reinforces A.V. Dicey's point that martial law in the English tradition never involved a suspension of laws, even in an emergency or in what some have called a 'state of exception'; though once common in the pre–1700 period, martial law had become deeply unfashionable in England, as the military customarily acted under the control, and in aid, of the civil powers. The Bostonians well remembered the Porteous affair in Edinburgh in 1736 when an officer had exceeded his legal authority.[60] For many Americans, therefore, legalism was also part of their culture of law, and repeatedly they felt that what was necessary was compelling the British government to follow the common rules. This continued into the revolutionary war when the 'law of nations' was frequently invoked by the Americans to oblige the British to observe the rules of war as understood by European nations.[61] As for the British government, the simple criminal prosecution of Aitken may have been deceptive. Despite a number of attempts to deploy the 1777 Act against Americans brought to London, none were successfully prosecuted. Exceptional times in fact proved remarkably difficult to incorporate in law (see Chapter 6). In 1971, when the death penalty was removed from the crime of arson in the royal dockyards, few in Parliament knew how this law had been created, or why it had been overlooked in the two earlier debates abolishing hanging for the far more serious offence of murder. Questions to the Home Secretary in 1966 had established that no one had been executed for this crime since criminal statistics began in 1856. Yet arson in dockyards was a crucial element in the politics of the 1770s in the Atlantic world.[62]

[59] David E. Engdahl, 'Soldiers, Riots and Revolution: The Law and History of Military Troops in Civil Disorders', *Iowa Law Review*, 57 (1) (1971), p. 28; Gage Proclamation in N. Niles, *Principles and Acts of the Revolution in America* (Baltimore, MD, 1822), pp. 136–8.
[60] David Dyzenhaus, '*Schmitt V. Dicey*: Are States of Emergency inside or outside the Legal Order?', *Cardozo Law Review*, 27 (5) (2008), pp. 2006–40; Porteous affair in Boston, Steven Wilf, 'Placing Blame: Criminal Law and Constitutional Narratives in Revolutionary Boston', *Crime, Histoire & Sociétés/Crime, History & Societies*, 4 (1) (2000), pp. 31–61.
[61] Gwenda Morgan, 'Rhetoric, Reality and Retaliation: The Problem of Implementing the Law of Nations', unpublished paper given at the Twentieth Annual Conference of the Omohundro Institute of Early American History and Culture, Halifax, Nova Scotia, June 2014.
[62] House of Commons, 21 December 1966, vol. 738 cc. 348-9W.

6

War, Kidnapped Americans and Treason

Despite, or perhaps because of, their failure to secure indictments in the colonies, the British authorities continued to explore the possibility of bringing treasonable offenders to England for trial. As we have seen, the 35 Henry VIII law was claimed as the legal licence for this, even though most historians have taken the view that all the legislation for that reign had been annulled. This chapter concerns the seizure of Americans and their legal treatment in London during the American Revolution, when there was in effect a state of war in existence, roughly 1775 onwards. Since no one officially declared war on the colonies, or even the 'rebels', the war has a somewhat uncertain beginning at Lexington and Concord. The legal measures taken in the year after the Declaration of Independence, however, make it clear the British government had taken that to be a declaration of war by itself. The Americans were already anxious about how their prisoners would be treated – and there was a popular fear in America of such a move, to try Americans in London, which can be demonstrated from the newspaper discussions of the Henry VIII law, as outlined in Chapter 5. There were also local myths circulating, shaping actions by otherwise loyal, that is, revolutionary Americans. In Isle of Wight County, Virginia, one man told the Committee of Safety that he had heard that anyone who signed the Continental Association 'would be sent for to England and be hanged'.[1] The suspension of habeas corpus in 1777 specifically for North Americans provided a greater legal clarity to potential proceedings, as it permitted the British government to bring those found on the high seas or in North America, and judged to be American rebels, to England, and hold them until it was convenient to prosecute them for treason. That this law was passed a year after the Declaration of Independence suggests that, even though the fighting had started, the British government was

---

[1] H.R. McIlwaine, ed., *Proceedings of the Committees of Safety Cumberland and Isle of White Counties Virginia, 1775–6* (Richmond, VA: State Libraries, 1919), p. 48, 27 July 1775; see p. 49 for the formula of recantation.

still to some extent viewing the American problem in terms of civil laws rather than the laws of war. Very quickly, there were, in addition to the individual suspected traitors, many sailors captured in wartime operations who were not initially treated as prisoners of war. They, too, were all potentially in danger of being convicted and executed for treason.

Treason and rebellion

Americans might proclaim their rights to the legal liberties of English law, as we saw in Chapter 2; the precise nature of those rights was a matter of contention both in London and in the colonies. Even so vital a guarantee as habeas corpus against wrongful imprisonment was of questionable status in the American colonies, in theory, but was often accepted in practice. Yet settlers were enabled to pass their own laws – and 'provincial control over provincial law' says Hulsebosch 'helps explain the absence of a unitary law for the empire', and why there was no 'Greater Britain' embracing the colonies as well as the metropole.[2] The movement of people accused of offences in one part of the empire to be tried in another threw up the question of unequal rights, rights that were essentially determined by the geography or origin of the accused. The judicial response to rebellion and treason, so obvious in the earlier risings by Scots and English against the Hanoverian dynasty in 1715 and 1745, was less clear with regard to the American Revolution. This was the first time the British Empire had faced a full-scale colonial revolt. Treason as a crime therefore had to be adaptable to the new situation. As Michael Head has emphasized:

> The history of crimes against the state is inglorious. In every epoch, the offences both common law and statutory, have become more draconian, far-reaching and severely punished whenever the ruling establishment felt threatened by domestic opposition, or by foreign rivals, especially once war loomed or armed

---

[2] A.H. Carpenter, 'Habeas Corpus in the Colonies', *The American Historical Review*, 8 (1) (1902), pp. 18–27; Eric R. Friedman, 'Habeas Corpus in Three Dimensions, I: Habeas Corpus as a Common Law Writ', *Harvard Civil Rights-Civil Liberties Law Review*, 46 (2011), pp. 591–618; Anthony Gregory, *The Power of Habeas Corpus in America: From the King's Prerogative to The War on Terror* (New York: Cambridge University Press/The Independent Institute, 2013). Daniel J. Hulsebosch, 'The Ancient Constitution and the Expanding Empire', *Law and History Review*, 21 (3) (2003), pp. 439–82, 479. See also p. 457: under Coke's reading of the 1608 *Calvin's Case*, says Hulsebosch, 'while subjects coming to England would enjoy English liberties, English liberties did not follow Englishman abroad'. As conquered lands, they did have the same rights as people in England, thought Blackstone p. 474. See also Craig Yirush, *Settlers, Liberty and Empire: The Roots of Early American Political Theory, 1675–1775* (Cambridge: Cambridge University Press, 2011).

hostilities broke out. Far from being fixed, or clearly defined by legal criteria, offences evolved and sharp shifts occurred in the frequency of prosecutions of various offences, in response to perceived political dangers.[3]

There were important precedents, again concerning the geography of law and prosecution. As was shown in Chapter 4, treason prosecutions had in effect been cut loose from the place of the alleged offences in the trials following the Jacobite rebellions, largely arising in Scotland, in 1715 and 1745. This broke the longstanding legal principle of a right to trial by your peers in the place or jurisdiction of the alleged crime.[4] The British authorities had failed to prosecute any Americans in the ten years before violence broke out in 1775 – not even for seditious publications, though they did manage to bring John Almon, a largely pro-American London publisher, to court in England for publishing the Junius letters. This was unsuccessful, and suggested that London juries were not easily persuaded of politically defined crimes. Even in the face of violent colonial resistance, as we have seen in the case of the burning of the *Gaspee*, the various laws of treason or arson could not be brought to bear on the suspects.[5] The British government had failed to extend British law to the colonies. The 1777 Act suspending *Habeas Corpus*, however, made it clear that it was designed to overcome these difficulties and facilitate the prosecution of suspected Americans in London rather than in the home territories. The focus of legal action had been removed from the location of the alleged actions, just as it was in the years following the '15 and the '45.

The authorities began with a legal assault on suspect Americans living in London, where they could be easily identified and seized. Arthur Lee, from Virginia and by the 1770s an alderman of the City of London, involved himself in defending the American patriot cause in print, and was largely left alone, but another long-term resident of London, banker Stephen Sayre, found himself accused of plotting treason. This has attracted some attention from historians, as it did at the time, as a reflection of the increasing suspicion of Americans in London, and perhaps also the official paranoia about subversive violence.

> The Orders for apprehending STEPHEN SAYRE, Esq; and seizing his Papers, upon a ridiculous, futile Charge of TREASON, ought to alarm every Man in the

---

[3] Michael Head, *Crimes against the State: From Treason to Terrorism* (Farnham: Ashgate, 2011), p. 21.
[4] Gwenda Morgan and Peter Rushton, *Banishment in the Early Atlantic World: Convicts, Rebels and Slaves* (London: Bloomsbury Academic, 2013).
[5] Gwenda Morgan and Peter Rushton, 'Arson, Treason and Plot: Britain, America and the Law, 1770–1777', *History*, 100 (341) (2015), pp. 374–91, and Chapter 5 here. Neil L. York, 'Imperial Impotence: Treason in 1774 Massachusetts', *Law and History Review*, 29 (2011), pp. 657–70.

Kingdom. The best and worthiest Men in England may fall a Sacrifice to those PARRICIDES, those TRAYTORS, those BLOOD-HOUNDS of Power, and their suborned Evidences, if a speedy Stop is not put to their infamous Proceedings by a general ASSOCIATION of the People.

There were allegations from a Guards officer, who claimed he had talked to Sayre, who was plotting to Kidnap George III. Francis Richardson, a fellow American, and Adjutant to the first Battalion of the first Regiment of Foot Guards, met Sayre at the Pennsylvania coffeehouse, and in a private room, Sayre tried to persuade him to stir up revolutionary feelings among the soldiers. He also is alleged to have said:

> The People were determined to take the Government into their hands and the time was near at hand. That they had a set of fine Fellows who were only waiting the opportunity and that as to tearing to peices [sic] Lord Mansfield, Lord North, Lord Bute etc it would be of no material consequence. They must strike at the fountainhead to which the Informant made answer, you do not means The King. The abovementioned Stephen Sayre replied yes, that the King was at the bottom of all, for he believes Lord North was heartily sick of the business. He then went on and said, the Design was to seize The King going to the House of Lords on the 26th instt., and to carry His Majesty to the Tower.

In addition, he alleged, 'The aforesaid Stephen Sayre inquired particularly into the situation of the Magazine of St James's Guard and the State of that in Hyde Park and finally concluded by saying the Attempt would intirely depend on their Opinion of the temper of the People that day.'[6] The case was clearly some kind of set-up, and failed in the courts, but it succeeded in another way in that most prominent Americans left London soon after, with Sayre ending up as the United States' envoy in a number of European capitals. He tried to sue the authorities in the shape of one government minister, and was later begging for a pension from the United States.

---

[6] *The Crisis: A Defense of American Rights, 1775–6*, ed. N. York (Indianapolis, IN: Liberty Fund, 2016), pp. 41 and 373 *The Trial of the Cause of an Action Brought by Stephen Sayre Esq., against the Right Honourable Earl of Rochford on Thursday 27 June 1776 … Published from Mr Gurney's Notes* (London: G.Kearsley, n.d.); *The Letters of Valens, (Which Originally Appeared in the London Evening Post) with Corrections, Explanatory Notes, and a Preface, by the Author*, William Burke, Richard Burke and Edmund Burke, 1729–1797. p. 42 Letter VI; James Lander, 'A Tale of Two Hoaxes in Britain and France in 1775', *The Historical Journal*, 49 (4) (2006), pp. 995–1024; also in York, 'Imperial Impotence'; Howell, *State Trials*, 20, pp. 1286–317 (Sayre against Rochford); Julie Flavell, *When London Was the Capital of America* (New Haven, CT: Yale University Press, 2010), pp. 143–63. TNA TS 11/542 Stephen Sayre, 1775 case, piece 4, 20th October 1775, the day after the alleged incident on the 19th.

In a letter from Paris in 1778, Benjamin Franklin, Silas Deane and Arthur Lee attempted to propose to Lord North an exchange of prisoners after the American victory at Saratoga the previous autumn. In the middle of their proposal there was, among many complaints of mistreatment, the allegation that Ethan Allen had been 'dragged in chains' to England.[7]

> Col, Parker, a gentleman of rank, was thrown into the common gaol in Boston, covered with wounds, where he perished, unpitied, for want of the common comforts which his situation, and humanity, required.
>
> Col. Ethan Allen, was dragged, in chains, from Canada to England, from England to Ireland, and from thence to New York; at a time when the officers taken from you, in the same expedition, were treated not only with lenity, but every possible indulgence.
>
> The barbarous treatment of Mr Lovel, in Boston, has no parallel. Of the prisoners made in Fort Washington, two-thirds of them perished by the unexampled cruelty and rigours of their captivity. Stripes have been inflicted on some, to make them commit the deepest of all crimes – the fighting against the liberties of their country. Numbers are now groaning in bondage in Africa and India, to which they were compelled by menaces of an immediate ignominious death; as contrary to every rule of war among civilized nations, as to every dictate of humanity

Allen had been captured during his disastrous raid on Canada, an act of private initiative and gross over-confidence following his capture of Fort Ticonderoga and its heavy artillery. He was a prisoner of war in the undeclared war of 1775, attacking Canada on his own initiative. The move was disastrous. Yet his own account of the events, and of his subsequent treatment by the British, made him famous. He became a celebrity on his arrival, as one historian has noted:

> He was the first high profile prisoner garnered by British forces after the outbreak of hostilities and Allen was among the first and only prisoners shipped to England. His presence immediately became a domestic British political issue and a rallying symbol for the opponents of King George's policies towards America. Given this fame, when it looked like Allen might lead Vermont back into allegiance with the Crown, he provided hope for a British turnaround and victory. Much of what the British people knew about Ethan Allen came from copious and widely disseminated newspaper articles.

---

[7] *Morning Chronicle*, 28 January 1778, back page has letter 12 December 1777, from B. Franklin, Silas Deane, Arthur Lee, from Paris to Lord North, proposing an exchange of prisoners; *London Evening Press*, 28 January 1778.

Certainly the London newspapers reported every detail.[8] Historians have had some difficulty in distinguishing the facts from his own myth-making, but the story of indecision and vacillation by the British authorities seems clear. From the start, it was unclear whether Allen and his fellow captives were rebels, traitors or prisoners of war.[9] The newspapers in London tracked events, speculated about Allen's likely treatment, and noted that he and other Americans had retained an experienced legal team, one that consistently acted against the government in the wartime period. Almost as soon as Allen's capture was reported, the press printed his letter to his captor, General Prescott, protesting against his treatment, and that on their arrival in London, he and thirty-two other prisoners were attempting to obtain a writ of *habeas corpus*. Thus, six months before the Declaration of Independence, a pattern, almost a template, had been established for American prisoners brought to London to follow.[10]

This chapter will now focus on the relatively small number of Americans who were arrested for treason in America or on the high during the course of the American Revolutionary War, brought to England, and who faced the prospect of trial in London. Prisoners such as Ebenezer Smith Platt, Samuel Curson and Isaac Gouverneur and others were deliberately targeted in military or naval operations and others such as John Witherspoon Jr., William Buckner and Charles Tomkies were picked up in the course of other operations. The biggest prize of all was Henry Laurens, former president of the US Congress and prospective ambassador to the Netherlands who was captured at sea en route to Europe from America to conclude a treaty with the Dutch. In addition, the case of John Trumbull is of interest, as he was arrested on his arrival in London in the middle of the war. All were charged with or suspected of treason. On arriving in England, each man was interrogated by a justice or court officer, then escorted to

---

[8] Gene Procknow, 'British Fascination with Ethan Allen', *Journal of the American Revolution*, 11 March 2015 (unpaginated, online); *A Narrative of Col. Ethan Allen's Captivity, from the Time of His Being Taken by the British, near Montreal, on the 25th Day of September, in the Year 1775, to the Time of His Exchange, on the 6th Day of May, 1778* (Isaiah Thomas and Alexander Thomas, 1807, registered in New Hampshire); John J. Duffy, and H. Nicholas Muller III, *Inventing Ethan Allen* (Hanover & London: University Press of New England, 2014).

[9] Amanda L. Tyler, 'Habeas Corpus and the American Revolution', *California Law Review*, 103 (2015), pp. 635–98, 649.

[10] *London Gazette*, 4 November 1775 (capture); *Lloyd's Evening Post*, 8 November (Allen's letter to Gen Prescott about his treatment, also in many others such as *Craftsman's* or *Say's Weekly Journal*, 11 November); *London Evening Post*, 23 December 1775, Ethan Allen 'and forty other prisoners' are brought to England; *Morning Chronicle*, 25 December 1775, speculates what the government intended to do with Allen given the prisoners in rebel hands; *London Evening Post*, 2 January 1776, reports that Allen and thirty-two others are trying to get a writ of *habeas corpus*; *The Gazetteer and New Daily Advertiser*, 6 January 1776, reports that Mr Dunning and Mr Alleyne had been retained by the prisoners 'lately brought from America'.

London or retained in London by one or more of the King's Messengers. These were a somewhat shadowy group of men who were employed in the service of the king by the office of the treasury solicitor. They were deployed in the detention, investigation and security of those involved in alleged treason cases.

Ebenezer Smith Platt

'The first American that [the] Government meddled with' as the *Annual Register* and the *Virginia Gazette* put it, was Ebenezer Smith Platt. Much depended on his fate. As the *Virginia Gazette* noted, derived from the London papers,

> If the administration should proceed with rigour against him, then every active man, who has been foremost in American Congresses and Committees, or in executing the orders of such meetings, must take care how he comes to Great Britain. The accusation against Mr Platt is founded on his having not only made free with his Majesty's stores at Savannah, but also traitorously supplied the enemy with a great quantity of ammunition.[11]

The most important aspects of the case were the lengthy legal proceedings, political concern on both sides of the Atlantic and the fact that, despite capturing a known rebel and gunrunner, the British authorities failed to prosecute him successfully. Initially, he had been committed in the West Indies for robbery on the high seas, but the Jamaica Attorney-General argued for a charge of high treason. The Royal Naval commander reported his capture on 30 March 1776:

> I am to acquaint their Lordships that I have seized one Mr Platt. He was a Committe Man at Georgia and is the Man that Boarded the *Philippa*, one Maitland, Master, of Georgia, last year and seized all the Government Gun Powder and carried it to the Rebels. I have had him some days in Irons, but could not get the identity of his Person sworn to untill this afternoon, which was from the Above Maitland and his People that was with him when the Powder was seiz'd, and is now here loading with sugar and as I have seized the above Platt at Port Royall, I presume he must be tryed on this Island for the Robery and Executed on this Island. I shall let his Excellency Sir Basil Keith know about him tomorrow morning and shall inform their Lordships by the next Packet what is done by the said Platt.[12]

---

[11] *Virginia Gazette* (Dixon), 9 May 1777; *Continental Journal*, 8 May 1777, datelined London 18 January.
[12] TNA PRO TS 11/1057/4710, 30 March 1776, Clark Gayton, Vice Admiral, Commander in Chief of HM Ships at Jamaica, Antelope, Port Royal, to Mr Stephens (some punctuation added).

The legal dilemma was compounded by the fact that the initial attack on the official stores occurred at sea, and the subsequent trial in Jamaica had resulted in an acquittal. The second effort by the authorities was therefore redirected to charges of treason which they argued could be tried in England. The Jamaica Attorney-General wrote to Governor Sir Basil Keith, mistaking Platt's first name:

> The affidavit I have submitted to the consideration of the Judge of the Admiralty, and we are both of opinion, that the offence therein charged being committed by a Person coming from shore while the ship lay off Savannah, which is within the body of the Province of Georgia arises out of the Adm[ira]lty jurisdiction and is notcognizable thereby, or by any other criminal Jurisdiction of this Island. The forcibly taking away stores, belonging to, or intended for, the use of the King's Forts, with intent to assist, in carrying on hostile measures then on foot against His Majesty, raises the Offence from Robbery to High Treason, which being committed in Georgia, is cognizable there on 25th Edward the 3d or in England by that Statute and the jurisdiction given by the 33d & 35th of Henry 8th. But the State of Georgia wherein the administration of civil and criminal justice, is silenced by arms, makes in effect this Offence triable, for the present in England only. Under these circumstances I am of Opinion, that William Platt cannot be in such proper and safe custody, as that of the Admiral, who, if he judge proper may send him to England, there to be dealt with according to Law. Had William [*sic*] Platt been apprehended by any civil Magistrate, I suppose the Admiral would have been applied to, through your Excellency to take him under his charge, and send him to England for the purpose aforesaid.

Platt was then sent to England, with the documentation the Jamaican authorities had acquired, namely several affidavits, including that of the captain of the ship from which the military stores had been seized, the *Philippa*.[13] When he arrived in England in November, Platt set about initiating a legal challenge to his arrest. He wrote to the captain of the *Pallas* requesting that an attorney be sent on board, 'in order to have the benefit of the Habeas Corpus Act, as I have been detained a Prisoner these Eight Months upon the accusation of one Capt. Maitland and want nothing but to be tried by the laws of my King and Country.'[14] In December, the Attorney and Solicitor Generals gave their opinion on this request, and also reviewed the evidence in the case against him, described as

---

[13] TNA PRO TS 11/1057/4710, 10 April 1776, Thomas Harrison and on back, 'Attorney General of Jamaica to Sir Basil Keith' – after Harrison's signature it says 'To his Excellency the Governor'; 25 July 1776, Letter from Vice Adm[ira]l Gayton Commander in Chief HM Ships at Jamaica, – inclosing the 'several affidavits relative to William Platt'; see also Sheldon S. Cohen, 'The Odyssey of Ebenezer Smith Platt', *Journal of American Studies*, 18 (2) (1984), pp. 255–74.

[14] TNA PRO TS 11/1057/4710, 4 October 1776, Ebenezer S. Platt to Capt. Hughes of the *Centaur*.

Platt 'late a committee man of the Province of Georgia', now 'sent to England as rebel Prisoner'. They said that it was unclear what the basis for the charges is since the documents do not show that the gunpowder was actually taken to the rebels: nor do they establish that Platt was there, or even on Cockspur Island. They went on,

> The Violence imputed to Platt and the rest at the Town of Savannah will amount to High Treason, if the Committee, under whose orders they professed to Act, can be *proved* to conduct the rebellion in Georgia, and it is understood, by report, that *in fact* they do; or if his violence can be referred in any other way, to a connection with the treasonable force which is in arms within that province. Supposing that to be the case, It will be proper to commit him for trial in the ordinary course; namely, by taking the Informations of the witnesses, issuing a warrant thereupon to bring him to be examined, and, if any of the charge appears well founded, commitment. The temper of our Laws certainly requires, that every Prisoner should be allowed the means of suing out a Habeas Corpus. But it seems fitter to proceed to his Examination; and to discharge him, if nothing appears in proof against him; or to commit him regularly if a sufficient foundation be laid for that.

In effect, they were unsure whether the evidence was strong enough, and were anxious to make sure that the accused's legal rights in treason cases (which alone guaranteed consultation and representation by a lawyer, unlike in ordinary felonies) were scrupulously observed. There were other similar issues at the same time: General Charles Lee, a British-American patriot, had been captured in America, and there was speculation about his likely fate:

> Many and various are the conjectures respecting the mode which Government will adopt for the trial of General Lee when he arrives. Some say he will be tried by the martial law, others that he will be indicted at the Old Bailey as a Rebel, and take his chance of the issue of an arraignment for High Treason. – Be the mode what it may, his fate seems to be pretty obvious.

This indicates the foregone conclusion likely in cases of American treason, in the eyes of the press, though in fact Lee was exchanged.[15]

In his story of the events after his trial in Jamaica, Platt himself described in the 8 January 1778 petition that he was brought to England aboard the frigate *Pallas*, and on his arrival at Portsmouth was moved from ship to ship to evade a writ of habeas corpus acquired by his friends on his behalf. Before it could

---

[15] TNA PRO TS 11/1057/4710, 10 December 1776, Mr Attorney and Solliciter General, signed E.Thurlow and A. Wedderburn, to Earl of Suffolk, in response to letter from the Lordships of the Admiralty, with ten enclosures. Underlining as in the original. *Morning Chronicle,* 14 February 1777.

be served, an express was sent from the Treasury by their solicitor and he was removed again to the *Centaur*. He was finally put ashore, examined by a justice, sent up to London and committed to Clerkenwell Bridewell for two days. He was brought before Sir John Fielding and Justice Addington, and committed by them on 23 January 1777 to Newgate prison where he remained in irons. His lawyer asserted to the authorities that 'Mr Platt is now confined in double irons'. 'It is in your power at least to prevent this Extrutiating Torment', he wrote, 'humanity I hope will direct you to write to … alleviate this Torture. I shall proceed in the Petition for tryal as expeditiously as possible'.[16] John Wilkes then raised his predicament in Parliament claiming that his commitment was illegal in view of the wording of the charge and in the light of the Habeas Corpus Act. In the debate over the 1777 legislation suspending habeas corpus for North Americans – in itself the first time that rights had been defined by geographic origin, Wilkes deployed the case of Platt as a dreadful warning of the consequences of the proposed law. In his speech on 17 February,

> There is now, Sir, actually in Newgate, an American merchant, named Ebenezer Smith Platt, who stands committed so lately as 23d of last January, charged with high treason at Savannah in the colony of Georgia in North America. He is committed by the well-known justice Addington and, as I was informed, was not allowed to see any of the witnesses against him, nor even to hear the affidavits read. He had before been tried on the same charge, at Kingston, Jamaica, and acquitted. I never saw him, but I have read an attested copy of the warrant of his commitment. He is charged generally with high treason, which I take to be an illegal commitment. I do not pretend, Sir, to a deep knowledge of the law. I have only the attentive reading of a private gentleman. I build my faith on some known and approved authorities, a Blackstone, a Burn and a very few others. Those authors agree, that every warrant of commitment ought to set forth the cause specially, that is to say, not for treason or felony in general, but for treason in compassing the death of the king, or levying war against his majesty in the realm, or counterfeiting the king's coin.

He went on:

> The case of Plat, Sir, gives us an instance of another violation of the law, an evasion of the Habeas Corpus Act, that holy statute, which ministers hold in abhorrence, and are allowed in England to evade with impunity, in America to

---

[16] TNA PRO TS 11/1057/4710, 25 January 1777, J. Colton, Symonds Inn, to Chamberlayne; 8 January 1778, Platt to the Earl of Suffolk. See the legal technicalities in Tyler, 'Habeas Corpus and the American Revolution', pp. 635–98.

suspend for nearly twelvemonth. The history of it is this: Plat was first confined to the *Antelope* for three months, then removed to the *Boreas* for three months, then carried on board the *Pallas* and in her brought in irons to England. On her arrival at Portsmouth he was removed on board the *Centaur* for three weeks, then to the *Barfleur*. On the 4th January, an Habeas Corpus was obtained, directed to the captain of the *Barfleur*; but before it could be served, an express was sent from the Treasury by their solicitor, and Plat was removed again to the *Centaur*, before the Habeas Corpus could arrive at Portsmouth. The return to the Habeas Corpus was thus eluded, but on his friends' being determined to sue out another, Plat was at last sent to the capital, and in the illegal mode, which I have stated, was committed to Newgate.

The lesson was obvious, said Wilkes, as this was all too reminiscent of the political control of the judicial process of the previous centuries: 'Can ministers, Sir, who are capable of thus trampling on our most sacred laws, be too narrowly watched, too deeply suspected, too strongly guarded against?'[17]

Two days later, Platt's lawyers brought his case before the judges of the Old Bailey, applying for his release on the grounds that, as he had not been indicted, he had a right to *habeas corpus*. The legal arguments by his counsel were countered by the Attorney-General and a colleague, with the argument that he had been ordered into custody on the evidence of two witnesses (from Savannah, Georgia) and, besides, the proper place for such a plea in cases of treason was the King's Bench, and not the equivalent of the assizes, the Old Bailey being the court of *oyer and terminer* shared by London and the county of Middlesex. They had a point, and the judges agreed that it was not within their powers to intervene. Platt's lawyers had pointed to the way that habeas corpus pleas concerning people accused of crimes in, for example, Yorkshire 200 miles away, were admissible in their court, as were writs for *a certiorari*, that is, removal to that jurisdiction. In reply, the Attorney-General emphasized the problems of an imperial power when faced with the problems of, for example, piracy. With an offence committed largely at sea, or on land where no court system existed, there was little choice but to try such cases in London, as had happened many times in the past, with regard to famous offenders such as Captain Kidd. The 1777 Act specified that Americans suspected of high treason or piracy on the high seas were liable to arrest and transportation to any place, to await trial at the

---

[17] *The Parliamentary History of England*, vol. 19 (London: T. Hansard, 1814), p. 30, also printed in *Morning Chronicle*, 25 February 1777.

King's pleasure, so the choice of analogy was carefully made. The issue of rights established by *Magna Carta*, to be tried by one's peers in the jurisdiction where the alleged offence had been committed, was central both to this case and to the increasing scope of London courts in the empire.[18] The result was that Platt was informed that bail would be forthcoming if he applied for it in the appropriate court – that of King's Bench, but in the meantime Parliament suspended *habeas corpus*. Platt himself was not hopeful. He wrote to Benjamin Franklin in Paris on 10 March:

> Since my Confinement here I have taken every Legal step to Indeavour to be brought to tryall but could not, and fear I shall not be, as I am now detained under that Accurs'd, and Arbitary Law, for the suspention of the Habeous Corpus Act until January 1778, until which time, if not longer I expect to remain, unless through the Blessings of God, the Americans shou'd Continue to go on with eaqual sucksess, as they have for these few months last past done, which I believe wou'd be the meanes of Discharging me and all others.

In parallel, his future wife Elizabeth Wright (whom he had met through her mother Patricia, one of several who visited and aided imprisoned Americans) wrote to Franklin to keep him appraised of the situation, informing him of Wilkes's speech, and conveying (via his daughter) Wilkes's regards.[19] Nevertheless, since he had been arrested before the passing of the Act, his lawyers brought a case in May at King's Bench before Lord Chief Justice Mansfield. The plea was unsuccessful, predictable given their 'disastrous' strategy, as Amanda Tyler has called it, since Mansfield concluded that Platt's case was exactly the kind that the Act was designed to deal with, a judgement that all the other judges supported.[20] Mansfield, claimed the newspaper reports, 'was clear, concise and decisive'.[21] This did not prevent Platt and his supporters from petitioning Parliament: in December the Duke of Richmond presented his document to the House of Lords during the debate on the Bill continuing the Act suspending *habeas corpus*, which was read and 'put on the table'. Platt's story, it was reported, was read 'one way, by two Dukes, of Richmond and Manchester', and 'in a very different manner' by the

---

[18] The Proceedings of the Old Bailey, 19 February 1777, Old Bailey online, Ref: f17770219-1.
[19] https://franklinpapers.org/ (accessed 9 May 2019); letters from Platt, 10 March, 6 May, 27 December 1777; from Wright, 10 March, 6 May, 10 November, 27 December: it seems that she wrote, enclosing his latters.
[20] Anon, *An Argument in the Case of Ebenezer Smith Platt, Now under Confinement for High Treason, by a Gentleman of the Law* (London: G. Kearsley, 1777). Tyler, 'Habeas Corpus and the American Revolution', p. 669.
[21] *Morning Chronicle*, 13 May 1777.

Earls of Suffolk and Sandwich.[22] The Lords, though, seemed to have requested copies of all the warrants and orders for imprisonment of Americans to be presented to them. In rebuttal of accusations of illegal activity, while admitting the failure to produce the documents, the cases of Ethan Allen and Ebenezer Platt were mentioned by Lord Suffolk. The American press noted the speech by the Duke of Richmond pointing to the failure to use Henry VIII Act with regard to Ethan Allen, 'who was bought home prisoner', having been found in arms. The failure to prosecute Allen, and his return to America to be exchanged, derived from 'motives of humanity', he claimed.[23] What in fact was not trumpeted by either side was a double failure, of the Habeas Corpus Act to guarantee freedom, and the Treason Act to guarantee a prosecution. In effect, both sides had failed in their key objectives, something that was to be repeated in subsequent cases.

In America, these events and proceedings were noted both in the press and in Congress. Much of the information in the American newspapers was filched from editions of London papers captured by privateers or traded from neutral sources. *The Morning Chronicle, General Evening Press, The Gazetteer and New Daily Advertiser*, among other newspapers, published full accounts of the debate at the Old Bailey, and an official transcription of the proceedings was printed in the sessions papers advertised at the end of March. Similarly, the King's Bench hearing and, particularly, Lord Mansfield's judgement in the case were given widespread publicity.[24] In August 1777, a petition for Platt reached the US Congress:

> The delegates of Georgia laid before Congress a letter from Ebenezer S. Platt, dated Newgate in London, 16th of May 1777, and directed to Seth Cuthbert, merchant in Georgia, representing that he had been apprehended and imprisoned on account of his having acted under the authority of Congress, and requesting to be supplied with a sum of money, and that he may be demanded in exchange; whereupon
>
> *Resolved*, That the American commissioners at the court of France be directed to supply the said Ebenezer S Platt with a sum not exceeding one hundred pounds sterling; and that they demand his person in exchange for some person in our power
>
> *Resolved*, That the sum so to be advanced be charged to the state of Georgia

---

[22] *London Evening Post* and *Morning Chronicle*, 9 December 1777.
[23] *Providence Gazette*, 13 July 1776 (page 2), also in *American Gazette*, 23 July 1776; *Morning Chronicle*, 3 March 1778.
[24] *The Morning Chronicle, General Evening Press, The Gazetteer and New Daily Advertiser*, 27 February 1777; *Morning Post*, 26 March 1777 for the advertisement for the printed sessions proceedings.

In parallel, therefore the American diplomats in Paris began a more sustained campaign on his behalf.[25] Thus, through the diplomatic efforts of Benjamin Franklin and the intervention of the Committee for the Support of American Prisoners, Platt was released in April 1778 and sent to Paris. In the London newspapers, he thanked the Committee and all the 'Friends to Liberty' who had contributed to his support during his confinement in Newgate. The Committee was certainly spending large sums of money – more than £150 on the expenses incurred by discharged prisoners alone, including Platt, they reported in May 1778. He was set at liberty, he complained, 'in a strange country, destitute of money, and every means of returning to his native country'. As one American newspaper report put it, in an 'Extract of letters from a young gentleman (a native of Pennsylvania) in London to his father in this city':

> I could with much more satisfaction endure all the hardships that I know you suffer, than to be in the enemy's country a tame spectator and witness of the more inhuman treatment of my countrymen – Some in irons in Newgate – some starving at Gosport, Plymouth etc. – some sent to Africa – some to the East Indies – and the more moderate, as it is termed, that of absolutely being obliged to take arms against their countrymen.

This was an exaggeration, but the plight of Americans in British hands was established by these images within a year of the outbreak of hostilities.[26]

John Trumbull

The warning contained in the *Virginia Gazette* on how people coming to England should be careful not to give rise to suspicion in the light of the treatment meted out to Platt was borne out by the subsequent experience of John Trumbull. Trumbull was the son of Jonathan Trumbull, the wartime Governor of Connecticut, and himself a former army officer in the Continental Army who resigned his commission in 1777 (at the age of twenty-one) due to dissatisfaction over his promotion prospects. Initially he travelled to France to work in a branch

---

[25] *Journals of Congress*, vol. 3 (New York: John Patterson, 1800), p. 348, 26 August.
[26] *Parliamentary History* 19, 3–53, 461–6, 560–2; Ebenezer Smith Platt to the Commissioners, *Chapters of John Adams*, 6, Paris 21 April 1778; *London Evening Press,* 19 March 1778, *Public Advertiser,* 8 May 1778 (Committee for the Support of American Prisoners); *Pennsylvania Packet*, 4 August 1778, copied in the *Massachusetts Spy*, 27 August from Philadelphia 4 August. Tyler, 'Habeas Corpus and the American Revolution', pp. 103, 635–98, 669–78).

of the family business but then moved to England in 1780 to study art under Benjamin West, having previously sought and received assurances that it would be safe for him to do so. In a period of high tension, however, he was arrested as a spy and imprisoned in Tothill Fields Bridewell on suspicion of high treason. He suspected that he might owe his arrest to the execution by the Americans of Colonel John André who really was a spy but it was more likely due to the company he kept. Trumbull attracted the attention of Edmund Burke, leading opposition critic of the war in parliament and William Hodgson who lobbied for his release and was discharged in August 1781 after a period of seven months in Tothill Fields Bridewell. Hodgson supplied him with money to support himself, get to France and return to America.[27]

The arrest and interrogation were reported widely in the London papers in November 1780, and their accounts were faithfully reproduced in the American press less than three months later. Turnbull had been arrested with two other men, one of them the Major Tyler who had been accompanying Winslow Warren to France when he had been captured. These events also ran in parallel with the reports of Henry Laurens's detention in the Tower of London (see below). The *London Courant* immediately drew a comparison with the 'vindictive, disgraceful and frivolous attacks' on Stephen Sayre and Ebenezer Platt, and warned of the dangers of these arrests – legally, they did not have to be justified, the paper said, and 'every prison becomes a bastille'. The English were not immune, it alleged, as this law was extended, and every 'public character in England obnoxious to their views, every distinguished friend to liberty, has long been proscribed'.[28]

The *American Journal and General Advertiser* in March 1781 went to the trouble of publishing very detailed texts from the London newspapers. They noted that in the examination of John Trumbull 'for High treason, at the Public Office, Bow Street, November 21, 1780', Trumbull, reported as 'son of the Rebel Governor Trumbull, of the province of Connecticut, in America', was brought up from New Prison for re-examination before Sampson Wright, Esq. and Mr Addington. On this occasion when three letters, amongst others found in

---

[27] John Trumbull, *American Remonstrances: Letters by John Trumbull* (London, New York and New Haven: 1841), pp. 40ff for resignation letter; Theodore Sizer, ed., *The Autobiography of Colonel John Trumbull: Patriot-Artist, 1756–1843* (New Haven: Yale University Press, 1841), p. 5; S.S. Cohen, *British Supporters of the American Revolution, 1775–1783: The Role of the 'Middling-level' Activists* (Woodbridge: The Boydell Press, 2004), p. 37. For Hodgson, see Sheldon S. Cohen, *Yankee Sailors in British Gaols: Prisoners of War at Forton and Mill, 1777–1783* (Newark, DE: University of Delaware Press, 1995), p. 196.

[28] *London Courant*, 22 November 1780; See also *New Annual Register 1780* (1781), and *The Gentleman's Magazine*, vol. 50 (1780), p. 584 for a full account, mentioning Benjamin West.

his possession, were produced and read in evidence against him. The papers faithfully printed them. One read:

> Dear Sir,
> I have this moment received your very friendly and polite letter and sincerely thank you for its contents. Your observations are very just, and I shall, in every particular, follow your advice.
>
> Since I wrote to you I had some conversation with my father, on the subject of my intended expedition; and as he strongly opposes my thoughts of going by way of the West Indies, ad at the same time warmly recommended our old route by Ostend and France: I am a little dubious how to act but shall, I believe, relinquish my original plan and adopt the last. In that case the providing myself with camp equipage here would be quite unnecessary, from the impossibility of conveying it with me, at the same time that I shall, in the kingdom of our dear and great Ally, be able to procure myself everything that is necessary, and as good in quality as in London. From these considerations, request our mutual friend Waters not to execute my late orders until he hears further from me; and if he has already given his directions, to stop them, as in the course of a few days I shall finally be resolved.
>
> I shall rejoice to join you in any plan that you and Waters may adopt, and hope in God, that your expectations may not be disappointed. A direct conveyance is certain of all others, to be preferred; but should your present hopes not be realized, what other schemes have you, and when do you expect to leave England? If you will not look upon one as an intruder, I will accompany you in any way that promises to lead to the desired port. I shall and will at any time leave this in twenty four hours. As I shall anxiously await the issue of your deliberations, be so obliging as to drop me a line on the receipt of this, and at the same time send me your direction.
> The papers mention that Mr. Laurens is permitted to walk about the Tower. Is the report founded in fact? Remember me kindly to Waters and Tyler.[29]

The men arresting Trumbull reported his demeanour at the occasion, when 'the prisoner behaved much like a gentleman, making no attempt to escape, only desiring to go to the necessary; which Mr Bond said he could not consent to, till he first delivered up the papers that were about him; under an apprehension, that he wanted by this pretext to make away with them'. The papers were scarcely hidden, being in the top of a bureau, and the arresting officer (Bond) seems not have trusted his prisoner very much.

---

[29] *American Journal and General Advertiser*, 7 March 1781.

Trumbull seems to have been a mixture of overconfidence and stupidity, but, despite his being a former officer in the American Continental Army, the British authorities had no evidence against him, and had to let him go. Whether he managed to study art for any great length of time with American Benjamin West is unclear, but he returned to become one of the most famous painters of revolutionary scenes and the key participants in American independence.

Winslow Warren

A second well-connected American apparently caught travelling to France by ship and brought to London 'as a prisoner of war' was from a passionately patriotic Boston family, the son of Mercy Otis Warren, who was by 1781 living in the house of former British governor Thomas Hutchinson, and who wrote one of the first histories of the American Revolution. As the London papers reported it,

> On Tuesday last Mr Winslow Warren, Son to Lieutenant-Governor Warren of Massachusetts, was apprehended at his Lodgings on a warrant for High Treason. Two Gentlemen then on a Visit to Mr Warren, were taken with him to Bow Street, after being very strictly searched by the Constables, and every Paper taken out of their Pockets. Mr Warren is a Lad of eighteen or nineteen Years of Age, taken some months ago on the Banks of Newfoundland, on a Voyage from Boston to France, and was brought to England as a Prisoner of War, in the Vessel, Captain Berkeley, about ten weeks ago, just before his School-fellow, Major Tiler, was apprehended; and it is more than probable the Information against him came from the same Quarter. He was set at Liberty after a short examination at Lord Hillsborough's, but was desired to wait upon his Lordship the next Evening. There was no Accusation whatever against him, but for a Correspondence with Major Tiler (the Letter of both of them being stopped and examined at the Post Office), and their Letters, chiefly on the Score of former Friendships, their Amours in London, Accounts of the Girls, and those Girls' Billet Doux afforded no small Share of Diversion and Laughter to the Magistrates.

Their initial imprisonment seems to have been token, and he acted as perhaps a young man in London at the time might act, enjoying what the city had to offer.

The dismissive tone of the last line seems to have reflected the authorities' response to this young man.[30] The presence of these young men in London may

---

[30] *Lloyds Evening Post*, 29–31 January 1781 and *London Courant*, 31 January 1781.

have become widespread knowledge, at least according to one report in the *Newport Mercury* (Rhode Island), apparently quoting a letter from a 'gentleman of character' in France, who says:

> I am sure if you and my other friends knew the importance of good intelligence on this side of the water, you would be more particular; for it is no less strange than true, that all the intelligence we get is from England; and this day we have an account that Col. Trumbull is actually confined, and that Major Tyler has made his [page1/page2] escape. Be assured, that so many Americans going to England has extremely disgusted the French.

The British authorities seem equally puzzled, and rather amused.[31]

Samuel Curson and Isaac Gouverneur

Like Platt, Samuel Curson and Isaac Gouverneur were arms dealers but they operated on a scale far larger and more systematically than Platt, having business dealings with the Dutch, the French and the Americans. Interest in their detention came about when James Lovell, chair of the Congressional Committee for Foreign Affairs in the US Congress, sought the cooperation of Benjamin Franklin, American Commissioner in France in locating the two men. Franklin's principal interest was American prisoners was in trying to establish cartels for the exchange of American sailors, but not soldiers, confined in British gaols and facing charges of treason and piracy under the 1777 North Act which suspended Habeas Corpus. In turn Franklin contacted William Hodgson, successful London merchant and head of the Committee for the Relief of American prisoners held primarily in Forten (Portsmouth) and Mill (Plymouth) gaols. One of the most conspicuous of the so-called 'American friends', William Hodgson, who handled large sums of money to assist prisoners, found that his first task was to find the two men before offering them financial aid at the insistence of Congress for their maintenance and defence. He was surprised to find they had no need of this support, at least not yet.

Curson and Platt were captured on St. Eustatius following the invasion of the Dutch island by Admiral Rodney and General Vaughan in February 1781. Writing home, Rodney declared that he was fully convinced 'that had it not been for their treasonable correspondence, the southern colonies must have long

[31] *Newport Mercury*, 17 March 1781.

since submitted'.³² The two men were 'stripped of every thing but their wearing apparel, their books, chapters and slaves having been taken from them and Mrs Gouverneur with a young Infant turned out of doors'. James Lovell supposed that 'special severity had been shewn to them in consequence of their acting as agents to Congress'. They were put on board the *Vengeance* man of war which anchored at Spithead on 28 June but the two men were kept on board and 'continued in confinement' until July 25.

Treason prosecutions were never a formality. In July 1781, the Secretary of State was writing to the Attorney and Solicitor Generals seeking their opinion on the nature of the crime with which the men were to be charged and how best to secure their conviction and punishment. A number of possibilities were explored but dismissed on the grounds that they were unsatisfactory. The question came down to this. If it could be proved that the goods they had shipped had arrived safely in the hands of the rebels 'they could be accused of treason in His Majesty's Colonies and committed on those grounds'.³³ On 25 July Curson and Gouverneur were

> put in the charge of two of the King's messengers and brought to the Earl of Hillsborough's office in Cleveland-row where after undergoing an examination, they were ordered into the custody of Mr Mann, the messenger and Friday night at ten o'clock, they were brought to the American department at Whitehall, where their conduct underwent a more severe regular inquiry before the Attorney and Solicitor Generals, Messrs Chamberlayne and White, Solicitors, and Mr Sampson Wright, the presiding magistrate in Bow Street. This examination lasted a considerable time, and several chapters were produced and read; after which Mr Gouverneur was committed to New-Prison, charged with high treason, in carrying on a correspondence with the American agent in Amsterdam John Adams, and furnishing the colonials with ammunition and every other species of military stores for the support of the war.

When the question was put 'Whether they had shipped such goods, producing one of their bill of lading books',

> which they both answered in the affirmative, and replied that since the first of their residence in St. Eustatia they had become Burghers of that island, and always considered their allegiance was to the States of Holland, and had acted uprightly and consistent with their government, for when the goods were

---

[32] Kenneth Breen, 'Sir George Rodney and St Eustatius in the American War: A Commercial and Naval Distraction, 1775–8', *Mariner's Mirror*, 84 (2) (1998), pp. 193–203, 197.
[33] TNA CO5/160, ff. 149–50 and 153–5.

shipped they were not published, nor under any restriction. In consequence of which Mr Gouverneur was conducted to the place of his confinement by two of the messengers under a warrant signed by Mr Wright – but his colleague Mr Curson, being very much indisposed, was indulged with the liberty of remaining in the custody of Mr Mann the messenger.

That Curson and Gouverneur claimed loyalty to the Dutch and the Dutch government protested their detention on the same grounds appears to have undermined the charge of treason against them but, as in the case of Platt and others their detention dragged on.[34]

Curson and Gouverneur were unaware of the progress of their case and sought information from Franklin in Paris. When William Hodgson attempted to meet Gouvereur at the New Prison to which he had been committed, he was denied access but had better luck with Curson, who seriously ill was housed by one of the king's messenger. 'When we shall be at liberty', they wrote to Franklin, 'God only knows, nothing of the kind, has yet come to our ears; if at any time it is in your power to give us any news on that score, you may easily conceive what singular satisfaction, it will afford us'. For over a year, both men were kept by one of the King's Messengers, Mr Mann who had been told to treat them well 'because of their rank'.[35]

The Dutch States General, reported the *London Courant*, remonstrated strongly against the unjust and cruel treatment the two men had experienced since the capture of St. Eustatius. The newspaper looked favourably on the case of the two young men and concluded that they were subjects of the Dutch considering how long they had lived on the island and the fact they were burghers, that is, full members of the merchant guild. A week later the same paper appeared even more sympathetic to Curson and Gouverneur declaring that it appeared 'very inconsistent' that they 'should now be confined for high treason committed in the colony of Pennsylvania. When they were living in St. Eustatia, and had been settled there before the war commenced'. Three weeks later the *Whitehall Evening Post* reported the remonstrance 'from their Mightinesses'. In March the *Morning Herald* reported that they were bailed 'on terms similar to Mr Laurens'. Writing from Ostend to Benjamin Franklin on 3 March William Alexander claimed that he had the good fortune to procure the liberty of Gouverneur and Carson after

---

[34] *St James's Chronicle*, 28 July 1781; *Morning Post*, 3 August 1781; *Newport Mercury*, 1 November 1781, from London, 9 August, online at http://fronklinchapters.org/franklin/framedVolumes.jsp?vol=36&page=092b (accessed 11 July 2015), vol. 35, p. 343, vol. 36, p. 92; Catherine M. Prelinger, 'Benjamin Franklin and the American Prisoners of War in England during the American Revolution', *William and Mary Quarterly*, 3rd ser., 32 (April 1975), pp. 261–94.
[35] TNA HO 42/48/104.

Mr Hodgson had tried and failed. On 11 May, the *St. James Chronicle* reported they were discharged from their recognizance in the Court of King's Bench. Their books and chapters, which had been sent home from Eustatia by Sir George Rodney, were at the same time returned to them at the Earl of Shelburne's office. Doubtless the fall of the North administration facilitated their release. Rumour had it that they proposed to bring an action against their prosecutors. There were other disputed aspects to the conquest of St. Eustatius, particularly the treatment and expulsion of the Jewish community, which left Rodney to become entangled in legal suits for years afterwards.[36]

John Witherspoon

Another captive acquired as a result of the invasion of St. Eustatius was John Witherspoon Jr, the son of the Reverend John Witherspoon, president of the College of New Jersey (Princeton), signatory to the Declaration of Independence and member of the US Congress. He was captured on a French privateering vessel the *De Graff*, on which he was serving as a surgeon, and carried to England. As an American serving aboard a French privateer he could have been incarcerated in Forten or Mill prisons and charged with treason. With some urging from the Committee on Foreign Affairs in Congress, and his father, negotiations for his release were opened in the summer of 1781. With financial assistance provided by William Hodgson and with aid from Franklin, Witherspoon travelled to Paris, there being no boats leaving for America from Britain.

In a letter dated 11 September 1781, Franklin informed Witherspoon that he had written immediately to London following the receipt of his letter of the 15th June in order to secure his son's liberty and have him supplied with money.

> I have now the pleasure to inform you that I have this day received an answer from thence, acquainting me that he is discharg'd, and that he has been furnish'd with the money he required and intends immediately to leave England: so that I hope you will soon have the Pleasure of seeing him. My grandson will acquaint you with the steps he has taken respecting the letter of credit you enclos'd to me.[37]

---

[36] *Whitehall Evening Post*, 7 February 1782; *Morning Herald*, 2 March 1782; *St James Chronicle*, 11 May 1782. The Amsterdam merchants protested at length, see TNA CO 246/1, ff. 217–20 is a long letter from a list of names headed by Jans Van der Soll, of the Committee of Merchants for the Affairs of St. Eustatius, 2 October 1781. In fact, their account books survive in the National Archive.

[37] James Lovell for the Committee for Foreign Affairs to Benjamin Franklin, vol. 33, p. 48; John Witherspoon to Benjamin Franklin, 15 June 1781, vol. 35, p. 464.

Charles Tomkies and William Buckner

Less well known is the case of Charles Tomkies and William Buckner, two Virginians who were seized by a royal navy ship in Chesapeake Bay and taken to England in July 1781 where they protested their lack of involvement in the war and stressed the plight of their families back home without their support. Out for a cruise in the Bay, they claimed, they had made a big mistake in approaching what they took to be a French man of war only to find it was a royal navy ship. When they reached England, the captain, Thomas Pye of the *Diligent* reported that they were men of considerable property, had never been to sea before, were not in arms when taken and held no office civil or military. They were ready to give their parole that they would not take up arms against Great Britain and requested that they be allowed to return to America on the first available ship.[38]

In their petition Tomkies and Buckner wrote that they had never known distress until now, that they had been cut off in a moment from their country, families and children without the least prospect of being restored to their distressed families. All their children were small and their situation on the River was within thirty miles of the place where the horrors of war were being carried on when they left Virginia.

> We have my lord experienced every kind of distress, indeed we have suffered for the want of the common comforts of life, but our greatest distress is our anxiety for our familys and children being without friends or money, or even an Acquaintance to whom we can apply to represent our situation of uncertainty. The justice told us our discharge should be sent but long have we waited with anxious expectation, but still remain in a state of suspense; this situation my lord is equal to death itself, we beg request in the most earnest manner that your lordship would be so human as to give directions for our exchange or that we may be suffered to return to our familys in some ship going to America which would be most desirable to us. An enquiry into the nature of our captivity would find that they were more unfortunate and hardly dealt with, than many of their Countrymen, who had already been discharged.[39]

Their petition was read by Lord Sandwich and Lord George Germain. The Governor of Virginia Thomas Nelson instructed the Virginia delegates in Congress of their capture but it is not certain that they received this letter. Unlike Platt, Curson and Gouverneur, Trumbull and Witherspoon, Tomkies

---

[38] TNA CO5/132/208.
[39] TNA CO5/132/206.

and Buckner's problem was that they lacked contacts in England, did not know William Hodgson and his organization or have any links with Benjamin Franklin in Paris. They lacked contacts, friends, access to funds and were not known to the Congress. What they shared with them was a lengthy period of confinement. Ironically despite the plausibility of their story, it was completely false. Tomkies was a captain in the 7th Virginia Regiment and Buckner, also a captain, was in the militia and a shipmaster in the Virginia navy, and they had been sent by General Steuben to welcome the French fleet. They subsequently applied for and received compensation for their imprisonment and Buckner's widow received a pension for his services.[40]

Henry Laurens

There was no such problem over the identity of Henry Laurens, a former president of the Congress who was taken prisoner at sea when his vessel the *Mercury* was captured by a British naval vessel. He had embarked on board the brigantine, a packet belonging to Congress with a sloop of war the *Saratoga* of sixteen guns. The expected escorts did not appear and Laurens ordered the *Mercury* and *Saratoga* to sea. The sloop proved too slow and Laurens recommended that it return to the Delaware, it being of little value for a defence. The *Mercury* was pursued by a British frigate of twenty-eight guns. It was poorly defended but Laurens had been anxious to be on his way to Europe to conclude a treaty with the Dutch and raise funds for the American War. When capture appeared inevitable, Laurens had thrown many of his chapters overboard keeping only a few, but they were recovered from the sea by sailors from the British ship.[41]

Laurens was landed at Dartmouth in the west country, put under the charge of Lieutenant Norris, who in a postchaise with four horses drove rapidly towards London where they arrived on 5 October. Some hours were taken up in collecting together two or three of the ministers, and a justice of the peace. Laurens described what happened next as follows:

> About 11 o'clock at night, I was sent under a strong guard, up three pair of stairs, in Scotland-Yard, into a very small chamber. Two king's messengers were placed

---

[40] The war pension application made by Tomkies's widow found at http://revwarapps.org/w6304.pdf (accessed 12 July 2018), a site maintained by William T. Graves, which also has the details of William Buckner – a pilot, and confirmation of service by witnesses etc. Buckner's pension application also survives on the same website.

[41] *Narrative of the Capture of Henry Laurens* (Charleston, 1857)

for the whole night at one door, and a subaltern's guard of soldiers at the other. As I was, and had been for some days, so ill as to be incapable of getting into or out of a carriage, or up or down stairs, without help. I looked upon all this parade to be calculated for intimidation.

The next morning, 6 October, from Scotland-Yard I was conducted again, under guard, to the secretary's office, White Hall, where were present, Lord Hillsborough, Lord Stormont, Lord George Germain, Mr Chamberlain, solicitor of the treasury, Mr Knox, under secretary, Mr Justice Addington, and others.

They established his identity and that a commission from Congress to him to borrow money in Europe signed by Samuel Huntington President and Charles Thomson Secretary was genuine. There were no further questions and he was told by Lord Stormont that he was to be committed to the Tower of London, not to a prison, 'you must have no idea of a prison'. The London papers reported his capture and confinement, but commented that, along with the defection of Benedict Arnold to the British cause, it 'does not appear to have harmed the Americans, or benefited the cause of this country'. Almost immediately, it was said that the strictures of his confinement were relaxed (in fact within a week, according to the newspapers, in contrast to that of Lord George Gordon, instigator of the eponymous riots).[42] According to Laurens's own account, the magistrate 'Mr Justice Addington' issued a warrant to the Lieutenant of the Tower, to 'receive and confine me'. Their 'Lordships' orders were

> to confine me a close prisoner; to be locked up every night; to be in the custody of two wardens, who were not to suffer me to be out of their sight one moment day or night; to allow me no liberty of speaking to any person to; to deprive me of the use of men and ink; to suffer no letter to be brought to me, nor any to go from me.

He remained a prisoner in the Tower for fifteen months during which time efforts were continually made to get him to accept a pardon which he rejected. Occasionally he was reported to have the freedom to walk inside the Tower gardens and ramparts. Much to Laurens's annoyance, Franklin was under the illusion that he was satisfied with his treatment and he rejected the offer of £100 which was made to him since, as he said, he had money of his own. 'This is the first voice of seeming consolation from my country, now near thirteen months confined in the tower, near fifteen months since Congress knew I was a prisoner: seeming consolation indeed.' The ministry, he had been informed, wished to get

---

[42] *London Evening Post*, 18–21 November 1781 and 21–23 November 1781.

rid of him but differed as to the proper means. Subsequently he arranged his own exchange with Lord Cornwallis who had in the meantime lost the battle of Yorktown.[43]

Conclusion

None of this ragbag of individuals, captured and brought to London as enemies or traitors, came to trial, though the British government undertook the preliminary stages of such prosecutions in several instances. The accused were usually interviewed at the port where they arrived, carried to London by King's Messengers, interrogated by ministers of state, often with the highest legal authorities, the treasury solicitor who was responsible for the King's Messengers, with a justice of the peace on hand to issue the necessary paperwork. With the exception of Tomkies and Buckner, the Committee of Foreign Affairs of the Congress raised these cases with Benjamin Franklin in Passy who in turn raised them with William Hodgson. The latter's assistance was most beneficial at the point when prisoners were released from their imprisonment and needed financial aid to leave the country. Details of their cases appeared in the English and American Press, often favourable to the Americans, but when raised by opposition figures in parliament such as Wilkes and Burke, it was not necessarily to their advantage. When Henry Laurens was belatedly recognized as one of the 'American unfortunates', he much resented the failure of Congress to recognize his ill treatment and lengthy imprisonment. The ministers of the crown lacked legal expertise and it would seem they also did not have the political will to pursue them. Their own laws did not help: if there *were* two witnesses against any of their captives, they were more than 3,000 miles away on the other side of the Atlantic. Revolutionary times proved no more conducive to the successful implementation of Britain's draconian treason laws than the decades preceding them. Yet the imprisonment for 'treason and piracy' was also a mass phenomenon: in contrast to the individuals discussed here, a large number of American sailors were captured and imprisoned. The procedure seems to have been to bring the most important – the officers – before a magistrate first who then ordered their incarceration for treason, and then this was extended to the rest. One Portsmouth magistrate called them 'traitors', 'damned rebels' and pirates, saying

[43] Laurens, *Narrative of the Capture*, pp. 26, 37, 39, 55; 50–1.

that they deserve no leniency. Yet the prisoners at Portsmouth were sometimes visited by David Hartley MP, who was assisting in negotiating their exchange as ordinary prisoners of war, though this was largely after Burgoyne's surrender at the end of 1781, when, recalled one prisoner Timothy Connor, conditions improved and there was more 'humanity' in their treatment. There were many attempts at escape, and even to volunteer for the Royal Navy, but the latter were refused because 'the Prisoners are committed by a Magistrate for treason or Piracies'. Even when, at the end of the war, Americans were finally treated as prisoners of war, George III still requested a list of them for him to pardon for their 'crimes'.[44] This illustrates the ambiguity of the different statuses of rebels, traitors and prisoners of war discussed in Chapter 2. The British government, partly because there were so many British soldiers in American hands, had to deal with the American authorities for purposes of prisoner exchange, as though with a foreign power like France. Yet, almost to the end of the war, the British also maintained the pretence that these men were rebels against a legitimate state, not fighters for a lawful, sovereign enemy. The law of treason was in effect useless in these circumstances.

---

[44] Cohen, *Yankee Sailors in British Gaols*, pp. 17 and 69; Timothy Connor, 'A Yankee Privateersman in Prison in England, 1777–1779', *New England Historical and Geneaological Register*, 30 (1876), pp. 174–8 and 343–52, 347 and 349. See Tyler, 'Habeas Corpus and the American Revolution', pp. 691–3 for the changing legal framework of British treatment of American prisoners at the end of the war.

7

Loyalism and Patriotism

Problems and interpretations of loyalism

Divided loyalties accompany all rebellions, and the American Revolution was no exception. This differed, though, in that the rebels in this instance managed to repress or expel their opponents who they defined as traitors. For the first time since the 1640s, the rebels were not the ones driven into exile. Figures are uncertain: perhaps 20–30 per cent of the population of the thirteen colonies were loyalists, not more than 300,000, and of those perhaps a fifth, around 61,000, left or were forced to leave, taking with them at least 15,000 slaves. About one in forty of the white residents left is one calculation.[1] Thus, some fought, some hid and some ran. Some loyalists may have suffered in silence, but many others formed regiments and fought alongside the troops from Britain. Many might be called 'disaffected' rather than loyal to Britain, a word often used in the eighteenth century to indicate sentiment rather than action. The extent of that feeling, of 'passive' loyalism, is not clear.[2] The extent of this 'treason' to a new nation pales when compared with the American Patriots' theoretical 'treason' to Britain. Yet treason, and the deployment of the laws of treason, was more discussed than acted upon through legal proceedings. Exile was rarely the outcome of a judicial sentence, though some were banished: others simply fled. Other forms of treatment such as imprisonment may have been ordered officially, but were only unusually the result of a full legal trial. The same was true of banishment of loyalists which was often achieved without formal legal

---

[1] M. Jasanoff, *Liberty's Exiles: American Loyalists in the Revolutionary World* (New York: Random House/Alfred A. Knopf, 2011); Harry M. Ward, *The War for Independence and the Transformation of American Society* (London: UCL Press, 1999), p. 35.
[2] Anne M. Ousterhout, *A State Divided: Opposition to the American Revolution* (New York: Greenwood Press, 1987) talks of the disaffected rather than loyalists, as few felt any particular loyalty to Britain. Richard A. Overfield, 'A Patriot Dilemma: The Treatment of Passive Loyalists and Neutrals in Revolutionary Maryland', *Maryland Historical Magazine*, 68 (2) (1973), pp. 140–59.

processes. Loyalism was viewed, but not treated judicially, as treason in most cases. The consequence is paradoxical: there were only a handful of treason trials in the American Revolution and, as far as records are sufficient, few executions. It was not only the British who failed to bring their opponents to court but only to jail (see Chapter 6 for the 'kidnapped' Americans in British hands).

Before the Revolution: 'Safety' and exclusion

Polarization in the years preceding the Declaration of Independence had already forged rival patriotisms in the American colonies. This is not the place to recapitulate the way historians have restored to loyalism its place in the story of the United States, but it is worth noting that what began as an attempt to rescue loyalists from the 'condescension of history', in which they had largely been forgotten, has resulted in to a modern situation of considerable historiographical understanding of the complex social, economic roots of loyalism. This was not a single movement, but emerges from recent studies as very local, personal and, in many areas, deeply felt. There is no simple view that can be taken of them, certainly not that of their contemporaries the American patriots.[3] Some historians have seen loyalists as victims:

> The British failed to restore royal authority in Georgia and South Carolina, not because Loyalists were too few, too passive, or too cruel, but because the rebels relentlessly murdered, imprisoned, abused, and intimidated those who supported the king's government. Many British officers recognized this situation and sympathized with the Loyalists' plight. 'The richest loyalist runs the risk of becoming a beggar' if left unprotected by the British army, a Hessian officer noted in 1778.

---

[3] See, as examples, of the early efforts, Claude H. Van Tyne, *The Loyalists in the American Revolution* (London: Macmillan, 1902) and James H. Stark, *The Loyalists of Massachusetts and the Other Side of the American Revolution* (Boston, MA: W. B. Clarke, 1910). More modern contributions (a selective list) are Robert M. Calhoon, *The Loyalists in Revolutionary America, 1760–1781* (1973), Phillip Papas, *That Ever Loyal Island: Staten Island and the American Revolution* (New York: New York University Press, 2007); Judith L. Van Buskirk, *Generous Enemies: Patriots and Loyalists in Revolutionary New York* (Philadelphia, PA: University of Pennsylvania Press, 2002); Joseph S. Tiedemann, Eugene R. Fingerhut, and Robert W. Venables, eds, *The Other Loyalists: Ordinary People, Royalism, and the Revolution in the Middle Colonies, 1763–1787* (Albany, NY: State University of New York Press, 2009); Mary Beth Norton, *The British-Americans: The Loyalist Exiles in England, 1774–1789* (Boston, MA: Little Brown and Co, 1972), Jim Piecuch, *Three Peoples, One King: Loyalists, Indians, and Slaves in the American Revolutionary South, 1775–1782* (Columbia, SC: University of South Carolina Press, 2008).

The issue of coercion and legitimacy pervaded the years of conflict between the British government and its North American colonies between 1774 and 1776.[4] The Coercive Acts against the unpacifiable people of Boston in 1774 – known, understandably as the Intolerable Acts to the Americans – made explicit the notion of legitimate force held among the British government ministers (these were the Administration of Justice Act; Massachusetts Government Act; Boston Port Bill). Benjamin Franklin may have lampooned them as laws made to enforce obedience to Parliament, but the British had already behaved as an occupying force – Richard Archer rightly pointed to the shock of the treatment of Boston. The resentment caused the formation of committees of safety at state and county level and the development of formal and informal systems of restriction and exclusion of loyalists. According to contemporary David Ramsay, it was at this time that Whigs and Tories became part of everyday language, designating the patriotic and the loyalist camps for the first time. 'No revolution was ever effected with greater unanimity, or with more order and regularity', wrote Ramsay later of his state of South Carolina: 'the Whigs acted by system, and in concert with their brethren in the adjacent states and were directed by a council of safety composed of the wisest men in the province. They easily carried every point – seized the leaders of the royalists and dispersed their followers.'[5] The conflict over loyalties and sovereignty took different forms, with the British relying on the supremacy of parliament, and the colonists asserting their rights on the basis of the colonial legislatures' orders and statutes to implement measures against loyalists. Mass popular violence became an instrument of extra-legal action, continuing a tradition that had been established by protests against the Stamp Act and its accompanying legislation. Holger Hoock puts such violence at the centre of the revolutionary process, but there was also a less emotional and more seriously sincere effort to seek a rationale in law and rights for the processes of commanding loyalty through coercive means.[6]

Other forces were at work, notably the undermining of the workings of the British state in the colonies as a means of resistance. Secure communications

---

[4] Piecuch, *Three Peoples, One King*, Kindle Loc. 258–62.
[5] Richard Archer, *As if an Enemy's Country: The British Occupation of Boston and the Origins of Revolution* (New York: Oxford University Press, 2010); D. Ramsay, *History of South Carolina*, 3 vols (Trenton, NJ: Isaac Collins, 1785), vol. I, pp. 258 and 260.
[6] A.M. Schlesinger, 'Political Mobs and the American Revolution, 1765–6', *Proceedings of the American Philosophical Society*, 99 (4) (1955), pp. 244–50. Holger Hoock, *Scars of Independence: America's Violent Birth* (New York: Penguin/Random House, 2018); Glenn A. Moots and Phillip Hamilton, eds, *Justifying Revolution: Law, Virtue, and Violence in the American War of Independence* (Political Violence in North America) (Norman, Oklahoma: University of Oklahoma Press, 2018).

became a priority for both sides in the 1770s, and the Congress and the British authorities fought to control the system to their advantage. In the case of the postal service, a mixture of coercion was followed by the exclusion of British officials. The postal service had proved vulnerable to interception for years, and at least one British governor of Massachusetts, Sir Francis Bernard, complained in 1769 that he was tired of seeing his letters from London in the newspapers almost before he had read them. This event ruined whatever reputation he had left in Massachusetts.[7] The British records of the post office indicate the state of fear and alarm these public servants felt by the mid-1770s, and reflect also the doubts and hesitations among their superiors as to how to respond. On the one hand, the British authorities could never be sure that their correspondence was not being read, and on the other, Congress and the leading Americans wanted to set up a rival service which *they* could trust. This was proposed and implemented in part by William Goddard, but to his great bitterness the job was given elsewhere. This system, reported in the London press as 'the Continental Posts', was in embryo in 1774 but beginning to replace the British system by 1775.[8] The situation of the British postal officials was now under dire pressure, and some of their difficulties emerge from their letters to their senior manager, Postmaster General Anthony Todd. Significantly, in New York Hugh Finlay had had to abandon his office after an attack, and had taken refuge aboard a British ship in the harbour when he wrote about the possibilities of him relocating to Canada:

> All communication by land between Canada and New York is now stopped; I cannot think of attempting to return by any way near the old route, but my knowledge of the country gives me hope of joining my family at any rate, as soon as I have performed all the duty as D[eputy] P[ost]Master General points out to me in the present situation of affairs; I most sincerely wish to be once more in a land where quiet, peace and good order yet reign; but how long Canada may enjoy a tranquil state, is very uncertain; it was rumoured in Albany that the Provincial troops had laid a plan to penetrate as far into Canada this summer as possible.

> Mr Foxcroft and I think it is very probable that the Post Office may be entirely shut up in a short time – we found that we could take no steps in these days of

---

[7] Colin Nicholson, 'Governor Francis Bernard, the Massachusetts Friends of Government, and the Advent of the Revolution', *Proc. Mass.Hist.Soc.*, 3rd ser., 103 (1991), pp. 24–113, 25.
[8] Richard R. John, *Spreading the News: The American Postal System from Franklin to Morse* (Cambridge, MA: Harvard University Press, 1995), pp. 130–1.

trouble and universal confusion to prevent the mails from being opened – Few men care to write by post, some because their letters are not safe in His Majesty's Mails; however, as long as our mails are permitted to pass to the Southward, unobstructed by constitutional Inspectors, we shall continue to keep the Post on foot although the Postage (we fear) will not defray the Costs of riding work.

He commented on the impossibility of getting letters through safely without interference:

> It is the intention of some of the Colonists to intercept his Majesties Packet boats with a design to obtain intelligence, all private correspondence will cease, no man will dare to write his sentiments on common subjects lest his meaning be misconstrued. If unhappily it is known that a man does not concur in every resolve of the different committees, and deem well done whatever is done, the Lord have mercy upon that poor man, he is held up immediately as an enemy to American liberty, he is declared to be a tool of the Ministry, then tar feathers and much worse is to be dreaded.
>
> The Presses are now all shut up against publications in favour of government. Poor Rivingtons (in this city) was the last, he stood singly for a long time but a few days after the sailing of the last Packet a Party of Horse headed by a Capt Sears and Capt Broome (formerly merchants here) came from Connecticut and seized his Types, for daring to publish an Explanation of Lord North's Motion.
>
> This Violence of the People is incredible and the leading Men have taken effectual means that nothing shall be said or wrote to open the Eyes of this Population.

Goddard himself was under legal consideration by the London authorities because of his management of postal affairs in Rhode Island: they reported to New York that the Attorney-General and another senior lawyer

> are both of opinion that it will be best to commence a prosecution against Goddard as soon as sufficient proof can he had against him to have the matter determined, whether he can be held to bail or not; if he cannot our Jurisdiction is so circumscribed that a prosecution will have no effect and the Law entirely evaded. In England the practice is to hold the persons to bail in all cases, but the prosecution there is in the Court of Exchequer, our practice here is quite different, therefore if he can't be held to bail application ought to be made to parliament for all persons offending against the Act of the 9th of Queen Anne to be held to bail otherwise any person moving out of the colony he [is] prosecuted in, to another, the action ceases of course.

This eloquently sums up the situation of many British administrators as the ground was cut from under them. In this instance, there was apparently prospect of any treason proceedings, only one for a minor fraud.⁹ This process of exclusion and replacement was also aimed at port officials and legal officers, implementing the formation of a nascent 'American' state within the shell of the British colonies. Non-cooperation (with, say, the demands for prosecution of offenders involved in disturbances such as the burning of *The Gaspee* or the Boston Tea Party) was accompanied by replacement of personnel if possible, at the level of magistrates and judges. As Aptheker has noted,

> In all the States, Tories were expelled from whatever public offices they may have been holding, and were barred from being elected to any. They were generally forbidden to serve as ministers, teachers, lawyers and doctors, either by law of by social practice. They were disenfranchised, by law, in five States, and by practice through the Revolutionary area.

Van Tyne came to the same conclusions from his survey of anti-loyalist measures, asserting that

> The average Patriot seemed unable to view the Loyalist in any other light than as a traitor. They finally came to make no distinction between Benedict Arnold and a Tory who had consistently opposed the Revolution from its very inception … On the ground that only citizens should be allowed the right to vote, and those who had not taken an oath of allegiance were not citizens, the Tory was early deprived of his vote in every citizens, the Tory was early deprived of his vote in every state.

The rights to legal redress, making a valid will, guardianship of orphans, in effect 'all legal actions' were denied to loyalists. New York State also attacked Tory members of the bar (in October 1779), and 'two years before, New Jersey had closed her courts to councillors and attorneys-at-law who were known as Loyalists', and the same measure was taken against teachers.¹⁰ Van Tyne overdoes his case here, mingling policies from different times and contexts, such as those

---

[9] TNA CO5 135, ff. 13–14 Hugh Finlay to Anthony Todd, on board the Kingfisher, 20 May 1775; f21C Foxcroft in New York to Todd, 6 December 1775; T 1/509/37-8, 5 April 1774; see *Public Advertiser*, 26 May and 2 June 1774; *Morning Chronicle*, 23 June 1774 for reports about Goddard's activities; see also POST 48/4; Anthony Todd to John Foxcroft and Hugh Finlay, 9 December 1774, Franklin Papers, Founders Online, National Archives, online at http://founders.archives.gov/documents/Franklin/01-21-02-0202 (last update: 2 November 2015) from *The Papers of Benjamin Franklin*, vol. 21, *January 1, 1774, through March 22, 1775*, ed. William B. Willcox. New Haven and London: Yale University Press, 1978, pp. 375–6.

[10] Herbert Aptheker, *The American Revolution, 1763–1783: A History of the American People* (New York: International Publishers, 1960, new ed. 1993), pp. 125–6; Van Tyne, *The Loyalists in the American Revolution*, pp. 190–2, 195–7.

adopted in 1774–5 along with many of those taken during the war. There was a shift in emphasis in wartime, as Ward rightly emphasizes:

> In the prosecution of the war, the American revolutionaries did not seek to recast definitions of treason and sedition. The realities of a civil war, with citizens of different persuasions in areas controlled by one or the other contending armies, necessitated the mitigation of severity of punishments, otherwise there would have been an endless bloodbath of retaliation. The greatest abridgement of rights came during the first year of the war from governmental authority exercised by makeshift committees of safety, extralegal provincial conventions and congresses, and implementation of martial law.[11]

As we shall see, prosecutions for treason increased once the shooting started, and most of those accused by the Americans were discovered working in some way for the British. Before 1776, there was a mixture of assertive power and coercion, deploying both force and law, directed by the committees of safety. Despite many individual cases of person assault and abuse, a certain level of legalistic caution made the committees of safety in the years after the attack on Boston adopt a quest for legitimacy as well as success in political dominance. Colin Williams argues that the committees of safety in the Hudson valley conducted many actions against loyalists, but these were often accompanied by doubts about their legitimacy, and committees tried to justify their arrests and imprisonment of suspects in legal terms, if only retrospectively.[12] Other forms of extra-legal action against opponents – particularly the use of public humiliation *charivari*-like punishments such as tarring-and-feathering, were particularly dangerous if not controlled. The embittering experience of Georgia loyalist Thomas Brown, tortured by patriots, left him both physically marked and disabled and a fiercely cruel opponent of American patriots. David Ramsay, in his history of South Carolina, accused him of cruelty and breaches of the rules of war, provoking a passionate response from Brown, then in his prosperous Caribbean retreat. Brown defended the executions of prisoners surrendered or captured in the field, and explained the context that provided (in his eyes) their justification.[13]

---

[11] Ward, *The War for Independence*, p. 49.
[12] Colin Williams, 'New York's Committees in the American Revolution', in James M. Johnson, Christopher Pryslopski and Andrew Villani (eds), *Key to the Northern Country: The Hudson River Valley in the American Revolution* (Albany, NY: State University of New York Press, 2013), pp. 48–83.
[13] Edward J. Cashin, *The King's Ranger: Thomas Brown and the American Revolution on the Southern Frontier* (Athens, GA: University of Georgia Press, 1989); Brown's response to Ramsay is in Rev. George White's *Historical Collections of Georgia: Containing the Most Interesting Facts, Traditions, Biographical Sketches, Anecdotes, etc., Relating to Its History and Antiquities, from the First Settlement to the Present* (New York City: Pudney and Russell, 1854), pp. 614–20. Ramsay continually denigrates Brown, see *History*, vol. 2, p. 237 among many others.

The committees of safety at the local level may have been concerned to bring this kind of mob violence under control. There is a much longer history here, says Gary Gestle, of the relation between loyalty, liberty and coercion in America.[14]

Force led both sides to conclude that the other had in some way induced their supporters to become followers of an unjustified cause: it was, for many, difficult to believe that could be sincere reasons for supporting the opposing side. Although personal animosity led many incidents to turn violent against individuals, both sides regarded the other as having been deluded in many ways. Until the end of the war, British commanders were sure that Americans had rebelled because they had been deceived by an elite who had their own interests in independence, and were equally confident that, given the opportunity, large numbers of loyalists would emerge to provide decisive assistance to the British cause. Lord Francis Rawdon wrote, 'It has been the fashion to say that the Loyalists were few in number, and that their activity in our cause was never as such as ought to have claimed our gratitude.' He thought of this as a 'most unjust opinion', pointing to the fact that 5,000 white people had left Charleston with the British withdrawal: 'this List of Sufferers surely is not be reckoned small'. American patriots, too, thought of loyalism as a kind of blindness and delusion which could be destroyed.[15]

Oaths and organizations

The role of oath-taking was highlighted in Chapter 2 as part of a common culture of loyalty performance in the British Atlantic. The enforcement of oaths, or the inducement of people to take them, intensified as states followed the instructions of Congress to introduce Test Acts, with penalties, in 1776.

As David Ramsay described it:

> Very soon after the declaration of independence, the danger of retaining men in the state, who wished to subvert its constitution, suggested. to the legislature of South-Carolina the necessity of securing itself against those who still abetted royal government, and wished for its re-establishment. A test-oath was therefore framed in 1776; but this was tendered only to those persons who had given some open evidence of their disaffection. The officers of the King, under the late regal

---

[14] Gary Geste, *Liberty and Coercion: The Paradox of American Government from the Founding to the Present* (Princeton NJ: Princeton University Press, 2015).
[15] Quoted in Piecuch, *Three Peoples*, Kindle Loc. 8545–51.

constitution, and a few others of suspected characters, having, on requisition, refused to take it, were obliged to leave the state. In the year 1778 the legislature enacted an oath or affirmation of allegiance, to be taken by every adult male, which was in the following words:

I, A B, do swear or affirm, that I will bear true faith and allegiance to the state of SouthCarolina, and will faithfully support, maintain and defend the same, against George the third, King of Great-Britain, his successors, abettors, and all other enemies and opposers whatsoever, and will, without delay, discover to the executive authority, or some one justice of the peace in this state, all plots and conspiracies that may come to my knowledge against the said state, or any other of the United States of America. So help me God.

In addition to this, an oath to abjure the King of Great-Britain was required of all officers of the state, both civil and military. They who refused the oath or affirmation above recited were obliged to depart the country. But they had a choice of either leaving their families, or of taking them away. They were also allowed to sell and carry off their estates, or to appoint attornies in their absence to take care of them. The defence of the country, requiring both the personal services and the contribution of its inhabitants, that all might be on an equal footing, the unsold estates of these gentlemen, in common with other absentees, were taxed double; but the idea of confiscation, at this period of the contest, was, by the legislature, uniformly reprobated. Notwithstanding this humane line of conduct, no indulgence with regard to property was given by British authority to the citizens of South Carolina after the reduction of Charleston. In vain was leave solicited in the capitulation, for those who chose it to sell their estates and leave the country. This was not only refused, but their estates were sequestered, and they deprived of the means of supporting themselves, unless they would submit to a government which many of them had abjured, and all of them had renounced.

In effect, the rule was swear the oath or leave. In fact, Ramsay remembered that many of the 'royalists' retreated to their plantations, to remain relatively unmolested.[16] Yet things were much more fraught in South Carolina, as armed groups formed and there was a danger of a local civil war. The surviving records confirm the basic wordage, and that the formula was already in place by early 1776, by which there had been clashes between rival armed groups. As Piecuch has shown, both sides were quick to arm themselves. An oath was designed for the previously insurgent, who had been disarmed, who had swear to 'to the best of my power, aid and support the authority of Congress, and every authority

---

[16] Ramsay, *History*, vol. 1, pp. 106–7.

derived from them: and also, that I will pay obedience to the Continental and Provincial Councils, according to the true meaning and spirit of the Association entered into by the Congress of this colony, on the 4th of June last. SO HELP ME GOD.'[17]

In New York, rather later than the other states, because of the interruptions caused in the autumn of 1776 by the war, the assembly ruled that:

> Whereas divers of the subjects of this State have been seduced from their allegiance to the same, by the arts of subtle and wicked emissaries from the enemy, and prevailed upon, by various and delusive promises, to leave their wives and children and join the army of the King of Great Britain, in direct violation of the great duties they owe to their country, their families and posterity. And whereas it hath been represented to this Convention, on the part of the said persons, that sundry of them having been deceived by the enemy, and instead of being protected, have either been totally neglected, or compelled to take up arms for the express purpose of enslaving and destroying their fellow citizens, are become sensible of their error, and very desirous of returning to their allegiance, and participating with their countrymen in the enjoyment of the inestimable rights and liberties secured to the good people of this State by the constitution and government thereof. And whereas divers of the said persons, as well as others, who have been guilty of treasonable acts against this State, for fear of the punishment due to their respective crimes, secrete themselves within the same.
>
> And whereas humanity directs that no means should be left unessayed to prevent the effusion of blood, and to give those an opportunity of resuming to their duty, who by wicked men may have been seduced therefrom. This Convention do, therefore, in the name and by the authority of the good people of this State, ordain, determine, declare and proclaim, that all such of the said delinquents above described, as shall on or before the first day of July next, voluntarily appear before any magistrate or field officer of the militia of this State, and take the following oath of allegiance to this State, viz:
>
> I, do most solemnly swear in the presence of Almighty God, that I will bear true allegiance to the State of New-York, and in all things do my duty as a good and faithful subject of the said State
>
> Ordered, That the same be published, and that Mr. Loudon be directed to print 1,000 copies, in handbills, and that he send them to this place as soon as possible.[18]

---

[17] *The State Records of South Carolina: Extracts from the Journals of the Provincial Congress of South Carolina, 1775-6*, ed. W.E. Hemphill and W.A. Wates (Columbia, SC: South Carolina State Archives Dept, 1960), p. 231, 13 March 1776; Piecuch, *Three Peoples, One King*.

[18] *Journals of the Provincial Congress, Provincial Convention, Committee of Safety and Council of Safety of the State of New York, 1775-1777*, vol. 1 (Albany: Thurlow Reed, Printer to the State, 1842), p. 920, 19 May 1777.

Civil disabilities were imposed gradually as these test oaths were introduced. In some ways these mirrored, but in an extreme and exaggerated way, the civil disabilities imposed in England on those who would not conform to the Church of England, but, without the tacit methods of inclusion that many groups benefited from there such as affirmation rather than oath and co-option onto administratively significant bodies. There was no intention to re-admit the loyalists by the back door. Significantly, though, refusal to take the oath rarely resulted in a potentially lethal prosecution for treason. Van Tyne in his 1902 history used dramatic language, discussing the processes, of the 'Inquisition' against loyalists, and 'reconcentration camps and banishment', a striking counter image when the concentration camp had only just been invented by the British in their South African (Boer) War of 1900–1, where 26,000 civilians had died of disease. Yet he pointed to the threatened consequences of refusing to take an oath of allegiance – such as 'banishment or imprisonment, but not death' in places such as South Carolina. He notes that the earliest test acts were directed at government officers, then professional men, then all free white male citizens, usually above sixteen, although Maryland and Pennsylvania above eighteen, Delaware twenty-one.[19] More recent studies confirm the essential progress of the test acts, but scholars such as Robert C. Doyle have also noted that as the war progressed, some states became much more severe: 'in January 1778 Massachusetts raised the stakes. Persons who joined the enemy after 19 April 1775 and were captured be committed to jail and then sent to the British lines. If they returned, the death penalty be imposed.' Similarly, New York might double-tax people who refused to appear to answer charges, and they could be removed to enemy lines. Confiscations progressed as well, and the properties added a source of income to some states such as Maryland and New York which made millions of dollars from sale of confiscated properties, which had been ordered by Congress under exile laws in 1778: 'Loyalists became exiles in their own country.'[20] The extent of opposition to the process is not clear in many instances, but in New Hampshire, Wilbur Siebert calculated that during the 'association test' of summer 1776, 8,199 men signed, and 773 refused, that is about 9 per cent or one in eleven. This did include 200 Quakers. Some Tories had already fled from the colony by then, including some prominent members of the House of

---

[19] Van Tyne, *The Loyalists in the American Revolution:* see the chapter on 'The Inquisition', and discussion of S Carolina pp. 65–7; targets of the oaths, pp. 130–2; 'under the ban of the law' (Ch. 9 p. 190), and 'reconcentration camps', pp. 201ff).
[20] Robert C. Doyle, *The Enemy in Our Hands: America's Treatment of Enemy Prisoners of War from the Revolution to the War on Terror* (Lexington, KY: University of Kentucky Press, 2011), pp. 38–40, 40.

Assembly who had been expelled.[21] On the other hand, this process of exclusion was not permanent, and there were ways of return available for many who changed their minds and took the oath. The resulting level of disenfranchisement of so many produced something of a crisis or democratic deficit in many states, and the mobilization of smaller farmers and artisans, particularly through the militias, led to campaigns for the reduction of property qualifications for the franchise. The war therefore saw many states reduce the property qualifications, and drives to continue the process continued after the war.[22]

Forbidden speech

If speaking the oaths was becoming compulsory through coercive measures, speaking against the United States or any of its constituents came under new forms of laws. In effect, both treason and sedition laws had to be amended to replace king and parliament with the United States, Congress or any of the States' constitutional arrangements. As Ward has rightly noted,

> the American patriots made no effort to alter the commonly understood notions of treason or sedition. Their only change was to replace the King with the United States and delete all the crimes involving sex with his family.

Many of the new states created new military regulations whereby the expression of dissent criticism became, for all ranks, punishable under military law (mostly fines of wages at the less serious end of the crime). Control over civilians was more problematical. As Van Tyne alleges, 'another kind of attack upon the Tory was the legislative prohibition of free speech and the free press. As a war measure, it had every excuse'. Connecticut had passed a law in the 16th Year of Geo III (1776) – the last to be designated in that way – making it an offence to

---

[21] Wilbur H. Siebert, *The Loyalist Refugees of New Hampshire* (Columbus: The Ohio State University Press, 1916), p. 3; see Josiah Smith's diary, particularly 1780-1 for those estates sequestered and people banished: Josiah Smith and Mabel L. Webber, 'Josiah Smith's Diary, 1780–1781 (Continued)', *The South Carolina Historical and Genealogical Magazine*, 34 (4) (October, 1933), pp. 194–210 (he was one of the exiles in St. Augustine); Thompson Westcott, *Names of the Persons Who Took the Oath of Allegiance to the State of Pennsylvania between the Years 1777 and 1789, with a History of the 'Test Laws' of Pennsylvania* (Philadelphia: John Campbell, no date).

[22] See David A. Bateman, *Disenfranchising Democracy: Constructing the Electorate in the United States* (Cambridge: Cambridge University Press, 2018); Charles Olsen, *Artisans for Independence; Philadelphia Mechanics and the American Revolution* (Syracuse, NY: University of Syracuse Press, 1975), Table 2.2, pp. 57 and 74.

speak, write or by any overt act libelled or defamed Congress or the acts of the state's General Assembly, punishable by fine, imprisonment or disenfranchised, and liable to costs of prosecution. 'There are abundant proofs in the Connecticut records that the law was vigorously prosecuted.' Five of the remaining states acted in the following year, 1777–8, and speaking against the Continental currency was punished too. In New Jersey, it was reported in August 1776, high treason was to be punished as by the 'antient laws', and anyone 'found guilty of reviling the government of this State, as by this Convention established, or of other seditious speeches, or practices, shall be punished in a like manner as by the former laws of this state'. A subsequent elaboration expanded the scope of the law: anyone who 'by speech, writing, open deed, or act, advisedly and wittingly maintain and defend the authority, jurisdiction or power of the King or Parliament of Great Britain' could be punished by a fine not more than 300 pounds, and imprisoned for not more than one year. Moreover, the same punishment could be inflicted upon

> any person who shall maliciously and advisedly revile, or speak contemptuously of the government of this state, or of the Honourable Congress of the United States of America, or of the measures adopted by the said Congress, or by the Legislature of this State, or who shall maliciously and advisedly say or do any thing whatever which will encourage disaffection, or manifestly tend to raise tumults and disorders in the State, or who shall maliciously and advisedly spread false rumours concerning the American forces, or the forces of the enemy, as will tend to alienate the affections of the people from the government or terrify or discourage the good subjects of this State or to dispose them to favour the pretensions of the enemy.[23]

Van Tyne's is an extreme view: committees of safety were more anxious about the organization of the 'disaffected', but they did hear instances of dangerous speech. Prosecutions seem to have been rare. One of the earliest was in Wilmington, North Carolina, where one James Hepburn, a lawyer from Cumberland County, tried to raise a company of men, spreading rumours that 50,000 Russian troops in the pay of the British,

> That the said James Hepburn, is a false scandalous, and seditious incendiary, who, destitute of property and influence, as he is of principle, basely and traitorously endeavors to make himself conspicuous in favor of tyranny and oppression, in

---

[23] Ward, *The War for Independence*, p. 49; Van Tyne, *The Loyalists in the American Revolution*, pp. 199–200; *New York Journal*, 1 August 1776; *New Gazette and Weekly Mercury*, 12 November 1776, New Jersey, an Act to Punish Traitors and Disaffected Persons, Princeton, 4 October 1777.

hopes, by violating the primary and fundamental laws of nature and the British Constitution, to raise a fortune to his family upon the subversion of Liberty, and the destruction of his country.

The 'Friends to Liberty' were urged to avoid all 'dealings and intercourse with such a wicked and detestable character'.[24] In New Jersey, for example, following the 1776 laws, there were a couple of cases in 1777 and 1778. It is likely that more were heard at local level:

> Isaac Carey Esq. appeared before the Board, and was examined touching certain seditious words, and expressions made use of by William Britton after and such his examination reduced to writing, and subscribed and sworn to by the said Isaac Carey.

In another case, a married couple were presented:

> Henry Desbrow and his wife appeared before the Board, pursuant to citation, and their several Examinations having been taken with respect to their uttering words tending to depreciate the Continental money Agreed that the Said Desbrow be permitted to carry his wife home on condition of his entering into recognizance in £300 to appear before the Board, tomorrow morning at ten O'clock, which being done he was accordingly dismissed.[25]

In February and March 1777, the New York authorities received reports of 'a certain Abraham Brinckerhoff' of New York had been distributing General Howe's proclamation to the Americans to return to British rule. Unfortunately, things did not go well. Brinckerhoff

> was exceeding industrious in propagating a certain seditious paper calculated to disunite the good people in this county from a strict adherence to the cause of liberty, in which we have the happiness to be nearly united; on which this committee resolved to have the said Abraham Brinckerhoff apprehended and conveyed to the committee already named; this was accordingly done, but our chairman, from unavoidable incidents, of which he hath informed us, did not send the crime to your committee as soon as should have been done; on this, Brinckerhoff is set at large, of which he makes no small triumph.

This was from the chair of the committee in Ulster County, complaining about the lapse. Brinckerhoff disappears from the records after that.[26]

---

[24] *Proceedings of the Safety Committee of Wilmington North Carolina, from 1774 to 1776*, ed. Thomas Loring (Ralegh, NC, 1844), pp. 39–40.
[25] *Minutes of the Council of Safety for the State of New Jersey* vol. 1 (Jersey City, NJ: John H. Lyon, 1872), pp. 79 (9 July 1777) and 264 (26 June 1778).
[26] *Journals of the Provincial Congress, Provincial Convention, Committee of Safety and Council of Safety of the State of New York, 1775–1777*, vol. 1 (Albany, NY: Thurlow reed, Printer to the State, 1842). NY, vol. 2, pp. 412–13; NY, vol. 1, p. 835, 13 March 1777.

Trials and outcomes

After Lexington, suggests Herbert Aptheker, persuasion gave way to compulsion, which took five main forms. These were (1) deprivation of all civil and some social rights, (2) confiscation of property, (3) exile, (4) confinement and (5) execution. The formation of local organizations through which to implement these policies was crucial, and was part of the essential patriotic strategy of 1775–6:

> The original basis for the anti-Tory campaign came from the revolutionary seizure of power by local and province-wide conventions and committees. The first nation-wide provision on this question is contained in a recommendation issued by the Continental Congress, in October 1775, that provincial Committees of Safety 'take into custody every person who, going at large, might in their opinion endanger the safety of the colony or the liberties of America'.

Yet, he concludes, 'the facts show that treason was never a serious danger to the Revolution – not even in the case of Benedict Arnold'.[27] This does not mean that there were no trials for treason, or that executions did not take place. The evidence is patchy, but in New York, the year following their legislation concerning treason in July 1776 produced many trials and a handful of executions. Two days after the Assembly's ruling, a list of imprisoned men was produced, with their crimes, namely 'treasonable practices against the States of America', 'treasonable practices' or being 'notoriously disaffected', or corresponding with the enemies of the United States: one was simply described with his crime being 'too good a pilot to be trusted at large'. The most important of the prisoners was David Mathews, mayor of New York City. While the governor did not possess the power to pardon those condemned for murder or treason, following the preceding British ruling, the 'commissioners', or the state committee of safety who were instructed to seek out conspiracies, were also empowered to both manage the prisoners and make final decisions on their fate. The petitions to the state Committee of Safety survive in large numbers, and the evidence accumulated for the trials of traitors is recorded in some detail. Though the evidence is incomplete, there are records of at least thirty condemned in the first twelve months, with all but a handful pardoned. The crimes, where details are given, were usually working for the British army, even recruiting for it, and being found among enemy prisoners captured during the fighting. There is slight evidence of a true conspiracy among them. At least four were hanged, but there seems that there was some reluctance

---

[27] Aptheker, *The American Revolution*, pp. 127–8.

to carry out large numbers of executions. Of nineteen men condemned in May 1777, fifteen were almost immediately pardoned, and after executions, the Committee recorded that 'it was carried that no more be hanged'. Yet a little after, in the cases of two men, James Hewetson and Arnoot Viele, they reported that they were 'determined to make public examples of them'.[28] New York shows how difficult it was to maintain legitimate procedures in war conditions. The practical difficulties of containing loyalist prisoners when their main jails were too close to British lines led to New York sending prisoners upcountry, sometimes to Connecticut, and holding them in very unsuitable conditions. Later in the war, the state tried to deport the families of those who were known to have joined the British. The use of the Simsbury mine in Connecticut for a prison became notorious among historians of loyalism.[29] Yet the occupation by the British in New York City for six years, and the presence of many loyalists in the British forces, posed great difficulties for the patriot side. In the face of the large-scale collapse of the normal judicial structures, the authorities resorted to court martials. There were precedents: in early 1776, a sentinel defecting to the enemy was prosecuted, and the Committee of Safety commented:

> That the courts of judicature in this Colony being as yet held by authority derived from the Crown of Great Britain, are for that reason incompetent to the full and impartial trial of the said sentinel for the offence wherewith he stands charged, and therefore that he must of necessity be tried by a court martial only.

In addition to the problem of the origins of their lawful authority, there soon developed the added problems caused by the chaos of the first stages of the fighting.

> Gentlemen – As this State is now attacked by the common enemy, and our jails are in general so near the sea coast and the banks of Hudson's river as to render it extremely imprudent to continue prisoners of a certain cast any longer in them, the Convention have therefore come to a resolution to send 13 prisoners, who are accused of notorious disaffection to the rights and liberties of the American States, of counterfeiting the currency of the States, of corresponding with the enemy, or of engaging in treasonable conspiracies, to be confined in your jail, till we shall have formed a civil Constitution and established courts of justice, that they may be brought to trial, which cannot be done while our whole attention is engaged about the means of resisting the enemy.

---

[28] *Journals of the Provincial Congress ... New York*, vol. 1, pp. 527; 530–1, 18 July 1776; 814, 914, 919, 925, 11 May 1777; 928, 969–71, 974, 24 June 1777; 987. See A. Reppy, 'The Spectre of Attainder in New York (Part 1)', *St. John's Law Review*, 23 (1) (1948), pp. 1–68, pp. 18–19.

[29] Van Tyne, *The Loyalists in the American Revolution*, pp. 233, 235–6.

The state had not yet organized a proper constitution, or created a source of legitimacy which replaced that of the preceding royal power. In addition, the war was very close to home and creating chaos in the administration of patriot affairs. In effect, the patriots were hanging on by their fingertips for many months in the autumn of 1776 and the early months of 1777. The court system had collapsed: in March 1777, it was resolved.

> Whereas, from the want of courts properly instituted for the trial of treasons and other offences against this State, the resolutions heretofore passed for the punishment of the same have not been executed, whereby divers persons in this State, who have been employed by the enemy as spies, or for the purpose of enlisting men into their service, or furnishing them with supplies or intelligence, many of whom were not punishable by the Continental articles of war, have escaped with impunity.
>
> Resolved, That all such persons as have been or shall be apprehended in this State, without the enemy's lines, by Continental or other American troops, as spies from the enemy, or for enlisting men into their service, or for furnishing supplies or intelligence to them, be tried for the said offences by martial law, and if found guilty, suffer death or other punishment at the discretion of a general court martial of the Continental army or of the militia of this State; provided that where any person shall have been convicted by a court martial by virtue of this resolution, that the sentence shall not be executed until approved by this Convention or a future Legislature of this State.
>
> Whereas a form of government will soon be established in this State, and proper courts organized for the trial of offences therein: Therefore,
>
> Resolved, That the resolution above mentioned continue in force until the first day of July next, unless sooner repealed by this Convention or the future Legislature of this State.

The procedure was that accusations were made by local committees of safety and the state committee requested the commanding general to form a court martial. For much of the time, this was General George Clinton, a well-known local figure who eventually departed to take part in the Saratoga campaign, but the process remained the same. In May the Convention was planning to hold courts of oyer and terminer, as part of the newly declared constitution, and they were determined also to restrict acts of attainder only to offences committed during the war. The military punctiliously handed back control of the legal processes, if not exactly on the due date, when General Putnam wrote to the council to confirm that ordinary prisoners accused of treason were to be handed over to the civil magistrates, but also that one of the captured spies, a man called Palmer, had been appropriately tried by court martial under the 'common rules of war'.[30] General George Clinton, organizer of the many court martials for treason, was not hesitant in expressing his opinion on the sentences: in the cases of Samuel Knapp and Samuel Divine in February 1777, he wrote:

> The gentlemen of the court are of opinion, and I perfectly agree with them, that if the latter sentences are approved and carried into execution, and the two former prisoners pardoned under the gallows, it will answer a better purpose than if they should be executed. Add to this, I am far from being clear that the evidence, as it is reported, (material parts of it being, I am sure, omitted through mistake,) will support the sentences. As the only use in punishment is to bring people to a proper sense of their duty, and as I flatter myself, from the effect even of convening this court only, has already had on the refractory and disobedient, that the end will be fully answered, though these wretches' lives be spared, nor have I the least doubt but that the Honourable Convention will extend mercy towards the first if it can (in their better judgment) be done consistent with the public good; on any other terms I do not wish it.
>
> I am much at a loss respecting some parts of my duty in this new business, in which I beg the advice and direction of the Convention.

He was uncertain, on this occasion, whether he should refer the sentences to George Washington, as would occur with military court martials, or approve or disapprove of the sentences himself. Throughout this period of court martials, the precise boundaries between civil and military authorities were blurred, if only because the offenders were often discovered in military circumstances wearing military clothing, or acting in a military way.[31] Later moves against loyalism seem to have attacked well-known persons through legislation, so a later development was the Act of Attainder of October 1779 which condemned the state's fifty-nine most obvious Tories to death if found within the borders of New York. Included in this group were the erstwhile Albany mayor. As late as February 1783, the county banned more than thirty loyalists for refusing to take the oath of allegiance.[32]

---

[30] *Journals of the Provincial Congress ... New York*, vol. 1, p. 531, 19 July 1776; pp. 856–7, 31 March 1777; see also p. 898, this legal process also included the offences listed on 16 July 1776 (above); p. 948, 29 May 1777; p. 1020, 29 July 1777; Reppy, 'The Spectre of Attainder in New York (Part 1)'.

[31] *Journals of the Provincial Congress ... New York*, vol. 1, pp. 468 (31 May 1776); 814 (20 February 1777).

[32] J.S. Tiedemann, Eugene R. Fingerhut, and Robert W. Venables, eds, *The Other Loyalists: Ordinary People, Royalism, and the Revolution in the Middle Colonies, 1763–1787* (Albany, NY: State University of New York Press, 2009); see also *Minutes of the Albany Committee of Correspondence, 1775–1778*, ed. James Sullivan (Albany, NY: University of the State of New York, 1923), The Division of Archives and History.

Like New York, New Jersey was under British attack and there was an ebb and flow of military control, ambivalence among many as to their loyalties and attempts by the British to raise loyalist troops. Like the other states, too, New Jersey had promulgated a law in July 1776 to deal with treason and counterfeiting. Richard C. Haskett comments on the neglected local sources available, that

> although a story taken from courtroom accounts obviously cannot be complete, it does provide a reliable outline of the clash between a patriot government and its tory enemies. The basic strategy of the state and the tactics employed by its attorney general are evident in the record of prosecutions; the early frustrations and final success of the patriot assault are revealed in the minute books of the courts where the battle took place.

The method adopted was reminiscent of the travels of the king's judges in the English assize courts: the Attorney-General William Paterson and the members of the council of safety together toured each county, and heard and tried cases as they went. 'Normal judicial safeguards were ignored in the emergency of the moment. In his dual role as a member of the council and Attorney-General, Paterson was able both to indict and to prosecute suspected tories.' In fact, historian Richard C. Haskett came to the conclusion that he was also able to profit from the property confiscations that followed the numerous convictions.[33] In some of the orders by the Council there is careful attention to traditional notions of jurisdictional responsibility, for example, in the case of two charges against one Thomas Fowler,

> Ordered, That Warrants of Commitment be issued against Thomas Fowler charged with High Treason, and with making an Assault upon one Lewis Bastedo, with an intent to murder. The said Warrant to be directed to the Gaoler of Sussex. The Assault was committed in the County of Burlington, the High Treason in Monmouth.

Eight men were pardoned on capture as they were willing to serve in the American forces. This became a standard procedure:

> Agreed That Harman Rosin, for going into the Enemy's lines since the Treason law, and returning into this State as a spy, have five days to consider whether he will enlist in our service, or be committed for his trial.

---

[33] *Minutes of the Provincial Congress and the Council of Safety of State of New Jersey* (Trenton, NJ: Naar, Day and Naar, 1979), pp. 561–2; Richard C. Haskett, 'Prosecuting the Revolution', *AHR*, 59 (3) (1954), pp. 578–87, 581; and 'William Paterson, Attorney General of New Jersey: Public Office and Private Profit in the American Revolution', *The William and Mary Quarterly*, 7 (1) (1950), pp. 26–38.

The overwhelming impression is that here, too, many of the accused agreed to serve in the American forces, and thereby escaped prosecution: some sensibly confessed on their arrest, suggesting that this had become a predictable policy of relative leniency.[34] There is little evidence of large numbers of executions, though the policy of enlistment did not always succeed. In August 1778, it was reported to the Council that

> Cornelius Bogert who had been sentenced to death and pardoned on Condition of enlisting into the continental Army during the War, having deserted from the same, was brought before the Board and being examined, gave information against the following persons who were enlisted at the same time and had in like manner deserted from their respective Corps, and who were now at their several homes, viz: Joseph Britain, John Shannon, James Neigh, Lawrence Fleming, Martin Sneider, Christian Sneider, & Nath[aniel] Parker, and was remanded to the Gaol.[35]

Pennsylvania – notorious but misleading?

The example of Pennsylvania has attracted a great deal of attention from historians, not least because the trials are well documented, and in the details of the proceedings there is serious debate about some of the key legal issues that a new regime was faced with when asserting its legitimacy. The most important aspect of the trials, as Carlton F.W. Larson has established, was the care given to their proper defence, though this depended on the courage of individual lawyers.[36] The judicial activities of Thomas McKean became famous among the Americans and notorious among the loyalists who sometimes expressed the loss of the 'loyal martyrs' he condemned. There were certainly measures taken against loyalists or tories, and pressure was maintained throughout the war.[37] Moreover, the expulsion of a number of Quakers from Philadelphia to western Virginia had few parallels elsewhere, although mistrust of the pacifist

---

[34] *Minutes of the Council of Safety for the State of New Jersey*, p. 25 (16 April 1777); p. 53 (23 May 1777); p. 192 (20 January 1778).
[35] *Minutes of the Council of Safety for the State of New Jersey*, p. 268 (3 August 1778).
[36] Carlton F.W. Larson, *The Trials of Allegiance: Treason, Juries and the American Revolution* (New York: Oxford University Press, 2019).
[37] A.M. Ousterhout, 'Controlling the Opposition in Pennsylvania during the American Revolution', *Pennsylvania Magazine of History and Biography*, 105 (1) (1981), pp. 1–34. *Black List: A List of Those Tories Who Took Part with Great-Britain in the Revolutionary War and Were Attainted of High Treason, Commonly Called the Black List* (Philadelphia, PA: the Proprietor, 1802); on McKean, see *Royal South Carolina Gazette*, 22 August 1781.

neutrality of Quakers was widespread. Banishment on this scale, with careful military control of the exiles during and at the end of their journey, was unique. It resembled the treatment of prisoners of war. Thus, while there are parallels with the dilemmas faced by Quakers elsewhere, the treatment in Pennsylvania – banished to one of Van Tyne's idea of a 'reconcentration' camp – was unique. Virginia did try to recruit them forcibly into the army (as the British did in the First World War), and sent them to Washington's camp near Philadelphia, but he promptly sent them back. In the end, they were permitted to find voluntary substitutes for their military service.[38] Though an entire group was never again identified in this way, there were still many individuals in Pennsylvania who were attainted for treason, more than 500, of whom about 400 forfeited their property. Some, almost forming a rebellious and loyalist gang led by the Doan family, were eventually subject to outlawry and hounded out of the country or to the gallows.[39]

There was a burst of trials following the withdrawal of the British from Philadelphia, and the restoration of a semblance of state law and government. Nearly all of these accused were defended by one man, James Wilson.

> Between September 1778 and April 1779, twenty-three men were tried for treason against the state of Pennsylvania by assisting the British occupation of Philadelphia. Although these men were charged with attempting to undo the very Revolution to which Wilson had pledged his life, his fortune, and his sacred honour, Wilson appeared in court not to prosecute them, but to defend them. And from the defence perspective, the results had been spectacular; Philadelphia juries acquitted nineteen of the twenty-three men, a high acquittal rate even in an age known for widespread jury leniency.

Thus was certainly a very high acquittal rate compared with the norm for other serious crimes, and if this was the total that Pennsylvania executed in the war, then it is a conservative one, compared with New York. This was in part the result of the hard work of defence counsel James Wilson, who subsequently came under physical attack by the local armed militia in his own home (with several

---

[38] Gwenda Morgan and Peter Rushton, *Banishment in the Early Atlantic World: Convicts, Rebels and Slaves* (London: Bloomsbury Academic, 2013), pp. 154–79; J.S. Tiedemann, Eugene R. Fingerhut, and Robert W. Venables, eds, *The Other Loyalists: Ordinary People, Royalism, and the Revolution in the Middle Colonies, 1763–1787* (Albany, NY: State University of New York Press, 2009).

[39] John M. Coleman, 'Thomas McKean and the Origins of an Independent Judiciary', *Pennsylvania History*, 34 (1967), pp. 111–30; p. 124 sometimes it seems to have been personal, as in the case of the Doan gang were pursued by McKean for several years until they fled; G.S. Rowe, 'Outlawry in Pennsylvania, 1782–1788, and the Achievement of an Independent State Judiciary', *American Journal of Legal History*, 20 (3) (1976), pp. 227–44.

deaths resulting).[40] Each of the well-known and widely discussed cases threw up legal issues that McKean had to resolve, and for these they are rightly famous. Despite the loyalist criticism, McKean paid careful attention to the problems, and had an eye on the judicial consequences. John Roberts was alleged to have joined the British forces, and tried to recruit others to do likewise. The absence of two witnesses to the latter – and the suggestion by the defence that *trying to persuade* was not treason unless he actually *did* persuade someone which would certainly be treason – produced serious debate. The fact of joining himself, and his confession, made it certain that he would be convicted and executed. Samuel Chapman, by contrast, had been attainted in 1778 and refused to surrender himself. His defence was that he had never been other than a British subject, and the question of whether he owed allegiance to Pennsylvania given the absence of a legitimate government. His defence counsel pointed out

> that on the 26th December, 1776, there was no government established in Pennsylvania, from which he could receive protection; and, consequently, there was none to which he could owe allegiance – protection and allegiance being political obligations of a reciprocal nature. The doctrine of perpetual allegiance to be found in the books, applies only to established and settled governments, not to the case of withdrawing from an old government, and erecting a distinct one. Then every member of the community has a right of election, to resort to which he pleases; and even after the new system is formed, he is entitled to express his dissent; and dissenting from a majority, to retire with impunity into another country. Upon this principle, it was asserted that the prisoner never was a subject of the state of Pennsylvania.

The point was that he had left the state or colony on that date, at least a month before Pennsylvania declared a full definition of what constituted treason. The question then arose whether the law could be seen as retrospectively applicable, which had few precedents. The discussion became very academic, with the defence counsel citing Locke, Pufendorf, Burlamaqui, Vattel and Blackstone as well as appropriate legal cases. 'The Attorney-General, to shew the definition of a nation, the relation which a citizen bears to the state, and the natural connexion between a state of society and the institution of a government', cited much the same range of authors. One key point was that the state had been constituted by the Declaration of Independence, and that the existing laws of

---

[40] Carlton F.W. Larson, 'The Revolutionary American Jury: A Case Study of the 1778–1779 Philadelphia Treason Trials', *SMU Law Review*, 61 (4) (2008), pp. 1441–529, p. 1443, and *The Trials of Allegiance*; Henry J. Young, 'Treason and Its Punishment in Revolutionary Pennsylvania', *The Pennsylvania Magazine of History and Biography*, 90 (3) (1966), 287–313.

the time were merely being reiterated in early 1777, not newly created. Yet the situation was one of civil war, argued the defence, not one where Pennsylvania was at war with another nation. In other cases, the awkwardness of the question of loyalty owed, was avoided, but the use of the law of outlawry against Aaron Doan, arrested initially for burglary, but acknowledged as a loyalist, led to a similar detailed examination of British precedents and legal doctrines.[41] The trials remained contentious in many ways, but, given the results, they were not in fact unusual. A high rate of acquittal, or of negotiated readmission of the accused through service in the American armed forces, kept executions to a low level in most states.

Aftermaths

The legal technicalities debated in the Pennsylvania cases were unusual, and have had a lasting impact on American legal thought. Other states were not so careful, or their judges were not so meticulous. New York, properly speaking, did not have a new constitution nor did it form new courts until the spring of 1777, by which time many court martials for treason had been conducted. There seems to have been little legal debate. Other states, such as Connecticut, seem to have detected and punished very few accused traitors.[42] The mixture of popular, political and legal measures taken against loyalists remains as a picture of what may happen when loyalties – and people – are divided in conditions of a civil war. Yet, in the midst of military violence and warfare, with nascent political institutions finding their way to an uncertain future, the impression is that the American patriots, when it came to court processes, were generally very scrupulous about the law and the legal niceties, and merciful in deploying its severity. There seems to have been a strong sense that too much judicial brutality would have been counterproductive, in terms of both reputation and relationships with loyalists, the disaffected or, most important, the neutrals. Nevertheless, after the war, there were doubts about what had taken place. One who questioned the processes of repression was Aedanus Burke, who, after the peace, wrote to the people of South Carolina, speaking movingly of

---

[41] A.J. Dallas, *Reports of Cases Ruled and Adjudged in the Courts of Pennsylvania, before and since the Revolution*, 2nd ed., 3 vols (Philadelphia, PA: P. Byrne, 1806), vol. 1, pp. 39–40 for John Roberts; pp. 53–60 for Samuel Chapman, 53–60 quotations pp. 53–4 and pp. 57–8; Doan pp. 86–8,
[42] Virginia DeJohn Anderson, *The Martyr and the Traitor: Nathan Hale, Moses Dunbar and the American Revolution* (New York: Oxford University Press, 2017).

innocent wives and children involved in the calamity of husbands and fathers, their widows are deprived of the right of dower, their children disinherited, and themselves banished for ever from this country. And this *without process, trial, examination,* or *hearing;* and without allowing them the sacred right of proving their innocence on a future day.

This plea may have had an effect, as one study has suggested that there was some reconciliation between patriots and loyalists in South Carolina, though how much return of confiscated property there was is unclear.[43] That other bitter conflicts also ended in eventual reconciliation may also be noted, particularly the final acceptance of the end of the Jacobite cause in Scotland with the death of the last possible Stuart claimant. They might disagree when it came to past history but could finally agree on the present.

---

[43] Aedanus Burke, as Cassius, *An Address to the Freemen of the State of South Carolina* (Philadelphia, PA: Robert Bell, 1783), p. 1; John C.Meleney, *The Public Life of Aedanus Burke: Revolutionary Republican in Post-Revolutionary South Carolina* (Columbia, SC: University of South Carolina Press, 1989); Rebecca Nathan Brannon, 'Reconciling the Revolution: Resolving Conflict and Rebuilding Community in the Wake of Civil War in South Carolina, 1775–1860' (unpublished Ph.D., University of Michigan, 2007); Aaron N. Coleman, 'Loyalists in War, Americans in Peace: The Reintegration of the Loyalists, 1775–1800' (Unpublished Ph.D., University of Kentucky, 2008).

8

After the Revolutions: Sedition, 'Revolution', Rebellion and Slavery

There were political trials in the 1790s in England, Scotland and Canada, and colonial conflicts in Grenada, St. Lucia, St. Vincent and Ireland, were followed by similar trials. While the domestic British prosecutions have rightly been studied in terms of the contexts of radical politics and suppression, a panic reaction by the authorities to the events of the French Revolution, the sense of a wider framework is usually missing. Seen in a wider Atlantic context, however, there appears a much more widespread panic about political dissent and the possibilities of revolution, and, by examining the legal methods adopted by the authorities, it can be seen that there are some plausible parallels in official tactics both between colonies and between the colonies and the metropolitan country. This is, perhaps, not to neglect some of the familiar people and prosecutions that have been so well studied by the likes of John Barrell and Michael Scrivener, nor to forget the emotional and philosophical background of some of the writers attacked in Britain who formed part of wider Romantic movement beyond that of purely Jacobin-influenced politics. The ferment caused by radical revolutionary thinking affected both the content and methods of the political reform movement in Britain *and* the drive for liberty in the Caribbean where the Haitian revolution pointed to new possibilities in anti-colonial struggles. Taking a broad overview of these events, however, does not indicate that the approach assumes that all these conflicts were similar nor that the responses of the authorities were the same everywhere. Context made a significant difference, as we shall see. It has been noted by Lisa Steffen that treason prosecutions at any one time reflect notions of national identity and, indeed, reinforce it. If the British learnt to be themselves in the face of repeated wars against the French, as Linda Colley has famously argued, then the non-revolutionary, pragmatic reformism of the British system owes its origins as an ideology and self-image to the rejection of many aspects of the French Revolution. Edmund Burke was not alone in seeing the revolutionaries as fanatics, and the authorities in Britain as cautious pragmatists who were reluctantly taking measures to keep order from falling into chaos (a self-image that survived into the twentieth century, that of the British as pragmatic gradualists rather than revolutionaries). The contest between alternative versions of patriotism, democracy, freedom and reform made the 1790s the first ideological conflict since the civil wars of the seventeenth century. Even the precise meanings of sedition and treason were undergoing challenge and modification, though official prosecutors, of not legislators, drew upon the traditional legal precedents.

At the core of the political conflicts and legal responses lay different kinds of *imagination*: the French Revolution and the Haitian Revolt fired the imagination of many looking for alternative social and political routes to, and forms of, liberty. Many were intellectuals, political campaigners and literary figures: others were slaves. In response, the British authorities in both and Canada attempted to extend the idea of 'constructive treason' to include those who campaigned for alternative models of democracy or who opposed the implementation of laws they judged to be oppressive: suggesting new political institutions, opposing old ones and criticizing legislation, all had to be included, with careful selectivity of individual targets, as treason. The dilemma for the government prosecutors was an ancient one: words had long been considered insufficient to constitute treason, which is why, in the 1790s, the prosecutions had mostly been for sedition, particularly concentrating on printed documents (see Chapter 3). Words had to be followed by some kind of action that demonstrated treasonable intent. As long ago as the fifteenth century, the creative extension of the 1352 legislation had involved a broader notion of 'encompassing the King's death', since, for example, to overthrow an institution – the church or an individual magnate – would necessarily mean the death of the king. Thus by a kind of logical extension, proposals for reform or replacement of an institution such as Parliament might be classified as treason, as this would necessitate making war on the King and his ministers.[1] John Barrell has called the legal cases of the 1790s as being based on 'fantasies of regicide', and noted that arguments of the state's prosecutors went against Matthew Hale's warning more than a century before of the dangers of making new treasons 'by construction and analogy'.[2]

The trials in London and Edinburgh made many men famous, and probably had the effect of making Tom Paine's writings even more widely read. Nevertheless,

---

[1] Samuel Rezneck, 'Constructive Treason by Words in the Fifteenth Century', *The American Historical Review*, 33 (3) (1928), pp. 544–52.
[2] John Barrell. *Imagining the King's Death: Figurative Treason, Fantasies of Regicide, 1793-1796* (Oxford: Oxford University Press, 2000), p. 382.

the prosecutions, even if largely unsuccessful, served to intimidate many critics of the established political system. London trials were inflicted on Thomas Hardy, John Horne Tooke, John Augustus Bonney, Stewart Kidd, Jeremiah Joyce, Thomas Wardle, Thomas Holcroft, John Richter, Matthew Moore, John Thelwall, Richard Hodgson and John Baxter – a mixed batch of members of the London Corresponding Society and the Society for Constitutional Information. Also publishers such as Daniel Isaac Eaton were prosecuted, in fact in his case twice in 1793 for printing seditious material (mostly Paine) and acquitted both times. With prosecutions for treason and sedition – there were about 200 of the latter, with perhaps a further 100 held in jail, the growing Jacobin movement was fragmented and broken (see Chapter 3). 'The established authorities crushed British Jacobinism and the reform movement in general with a massive if also inefficient repression. Whether the movement was really as dangerous as the Pitt government thought is another question.'[3] In a number of trials, defence council mentioned the armed character of their vigilante anti-Jacobin opponents, the 'Church and King' mobs, about which the government conveniently did nothing. In fact their threat actually grew worse after the bulk of the treason and sedition prosecutions in 1793–4, with 1796–7 seeing many physical attacks. The trials may have encouraged or even legitimized the extremes of the mob. Yet it has been observed that the Jacobin effort had not been without long-term effects. The Jacobin-influenced critics raised fundamental questions about a huge range of topics, from slavery to women's rights to representative democracy. Feeding into a broader development of romanticism, they also enabled a critique of cruelty both against humans and animals. New types of writing, experimental styles of novels and plays, were developed alongside the more explicitly political debates. 'Jacobinism exerted considerable power in Britain. In terms of political theory and models of political organizing, the Jacobins set a pattern and established paradigms that were sustained by an important minority into the Reform agitation of 1830–32, the war of the unstamped in the 1830s, and Chartism.'[4]

---

[3] L. Steffen, *Defining a British State: Treason and National Identity, 1608–1820* (Houndmills, Basingstoke: Palgrave Macmillan, 2001), p. 106; Michael T. Davis, '"That Odious Class of Men Called Democrats": Daniel Isaac Eaton and the Romantics, 1704–1795', *History*, 84 (273) (1999), pp. 74–92, 76; Michael Scrivener, *Seditious Allegories: John Thelwall and Jacobin Writing* (University Park, PA: Penn UP, 2001), p. 7; Clive Emsley, 'Repression, "Terror" and the Rule of Law in England during the Decade of the French Revolution', *The English Historical Review*, 100 (397) (1985), pp. 801–25, p. 824 and 'An Aspect of Pitt's "Terror": Prosecutions for Sedition during the 1790s', *Social History*, 6 (2) (May, 1981), pp. 155–84.

[4] Steve Pool, ed., *John Thelwall: Radical Romantic and Acquitted Felon* (London: Pickering and Chatto, 2009), pp. 1–2 the phrase was used against him, 'acquitted felon' by opponents; pp. 66 and 171 fear of 'Church and King' mobs; Scrivener, *Seditious Allegories*, p. 4.

The response of the legal authorities was to deploy some of the traditional legal weapons of the law, as well as introducing new forms of control over areas such as printing and publishing. Like their predecessors, in other words, the 1790s authorities often used the laws of treason and sedition while arguing for an extension, particularly of treason, to include ideas and proposed plans for a reformed constitution, and demands for new forms of rights. The legal issues raised by the trials are the key to understanding the adaptability of the British state to new situations, and the ability of the authorities to come up with new ways of suppressing the opposition and maintain control. The statement that was popular with prosecutors, as a means of persuading juries that the defendants' actions were treason, was that of Sir Michael Forster, quoted for example in Downie's case in Edinburgh in 1794.

> Insurrections in order to throw down all inclosures, to alter the established law, or change religion; to enhance the price of all labour; or to open all prisons; all risings, in order to effect these innovations, of a public and general concern, by an armed force are, in construction of law, high treason within the clause of levying war. For, though they are not levelled at the person of the king, they are against his royal majesty. And besides, they have a direct tendency to dissolve the bonds of society, and to destroy all property, and all government too by numbers and an armed force. Insurrections, likewise, for redressing national grievances, or for the expulsion of foreigners or indeed of any single nation living here under the protection of the king, or for the reformation of real or imaginary evils of a public nature, and in which the insurgents have no special interest, risings to effect these ends, by force and numbers, are, by construction of law, within the clause of levying war. For they are levelled at the king's crown and royal dignity.

In a century which had seen the beginnings of organized labour, from Spitalfields silk weavers on the outskirts of London to keelmen in the northeast of England loading coal on ships heading to that city, the inclusion of strikes – 'insurrections' that aimed 'to enhance the price of all labour' – is very significant. Even an attempt to 'redress national grievances' could be treason. There is a key let-out, however: these actions are treasonable where the 'insurgents have no special interest'; in other words, if a strike took place in one industry to support workers in another, it could be construed as treasonable. Oddly enough, secondary strikes in sympathy with other workers became illegal under Mrs Thatcher's government in the 1980s. The reference to attacks on resident foreigners given protection by the king reflected the arrival, in London particularly, of new people such as Huguenots from France, and the return of a Jewish community. Foster's remarks are also interesting because they reflect the very different range of threats and opposition experienced by governments – and employers – in the eighteenth century: the scene of actions had changed significantly since the Restoration writings of Matthew Hale. This statement, written in 1762, and perhaps significantly published in a third, larger edition in 1792, seems to have shaped legal views in the 1790s. It was quoted in one of the few treason cases in Canada (see below).[5]

In subsequent elaborations, local cases were integrated into this framework, expanding the scope of 'constructive treason' even further. East's *Pleas of the Crown*, published in 1803, reflected on some of the events since the 1746 Jacobite rising:

> On the trial of Lord George Gordon the court of King's Bench declared their unanimous opinion that an attempt, by intimidation and violence to force the repeal of a law was a levying war against the king. The statute in question was the 18 Geo. 3. c. 60. for relieving Roman Catholics from certain penalties; and the treasonable acts given in evidence against the prisoner was the assembling a great multitude of people, and encouraging them to surround the two houses of parliament and commit different acts of violence there and elsewhere, with a view to intimidate them to a repeal of the statute. Insurrections of this nature, though not levelled directly against the person of the king, are yet an attack upon his regal office, and tend to dissolve all government, society, and order. The king is bound in duty to enforce the acts of the legislature and uphold their authority: any resistance, therefore, to these, must, in its consequences, extend to the endangering of his person and government, by involving the state in a general distraction; on which account this species of treason falls properly within the clause of levying war against the king. Upon this principle the Yorkshire and Northumberland rioters, who opposed the militia laws, were convicted of high treason and several of them were executed. But under this branch a bare conspiracy to levy such a war is not treason, unless the war be actually levied; in which case the conspirators, as well as the actors, would be all equally guilty.

The northeast cases referred to involved widespread opposition to the compulsory registration of men for service in the militia regiments. Militia riots ran through Yorkshire and then the northeast in the late 1750s and early 1760s, culminating in the Hexham riot of 1761, where dozens were killed or injured by troops (ironically, by militia soldiers). The public fear was that these local troops

---

[5] Sir Michael Foster, *A Report of Some of the Proceedings of the Commission for the Trial of the Rebels in the Year 1746, in the County of Surrey and of Other Crown Cases*, 3rd ed., ed. Michael Dobson (1792), p. 211, originally 1762; see Downie's case, T.B. Howell, *State Trials*, vol. 24, col. 129 (London: Howells, 1820).

would be sent abroad to fight. Two men, who were not at the riot, but who took part in an attack on the militia's administrative records in Northumberland, were prosecuted in 1761 for treason. They had destroyed the key documents, the lists of local men liable to be called up to serve in the militia. One, Peter Patterson, was executed eventually on a second attempt, after a rope had broken, and, after being allowed to hang for some time, dismembered. William Elder, the other defendant, was convicted but pardoned. As in the case of the Gordon riots, it was the use of direct action to oppose or change a law that was held to have constituted treason.[6]

Colonial treason

The problems of defining treason were extensively debated in the case of David McLane or MacLane in Canada in 1797, where the nature of treason and of jurisdictional rights – he was an American – had to be established in one of the first peacetime prosecutions there. The trial exhibited all the anxieties and insecurities of the authorities which they shared with their contemporaries in Britain. It was assumed that recent disturbances and protests were entirely the result of outside agitations originating with the French, and that the violence of the French Revolution was about to break out locally. There were conflicts over turnpikes under a recent Road Act, and some of the colonial judges and others were eager to see at least some of this as treasonable. Angry farmers meeting at night might seem more like potential rioters, but there was the additional factor that these were mostly French speakers. At the same time, there were rumours of a French fleet off the coast and plots coming from French officials in the United States. As F. Murray Greenwood has noted, 'The sense of imminent peril among English-speakers in Lower Canada generated an elastic definition of treason. This hard attitude, fed by alarm, was particularly evident during the trial of David McLane.'[7] The trial of American McLane or MacLane turned on a number of issues, with plenty of evidence of questionable activities including apparent intelligence gathering, and a plot to surrender Montreal to the French.

---

[6] E.H. East, *Treatise of the Pleas of the Crown*, 2 vols (London: J. Butterworth, 1803), vol. 1, pp. 72–3; G. Morgan and P. Rushton, *Rogues, Thieves and the Rule of Law: The Problem of Law Enforcement in North-East England, 1718–1800* (London: UCL Press, 1998), pp. 141, 148, and 210.

[7] F. Murray Greenwood, *Legacies of Fear: Law and Politics in the Era of the French Revolution* (Toronto: University of Toronto Press, 1993), p. 138; I have followed Greenwood's usage of 'McLane', though he is 'MacLane' in the *State Trials*, vol. 26, col. 721.

Yet, as an alien, he was judged to be triable as a treacherous British subject. In addition, the context of agitation in Quebec clearly required clarification of the treason law, which the McLane case conveniently provided.

The presiding judge, James Monk, Justice of the King's Bench for Montreal, set the scene very carefully in his preamble to the court, establishing that they were faced with an entirely unprecedented time in Canadian history:

> 'Till this period, the Canadians, convinced by experience that they had the full enjoyment of every privilege to which their ancestors had been accustomed, and that they were also exempted from many rigorous services incident to a government purely monarchical, contentedly lived under the king's mild dominion, and showed their satisfaction by a cheerful submission to the laws. It need hardly be mentioned that the period to which I allude is that of the sanguinary revolution in France, since which time emissaries have been sent forth, as well native as proselytes, under the pretence of diffusing liberty, to disturb the quiet of all settled government. Every symptom of disobedience, and the few instances of marked disaffection, that have appeared in this colony, may be traced to this cause of delusion. It is therefore some consolation to reflect that the evil is not of native growth, but has been introduced by the insidious arts of mischievous foreigners, practising on the minds of the ignorant and credulous natives.

Thus was established the unnaturalness of treason, and its alien origin and character, at the outset. Treason derived from the outside corruption of the new, false preachers of liberty. Later in the trial, the Attorney-General noted its historic importance in British North America:

> This is certainly the first trial for high treason, which has taken place in Canada, perhaps in America, if we except the shameful proceedings had in the year 1701, against colonel Nicholas Bayard in the late province of New York; and even this is not a case similar to the present, as his indictment was drawn upon a local statute.

This was not quite the case, but they were probably relying on the available published sources – Bayard's trial was also included in *State Trials* by their first editor, William Cobbett.[8] In his preamble Monk therefore established the nature of 'levying war' on the king, and it cannot have been accidental that, in a time of turnpike protests, he deliberately mentioned them:

---

[8] *State Trials*, vol. 26, col. 728 and col. 815.

Another head of treason is that of levying war against the king in his realm: this is either positive, or constructive. It is positive so far as it applies to any rebellious insurrection by a pretender to the throne or factious demagogue, with drums or trumpets, in martial array, either to dethrone the king, as to take him into their power. under pretence of altering the measures of government, or of removing evil counsellors. By construction of law it extends to those cases where insurgents move not immediately against the king's person, but for the purpose of carrying into execution any general and illegal design, such as to pull down all turnpikes, to destroy all meeting houses, to expel all foreigners, to reform any real or imaginary grievance of a public nature, in which the insurgents have no particular interests (for the law has provided a peaceable mode of seeking redress in these cases by petition to either branch of the legislature). But, as it was solemnly resolved in a recent case, every attempt, by intimidation or violence to obtain the repeal of a law, comes within this branch of the statute, and is treason.

This lifted many phrases from the statement by Sir Michael Foster, without attribution.[9] There were fourteen counts in the charge sheet, an almost endless list of accusations that were repeated frequently, mainly alleging that on numerous different days McLane tried to invite the French into Quebec, through Montreal, and stirred people to rebellion to handover the city to the French.[10]

The defence was not very stout: defence counsel Pyke questioned whether the English treason law had been introduced under the 1774 Quebec Act. It had not been specifically mentioned, and therefore there should have been legislation in the provincial assembly to reaffirm its validity. In addition, there was the absurdity of counting an 'alien' as a British subject: McLane was from Rhode Island in the United States, and had been through no naturalization process. He might be an enemy alien, but not a traitor. The trial went on all day, starting at 7 am and ending at 9 am. The result was scarcely a surprise, as the panel of judges had been carefully selected from the members of the Executive Council, with or without legal training, though the Anglican bishop was excepted. McLane was executed, with hanging and beheading. This presaged further trials in the nineteenth century, as forms of unrest were frequent in Canada, particularly Francophone Canada, and the precedent had been set.[11]

---

[9] *State Trials*, vol. 26, p. 727.
[10] *State Trials*, vol. 26, 721–828, 733–47; there were fourteen charges in the end, summarized, 752–3; see Murray Greenwood, 'The Treason Trial and Execution of David McLane', *Manitoba Law Journal*, 20 (1991), pp. 3–14.
[11] *State Trials*, vol. 26, col. 822, and the 1774 Quebec Act was specifically mentioned by the Attorney General, col. 817 and 826; Greenwood, 'Treason Trial', p. 6; Barry Cahill, 'Sedition in Nova Scotia: R. v. Howe and the Contested Legality of Seditious Libel', *U.N.B.L.J.* [*University of New Brunswick Law Journal*], 51 (2002), pp. 95–140.

It is fitting that the study of the arguments in formal legal proceeding ends with a colonial example. In many ways, rebellion and treason became predominantly colonial phenomena after 1800, with only a handful of prosecutions in Britain itself. By the 1790s 'constructive treason' was in great danger of losing all the cautious safeguards of earlier times, and had become a catch-all to be turned into a weapon against those the authorities feared most. This may be a slight exaggeration, but the sense of the 'enemy within' had changed from religious or dynastic rebels to ones who wished to transform the political system and even society itself. Almost any rational criticism of the established system could be defined as seditious, though convincing a jury proved more difficult. In addition, the proposal for replacing current institutions could be recast as a threat to the monarchy itself, by reference to the executions of the French king and queen in 1793, and prosecutions brought. There were alternatives when it came to violent protests, in the 1715 Riot Act and other laws, but the organizers would always stand in danger of a treason prosecution in the age of revolution.

Rebellions, slaves and maroons

Parallel but apparently rather different events occurred in the military and legal actions in the Caribbean against political rebellions and maroon communities. Yet there are striking similarities in the general context: the difference lies in the levels of violence. In the 1790s, in part because of the double shock of the French and the Haitian Revolutions, there was widespread panic in the British Atlantic and, at the same time, in the newly independent American Republic. The threat to the very existence of slavery provoked ferocious responses from the British and French authorities in the Caribbean, and the exile of the French slaveowning class in North America in cities such as Charleston provided a proof of the consequences of dispossession and revolution. Yet the 'rebellions' which the British authorities faced in some of their Caribbean colonies in the 1790s were not a simple pattern of slave revolts; nor was slavery the only issue. The key problem, from the point of view of the British, was the questionable loyalty of 'new' colonial subjects in the formerly French colonies, and the trustworthiness of the uncontrolled populations of free peoples of African and Carib descent. The British rightly feared that some of their French-speaking colonists, even if formally free, might be tempted by the lure of the French Revolution, or perhaps simply by their alienation from British identity, demanding their rights to be French, as many people found themselves marginalized as French speakers in an Anglophone empire, without the guarantees offered to the *Quebecois* in the 1770s. In addition, the British seem to find the idea of *any* free population other than white Britons a kind of threat, and the two maroon wars pursued in the 1790s in St. Vincent and Jamaica seem to have arisen from local paranoia rather than from any demonstrable threat from those communities. These exercises in ethnic cleansing of untrustworthy populations reflect a fear of treacherous identities. Simple models, of either slave revolt or revolutionary impulse, therefore come up against factors of local complexity and national and racial differences. In the context of the Haitian rising, the British authorities – and those in slave societies across the Americas – became more alert and anxious about threats from below. While the British intervention in Haiti itself is beyond the scope of this study, we will discuss here the general fear of revolution, which did much to shape British domestic politics in the 1790s, and the response to the Irish revolt of 1798 (see below). In the slave colonies, the mixture of white, black and mixed race, of slave and free, gave a particular flavour to several of the conflicts in this period. As in the American Revolution in the southern colonies, the fear of slave revolts in the British Caribbean after the Haitian Revolution erupted in 1791 led to severe political repression. Not for the first time, the rulers of a British colony had resorted to repression under conditions of a paranoid style of politics, in this period after 1789 matching that to the authorities in Britain.[12]

The violence in the Caribbean was directed against what appeared to be insurgent populations of white and mixed race peoples. The role of the free, mostly French-speaking, smallholders in framing the grievances and leading the resistance was the most notable feature of actions in both Grenada and St. Lucia. Some were of mixed African and European ancestry. Though the English-speaking planters were convinced their opponents were stirred up and led by agents of the French Republic, with predictable revolutionary aims, it is equally likely that the marginalization of the French language and the Catholic Church over many years lay behind the initial disaffection. These men were not rich, and were often engaged in producing commodities such as coffee rather than sugar. As in other colonies, the mixed race and freed black population were increasingly regarded as deserving lesser status and fewer legal or civil rights. The role of slaves is rather more problematic: many clearly ran from the larger plantations to the rebel areas, but their places of work were being destroyed

---

[12] For a wider context, see Gaspar, D.G. and Geggus, D.P., eds, *A Turbulent Time: The French Revolution and the Greater Caribbean* (Bloomington, IN: Indiana University Press, 1997); Wim Klooster and Gert Oostindie, eds, *Curaçao in the Age of Revolutions, 1795-1800* (Leiden: KITLV Press, 2011).

in the rebellion. White planters had left their estates to trustworthy slaves and others, and these people were vulnerable in the fighting. Some have suggested that slaves formed a key part of the fighting force in places like Grenada and St. Lucia. As Craton summarizes the situation: what may have begun as protests by smaller settlers also led to the unleashing of a large slave uprising.

> The most remarkable episode ... was the rebellion led by the coloured planter Julien Fédon, which paralysed Grenada for almost two years. More than 7,000 slaves were actively involved, half of the island total, but the leaders were undoubtedly the 150 or more French-speaking coffee planters and smallholders who, like Fédon, felt oppressed by the British regime and looked to the French Revolution for redress and revenge.[13]

Julien Fédon was the nominal leader and achieved a rapid impact when, after killing a number of English-speaking white planters, he and his men took about forty prisoners, among them Lieutenant Governor Ninian Home, held on Fédon's family estate. When Fédon's emissaries, Joachim (or Joachin) Phillip and Charles Nogues, met the president and Privy Council of the island in March 1795, they demanded that the British surrender. They were in a relatively strong position. The two men were themselves from relatively affluent backgrounds, and like Fédon himself, Phillip in particular coming from a family with extensive holdings in land and slaves. They impressed by their appearance in blue French uniforms with the tricolour sash of the revolution around their waists. In their pronouncements to the council, they pointed to the demands of the French government agent, Victor Hugues, who had been decisive in defeating the British forces in Guadaloupe, that the British surrender their possessions in the Caribbean. Yet, although this sounds like a traditional military move by the French against the British in the region, masquerading as a wave of revolutionary activity, there were complex social and historical factors behind the insurgency in Grenada.[14]

Anderson highlights the many contradictions of free and unfree, French and English, white, black and inbetween categories, fissions that undermined any possibility of a coherent society, not even a slave society, on the island:

---

[13] M. Craton, *Testing the Chains: Resistance to Slavery in the British West Indies* (Ithaca NY: Cornell University Press, 1982), pp. 180–202, p. 183, and K. Candlin (2018), 'The Role of the enslaved in the "Fédon Rebellion" of 1795', *Slavery and Abolition*, published online April 2018; see also, E.L. Cox, 'Fédon's Rebellion 1795–96: Causes and Consequences', *The Journal of Negro History*, 67 (1) (1982), pp. 7–19.
[14] Cox, 'Fédon's Rebellion'; K. Candlin, *The Last Caribbean Frontier, 1795–1815* (Houndmills, Basingstoke: Palgrave Macmillan).

The island, until recently a French possession, had crisscrossing fault lines dividing Catholic and Protestant; French-speaking and Anglophone; slave and free; black, white, and mixed-race. These groups clashed repeatedly over the questions of who was to enjoy the rights of a British subject, and who was to shoulder its obligations. In 1795, slave and free coloured resistance incited by the French and Haitian Revolutions combined with simmering Anglo-French resentment on Grenada in Fédon's Rebellion, a 16-month uprising that at its height boasted an estimated 7,200 adherents—black, white, slave and free—and controlled nearly all the island before its suppression in the summer of 1796.

She raises the question of the concept of citizenship and rights in this ferment of contrasting identities.[15] The 'French' had had 'Britishness' forced on them by conquest some years earlier. Yet discrimination and a frustrated economic position saw them become insurgents. Convinced that they faced a major threat to both British control and slavery itself, the authorities declared martial law, which provoked from Fédon both indignation and a threat to execute hostages. As the British mustered troops and began to intrude into rebel areas, Fédon carried out his threat to execute forty-eight of the fifty-one hostages, including Lieutenant Governor Home. Fédon's strategy of menacing the large slave plantations forced most of the Anglophone white planters to abandon their estates and seek refuge in the island's capital, where they made demands for more aggressive military action. The British authorities had to import more than 1,000 troops and, in June 1796, fifteen months after the rebellion began, decisively defeated the rebels.

Hundreds of prisoners were taken at the end of the fighting, including Fédon – the surviving list of those held by the authorities has more than 400 names. The legal proceedings in Grenada were rather unorthodox, with suspects named following the legislature passing an Act of Attainder, which was a form of conviction by the legislative body (such as the British Parliament), and reduced subsequent legal proceedings to the identification of those named in the Act, and a choice of sentence in most cases – chosen by the decision of a panel of judges. This replaced the formal adversarial trial by jury with legal representation on both sides, as specified under the 1696 Treason Act, which was supposed to enforce due processes in these essentially political trials. At least 100 of the accused were sentenced to death and others order to be transported

---

[15] C. Anderson, 'Old Subjects, New Subjects and Non-Subjects: Silences and Subjecthood in Fédon's Rebellion, Grenada, 1795–96', in R. Bessel and N. Guyatt (eds), *War, Empire and Slavery, 1770–1830* (Houndmills, Basingstoke: Palgrave Macmillan, 2010), pp. 201–17, 202.

out of the colony. In this practice of banishment, the British authorities were pursuing a much older tradition of removing rebellious slaves, who had not been condemned to death, from the colony of the revolt. This had been the practice in the 1741 New York conspiracy, for example, and in slave states after American independence. It was a way of purging a slave society of its internal enemies.[16] One contemporary writer Turnbull thought the rebels were 'fellow-subjects' who had committed treason, though a number may have been French: most were of local origin, though he noted that four 'execrable traitors' were born of British parents. Contemporary accounts of the Grenada fighting were largely from the viewpoint of those whom Craton calls the 'plantocracy', like Turnbull. None had any doubts about the threat and the treachery of the accused.[17] Most were charged with treason – in the words of the accusations, 'not only of subverting His Majesty's Government but of totally extirpating His Loyal Subjects of this Island', and many others with either murder or manslaughter. The treason charges may have functioned as the modern equivalent of 'attempted murder', which was not on the statute book until the mid-nineteenth century. There were few doubts about the main participants' guilt, but some of the accused made the only objection or defence available to them and asserted that they were not the people named in the Act of Attainder. Nearly all these arguments were dismissed. Those who were accused of manslaughter, if convicted, were branded on their hands, while others were fined for committing assaults. Even if not convicted, a handful of the accused were only released from jail on condition of their 'on their shipping themselves off the Island', an interesting use of voluntary self-banishment previously deployed for the more affluent Jacobites. The racial pattern of punishment was striking. As Cox has observed,

> Of the guilty, most of those condemned to death and actually executed were free coloureds, while the whites were reprieved. Those guilty free coloreds who were not executed, together with whites who were reprieved, were shipped to non-British territories along the coast of Honduras. The feeling was that under no circumstances should such 'dangerous persons' remain in the island, and

---

[16] Court of Oyer and Terminer (Grenada), 1796, transcribed, Lawrence Brown, EAP295/2/6/1 Court of Oyer and Terminer for Trial of Attained Traitors record book [1796], transcription, online at https://eap.bl.uk/sites/default/files/legacy-eap/downloads/eap295_2_6_1_transcription.pdf (accessed 9 August 2018); J. Lepore, *New York Burning: Liberty, Slavery, and Conspiracy in Eighteenth-Century Manhattan* (New York: Alfred A. Knopf, 2005) and Daniel Horsmanden, The New York Conspiracy, or the *History of the Negro Plot, with the Journal of the Proceedings against the Conspirators at New-York in the Years 1741–2* (New York: Southwick and Pelsue, 1810, originally 1744).

[17] Gordon Turnbull, *A Narrative of the Revolt and Insurrection of the French Inhabitants of Grenada, by an Eye-Witness* (Edinburgh: Constable, 1795), pp. 161 and 210.

when in May, 1797, some female relatives attempted to reenter the island from Trinidad, the public outcry against them was so loud that Governor Charles Green accepted Council's advice in refusing them permission to land.

With attainder and conviction went the seizure of the convicts' properties, and this brought hundreds of Grenadan slaves into ownership by the Crown.[18] When the rising began, some slaves took part, and at least one slave was listed among the 'traitors': this raised questions of them having duties as citizens or subjects, above those due to masters, that is, loyalty to the state or crown, as though they were free. Prosecuting them in this way suggested that they possessed agency and were in fact free and capable of freedom, since they were acting as citizens or subjects, not chattels. This had been an issue in revolutionary Virginia in the War of Independence, when one slave fighting in the Royal Navy was seized as a traitor by the Virginia authorities. Advisedly, Thomas Jefferson, then governor of Virginia, decided against prosecution, on the grounds that this would have treated the slave as a free, if offending, citizen. There were limits to both rights and the duty of loyalty, confined to the free alone.[19]

The maroon wars are in a sense outside the scope of a book on the application of the laws of treason, because legal proceedings were notably absent against these groups of free black and mixed-race people. The view of them seems to presage the whole designation of peoples in the subsequent second British Empire, such as the Criminal Tribes laws of late nineteenth-century British-ruled India. The reactions of the British authorities in 1795–6 were vigorous but ineffective military invasions of rebel-held territories. Troops were rushed to Barbados and thence allocated to the different troublespots. In St. Lucia, the promising career of John Moore (famous for his retreat to Corunna fifteen years later) was almost stifled by his inability to bring the 'Brigands' or rebels to a decisive battle. In St. Vincent, the 'Black Caribs', a term which the British authorities used to designate African slaves and runaways, while the relatively few 'Yellow Caribs' were regarded as genuine indigenous people, almost overran the capital of the island, and the situation was saved only by heroic defence, and, eventually, by a level of savagery that British participants thought unprecedented. As in Grenada and St. Lucia, the alliance with French smallholders, equally disaffected from British rule, provided the Black Caribs with crucial intelligence as well as military support. In political ideals, too, there were elements of French republican rhetoric, but the key factor was the British determination to abolish

---

[18] Cox, 'Fédon's Rebellion', p. 16.
[19] See Anderson, 'Old Subjects, New Subjects and Non-Subjects'.

a zone of freedom, into which it was believed French government agents were infiltrating, and suppress a group who did not acknowledge British authority or legitimacy. The second Carib War in St. Vincent was therefore aimed at the entire removal of an entire people, a form of ethnic cleansing recalling the treatment of the Nova Scotia Acadians in 1755. There was clear designation of Black Caribs as a treasonable *people*, who had to be removed. Also, there was an element of seeing in this maroon, free, black, population, a force that was anomalous in the context of white/black structures. As in eighteenth-century Virginia, the existence of a free black population, however passive in these islands and, in the matter of slave runaways, cooperative, seems to have stirred up mistrust and anxiety. In both St. Vincent and Jamaica, there was an air of unfinished business being taken up and concluded in the 1790s expulsions.[20]

As the fighting progressed, the 'inhabitants' (white, Anglophone settlers) petitioned the authorities:

> In various instances the Cultivation of the lands has been greatly retarded by the Negroes inhabiting the Windward Coasts of this Island, a Race of People who have been vulgarly and most improperly stiled Charibs; but who are really and strictly nothing but Negroes and Intruders into this Country.

Alleging terrible crimes committed by these supposed Caribs, they pointed out that 'hundreds' of British people had been transported to the colonies for a lot less serious crimes, and pleaded for the complete removal of 'these merciless and faithless Savages'. The colony's governor and military commander General Ralph Abercrombie explored the possibilities for more than 4,700 people, suggesting that

> if there is a Spanish War, send them to Rattan, or any of the part of the Main considerably to Leeward. If there is not, land them upon St. Domingo when the Spaniards have given it up – perhaps the Island of Samana ... The yellow Charibs who are few in number, and innocent of the late War, may safely and properly be allowed to remain. They are the origines of the island.[21]

For the Black Caribs, 'Rattan', more properly Roatán, an island off what is now Honduras, was chosen. At least 1,300 of the Black Caribs died before arriving in Latin America, as they were moved from one waterless island to another: apart from the removal of the Acadians from Nova Scotia in 1755, this was the worst instance of ethnic cleansing since Cromwell's policies in Ireland in the

---

[20] Craton, *Testing the Chains*, p. 192.
[21] TNA, WO 1/82/423-6 Petition of the inhabitants of St. Vincent, 11 September 1795; 583–6, R. Abercrombie's report and recommendations about the Black Caribs, 1795.

1650s. Like the 'cajuns', though, these people – the Garifuna – have survived, with their own language (in part derived from Arawak, one of the native Carib languages) and their own distinctive style of music, both in central America and as a diaspora culture in places such as New York.[22]

At the same time, in Jamaica, the Second Maroon War saw the authorities turn on the Trelawny Maroons who had observed the peace settlement of 1739 without any real breaches. If the British had in effect been forced to make peace in the 1730s at the end of the First Maroon War, they clearly felt that there needed to be a final settlement of the issue. One longstanding grievance of the slaveowners was that the maroons had not fulfilled the agreement to recapture and return runaway slaves. This was despite repeated severe legislation, making the harbouring of runaways punishable by transportation (which in fact meant re-enslavement for a maroon, being sold outside the colony). As one contemporary author put it, 'that the Maroons had proved themselves a useful body, cannot be denied. Besides their utility in preventing assemblages of fugitives, they had been active in the suppression of rebellions'. By the 1790s, however, the mutual trust and practical coexistence of maroon and slave societies had broken down. With the dominant white plantation owners hostile to them, and under increasing pressure from the authorities, the maroons in effect declared war in 1795 after a nasty incident in which two of their members had been flogged for pig-stealing, and began raiding white properties.[23] In one view, the maroons had

> flagrantly reneged and encroached on the treaty arrangements, resulting in the second Maroon War (1795–1796), in which the Trelawny Maroons (the largest group ...) declared war on the British. The Trelawny Maroons went on a bloody rampage of killing, plundering, and burning that resulted in the death of many people and farm animals, and the destruction of a large number of farms ... Quite apprehensive, Alexander Lindsay, the Duke of Balcarres, the Governor of Jamaica in 1796, was determined to save the island from the Maroons' destructiveness; his prescription for this was a simple one: it was to deport the Trelawny Town Maroons, in spite of the fact that they had laid down their arms under pledge that they would not be deported from the colony.[24]

This was very much the view of the other major account at the time by Edwards (1801), who included his Jamaica story in a more condemnatory account of

---

[22] C. Taylor, *The Black Carib Wars: Freedom, Survival and the Making of the Garifuna* (Oxford: Signal Books, 2012); A.O. Thompson, *Flight to Freedom: African Runaways and Maroons in the Americas* (Jamaica: University of the West Indies Press, 2006).
[23] R.C. Dallas, *A History of the Maroons* (London: A. Strahan, 1804), vol. I, pp. 97 and 101.
[24] J.D. Lockett, 'The Deportation of the Maroons of Trelawny Town to Nova Scotia and then back to Africa', *Journal of Black Studies*, 30 (1) (1999), pp. 5–14, p. 9.

Haiti and revolutionary activity in the Caribbean, and had few doubts about their threat to disorder and violence. It is clear from both Dallas and Edwards that one problem for the white authorities was the mobility of these maroons, who moved out of their area for economic and social reasons, wandering from estate to estate. Their freedom contrasted with the restrictions imposed on slave who could not leave a plantation without a pass signed by their owner or his overseer. The maroons were in some ways an anomaly in a highly controlled slave society. Exactly how many were in Trelawny Town and involved in the deportation is not entirely clear: the population was estimated at 1,400 in 1788. They were sent to Nova Scotia, to the surprise of the governor who published his protesting correspondence on the subject, and proved expensive to maintain there. After three years suffering Canadian winters, 538 were sent to Sierra Leone from Nova Scotia, of perhaps 600 who had been sent from Jamaica. Return to Jamaica was impossible, becoming a serious crime under a 1796 Act making it a hanging offence to return or even to *receive* a returner – even if the maroons had been able to arrange it. The second group, the Accompong Maroons, remained uninvolved, and have survived the subsequent two centuries.[25]

These policies were in effect ethnic cleansing at the command of the local rich landowners, but in the Grenada fighting, the engagement with so many free – and landholding – insurgents forced the British authorities to deploy the laws of crime, assault and treason to a very large extent. The thousands of slaves involved are hardly ever referred to after the defeat of the revolts, but the fear of slave revolt continued until the abolition of slavery. Colonial courtesies, the extension of legal rights to the insurgents, were clearly based on race and class in these Caribbean events. Property holders and white free men were likely to face at least some form of legal process, while free blacks or native Indians (and the Black Caribs probably had some native Carib ancestry) were not. In many ways, this became the pattern in Britain's empire until the mid-twentieth century.

Ireland 1798: The first modern nationalist revolt?

Ireland, though not strictly a colony, was an exceptional state with its own legislature and a hugely unequal social structure divided largely on religious grounds. The year 1798 marked a new phase in its history and national identity,

---

[25] Dallas, *History,* vol. 2, pp. 120 and 249; Lockett, 'Deportation', p. 12; B. Edwards, *An Historical Survey of the Island of Saint Domingo, together with an Account Negroes of the Island of Jamaica* .... London: John Stockdale, 1801), p. 355

and some historians have seen all the disturbances in eighteenth-century Ireland (as discussed in Chapter 4) as mere precursors to the main event, the drive to independence in the 1790s. Only a few remarks can be made here, in the face of a progressively complex and impressive historiography exploring the diversity of the events, and the different experiences of the different counties and groups engaged in the conflict. Continuities with earlier issues certainly existed over rural land and the recruitment to the militia, but new grievances, and new bodies of the aggrieved, had been added to the mix by the 1790s.[26] Ulster linen workers as well as farmers were angry, accompanied by a new form of Protestant radicalism, and, equally important, by the 1780s a newly confident Catholic urban class was beginning to assert itself. As Ian McBride notes, by the 1790s, 'The spectacular realignments within and between the three major confessional blocs overturned a hundred years of entrenched hostilities. The alliance of advanced reformers from the Protestant middle classes with their counterparts in the Catholic Committee, signalled by the formation of the Society of United Irishmen in 1791, would have seemed unimaginable just a decade before.'[27] This unity was recognized by the authorities as unprecedented and, by 1797, with rumours of a French landing imminent, savage repression was unleashed on Ulster in particular, as rumours of rebellion there spread. This left the support for the 1798 landing and rising weakened, and the threat was overwhelmed by loyalist forces within a few weeks. That did not end the killing, and it is estimated that at least 5,600 were killed in fighting, arbitrary executions and casual slaughter, particularly in Wexford. The figure, it has been suggested, could have been as high as 20,000. McBride notes that the new governor, Lord Cornwallis, perhaps because of his American experience, did not treat all Catholics or inhabitants of rebel areas as enemies: the British army had spent a great deal of effort recruiting Catholics, to regiments that generally fought very successfully in Britain's wars.[28] Legal repression, though, inevitably followed, with well-known leaders such as Theobald Wolfe Tone put on trial (in his French uniform), and James Kelly points to the continuation of the punishment of the body under treason law in the aftermath. 'It has been calculated that 378

---

[26] Martyn J. Powell, 'Ireland's Urban Houghers: Moral Economy Is Popular Protest in Late Eighteenth Ireland', in S.P. Finland and M. Boswell (eds), *The Laws and Other Legalities of Ireland, 1689–1850* (Farnham: Ashgate, 2011), pp. 231–300.

[27] Ian McBride, *Eighteenth-Century Ireland: The Isle of Slaves* (Dublin: Gill & Macmillan, 2009/2014), Kindle Loc. 8523; see also John Gibney, ed., *The United Irishmen, Rebellion and the Act of Union 1798–1803* (Barnsley: Pen and Sword, 2018) in association with *History Ireland*.

[28] Daniel Gahan, *The People's Rising: Wexford 1798* (Dublin: Gill and Macmillan, 1995); McBride, *Eighteenth-Century Ireland*, Kindle Loc. 8984.

(out of 1,358 who were convicted by a variety of military and civil tribunals) were hanged, but the number summarily executed was far larger.' The heads of 'traitors' were frequently struck off and publicly displayed. When in May 1799 Walter Devereux of County Wexford was found guilty of 'being a leader of rebellion, and concerned in the murder of different persons that were made prisoner by the rebels who acted under his authority', the court ordered 'that his head should be severed from his body, and exposed as the head of a traitor, his heart burned, and his body either quartered or given for dissection'. Others were transported to Australia, unusually for supposed traitors: 'in 1799 the *Minerva* and the *Friendship* sailed with two consignments of this sort, totalling about 230 prisoners'. Those sent included at least three Catholic priests. By the early 1800s about a quarter of those in Botany Bay were Irish.[29]

There were many aspects to this rising which distinguished it from previous actions in Ireland. Many sectarian divisions were overcome, and women were prominent in some of the disturbances. They were also numerous among property holders making claims of compensation for damaged property and other losses to the government afterwards.[30] Above all, the demand for national independence reflected a new sensibility about nationhood and identity that was influenced by the conflicts of both the American and the French Revolutions. For the British authorities, this was too close to home for comfort, and the reliance of the rebels on military aid from France was reminiscent of previous interventions in the Jacobite risings earlier in the century. Yet now, the intervention threatened more than a dynasty: the threat was to the British state itself. Consequently, there was a general panic in official circles that meant that any gathering of Irishmen was suspect. In England a group of Irish men in Kent were tried for treason in 1798, allegedly for working with the French for an invasion. Of the five men, tried by a special commission for treason, only one Quigley or O'Coigly, sometimes known as Father Quigley, was convicted and sentenced to death, and he was duly hanged and beheaded. Much of the evidence centred on their attempts to commission a ship to go to Holland or France – something that had become illegal without special permission (since war had broken out in 1793),

---

[29] Quotations cited from James Kelly, 'Punishing the Dead: Execution and the Executed Body in Eighteenth-Century Ireland' in Richard Ward (ed.), *A Global History of Execution and the Criminal Corpse* (Houndmills, Basingstoke: Palgrave Macmillan, 2015), pp. 37–70, 60; Thomas Pakenham, *The Year of Liberty: The Great Irish Rebellion of 1798* (London: Little Brown, 1969/1997), pp. 349–50. On Wolfe Tone, See McBride, *Eighteenth-Century Ireland*, Chapter 10.

[30] Catherine O'Connor, 'Women and the Rebellion, Wexford 1798', *History Studies*, 4 (2003), 1–16, p. 12; Daire Keogh and Nicholas Furlong, eds, *The Women of 1798* (Dublin, 1998).

and communicate directly with the Directory in Paris inviting them to invade England.[31] The level of surveillance as well as the attempts to convict for high treason suggests a degree of anxiety and vigilance in official circles at this time. Although it was possible to publish generally sympathetic accounts of the 1798 rebellion, attributing the desperation and the violence to the previous pattern of repression by the British authorities, as an anonymous Irish emigrant did in the aftermath 'in an address to the People of England', the Irish and their connection with their French allies induced panic reactions among the authorities on both sides of the Irish Sea.[32] Treason was everywhere, and the law, at least in England, was carefully observed in the trial process. Elsewhere, there were looser standards under conditions of greater violent conflicts. Ireland, like the West Indies, saw many casual extra-judicial killings in a context that was closer to a civil war than a defensive action against invasion. In this sense Ireland was increasingly treated as a colony, and the abolition of the Irish parliament soon after the 1798 rising signified a desire in London for tighter control of what might be seen as the backdoor to Britain, a policy reminiscent of the Act of Union between England and Scotland 100 years earlier. At the end of the eighteenth century, Ireland therefore shared a common experience of panic and repression with many other areas under British rule in the North Atlantic. Revolution and the threat of it provoked more than a crisis of the state: it was a crisis of empire.[33]

Revolutionary dreams: 'Bliss was it to be alive'

By 1800, the British Atlantic world had seen a transformation in the nature of threats from treason and rebellion. In Britain, there were no longer any dynastic rivals to the Hanoverian monarchy, and little scope for those rivals, even if they could be found, to be supported by culturally distinctive populations in the remoter, less developed areas of Scotland, Ireland or England. For the governing circles of Britain, the anxiety had shifted, from *rebellion* to *revolution*. Yet political repression of these aspirations also had a cultural dimension: in Ireland,

---

[31] Joseph Gurney, *The Trial of James O'Coigly, Otherwise Called James Quigley, Otherwise Called James John Fivey, Arthur O'Connor, John Binns, John Allen, and Jeremiah Leary for High Treason under a Special Commission at Maidstone in Kent* (London: M.Gurney, 1798); Howell, State Trials, vol. 27, pp. 1–254.

[32] See Anonymous, *The Causes of the Rebellion in Ireland Disclosed, in an Address to the People of England* (London: J.S. Jordan, 1799 according to the ESTC).

[33] See Michael T. Davis, Emma Macleod and Gordon Pentland, eds, *Political Trials in an Age of Revolutions: Britain and North Atlantic, 1793–1848* (Houndmills, Basingstoke: Palgrave Macmillan, 2019).

the colonial rule of coercive acts and the suppression of culture and religion continued there as it had once ruled in the Scottish Highlands. Revolution, though, threatened the narrowly based, propertied democracy that had triumphed over the monarchy in 1688. The Glorious Revolution did not change the structure of the franchise or the social composition of the members in Parliament. As the population grew after 1800, fewer and fewer people (men only) were in fact participating in the oldest democracy in the world. The authorities, beginning in the 1790s, reacted repressively to any sign of self-organization among the excluded, and up to the 1840s pursued writers, agitators, trade unionists and others for their critical, 'seditious' publications and campaigns.

This book was written in the bicentennial year of Manchester's 1819 Peterloo Massacre, when a peaceful gathering was violently attacked by cavalry troops, with many deaths and injuries. This might serve as a reminder of the violence of the early British state, but it seems very insignificant given some of the preceding violent conflicts such as those against the Jacobites in the first half of the eighteenth century, the ethnic cleansing of Caribs and maroons, and the use of extrajudicial killing by military forces in some of the violent episodes and conflicts in British colonies. In many ways, the legal practices developed in Britain were of limited applicability in the colonies. Mass banishments of rebels of traitors, for example, were impossible, as there was nowhere else to send them. A handful could be transported, to other colonies, eventually to Australia, but only in the case of the ethnic cleansing of the Black Caribs of St. Vincent was a policy of ejection beyond the boundaries of the British Empire implemented. At the close of the eighteenth century, the empire was troubled, or, to be more precise, its management was. Everywhere a different kind of freedom was being discussed, and such visions of a different future could not be suppressed. Yet the British authorities were clearly anxious to demonstrate their lawfulness, in effect having to prove their legitimacy in each treason case in the courts. In treason, the state itself is on trial along with those it prosecutes. Lisa Steffen proposed that it was through the treason laws that the British state and national identity were defined, and there is something to that view. By extension, it might be concluded that treason was also crucial in defining a specifically British identity throughout the empire, above all in the Atlantic world, and through treason trials the requirements of loyalty and Britishness were clarified and defined.[34]

---

[34] Steffen, *Defining a British State*.

References

PRINTED PRIMARY SOURCES:

American Sources:

Connecticut:

Public Records of the Colony of Connecticut, vol. 1 1665, vol. 2 *1675 to 1678*, ed. J.H. Trumbull (Hartford, CT: F.A. Brown, 1850 and 1852).

The Public Records of the Colony of Connecticut from October, 1706 to October, 1716, ed. Charles J. Hoadly (Hartford, CT: Case, Lockwood and Brainard, 1870).

Acts and Laws of His Majesties Colony of Connecticut (Boston, MA: Bartholomew Green and John Allen, 1702)

The Public Records of the Colony of Connecticut from May, 1775 to June 1776…, ed. Charles J. Hoadly (Hartford, CT: Lockwood and Brainard, 1890).

The Public Records of the State of Connecticut, from October, 1776 to February, 1778, inclusive, ed. Charles J. Hoadly (Hartford, CT: Press of the Case, Lockwood and Brainard, 1894).

The Public Records of the State of Connecticut, from May 18 1778 to April 23 1780, Inclusive, ed. Charles J. Hoadly (Hartford, CT: Press of the Case, Lockwood and Brainard, 1895).

Delaware:

Laws of the State of Delaware, 2 vols (Newcastle, DE: Samuel and John Adams, 1797).

Georgia:

Digest of the Laws of Georgia, 1755–1798, ed. Robert and George Watkins (Philadelphia, PA: R. Atken, 1800).

Maryland:

Bacon, Thomas, *Laws of Maryland at Large* (Annapolis, MD: Jonas Green, 1765).

Chancellor W. Kilty, *A Report of All Such English Statutes as Existed at the Time of the First Emigration of the People of Maryland and Which by Experience Have Been Found Applicable to the Local and Other Circumstances* (Annapolis, MD: J. Chandler, 1811).

Proceedings of the Council of Maryland, August 10, 1753–March 30, 1761, ed. William Hand Browne (Baltimore, MD: Maryland Historical Society, 1911), Archives of Maryland, vol. 31.

Journal and Correspondence of the Council of Safety, January 1–March 20, 1777, Journal and Correspondence of the State Council, March 20, 1777 to March 28, 1778, ed. W.H. Browne (Baltimore, MD: Maryland Historical Society, 1897 Archives of Maryland vol. 16).

Massachusetts:

Records of the Court of Assistants of the Colony of the Massachusetts Bay, 1630–1692, Printed for J. Noble, 3 vols (Boston, MA: Suffolk County, 1904).

The Records and Files of the Quarterly Courts of Essex County Massachusetts, vol. 1, 1636–1656 (Salem, MA: Essex Institute, 1911), vol. 2, 1656–1662 (Salem, MA: Essex Institute, 1912).

Speeches of the Governors of Massachusetts, 1765–1775; the Answers of the House of Representatives Thereto, ed. Alden Bradford (New York: da Capo Press, 1971; unabridged reprint of 1818 (Boston) edition, originally Boston: Russell and Gardner, 1818).

The Colonial Laws of Massachusetts, Reprinted from the Edition of 1672, with the Supplements through 1686, ed. William H. Whitmore (Boston, MA: Rockwell and Churchill, 1890).

Records of the Governor and Colony of the Massachusetts Bay in New England, *Vol. 4 1664–1674*, part I (Boston, MA: William White, 1854).

Worcester Town Records from 1753 to 1783, ed. Franklin R. Rice (Worcester, MA: Worcester Society of Antiquity, 1882).

New Plymouth, N.D. Shurtleff, eds, *Records of the Colony of New Plymouth in New England*, vol. 5 Court Orders, 1666–78 (Boston, MA: William White, 1856).

New Jersey:

Documents Relating to the Colonial History of the State of New Jersey, vol. 1, 1631–1687, ed. William A. Whiteread (Newark, NJ: Daily Journal, 1880).

Documents Relative to the Colonial History of the State of New Jersey, Vol. 7, 1746–51, ed. W.A. Whitehead (Newark, NJ: Daily Advertiser Printing House, 1883).

Minutes of the Provincial Congress and the Council of Safety for the State of New Jersey (Trenton, NJ: Naar, Day and Naar, 1879).

Minutes of the Council of Safety for the State of New Jersey, vol. 1 (Jersey City, NJ: John H. Lyon, 1872).

New York:

Colonial Laws of New York, vol. 1 (Albany, NY: James B. Lyon, 1894).

Journals of the Provincial Congress, Provincial Convention, Committee of Safety and Council of Safety of the State of New York, 1775–1777, vol. 1 (Albany, NY: Thurlow reed, Printer to the State, 1842).

Minutes of the Albany Committee of Correspondence, 1775–1778, ed. James Sullivan (Albany, NY: University of the State of New York, 1923), The Division of Archives and History.

The Montresor Journals, ed. G.D. Scull, John Montrésor, James Gabriel Montrésor (New York Historical Society, 1881).

North Carolina:

A Complete Revisal of all the Acts of the Assembly of North Carolina (New Bern, NC: James Davis, 1774).

Proceedings of the Safety Committee of Wilmington North Carolina, from 1774 to 1776, ed. Thomas Loring (Ralegh, NC: 1844).

Pennsylvania:

Statutes at Large, Pennsylvania, vol. 3, 1711–1724 (Philadelphia, PA: Clarence H. Busch, State Printer, 1896).

Thompson Westcott, *Names of the Persons Who Took the Oath of Allegiance to the State of Pennsylvania between the Years 1777 and 1789, with a History of the 'Test Laws' of Pennsylvania* (Philadelphia, PA: John Campbell, no date).

Black List: A List of Those Tories Who Took Part with Great-Britain in the Revolutionary War and Were Attainted of High Treason, Common Called the Black List (Philadelphia, PA: the Proprietor, 1802).

A.J. Dallas, *Reports of Cases Ruled and Adjudged in the Courts of Pennsylvania, before and since the Revolution*, 3 vols, 2nd ed. (Philadelphia, PA: P. Byrne, 1806).

Rhode Island

Acts and Laws of The English Colony of Rhode Island… Made and Passed since the Revision in June 1767 (Newport, RI: Solomon Southwick, 1772).

Rhode Island, *The Early Records of the Town of Providence*, ed. H. Rogers and G. Fields, vol. 15 (Providence, RI: Snow and Farnham, City Printers, 1899).

Records of the Colony of Rhode Island and Providence Plantations in New England, ed. J.R. Bartlett, vol. 2 (Providence, RI: Crawford Greene and Brother, State Printers, 1857).

South Carolina:

Statutes at Large in South Carolina, 3 vols, ed. Thomas Cooper (Columbia, SC: A.S. Johnson, 1838).

J.F. Grimké, *Public Laws of the State of South-Carolina* (Philadelphia: R. Aitken, 1790).

The State Records of South Carolina: Extracts from the Journals of the Provincial Congress of South Carolina, 1775–6, ed. W.E. Hemphill and W.A. Wates (Columbia, SC: South Carolina State Archives Department, 1960).

Virginia:

Calendar of Virginia State Papers, 1652–1781, vol. 1, ed. W.P. Palmer (Richmond, VA: R.F. Walker, 1875).

Hening, W.W., *The Statutes at Large, Being a Collection of the Laws of Virginia, from the First Session of the Legislature in the Year 1619, Statutes*, vol. 2 (New York, R., G. and W. Bartow, 1823).

Kennedy, John P., ed., *Journals of the House of Burgesses of Virginia, 1766–69* (Richmond, VA: Virginia State Library, 1905), vol. 11.

Executive Journals of the Council of Colonial Virginia, ed. H.R. McIlwaine, vol. 3 (Richmond, VA: D. Bottom, 1938).

H.R. McIlwaine, ed., *Proceedings of the Committees of Safety Cumberland and Isle of White Counties Virginia, 1775–6* (Richmond, VA: State Libraries, 1919).

General British and the Caribbean:

Mr. Aislabie's Two Speeches Considered: With his Tryal at Large in Both Houses of Parliament… (London: A. Moore, 1721).

Allardyce, J., *Historical Papers Relating to the Jacobite Period, 1699–1750*, 2 vols (Aberdeen: The New Spalding Club, 1895).

Allen, Ethan, *A Narrative of Col. Ethan Allen's Captivity, from the Time of His Being Taken by the British, Near Montreal, on the 25th Day of September, in the Year 1775 to the Time of His Exchange, on the 6th Day of May, 1778* (Isaiah Thomas and Alexander Thomas, 1807, registered in New Hampshire).

Amhurst, Nicholas, *The Doctrine of Innuendo's Discussed or the Liberty of the Press Maintain'd* anon, sometimes attributed to Nicholas Amhurst (London, 1731).

Anonymous, *The Causes of the Rebellion in Ireland Disclosed, in an Address to the People of England* (London: J.S. Jordan, 1799 according to the ESTC).

Besse, J., *A Collection of the Sufferings of the People Called Quakers…*, 3 vols (London: Luke Hindle, 1753).

Blackstone, W., *Commentaries on the Laws of England*, 4 vols (Oxford: Clarendon Press, 1765–9).

Britain, Jonathan, *The Rev Mr Talbot's Narrative of the Whole of His Proceedings Relative to Jonathan Britain* (Bristol, 1772).

Britain, Jonathan, *Some Particulars of the Life and Death of Jonathan Britain Who Was Executed at Bristol for Forgery, by a Gentleman Who Attended Him, with a Preface by the Rev Mr. Rouquet* (Bristol, 1772).

'Britannus', *An Answer to Mr. Mist's Journal of the Twenty-Eighth of January, No. 93*, by 'Britannus' (London: N. Blandford, 1727).

Burgoyne, *A State of the Expedition from Canada as Laid before the House of Commons, by Lieutenant-General Burgoyne*, 2nd ed. (London: 1780).

Burke, A., Aedanus Burke, as Cassius, *An Address to the Freemen of the State of South Carolina* (Philadelphia, PA: Robert Bell, 1783).

Burke, Edmund, *The Works of Edmund Burke* (Boston, MA, 1836), vol. I.

Burke, Edmund, 'A Letter to John Farr and John Harris, Sheriffs of the City of Bristol on the Affairs in America' (1777), in *The Works of the Right Honourable Edmund Burke* (London: Abel, Daldy, 1864), vol. 2.

Burrough, G., *A Declaration of the Sad and Great Persecution and Martyrdom of the People of God Called Quakers, in New England for the Worshipping of God* (Boston and London, 1661).

Coad, J., *Memorandum of the Wonderful Providences of God to a Poor Unworthy Creature, during the Time of the Duke of Monmouth's Rebellion and to the Revolution in 1688. By John Goad, One of the Sufferers* (London: Longman, Brown, Green, & Longmans, 1849).

Cobbett, *The Parliamentary History of England, vol. 19* (London: T. Hansard, 1814).

Connor, Timothy, 'A Yankee Privateersman in Prison in England, 1777–1779', *New England Historical and Geneaological Register*, 30 (1876), 174–8 (part 1); 343–52 (part 2).

Dallas, R.C., *A History of the Maroons* (London: A. Strahan, 1804).

Defoe, D., *The Proceedings of the Government against the Rebels, Compared with Persecutions of the Late Reigns* (1716, attributed to Daniel Defoe).

Defoe, D., *The Mercy of the Government Vindicated, to Which Are Added Remarks upon a Late Pamphlet Entituled an Argument to Prove the Affections of the People the Best Security of the Government* (London: James Roberts, 1716, attributed to Defoe).

The Notebook of Robert Doughty, 1662–1665, ed. James M. Rosenheim, Norfolk Record Society, vol. 54 (1989, printed Aberystwyth, 1991).

Douglas, F., *The History of the Rebellion in 1745 and 1746, Extracted from the Scots Magazine; with an Appendix, Containing an Account of the Trials of the Rebels; the Pretender and His Sons Declarations etc.* (Aberdeen: F. Douglass and W. Murray, 1755).

Drayton, John, *Memoirs of the American Revolution from Its Commencement to the Year 1776, Inclusive, as Relating to the State of South Carolina*, 2 vols (Charleston, SC: A.E. Miller, 1821).

Dudley, Joshua, *Memoirs of the Life of Joshua Dudley Explaining amongst Other Particulars the Motives of His Pretended Discovery of the Persons Concerned in Setting Fire to the Dock-Yard at Portsmouth in July 1770 Written by Himself* (London, 1772).

East, E.H., *Treatise of the Pleas of the Crown 2 vols* (London: J. Butterworth, 1803).

Edwards, B., *An Historical Survey of the Island of Saint Domingo, Together with an Account of the Maroon Negroes of the Island of Jamaica…* (London: John Stockdale, 1801).

Forbes, D.G., *Culloden Papers: Comprising an Extensive and Interesting Correspondence from the Year 1625 to 1746… from the Originals in the Possession of Duncan George Forbes of Culloden* (London: T. Cadell and W. Davies, 1815).

Forbes, R., *The Lyon in Mourning, or a Collection of Speeches, Letters, Journals etc. Relative to the Affairs of Prince Charles Edward Stuart, by the Rev. Robert Forbes, A.M., Bishop of Ross and Caithness, 1745–1775*, edited from his Manuscript, with a Preface, by Henry Paton, M.A., 3 vols (1895; reprinted, Edinburgh: Scottish Academic Press, 1975, The Scottish History Society).

Forster, Sir M., *A Report of Some of the Proceedings of the Commission for the Trial of the Rebels in the Year 1746, in the County of Surrey and of Other Crown Cases*, 3rd ed., ed. Michael Dobson (London: 1792, originally 1762).

Fortescue, Lord John, *Reports of Select Cases of all the Courts of Westminster-Hall…* (London: Henry Lintot, 1738).

The Tryal of Richard Francklin for a Misdemeanor … (Edinburgh: Gavin Hamilton and Company, 1731).

The Papers of Benjamin Franklin, vol. 21, *January 1, 1774, through March 22, 1775*, ed. William B. Willcox (New Haven and London: Yale University Press, 1978).

Gordon, W., *The History of the Rise, Progress and Establishment of the Independence of the United States of America*, 3rd ed. (New York, 1801).

Graham, E.R., 'Letters from a Jacobite transported to Virginia after the 1715 Rebellion', *Scottish Local History*, 78 (Spring 2010), n.d.

Gurney, Joseph, *The Trial of James O'Coigly, Otherwise Called James Quigley, Otherwise Called James John Fivey, Arthur O'Connor, John Binns, John Allen, and Jeremiah Leary for High Treason under a Special Commission at Maidstone in Kent* (London: M. Gurney, 1798).

Holt, Sir J., *A Report of All the Case Determined by Sir John Holt, Kt., from 1688 to 1710, Which Time He Was Lord Chief Justice of England* (London: E. and R. Nutt and R. Gosling, 1738).

Horsmanden, D., *The New York Conspiracy, or a History of the Negro Plot, with the Journal of the Proceedings against the Conspirators at New York in the Years 1741–1742* (originally 1744; New York: Southwick and Pelsue, 1810).

Jacob's Law Dictionary, ed. T.E. Tomlins, *The Law Dictionary, originally Complied by Giles Jacobs* (London, 1809).

John The Painter

Joseph Gurney, *The Trial of James Hill al. James Hinde or James Aitkin (Known Also by the Name of John the Painter) for Feloniously… Setting Fire to the Rope House of HM's Dock-yard… 6 March 17 Geo III, 1777 John The Painter's Ghost: How He Appeared on the Night of His Execution to Lord Temple* (London, 1777).

A Short Account of the Motives Which Determined the Man Called John the Painter and Justification of His Conduct, Written by Himself and Sent to His Friend Mr A. Tomkins, with a Request to Publish It after His Execution (London, 1777).

The Trial of James Hill, Alias John the Painter, for Wilfully Setting Fire to the Ropehouse in the King's Yard at Portsmouth… (London, 1777).

The Trial of James Aitken, Commonly Called John the Painter, an Incendiary… (London: 1777).

The Trial at Large of James Hill Otherwise James Hind, Otherwise James Aitken, Commonly Known by the Name of John the Painter… (1777).

Home Office Papers (George III): 1770–2 (1881).

Journal of the House of Commons, vol. 33.

Journal of the House of Lords, vol. 21, 1718–1721 (London, 1767–1830).

Horsmanden, D., *The New York Conspiracy, or the History of the Negro Plot, with the Journal of the Proceedings against the Conspirators at New York in the Years 1741–2* (New York: Southwick and Pelsue, 1810, originally 1744).

Howell, T.B., *A Complete Collection of State Trials and Proceedings for High Treason and Other Crime and Misdemenors….Vol. 17, 12 George I to 17 George I, 1726–1743* (London: for Longman etc, 1816).

Hutchins, P.O., *Diary and Letters of Thomas Hutchinson* (Boston, 1884).

Laurens, Henry, *Narrative of the Capture of Henry Laurens* (Charleston, 1857).

Levot, P., *Procès d'Alexandre Gordon, Espion Anglais, Décapité a Brest en 1769* (Brest, 1861).

Middlesex, Calendar of Sessions Books, 1689 to 1709, ed. W.J. Hardy (Westminster, 1905).

The Case of the Honourable Alexander Murray Esq… (London: C. Pugh, 1751).

Niles, N., *Principles and Acts of the Revolution in America* (Baltimore, MD, 1822).

North Riding Quarter Sessions Records, 9 vols, ed. Rev J. Atkinson (North Riding Record Society), vol. 5: 1887; vol. 6: 1888; vol. 8: 1889.

Pitman, H., *A Relation of the Great Suffering and Strange Adventures of Henry Pitman* (London: Andrew Sowle, 1689).

Ramsay, D., *History of South Carolina*, 3 vols (Trenton, NJ: Isaac Collins, 1785).

Rawlin, William, *The Laws of Barbados Collected by William Rawlin of the Middle Temple, London Esq., and Now Clerk to the Assembly of the Said Island* (London: William Rawlin, 1699).

The Trial of the Cause of an Action Brought by Stephen Sayre Esq., against the Right Honourable Earl of Rochford on Thursday 27 June 1776…Published from Mr Gurney's Notes (London: G. Kearsley, n.d.).

Scharf, T., *A History of Maryland*, 3 vols (Baltimore, ND: John B. Piet, 1879).

Seton, Sir B.G., and Jean Gordon Arnot, *The Prisoners of the '45, edited from the State Papers*, 3 vols (Edinburgh UP for the Scottish Historical Society, 1929).

Shropshire: Abstract of the Orders Made by the Court of Quarter Sessions for Shropshire, Vol. 1, 1638–1709, ed. R. Lloyd Kenyon (Shropshire: no date).

Simmons, R.C., and P.D.G. Thomas, eds, *Proceedings and Debates of the British Parliaments Respecting North America 1754–1783, 6 vols*. (White Plains, NY, 1984).

Sizer, T., ed., *The Autobiography of Colonel John Trumbull: Patriot-Artist, 1756–1843* (New Haven: Yale University Press, 1841).

Star Chamber, *A Decree of the Star Chamber Concerning Printing* (originally London, Robert Barker, 1637, reprinted The Grolier Club, 1884).

State Trials, ed. T.B. Howell, Vols 26 and 27 (London: Howells, 1820).

The Statutes at Large from the First Year of the Reign of George the First to the Third Year of the Reign of King George the Second 5 vols, ed. Owen Ruffhead (London: Mark Basket, 1763).

Statutes of the Realm, Charles Eyre and William Strahan (1786).

Statutes of the Realm, ed. John Raithby (1819).

Thomas, Isaiah, *The History of Printing in America, with a Biography of Printers…*, 2 vols (Worcester, MA: I. Thomas, June 1810).

Thrale, Mary, *Selections from the Papers of the London Corresponding Society, 1792–1799* (Cambridge University Press, 1993).

Tindall, N., *The Continuation of Mr Rapin's History of England from the Revolution to the Present Times*, 6th ed., vol. 14 (4th of the Continuation) (London: Mr. Knapton, 1758).

Treasury, *Calendar of Treasury Books, Volume 8: 1685–1689*, part 1, ed. William A. Shaw (London: HMSO, 1923).

John Trumbull, *American Remonstrances: Letters by John Trumbull* (London, New York and New Haven, 1841).

Turnbull, G., *A Narrative of the Revolt and Insurrection of the French Inhabitants of Grenada, by an Eye-Witness* (Edinburgh: Constable, 1795).

Tutchin, John, *The Western Martyrology; or Bloody Assizes* (orig. 1795; 5th ed., reprinted, London: James Blackwood, 1883).

Tutchin, *The Trial of Mr John Tutchin for Writing a Certain Libel Called the Observator* (London: Thomas Spring, 1704).

Tutchin, *The Trackers Vindicated or, an Answer to the Whigs' New Black List… and a Word to Mr John Tutchin about His Scandalous Ballad…* (London: n.d., 1705).

Tutchin, *An Account of the Birth, Education, Life and Conversation of That Notorious and Bold Scribbler, the Observator…* (Licensed, according to order, London, 1705).

The Letters of Valens, (Which Originally Appeared in the London Evening Post) with Corrections, Explanatory Notes, and a Preface, by the Author (Burke, William, Burke, Richard, and Burke, Edmund, 1729–1797).

Wheeler, A., 'Adam Wheeler: His Account of 1685', in H.E. Malden (ed.), *Camden Miscellany* 8 (London, 1910), 153–68.

White, Rev. G., *Historical Collections of Georgia: Containing the Most Interesting Facts, Traditions, Biographical Sketches, Anecdotes, etc., Relating to Its History and Antiquities, from the First Settlement to the Present* (New York City Pudney and Russell, 1854).

Wigfield, W.M., *The Monmouth Rebels, 1685* (Taunton: Somerset Record Society, 1985).

Zenger, *Remarks on the Trial of John Peter Zenger, Printer of the New York Weekly Journal Who Was Lately Tried and Acquitting for Publishing and Printing Two Libels against the Government of that Province* (London: J. Roberts, 1738).

Zenger, *The Tryal of John Peter Zenger, of New York, Printer…* (London: J.Wilford, 1738).

Zenger, *The Trial of John Peter Zenger, of New York, Printer,… to Which Is Now Added, Being Never Printed before, the Trial of Mr William Owen, Bookseller* (London: J. Almon, 1765).

PRINTED SECONDARY SOURCES:

Adam, M.I., 'Eighteenth-Century Landlords and the Poverty Problem', Part 1, *The Scottish Historical Review*, 19 (73) (1921), 1–20, and Part 2, 19 (75) (1922), 161–79.

Aljunied, K., 'Coffee-Shops in Colonial Singapore: Domains of Contentious Politics', *History Workshop Journal*, LXXVII (2014), 66–85.

Alden, J.R., *Stephen Sayre: American Revolutionary Adventurer* (Baton Rouge: Louisiana State University Press, 1983).

Anderson, C., 'Old Subjects, New Subjects and Non-Subjects: Silences and Subjecthood in Fédon's Rebellion, Grenada, 1795–96', in R. Bessel and N. Guyatt (eds), *War, Empire and Slavery, 1770–1830* (Houndmills, Basingstoke: Palgrave Macmillan, 2010), 201–17.

Anderson, V.D., *The Martyr and the Traitor: Nathan Hale, Moses Dunbar and the American Revolution* (New York: Oxford University Press, 2017).

Aptheker, H., *The American Revolution, 1763–1783: A History of the American People* (New York: International Publishers, 1960, new ed. 1993).

Archer, R., *As If an Enemy Country: The British Occupation of Boston and the Origins of Revolution* (New York: Oxford University Press, 2010).

Armitage, D., *The Declaration of Independence: A Global History* (Cambridge, MA: Harvard University Press, 2007).

Australian Law Reform Commission, *Fighting Words: A Review of Sedition Laws in Australia* (Commonwealth of Australia, 2006).

Baker, Sir J., *The Oxford History of the Laws of England, Vol. 6, 1483–1558* (Oxford University Press, 2003).

Barnard, T.C., 'Athlone, 1685: Limerick, 1710: Religious Riots or Charivaris?', *Studia Hibernica*, 27 (1993), 68–9.

Barnes, V.F., 'Francis Legge, Governor of Loyalist Nova Scotia 1773–1776', *New England Quarterly*, 4 (3) (1931), 420–47.

Barrell, J., *Imagining the King's Death: Figurative Treason, Fantasies of Regicide, 1993–1796* (Oxford University Press, 2000).

Barrell, J., *The Spirit of Despotism: Invasions of Privacy in the 1790s* (Oxford University Press, 2006).

Bartlett, T., 'An End to Moral Economy: The Irish Militia Disturbances of 1793', *Past and Present*, 99 (1983), 41–64.

Bateman, D.A., *Disenfranchising Democracy: Constructing the Electorate in the United States* (Cambridge University Press, 2018).

Baugh, D.A., 'Maritime Strength and Atlantic Commerce: The Uses of "a Grand Maritime Empire"', in Lawrence Stone (ed.), *An Imperial State at War: Britain from 1689 to 1815* (London: Routledge, 1994), 185–223.

Baugh, D.A., *The Global Seven Years War: Britain and France in a Great Power Contest* (London: Routledge, 2011).

Beatttie, J.M., *Policing and Prosecution in London: Urban Crime and the Limits of Terror* (Oxford, Oxford University Press, 2001).

Becker, H., *The Outsiders: Studies in the Sociology of Deviance* (New York: Free Press, 1963).

Beedell, A.V., 'John Reeves's Prosecution for a Seditious Libel, 1795-6: A Study in Political Cynicism', *Historical Journal*, 36 (1993), 790–824.

Bellamy, J.G., *The Tudor Law of Treason* (London: Routledge Kegan Paul, 1979).

Bellany, A., 'Singing Libel in Early Stuart England: The Case of the Staines Fiddlers, 1627', *Huntington Library Quarterly*, 69 (2006): 177–93.

Bellany, A., 'Libels in Action: Ritual, Subversion and the English Literary Underground, 1603-42', in P. Griffiths (ed.), *The Politics of the Excluded, c. 1500-1850* (Houndmills, Basingstoke: Palgrave, 2001), 99–125.

Bellany, A., 'Railing Rhymes Revisited: Libels, Scandals, and Early Stuart Politics', *History Compass*, 5 (4) (2007), 1136–79.

Benton, L., *Law and Colonial Cultures: Legal Regimes in World History, 1400-1900* (New York and Cambridge: Cambridge University Press, 2002).

Benton, L., *A Search for Sovereignty: Law and Geography in European Empires* (New York: Cambridge University Press, 2010).

Benton, L., and R.J. Ross, eds, *Legal Pluralism and Empires, 1500-1850* (New York University Press, 2013).

Berger, R., 'Bills of Attainder: A Study of Amendment by the Court', *Cornell University Law Review*, 63 (3) (1978), 355–404.

Bickham, T.O., 'Sympathizing with Sedition? George Washington, the British Press, and British Attitudes during the American War of Independence', *The William and Mary Quarterly*, 3rd ser., 59 (2002), 101–22.

Bielinski, S., 'Albany County', in Tiedermann et al. (eds), *The Other Loyalists*, 155–73.

Bilder, M.S., *Transatlantic Constitution: Colonial Legal Culture and the Empire* (Cambridge, MA: Harvard University Press, 2004).

Billings, W.M., 'The Transfer of English Law to Virginia, 1606-50', in K.R. Andrews, N.P. Canny and P.E.H. Hair (eds), *Westward Enterprise: English Activities in Ireland, the Atlantic, and America, 1480-1650* (Liverpool: Liverpool University Press, 1978), 215–44.

Black, J., *Natural and Necessary Enemies: Anglo-French Relations in the Eighteenth Century* (London: Gerald Duckworth, 1986).

Black, J., *British Diplomats and Diplomacy, 1688–1800* (Liverpool University Press, 2001).

Blackstone, W., *Commentaries on the Laws of England, 4 vols* (Oxford: Clarendon Press, 1770).

Blumberg, P.I., *Repressive Jurisprudence in the Early American Republic: The First Amendment and the Legacy of English Law* (Cambridge: Cambridge University Press, 2010).

Boudin, L.B., '"Seditious Doctrines" and the "Clear and Present Danger" Rule: Part I', *Virginia Law Review*, 38 (1952), 143–86.

Brannon, R.N., 'Reconciling the Revolution: Resolving Conflict and Rebuilding Community in the Wake of Civil War in South Carolina, 1775–1860' (unpublished Ph.D., University of Michigan, 2007).

Breen, K., 'Sir George Rodney and St Eustatius in the American War: A Commercial and Naval Distraction, 1775–8', *Mariner's Mirror*, 84 (2) (1998), 193–203.

Bromley, J.S., *Corsairs and Navies, 1600–1760* (London: The Hambledon Press, 1987).

Brooks, C.W., *Law, Politics and Society in Early Modern England* (Cambridge University Press, 2008).

Bryan, I., 'Unpalatable in Word or Deed: Hostility, Difference and Free Expression', *Crimes and Misdemeanours*, 1 (2007), 126–53.

Butler, D., and D. Kavanagh, *The British Election of October, 1974* (Houndmills, Basingstoke: Palgrave Macmillan, 1975).

Cahill, B., 'The Sedition Trial of Timothy Houghton: Repression in a Marginal New England Planter Township during the Revolutionary Years', *Acadiensis*, 24 (1994), 35–58.

Cahill, B., 'Sedition in Nova Scotia: R. V. Howe and the Contested Legality of Seditious Libel', *U.N.B.L.J.[University of New Brunswick Law Journal]*, 51 (2002), 95–140.

Cahn, M.D., 'Punishment, Discretion, and the Codification of Prescribed Penalties in Colonial Massachusetts', *American Journal of Legal History*, 33 (1989), 107–33.

Calhoon, R.M., *The Loyalists in Revolutionary America, 1760–1781 (1973)* (New York: Harcourt Brace Jovanovich, 1973).

Calloway, C.G., *The Revolution in Indian Country: Crisis and Diversity in Indian Communities* (New York: Cambridge University Press, 1995).

Calloway, C.G., *White People, Indians and Highlanders: Tribal Peoples and Colonial Encounters in Scotland and America* (New York: Oxford University Press, 2008).

Campbell, R., 'Sentence of Death by Burning for Women', *Journal of Legal History*, 5 (1), 44–59.

Candlin, K., *The Last Caribbean Frontier, 1795–1815* (Houndmills, Basingstoke: Palgrave Macmillan, 2012).

Candlin, K. (2018), 'The Role of the Enslaved in the "Fédon Rebellion" of 1795', *Slavery and Abolition*, published online April 2018.

Carnell, R., *A Political Biography of Delarivier Manley* (London: Pickering and Chatto, 2008).

Carp, B.L., *Defiance of the Patriots: The Boston Tea Party in the Making of America* (New Haven, CT: Yale University Press, 2010).

Carpenter, A.H., 'Habeas Corpus in the Colonies', *The American Historical Review*, 8 (1) (October., 1902), 18–27.

Carroll, K.L., 'Persecution and Persecutors of Maryland Quakers, 1658–1661', *Quaker History*, 99 (2010), 15–31.

Cash, A.H., *John Wilkes: The Scandalous Father of Civil Liberty* (New Haven, CT: Yale University Press, 2006).

Cashin, E.J., *The King's Ranger: Thomas Brown and the American Revolution on the Southern Frontier* (Athens, GA: University of Georgia Press, 1989).

Cavanagh, D., and T. Kirk, eds, *Subversion and Scurrility: Popular Discourse in Europe from 1500 to the Present* (Aldershot, 2000).

Childs, J., 'The Laws of War in Seventeenth-Century Europe and Their Application during the Jacobite War in Ireland', in David Edwards, Padraig Lenihan and Clodagh Tait (eds), *Age of Atrocity: Violence and Political Conflict in Early Modern Ireland* (Dublin: Four Courts Press, 2007), 283–300.

Chapin, B., 'The American Revolution as Lèse Majesty', *Pennsylvania Magazine of History and Biography*, 79 (3) (1955), 318–21.

Cohen, S.S., 'The Odyssey of Ebenezer Smith Platt', *Journal of American Studies*, 18 (2) (1984), 255–74.

Cohen, S.S., *Yankee Sailors in British Gaols: Prisoners of War at Forton and Mill, 1777–1783* (Newark, DE: University of Delaware Press, 1995).

Cohen, S.S., *British Supporters of the American Revolution, 1775–1783: The Role of the 'Middling-level' Activists* (Woodbridge: The Boydell Press, 2004).

Coleman, A.N., 'Loyalists in War, Americans in Peace: The Reintegration of the Loyalists, 1775–1800' (Unpublished Ph.D., University of Kentucky, 2008).

Coleman, J.M., 'Thomas McKean and the Origins of an Independent Judiciary', *Penn. History*, 34 (1967), 111–30.

Colley, L., *Britons: Forging the Nation, 1707–1737* (New Haven, CT: Yale University Press, 1992).

Colley, L., *Captives: Britain, Empire and the World* (New York/London: Random House, 2002).

Collins, J.M., *Martial Law and English Laws, c. 1500–1700* (CUP, 2017).

Colonial Origins of the American Constitution: A Documentary History, ed. Donald S. Lutz (Indianapolis: Liberty Fund 1998), online at http://oll.libertyfund.org/EBooks/Misc-AmericanColonialDocs_0013.pdf.

Cox, E.L., 'Fédon's Rebellion 1795–96: Causes and Consequences', *The Journal of Negro History*, 67 (1) (1982), 7–19.

Craton, M., *Testing the Chains: Resistance to Slavery in the British West Indies* (Ithaca, NY: Cornell University Press, 1982).

Cressy, D., *Dangerous Talk: Scandalous, Seditious and Treasonable Speech in Pre-Modern England* (Oxford: Oxford University Press, 2010).

Crothers, A.G., 'Northern Virginia's Quakers and the War for Independence: Negotiating a Path of Virtue in a Revolutionary World', in Tiedemann et al. (eds), *The Other Loyalists*, 105–30.

Daniels, C., '"Liberty to Complaine": Servant Petitions in Maryland, 1652–1797', in C.L. Tomlins and B.H. Mann (eds), *The Many Legalities of Early America* (Chapel Hill, NC: University of North Carolina Press/Omohundro Institute of Early American History and Culture, 2001), 219–49.

Davidson, N., 'The Scottish Path to Capitalist Agriculture 1: From the Crisis of Feudalism to the Origins of Agrarian Transformation (1688–1746)', *Journal of Agrarian Change*, 4 (3) (2004), 227–68.

Davis, J., 'The London Garotting Panic of 1862: A Moral Panic and the Creation of a Criminal Class in Mid-Victorian England', in V.A.C. Gatrell, B. Lenman and G. Parker (eds), *Crime and the Law: A Social History of Crime in Western Europe since 1500* (London: Europa Publications, 1980), 190–213.

Davis, M.T., '"That Odious Class of Men Called Democrats": Daniel Isaac Eaton and the Romantics, 1704–1795', *History*, 84 (273) (1999), 74–92.

Davis, M.T., 'The British Jacobins: Folk Devils in the Age of Counter-Revolution?', in David Lemmings and Claire Walker (eds), *Moral Panics, the Media and the Law in Early Modern England*, (Houndmills, Basingstoke: Palgrave Macmillan, 2009), 221–44.

Davis, M.T., E. Macleod and G. Pentland, eds, *Political Trials in an Age of Revolutions: Britain and North Atlantic, 1793–1848* (Houndmills, Basingstoke: Palgrave Macmillan, 2019).

de Armond, A.J., 'Andrew Bradford', *Pennsylvania Magazine of History and Biography*, 62 (1938), 463–87.

De Beer, E.S., 'Executions Following the "Bloody Assize"', *Bulletin of the Institute of Historical Research*, 4 (1926–7), 36–9.

De Vattel, E., *The Law of Nations or the Principles of the Law of Nature*, edited and with an Introduction by Be´la Kapossy and Richard Whatmore (Indianapolis, IN: Liberty Fund, 2008).

Deng, S., *Coinage and State Formation in Early Modern England* (New York: Palgrave Macmillan, 2011).

Devereaux, S., 'The Abolition of the Burning of Women in England Reconsidered', *Crime, Histoire & Sociétés / Crime, History & Societies* [online], 9 (2) (2005), online since 26 February 2009, URL: http://journals.openedition.org/chs/293, DOI: 10.4000/chs.293 (accessed 11 November 2019).

Dobson, D., *Directory of Scots Banished to the American Plantations, 1650–1775* (Baltimore, MD: Genealogical Publishing Co, 1984).

Donnelly, J.S., 'The Whiteboy Movement, 1761–5', *Irish Historical Studies*, vol. 21, no. 81 (March, 1978), 20–54.

Donnelly, J.S., 'Irish Agrarian Rebellion: The Whiteboys of 1769–76', *Proceedings of the Royal Irish Academy: Archaeology, Culture, History, Literature*, vol. 83 (1983), 293–31.

Doyle, R.C., *The Enemy in Our Hands: America's Treatment of Enemy Prisoners of War from the Revolution to the War on Terror* (Lexington, Kentucky: University of Kentucky Press, 2011).

Duffy, J.J., and H.N. Muller III, *Inventing Ethan Allen* (Hanover and London: University Press of New England, 2014).

Dyzenhaus, D., '*Schmitt V. Dicey:* Are States of Emergency inside or outside the Legal Order?', *Cardozo Law Review*, 27 (5) (2008), 2006–40.

Earle, P., *Monmouth's Rebels: The Road to Sedgemoor, 1685* (New York: St. Martin's Press, 1977).

Eastwood, D., 'John Reeves and the Contested Idea of Constitution', *J. for Eighteenth-Century Studies*, 16 (2) (1993), 197–212.

Eder, M., *At the Instigation of the Devil': Capital Punishment and the Assize in Early Modern England* (Germany: Hilgertshausen-Tandern, 2009).

Eldridge, L.D., *A Distant Heritage: The Growth of Free Speech in Early America* (New York: New York University Press, 1994).

Eldridge, L.D., 'Before Zenger: Truth and Seditious Speech in Colonial America, 1607–1700', *The American Journal of Legal History*, 39 (3) (1995), 337–58.

Ellet, E.F., *Revolutionary Women in the War for American Independence* (New York: Baker and Scribner, 1848).

Eloranta, J., and J. Land, 'Hollow Victory? Britain's Public Debt and the Seven Years' War', *Essays in Economic & Business History*, 29 (2011), 101–18.

Emsley, C., 'An Aspect of Pitt's "Terror": Prosecutions for Sedition during the 1790s', *Social History*, 6 (2) (1981), 155–84.

Emsley, C., 'Repression, "Terror" and the Rule of Law in England during the Decade of the French Revolution', *The English Historical Review*, 100 (397) (1985), 801–25.

Engdahl, D.E., 'Soldiers, Riots and Revolution: The Law and History of Military Troops in Civil Disorders', *Iowa Law Review*, 57/1 (1971), 1–73.

Evans, C., 'Oaths of Allegiance in Colonial New England', *Proceedings of the American Antiquarian Society*, 31 (2) (1922), 377–438.

Farmer, L., *Criminal Law, Tradition and Legal Order: Crime, and the Genius of Scots Law, 1747 to the Present* (Cambridge University Press, 1997).

Finkelman, P., 'The Zenger Case: Prototype of a Political Trial', in Michael R. Belknap (ed.), *American Political Trials* (Greenwood Press, 1994).

Fisher, L.D., '"Why Shall Wee Have Peace to Bee Made Slaves": Indian Surrenderers during and after King Philip's War', *Ethnohistory*, 64 (1) (2017), 91–114.

Flavell, F., 'The Plot to Kidnap George III', *BBC History*, November 2006, 13–16.

Flavell, J., *When London Was the Capital of America* (New Haven, CT: Yale University Press, 2010).

Fox, A., 'Ballads, Libels and Popular Ridicule in Jacobean England', *Past and Present*, 145 (1994), 47–83.

Fox, A., 'Rumour, News and Popular Political Opinion in Elizabethan and Early Stuart England', *The Historical Journal*, 40 (1997), 597–620.

Friedman, E.R., 'Habeas Corpus in Three Dimensions, I: Habeas Corpus as a Common Law Writ', *Harvard Civil Rights-Civil Liberties Law Review*, 46 (2011), 591–618.

Gahan, D., *The People's Rising: Wexford 1798* (Dublin: Gill and Macmillan, 1995).

Gallay, A., *The Rise of the English Empire in the American South, 1670–1717* (New Haven, CT: Yale University Press, 2002).

Carrier, J.G., 'Moral Economy: What's in a Name?', *Anthropologival Theory*, 18 (1) (2018), 18–35.

Garnham, N., *Courts, Crime and the Criminal Law in Ireland,1692–1760* (Dublin: Irish Academic Press, 1996).

Garnham, N., 'Police and Public Order and Eighteenth-Century Dublin', *Proceedings of the British Academy*, 107 (2001), 81–91.

Gaspar, D.G., and D.P. Geggus, eds, *A Turbulent Time: The French Revolution and the Greater Caribbean* (Bloomington, IN: Indiana University Press, 1997).

Gaskill, M., *Crime and Mentalities in Early Modern England* (Cambridge University Press, 2000).

Geste, G., *Liberty and Coercion: The Paradox of American Government from the Founding to the Present* (Princeton NJ: Princeton University Press, 2015).

Gibbs, G.C., 'Press and Public Opinion: Prospective', in J.R. Jones (ed.), *Liberty Secured?* (Stanford, CA: Stanford University Press, 1992), 231–64.

Gibney, J., ed., *The United Irishmen, Rebellion and the Act of Union 1798–1803* (Barnsley: Pen and Sword, 2018) in association with *History Ireland*.

Goolrick, J.T., *The Life of General Hugh Mercer* (New York: The Neal Publishing Company, 1906).

Gould, E.H., 'Zones of Law, Zones of Violence: The Legal Geography of the British Atlantic, circa 1772', *The William and Mary Quarterly*, 60 (3) (July, 2003), 471–510.

Gould, E.H., 'Entangled Atlantic Histories: A Response from the Anglo-American Periphery', *American History Review*, 112 (2007), 764–86.

Grayling, A.C., *Towards the Light: The Story of the Struggles for Liberty and Rights That Made the Modern World* (London: Bloomsbury, 2007).

Green, T.H., *Verdict According to Conscience: Perspectives on the English Trial Jury* (Chicago: University of Chicago Press, 1985).

Green, T.H., 'The Jury, Seditious Libel and the Criminal Law', in R.H. Helmholtz and Thomas A. Green (eds), *Juries, Libel and Justice: The Role of English Juries in Seventeenth- and Eighteenth-Century Trials for Libel and Slander* (Los Angeles, CA: William Andrews Memorial Library, 1986), 39–91.

Greene, J.P., *Exclusionary Empire: English Liberty Overseas, 1600–1900* (Cambridge University Press, 2010).

Greenwood, F.M., 'The Treason Trial and Execution of David McLane', *Manitoba Law Journal*, 20 (1991), 3–14.

Greenwood, F.M., *Legacies of Fear: Law and Politics in the Era of the French Revolution* (Toronto: University of Toronto Press, 1993).

Gregory, A., *The Power of Habeas Corpus in America: From the King's Prerogative to the War on Terror* (New York: Cambridge University Press/The Independent Institute, 2013).

Hadfield, A., *Lying in Early Modern English Culture: From the Oath of Supremacy to the Oath of Allegiance* (Oxford University Press, 2017).

Halliday, P.D., *Habeas Corpus: From England to Empire* (Cambridge, MA: The Belknap Press of Harvard University Press, 2010).

Hamburger, P., 'The Development of the Law of Seditious Libel and the Control of the Press', *Stanford Law Review*, 37 (1985), 661–762.

Harris, M., *London Newspapers in the Age of Walpole: A Study of the Origins of the Modern English Press* (London and Toronto: Associated University Presses, 1987).

Harris, T., ed., *The Politics of the Excluded, c. 1500–1850* (Houndmills, Basingstoke: Palgrave, 2001).

Harris, T., *Revolution: The Great Crisis of the British Monarchy, 1685–1720* (London: Penguin, 2007).

Haskett, R.C., 'Prosecuting the Revolution', *AHR*, 59 (3) (1954), 578–87.

Haskett, R.C., 'William Paterson, Attorney General of New Jersey: Public Office and Private Profit in the American Revolution', *The William and Mary Quarterly*, 7 (1) (1950), 26–38.

Haskins, G.L., *Law and Authority in Early Massachusetts: A Study in Tradition and Design,* 2nd ed. (Lanham MD: University Press of America, 1985).

Hay, D. and P. Craven, eds, *Masters, Servants and Magistrates in Britain and the Empire, 1562–1955* (Chapel Hill, NC: University of North Carolina Press, 2004).

Hayton, D., 'Parliament and the Established Church', in D.W. Hayton, James Kelly and John Bergin (eds), *The Eighteenth-Century Composite State: Representative Institutions in Ireland and Europe, 1689–1800* (Houndmills, Basingstoke: Palgrave Macmillan, 2010), 78–106.

Head, M., *Crimes against the State: From Treason to Terrorism* (Farnham: Ashgate, 2011).

Heinzelman, S.S., *Riding the Black Ram: Law, Literature and Gender* (Stanford, CA: Stanford Law Books, 2010).

Hencke, D., and F. Beckett, *Marching to the Fault Line: The 1984 Miners Strike and the Death of Industrial Britain* (London: Constable and Robinson, 2009).

Henshaw, V., *Scotland and the British Army, 1700–1750: Defending the Union* (London: Bloomsbury, 2014).

Hill, L.M., 'The Two-Witness Rule in English Treason Trials: Some Comments on the Emergence of Procedural Law', *The American Journal of Legal History*, 12 (1968), 95–111.

Holdsworth, W., *History of English Law 17 vols 1903–1966* (London: Methuen/Sweet and Maxwell, 1945), vol. 4.

Hoock, H., *Scars of Independence: America's Violent Birth* (New York: Penguin/Random House, 2018).

Hoppit, J., *A Land of Liberty? England, 1689–1727* (Oxford University Press, 2000).

Horle, C.W., *Quakers and the English Legal System, 1660–1668* (Philadelphia: University of Pennsylvania Press, 1988).

Hostettler, J., *The Criminal Jury Old and New: Jury Power from Early Times to the Present Day* (Winchester: Waterside Press, 2004).

Howard, S., 'Crime, Communities and Authority in Early Modern Wales: Denbighshire, 1660–1730' (unpublished Ph.D. thesis, University of Wales, Aberystwyth, 2003).

Huffman, J.M., 'Americans on Paper: Identity and Identification in the American Revolution', (unpublished Ph.D., Harvard, 2013).

Hulsebosch, D.J., 'The Ancient Constitution and the Expanding Empire', *Law and History Review*, 21 (3) (2003), 439–82.

Hulsebosch, D.J., *Constituting Empire: New York and the Transformation of Constitutionalism in the Atlantic World, 1664–1830* (Chapel Hill: University of North Carolina Press, 2005).

Hulsebosch, D.J., 'English Liberties outside England: Floors, Doors, Windows and Ceilings in the Legal Architecture of Empire', *New York University Public Law and Legal Working Papers No. 571* (2016).

Humphrey, T.J., 'William Prendergast and the Revolution in the Hudson River Valley: "Poor Men Were Always Oppressed by the Rich"', in Nancy L. Roden and Ian K. Steele (eds), *The Human Tradition in the American Revolution* (Wilmington, DE: Scholarly Resources, 2000), 81–98.

Humphrey, T.J., 'Crowd and Court: Rough Music and Popular Justice in Colonial New York', in William Pencak, Matthew Dennis and Simon P. Newman (eds), *Riot and Revelry in Early America* (University Park, PA: University of Pennsylvania Press, 2002), 107–24.

Hurst, W., 'Treason in the United States: I. Treason Down to the Constitution', *Harvard Law Review*, 58 (1944), 226–72.

Hyman, H.M., *To Try Men's Souls: Loyalty Tests in American History* (Berkeley, CA: University of California Press, 1959).

Inderwick, F.A., *Side-Lights on the Stuarts*, 2nd ed. (London: Sampson Low, Marston, Searle and Rivington, 1891).

Irving, H.B., *The Life of Judge Jeffreys* (New York: Longman, Green and Co, 1898).

Jansen, S.L., *Dangerous Talk and Strange Behaviour: Women and Popular Resistance to the Reforms of Henry VIII* (Houndmills, Basingstoke: Macmillan, 1996).

Jasanoff, M., *Liberty's Exiles: American Loyalists in the Revolutionary World* (New York: Random House/Alfred A. Knopf, 2011).

Jenkins, D., 'The Sedition Act of 1798 and the Incorporation of Seditious Libel into First Amendment Jurisprudence', *American Journal of Legal History*, 45 (2001), 154–213.

John, R.R., *Spreading the News: The American Postal System from Franklin to Morse* (Cambridge, MA: Harvard University Press, 1995).

Johnson, H.A., 'English Statutes in Colonial New York', *New York History*, 58 (3) (1977), 277–96.

Johnson, H.A., 'The Rule of Law in the Realm and the Province of New York: Prelude to the American Revolution', *History*, 91 (1) (301) (2006), 3–23.

Jones, D.M., *Conscience and Allegiance in Seventeenth-Century England: The Political Significance of Oaths and Engagements* (Rochester, NY: University of Rochester Press, 1999).

Kaplan, M.L., *The Culture of Slander in Early Modern England* (Cambridge University Press, 1997).

Kars, M., *Breaking Loose Together the Regulator Rebellion in Pre-Revolutionary North Carolina* (Chapel Hill and London: The University of North Carolina Press, 2002).

Kelly, J., 'Punishing the Dead: Execution and the Executed Body in Eighteenth-Century Ireland', in Richard Ward (ed.), *A Global History of Execution and the Criminal Corpse* (Palgrave Macmillan, 2015), 37–70.

Keogh, D., and Nicholas Furlong, eds, *The Women of 1798* (Dublin: Four Courts Press, 1998).

Kerchner, B., 'Perish or Prosper: The Law and Convict Transportation in the British Empire, 1700–1850', *Law and History Review*, 21 (3) (2003), 527–84.

Kesselring, K., '"Negroes of the Crown": The Management of Slaves Forfeited by Grenadian Rebels, 1796–1831', *Journal of the Canadian Historical Association*, 22 (2) (2011), 1–29.

Kidd, C., 'Gaelic Antiquity and National Identity in Enlightenment Ireland and Scotland', *English Historical Review*, 109 (434) (1994), 1197–214.

Kindleberger, C.P., and R.Z. Aliber, *Manias, Panics, and Crashes: A History of Financial Crises*, 5th ed. (Hoboken, NJ: John Wiley, 2005).

Klooster, K., and Gert Oostindie, eds, *Curaçao in the Age of Revolutions, 1795–1800* (Leiden: KITLV Press, 2011).

Klug, K., K. Starmer and S. Weir, *Three Pillars of Liberty* (London: Routledge, 1996).

Konig, D.T., 'Dale's Laws and the Non-Common Law Origins of Criminal Justice in Virginia', *American Journal of Legal History*, 26 (1982), 354–75.

Konig, D.T., 'Regionalism in Early American Law', in Michael Grossberg and Christopher L. Tomlins (eds), *The Cambridge History of Law in America,* 2 vols (Cambridge: Cambridge University Press, 2008), vol. 1, *Early America (1580–1815)* 144–77.

Kramnick, I., and Barry Sheerman, *Harold Laski: A Life on the Left* (London: Allen Lane, 1993).

Labaree, L.W., *Royal Instructions to British Colonial Governors 1670–1776*, 2 vols (New Haven CT: Yale University Press, 1930).

Lander, J., 'A Tale of Two Hoaxes in Britain and France in 1775', *The Historical Journal*, 49 (4) (2006), 995–1024.

Langbein, J.H., *The Origins of the Adversary Criminal Trial* (Oxford University Press, 2003).

Larson, C.F.W., 'The Revolutionary American Jury: A Case Study of the 1778–1779 Philadelphia Treason Trials', *SMU Law Review*, 61 (4) (2008), 1441–529.

Larson, C.F.W., *The Trials of Allegiance: Treason, Juries and the American Revolution* (New York: Oxford University Press, 2019).

Lassiter, L.C., 'Defamation of Peers: The Rise and Decline of the Action for *Scandalum Magnatum*, 1497–1773', *The American Journal of Legal History*, 22 (1978), 216–36.

Lauber, A.W., *Slavery in Colonial Times within the Present Limits of the United States* (NewYork: Columbia University/Longmans Green and Co., 1913).

Lemmings, D., and Claire Walker, eds, *Moral Panics, the Media and the Law in Early Modern England* (Houndmills, Basingstoke: Palgrave Macmillan, 2009).

Lepore, J., *New York Burning: Liberty, Slavery, and Conspiracy in Eighteenth-Century Manhattan* (New York: Alfred A. Knopf, 2005).

Leslie, W.R., 'The Gaspee Affair: A Study of Its Constitutional Significance', *Mississippi Valley Historical Review*, 39 (1952), 233–56.

Levy, L.W., 'Did the Zenger Case Really Matter? Freedom of the Press in Colonial New York', *William and Mary Quarterly*, 3rd ser., 17 (1960), 35–50.

Levy, L.W., *Freedom of Speech and Press in Early American History: Legacy of Suppression*, 2nd ed. (New York: Harper and Row Torchbook, 1963).

Lewis, G.C., *On Local Disturbances in Ireland and on the Church of Ireland Question* (London: B. Fellowes, 1836).

Lieberman, D., *The Province of Legislation Determined: Legal Theory in Eighteenth-Century Britain* (Cambridge University Press, 1989).

Linebaugh, P., and Marcus Rediker, *The Many-Headed Hydra: Sailors, Slaves, Commoners and the Hidden History of the Revolutionary Atlantic* (Boston, MA: Beacon Press, 2002).

Loane, J.B., 'Treason and Aiding the Enemy', *Military Law Review*, 30 (1965) 43–81.

Lock, A., 'Reform, Radicalism and Revolution: Magna Carta in Eighteenth-Century and Nineteenth-Century Britain', in Lawrence Goldman (ed.), *Magna Carta: History, Context and Influence* (London: Institute of Historical Research, 2018), 101–16.

Lockett, J.D., 'The Deportation of the Maroons of Trelawny Town to Nova Scotia and Then back to Africa', *Journal of Black Studies*, 30 (1) (1999), 5–14.

Lockwood, M., 'From Treason to Homicide: Changing Conceptions of the Law of Petty Treason in Early Modern England', *Journal of Legal History*, 34 (1) (2013), 31–49.

Lustig, M.L., *Privilege and Prerogative: New York's Provincial Elite, 1710–1776* (Cranbury, NJ: Associated University Presses, 1995).

Macaulay, T.B., *History of England from the Accession of James II*, 4 vols, Introduction by Douglas Jerrold (London: J.M. Dent and Sons, Everyman Library, 1906).

MacLachlan, C.J.M., ed., *Crossing the Highland Line : Cross-Currents in Eighteenth-Century Scottish Writing* (Association for Scottish Literary Studies, 2009; selected papers from the 2005 ASLS Annual Conference).

Maher, L.W., 'Modernising the Crime of Sedition?' *Labour History*, 90 (2006): 201–9, online at http://historycooperative.org/journals/lab/90/maher.html (accessed 14 June 2010).

Manning, B., 'The Origins of the Doctrine of Sedition', *Albion*, 12 (1980), 99–121.

McBride, I., *Eighteenth-Century Ireland : The Isle of Slaves* (Dublin: Gill & Macmillan 2009/2014).
Meleney, J.M., *The Public Life of Aedanus Burke: Revolutionary Republican in Post-Revolutionary South Carolina* (Columbia, SC: University of South Carolina Press, 1989).
Miller, K.A., *Emigrants and Exiles: Ireland and the Irish Exodus to North America* (Oxford University Press, 1985).
Moots, G.A., and P. Hamilton, eds, *Justifying Revolution: Law, Virtue, and Violence in the American War of Independence* (Political Violence in North America) (Norman, Oklahoma: University of Oklahoma Press, 2018).
Morgan, G., 'Sold into Slavery in Retribution against the Nanziattico Indians', *Virginia Cavalcade*, 33 (4) (1984), 168–73.
Morgan, G., *The Debate on the American Revolution* (Manchester: Manchester University Press, 2007).
Morgan, G., and P. Rushton, *Rogues, Thieves and the Rule of Law: The Problem of Law Enforcement in North-East England, 1718–1800* (London: UCL Press, 1998).
Morgan, G., and P. Rushton, *Eighteenth-Century Criminal Transportation: The Formation of the Criminal Atlantic* (Houndmills, Basingstoke: Palgrave Macmillan, 2004).
Morgan, G., and P. Rushton, *Banishment in the Early Atlantic World: Convicts, Rebels and Slaves* (London: Bloomsbury Academic, 2013).
Morgan, G. and P. Rushton, *The British and French in the Atlantic 1650–1800: Comparisons and Contrasts* (London: Routledge, 2019).
Murdoch, A., *British History, 1660–1832: National Identity and Local Culture* (Houndmills, Basingstoke: Macmillan, 1998).
Murphy, K.S., 'Judge, Jury, Magistrate and Soldier: Rethinking Law and Authority in Late Eighteenth-Century Ireland', *American Journal of Legal History*, 44 (2000), 231–56.
Nash, D., *Blasphemy in Modern Britain: 1789 to the Present* (Aldershot: Ashgate, 1999).
Nash, D., *Blasphemy in the Christian* World (Oxford University Press, 2007).
Nicholson, B.J., 'Legal Borrowing and the Origins of Slave Law in the British Colonies', *The American Journal of Legal History*, 39 (1994), 38–53.
Nicholson, C., 'Governor Francis Bernard, the Massachusetts Friends of Government, and the Advent of the Revolution', *Proc. Mass.Hist.Soc.*, 3rd ser., 103 (1991), 24–113.
Norton, M.B., *The British-Americans: The Loyalist Exiles in England, 1774–1789* (Boston, MA: Little Brown, 1972).
O'Connor, C., 'Women and the Rebellion, Wexford 1798', *History Studies*, 4 (2003), 1–16.
Ogborn, M., 'Orality, Oaths and Evidence in the British Atlantic World, 1650–1800', *Trans.Proc.Inst.Brit.Geographers*, NS 36 (1) (2011), 109–25.
Oldham, J., *English Common Law in the Age of Mansfield* (Chapel Hill: University of North Carolina Press, 2004).
Olsen, C., *Artisans for Independence; Philadelphia Mechanics and the American Revolution* (University of Syracuse Press, 1975).

Olson, A., 'The Zenger Case Revisited: Satire, Sedition and Political Debate in Eighteenth-Century America', *Early American Literature*, 35 (2000), 223–45.

Ossipow, W., and D. Gerber, 'The Reception of Vattel's *Law of Nations* in the American Colonies: From James Otis and John Adams to the Declaration of Independence', *American Journal of Legal History*, 57 (4) (2017), 521–55.

Ousterhout, A.M., 'Controlling the Opposition in Pennsylvania during the American Revolution', *Pennsylvania Magazine of History and Biography*, 105 (1) (1981), 3–34.

Ousterhout, A.M., *A State Divided: Opposition to the American Revolution* (New York: Greenwood Press, 1987).

Overfield, R.A., 'A Patriot Dilemma: The Treatment of Passive Loyalists and Neutrals in Revolutionary Maryland', *Maryland Historical Magazine*, 68 (2) (1973), 140–159.

Pagan, J.R., 'English Statutes in Virginia, 1660–1714', in Warren M. Billings and Brent Tarter (eds), *'Esteemed Bookes of Lawe' and the Legal Culture of Early Virginia* (Charlottesville, VA: University of Virginia Press, 2017), 58–94.

Pakenham, T., *The Year of Liberty: The Great Irish Rebellion of 1798* (London: Little Brown, 1969/1997).

Papas, P., *That ever Loyal Island: Staten Island and the American Revolution* (New York University Press, 2007).

Parker, E., 'Implementation of the UK Terrorist Act 2006 – The Relationship between Counterterrorism Law, Free Speech, and the Muslim Community in the United Kingdom versus the United States', *Emory International Law Review*, 21 (2007), 711–57.

Parpworth, N., 'The Abolition of the Blasphemy Laws', *Justice of the Peace*, 172 (15 March 2005), 164–7.

Peakman, J., *Mighty Lewd Books: The Development of Pornography in Eighteenth-Century England* (Houndmills, Basingstoke: Palgrave Macmillan, 2003).

Pencak, W., M. Dennis and S.P. Newman, eds, *Riot and Revelry in Early America* (University Park, PA: Pennsylvania State University, 2002).

Pestana, C.G., 'The City upon a Hill under Siege: The Puritan Perception of the Quaker Threat to Massachusetts Bay', *The New England Quarterly*, 56 (1983), 323–53.

Pestana, C.G., 'The Quaker Executions as Myth and History', *The Journal of American History*, 80 (1993), 441–69.

Pestana, C.G., *The English Atlantic in an Age of Revolution, 1640–1661* (Cambridge, MA: Harvard University Press, 2004).

Piecuch, J., *Three Peoples, One King: Loyalists, Indians, and Slaves in the American Revolutionary South, 1775–1782* (Columbia, SC: University of South Carolina Press, 2008).

Pittock, M., *Poetry and Jacobite Politics in Eighteenth-Century Britain and Ireland* (Cambridge University Press, 1994).

Plank, G., *Rebellion and Savagery: The Jacobite Rising of 1745 and the British Empire* (Philadelphia, PA: University of Pennsylvania Press, 2006).

Pool, S., ed., *John Thelwall: Radical Romantic and Acquitted Felon* (London: Pickering and Chatto, 2009).

Potts, L.W., *Arthur Lee: A Virtuous Revolutionary* (Baton Rouge, LA: Louisiana State University Press, 1981).

Powell, M.J., 'Ireland's Urban Houghers: Moral Economy Is Popular Protest in Late Eighteenth Ireland', in S.P. Finland and M. Boswell (eds), *The Laws and Other Legalities of Ireland, 1689-1850* (Farnham: Ashgate, 2011), 231-300.

Prelinger, C.M., 'Benjamin Franklin and the American Prisoners of War in England during the American Revolution', *William and Mary Quarterly*, 3rd ser., (April 1975), 261-94.

Preyer, K., 'Penal Measures in the American Colonies: An Overview', *The American Journal of Legal History*, 26 (1982), 326-53.

Procknow, G., 'British Fascination with Ethan Allen', *Journal of the American Revolution*, 11 March 2015 (unpaginated, online).

Reppy, A., 'The Spectre of Attainder in New York', *St. John's Law Review*, 23 (1) (2013), Part 1, 1-67, Part 2, 243-90.

Rezneck, S., 'Constructive Treason by Words in the Fifteenth Century', *Am.Hist.Rev.*, 33 (3) (1928), 544-52.

Roberts, G., *The Life, Progresses and Rebellions of James, Duke of Monmouth*, 2 vols (London: Longman, 1844).

Rogers, P., 'Nathaniel Mist, Daniel Defoe and the Perils of Publishing', *The Library*, 10 (2009), 298-313.

Rose, M., 'The Author in Court: Pope v. Curll (1741)', *Cultural Critique*, 21 (Spring 1992), 197-217.

Ross, R.J., 'The Legal Past of Early New England: Notes for the Study of Law, Legal Culture, and Intellectual History', *The William and Mary Quarterly* 3rd ser., 50 (1993), 28-41.

Ross, R.J., 'Puritan Godly Discipline in Comparative Perspective: Legal Pluralism and the Sources of "Intensity"', *American Historical Review*, 113 (2008), 975-1002.

Rowe, G.S., 'Outlawry in Pennsylvania, 1782-1788, and the Achievement of an Independent State Judiciary', *Am.J.Legal Hist.*, 20 (3) (1976), 227-44.

Rushton, P., 'The Rise and Fall of Seditious Words, 1650-1750', *Northern History*, 52 (1) (2015), 68-84.

Rutherford, L., *John Peter Zenger: His Press, His Trial and a Bibliography of Zenger Imprints* (New York: Dodd, Mead and Co, 1904).

Sandberg, R., and N. Doe, 'The Strange Death of Blasphemy', *The Modern Law Review*, 71 (2008), 971-86.

Sankey, M.M., *Jacobite Prisoners of the 1715 Rebellion: Preventing and Punishing Insurrection in Early Hanoverian Britain* (Burlington: Ashgate, 2005).

Scheflin, A., and J. Van Dyke, 'Jury Nullification: The Contours of a Controversy', *Law and Contemporary Problems*, 43 (1980), 51-115.

Schlesinger, A.M., 'Political Mobs and the American Revolution, 1765-6', *Proceedings of the American Philosophical Society*, 99 (4) (1955), 244-50.

Schmitt, Carl, Tracy B. Strong and Georg Schwab, eds, *Political Theology: Four Chapters on the Concept of Sovereignty* (University of Chicago Press, 2006)

Schmittroth, L., L.W. Baker and S. McConnell, eds, *American Revolution : Primary Sources* (Farmington Mills, MI: The Gale Group, 2000).

Schwartz, B., 'Holmes versus Hand: Clear and Present Danger or Advocacy of Unlawful Action?', *The Supreme Court Review* (1994), 209-45.

Schwoerer, L.G., 'Liberty of the Press and Public Opinion, 1660-1695', in J.R. Jones (ed.), *Liberty Secured? Britain after 1688* (Stanford, CA: Stanford University Press, 1992).

Schwoerer, L.G., *The Ingenious Mr Henry Care, Restoration Publicist* (Baltimore, MD: The Johns Hopkins University Press, 2001).

Scott, J., *Algernon Sidney and the Restoration Crisis, 1677-1683* (Raleigh, NC: Cambridge University Press, 1991).

Scott, K., 'Counterfeiting in Colonial Virginia', *VMHB*, 61 (1) (1953), 3-33.

Scrivener, M., *Seditious Allegories: John Thelwall and Jacobin Writing* (University Park, PA: University of Pennsylania Press, 2001).

Shagan, E.H., 'Rumours and Popular Politics in the Reign of Henry VIII', in Tim Harris (ed.), *The Politics of the Excluded, c. 1500-1850* (Houndmills, Basingstoke: Palgrave Macmillan, 2001), 30-66.

Schama, S., *A History of Britain: The British Wars 1603-1776* (The Bodley Head, 2009) vol. 2 of *The History of Britain*.

Shuger, D., *Censorship and Cultural Sensibility: The Regulation of Language in Tudor-Stuart England* (University Park, PA: University of Pennsylvania Press, 2006).

Siebert, W.H., *The Loyalist Refugees of New Hampshire* (Columbus: The Ohio State University Press, 1916).

Smith, B.P., 'Imperial Borrowing: A Review', of D. Hay and P. Craven (eds), *Masters, Servants and Magistrates in Britain and the Empire, 1562-1955* (Chapel Hill, NC: University of North Carolina Press, 2004), in *Comparative Labour Law and Policy*, 25 (2004), 447-62.

Smith, J., *Europe and the Americas: State Formation, Capitalism and Civilizations in Atlantic Modernity* (Leiden and Boston: Brill, 2006).

Smith, J., and Mabel L. Webber, 'Josiah Smith's Diary, 1780-1781 (Continued)', *The South Carolina Historical and Genealogical Magazine*, 34 (4) (1933), 194-210.

Smith, J.M., 'The Sedition Law, Free Speech and the American Political Process', *William and Mary Quarterly*, 3rd ser., 9 (1952), 497-511.

Smith J.H., and Leo Hershowitz, 'Courts of Equity in the Province of New York: The Cosby Controversy, 1732-1736', *The American Journal of Legal History*, 16 (1972), 1-50.

Sorial, S., 'Sedition and the Question of Freedom of Speech', *Current Issues in Criminal Justice*, 18 (2007): 431-48.

Spindell, D.J., 'The Law of Words: Verbal Abuse in North Carolina to 1730', *American Journal of Legal History*, 39 (1995), 25–42.

Stanlis, P.J., 'Edmund Burke's Legal Erudition and Practical Politics: Ireland and the American Revolution', *Political Science Reviewer*, 25 (1) (2006), 82–3.

Stark, J.H., *The Loyalists of Massachusetts and the Other Side of the American Revolution* (Boston, MA: W. B. Clarke, 1910).

Stauch, T.T., 'Oaths and Christian Belief in the New Nation, 1776–1789', in J.B. Stein and S.G. Donabed (eds), *Religion and the State: Europe and North America in the Seventeenth and Eighteenth Centuries* (Lexington Books, 2012), 127–41.

Stauch, T.T., 'Taking Oaths and Giving Thanks: Ritual and Religion in Revolutionary America', (Unpublished PhD, University of South Carolina, 2013).

Steele, I.K., *The English Atlantic: 1675–1740: An Exploration of Communication and Community* (New York: Oxford University Press, 1986).

Steffen, L., *Defining a British State: Treason and National Identity, 1608–1820* (Houndmills, Basingstoke: Palgrave Macmillan, 2001).

Stoebuck, W.B., 'Reception of English Common Law in the American Colonies', *William and Mary Law Review*, 10 (1968), 393–426.

Stone, G.R., 'Sex, Violence and the First Amendment', *University of Chicago Law Review*, 74 (2007), 1857–71.

Stroh, S., *Gaelic Scotland in the Colonial Imagination: Anglophone Writing from 1600 to 1900* (Evanston, IL: Northwestern University Press, 2017).

Taylor, C., *The Black Carib Wars: Freedom, Survival and the Making of the Garifuna* (Oxford: Signal Books, 2012).

Thomas, D., *A Long Time Burning: The History of Literary Censorship in England* (London: Routledge Kegan Paul, 1969).

Thomas, P.D.G., *The Townshend Duties Crisis: The Second Phase of the American Revolution* (Oxford University Press, 1967).

Thomas, P.D.G., *Tea Party to Independence: The Third Phase of the American Revolution 1773–1776* (Oxford University Press, 1991).

Thompson, A.O., *Flight to Freedom: African Runaways and Maroons in the Americas* (Jamaica: University of the West Indies Press, 2006).

Thompson, E.P., 'The Crime of Anonymity', in Peter Linebaugh, John G. Rule, E.P. Thompson and Cal Winslow (eds), *Albion's Fatal Tree: Crime and Society in Eighteenth-Century England* (Harmondsworth: Penguin, 1977), 255–344.

Thompson, R., '"Holy Watchfulness" and Communal Conformism: The Functions of Defamation in Early New England Communities', *The New England Quarterly*, 56 (1983), 504–22.

Tiedemann, J.S., Eugene R. Fingerhut, and Robert W. Venables, eds, *The Other Loyalists: Ordinary People, Royalism, and the Revolution in the Middle* Colonies, *1763–1787* (Albany, NY: State University of New York Press, 2009).

Timmons, S.A., 'Executions Following Monmouth's Rebellion: A Missing Link', *Historical Research*, 76 (192) (2003), 286–91.

Troxler, C.W., *Farming Dissenters: The Regulator Movement in Piedmont North Carolina* (The North Carolina Office of Archives and History, 2011).

Truxes, T.S., *Defying Empire: Trading with the Enemy in Colonial New York* (New Haven, CT: Yale University Press, 2008).

Vallance, E., *Revolutionary England and the National Covenant: State Oaths, Protestantism and the Political Nation, 1553–1682* (Woodbridge: Boydell Press, 2005).

Vallance, E., *The 1723 Oath Rolls in England: An Electronic Finding List* (University of Roehampton, 2014).

Vallance, E., 'Women, Politics, and the 1723 Oaths of Allegiance to George I', *Historical Journal*, 59 (4) (2016), 975–99.

Van Buskirk, J.L., *Generous Enemies: Patriots and Loyalists in Revolutionary New York* (Philadelphia, PA: University of Pennsylvania Press, 2002).

Van Tyne, C.H., *The Loyalists in the American Revolution* (New York: The Macmillan Company, 1902).

Vaughan, T., and E.W. Clark, *Puritans among the Indians: Accounts of Captivity and Redemption, 1676–1724* (Cambridge, MA: Belknap Press, 1981).

Visconsi, E., 'The Invention of Criminal Blasphemy: Rex v. Taylor (1676)', *Representations*, 103 (2008), 30–52.

Waldenmaier, N.P., *Some of the Earliest Oaths of Allegiance to the United States of America* (Lancaster, PA, 1944).

Walter, J., *Covenanting Citizens: The Protestation Oath and Popular Political Culture in the English Revolution* (Oxford University Press, 2016).

Ward, H.W., *The War for Independence and the Transformation of American Society* (London: UCL Press, 1999).

Warner, J., *John the Painter: The First Modern Terrorist* (London: Profile Books, 2004).

Warren, M.O., *History of the Rise, Progress and Termination of the American Revolution*, ed. Lester H. Cohen (Indianapolis, IN: Liberty Fund, 1988 [originally, Boston: Manning and Loring, 1805]).

Watt, T.D., *Popular Protest and Policing in Ascendancy Ireland, 1691–1761* (Woodbridge: The Boydell Press, 2018).

Wilf, S., 'Placing Blame : Criminal Law and Constitutional Narratives in Revolutionary Boston', *Crime, Histoire & Sociétés / Crime, History & Societies*, 4 (1) (2000), 31–61.

Wilkes Jr., D.E., 'From Oglethorpe to the Overthrow of the Confederacy: Habeas Corpus in Georgia, 1733–1865', *Georgia Law Review*, 45 (2011), 1015–72.

Williams, C., 'New York's Committees in the American Revolution', in James M. Johnson, Christopher Pryslopski and Andrew Villani (eds), *Key to the Northern Country: The Hudson River Valley in the American Revolution* (Albany, NY: State University of New York Press, 2013), 48–83.

Wilson, B., *The Laughter of Triumph: William Hone and the Fight for the Free Press* (London: Faber and Faber, 2005).

Wilson, B., *What Price Liberty? How Freedom Was Won and Is Being Lost* (London: Faber and Faber, 2009).

Wilson, K., *The Sense of the People: Politics, Culture and Imperialism in England, 1715-1785* (Cambridge: Cambridge University Press, 1998).

Wood, G.S., 'Conspiracy and the Paranoid Style: Causality and Deceit in the Eighteenth Century', *William and Mary Quarterly*, 39 (3) (1982), 401-42.

Wood, G.S., 'Classical Republicanism and the American Revolution', *Chicago-Kent Law Review*, 66 (1990), 13-38.

Yirush, C., *Settlers, Liberty and Empire: The Roots of Early American Political Theory, 1675-1775* (Cambridge University Press, 2011).

York, N.L., 'The Uses of Law and the *Gaspee Affair*', *Rhode Island History*, 50 (1992), 1-22.

York, N.L., *Burning the Dockyard: John the Painter and the American Revolution* (Portsmouth, 2001).

York, N.L., 'George III, Tyrant: "The Crisis" as Critic of Empire, 1775-1776', *History*, 94 (4) (316) (2009): 434-60.

York, N.L., 'Imperial Impotence: Treason in 1774 Massachusetts', *Law and History Review*, 29 (2011), 657-70.

Young, H.J., 'Treason and Its Punishment in Revolutionary Pennsylvania', *The Pennsylvania Magazine of History and Biography*, 90 (3) (1966), 287-313.

Zook, M., '"The Bloody Assizes": Whig Martyrdom and Memory after the Glorious Revolution', *Albion*, 27 (3) (1995), 373-96.

Index

Abercrombie, General Ralph 213
Aberdeen 104
Acadians 42, 212
Aitken, James (*alias* John the Painter) 143–6
Allen, Ethan 153–4
Almon, John 77, 151
American Prisoners, Committee for the Support of 162
Anderson, C. 209–10
Apprentices/apprenticeship 28
Aptheker, Herbert 189
Archer, Richard 27
Arnot, Jean Gordon 115–16
Attainder, Act of (Grenada) 210
Australia 28, 47

Bacon, Nathaniel 7
Bacon's Rebellion (Virginia) 7, 67, 125, 126
Barbados 33, 36, 75
Barrell, John 200
Baxter, John 201
Bayard, Nicholas 30, 125, 205
Beare's Case (*R. v. Beare*) 59, 60
Beattie, John S. 34
Bentham, Jeremy 131
Benton, Lauren 3, 25, 51
Berkeley, Sir William 35
Bernard, Governor Francis (Massachusetts) 78
Bilder, M.S. 24, 27, 29, 51
Billings, Warren M. 66
Blackstone, William 5, 6
Blankard's Case 27
Blasphemy 55, 64
Board of Trade 28
Bonney, John Augustus 201
Boston Gazette 78–8
Boston Tea Party 143
Bradford, William 66
Britain, Jonathan (*alias* William Unthank) 133–6

'Britannus', *see* Curll, Edmund
Brown, Thomas 181
Buckner, William 170
Burke, Aedanus 197–8
Burke, Edmund 14, 139

Cahn, Mark D. 64
Calloway, Colin 103, 119–20
Calvin's Case 24
Canada 204–6
Caribs Black 212, 219
Caribs 'Yellow' 212
Carlisle 104, 117
Carpenter, Lt. Gen. 104
Cary Rebellion (North Carolina) 66
Chapman, Samuel 196
Charles I, King 34
Charles II, Restoration 54–5, 57–8
Charlie, Bonnie Prince (Prince Charles Edward Stuart) 13, 115
Chartism 201
Chesapeake 53, 170
Chester 108-9, 117
Church and King Mobs 201
Civil Wars, British 4
Clarke, Richard 36–7
Clinton, General George 191–2
Coad, John 98
Code Noire 23
coffee houses 83–4
Coke, Edward 6, 56–7
Committee of Safety 149, 181, 190
Commons, House of (Parliament) 8, 72
Connecticut 13, 71, 86, 126, 186–7, 197
Connor, Timothy 174
County Durham 83–4
Cox, E.L. 211–12
Craftsman, The 59, 62, 75, 84
Craton, Michael 209, 211
Crawford, Gideon 84–5
criminal tribes (India) 212
Cromwell, Oliver 4, 35, 64, 92

Cumming, William 112
Curll, Edmund 60-1
Curson, Samuel 166

Dale, Sir Thomas 66
Dartmouth, Earl of 143
David, Jacques-Louis 44
Davidson, Neil 101
De Libellis Famosuis (Edward Coke) 57
De Vattel, Emer 10, 11, 12, 103-4
Declaration of Independence of the United States 149
Defoe, Daniel 70, 96, 130
Delaware 38-9
Devereux, Walter 217
Devon 41
Dicey, A.V. 148
Doan Gang (Pennsylvania) 195
Donegan, Barbara 4
Donnell, J.S. 122
Doughty, Robert 55
Douglas, Francis 104
Doyle, Robert C. 185
Drayton, William Henry 73-4
Drogheda 4
Dudley, Joshua 133-6
Duke of Cumberland 83, 115
Dunmore, Lord 7, 15
Dutch States General 168

Earle, Peter 96-7
Eder, Markus 97
Edinburgh 84-5
Elizabeth I 54-5

Fédon, Julien 10, 100-209
Forgery 39-40
Forster, 'General' Thomas 110
Foster, Sir Michael 202, 206
Fox, Charles James 145
Franklin, Benjamin 12, 153, 166, 169
Franklin, James 74
Franklin, Richard 59, 62, 72

Gage, Thomas 7, 148
Garifuna 214
Garnham, Neal 121
Garstang 110
Gaspee 131, 137, 140-3

Georgia 38-9
Gestle, Gary 182
Glastonbury 94
Glorious Revolution 7, 8, 30, 35, 92
Goddard, William 178-9
Gould, Eliga 11
Gouverneur, Isaac 166
Governors, colonial 34
Grayling, A.C. 50
Greene, Jack P. 16
Greenwood, F. Murray 204
Grenada 199, 208

Haiti 200
Haitian Revolution 207
Hale, Matthew (Lord Chief Justice) 33, 55, 59, 200, 203
Hamburger, P. 58
Hamilton, Andrew 75
Hardy, Thomas 201
Haskett, Richard C. 193
Hay, Douglas 92
Head, Michael 150
Heath, Edward 9
Henry VIII 54
Henry, Patrick 7
Hexham Riot (1761) 203
Highlands, The Scottish 99-103
Hodgson, Richard 201
Hodgson, William 166, 168
Hogg, Quintin (Lord Hailsham) 9
Holcroft, Thomas 201
Holdsworth, William 5, 55-6
Holt, Sir James (Lord Chief Justice) 59, 60-1
Home, Lt. Governor Ninian (Grenada) 209-10
Hoock, Holger 177
Hoppit, Julian 130
Horsmanden, Daniel 127
Hudson Valley (New York) 181
Hugues, Victor 209
Hulsebosch, Daniel J. 24, 31-2, 51, 150
Hungary, Queen of 83
Hurst, W. 36

Ilchester 96
Ingle, Richard 35
Ireland 120-4, 215-17
Ireland, Church of 122

Jacobinism 201–2
Jacobites/Jacobite Risings 11, 13, 14
Jamaica 32, 36, 156, 208, 214–15
Jefferson, Thomas 212
Jeffreys, Lord Chief Justice George 60, 92
John the Painter, *see* James Aitken
Johnson, Herbert 30–1
Joyce, Jeremiah 201
Junius Letters 77, 151

Keith, Governor Sir Basil (Jamaica) 156
Kelly, Edward 70–1
Kelly, James 124, 216–7
Kent (England) 217
Kidd, Stewart 201
Kilty, W. 36–7
King's Bench 54–5, 59, 63, 69, 79, 160
Konig, David T. 51

Lancaster 108
Larson, Carlton F.W. 23, 117, 194
Laurens, Henry 171–3
Laws
    3 Edward I (1275) 59
    35 Henry VIII 6, 138–40
    Act for the More Easy and Speedy Trial of Rebels (1746) 110
    Artificers, Statute of (1563) 28
    Dock-Yards Act (1772) 69, 132, 136–7
    Fox's Libel Act 81
    Habeas Corpus (writs) 4, 26, 36–7, 39
    Juries Act (1730) 62
    Licensing Acts 54
    Martial Law, 7–9
    Navigation Acts 40–1
    Quebec Act (1774) 206
    Riot Act (1715) North Carolina (1769) 125–6, 128
    scandalum magnatum 57
    Theft from Warehouses and Shops 34
    Toleration Act (1690) 32
    Treason Act 1352, 5, 7, 9, 34, 132
    Treason Trials Act 1696, 4, 7, 36, 38, 58, 210
Lee, Arthur 142, 151
Lee, General Charles 157
Leicester 84
Leisler, Jacob 30, 35, 125
Lemmings, David 131

Leslie, William 140, 142
'Levellers' 123, 127
Levy, Leonard W. 50
Lewis, George Cornewall 122
Lincoln 117
Linebaugh, Peter 92
Liverpool 110, 117
London Corresponding Society 80, 201
Lords, House of (Parliament) 70, 73
Loyalists 175–6, 180–1

Macaulay, Thomas Babington 96
Magna Carta 26, 33
Malaysia 47
Manchester 110, 116–17
Manley, Mary Delarivier 63
Mansfield, Lord Chief Justice 77, 160
Marion, Francis 16
Maroons 214–15
Maryland 34–6, 64, 86, 118–19
Massachusetts 32, 36, 40–2, 64, 66, 69, 73, 87
McBride, Ian 124, 216
McCrae 15
McDougall, Alexander 76–9
McKean, Thomas 11, 194
McLane (MacLane), David 204
Mercer, Hugh 118–19
Messengers, King's 79
Middlesex (England0 82
militia riots 203
Mist, Nathaniel 62, 63
Monk, James (Justice of the King's Bench, Montreal) 205
Monmouth, Duke of 92
Monmouth Rebellion 7, 92–8
Montresor, John 127
Moore, John 212
Moore, Matthew 201
Murphy, Kathleen S. 121
Murray, Alexander 71

Nanziatticos (Virginia) 22
Native Americans ('Indians') 21–2, 40
New England 53, 69
New England Courant 74
New Hampshire 185
New Haven 35
New Jersey 66, 188, 193–4

New York 24, 30, 35, 68, 75–6, 188–92
Newcastle Courant 84
Newcastle-upon-Tyne 82–3
Newfoundland 32
Nogues, Charles 209
North Carolina 66, 85–6, 125, 187
Northumberland 113–14, 204
Nova Scotia 42

Oaths 41–4, (America) 182–6
Oaths (Scotland) 42
Oglethorpe, General James 103
Oldham, James 58
Ottoman Empire 4
Owen, William 8, 71, 75, 79

Paine, Tom 200
Paterson, William (Attorney-General, New Jersey) 193
Paxton Boys 125–6
Pennsylvania 11–12, 37, 66, 118, 194–7
Philadelphia 126
Piecuch, J. 15
piracy 36
Pitman, Henry 94–5
Platt, Ebenezer Smith 155–62
Pluralism, legal 25
Portsmouth 131–4, 174
Post Office (American colonies) 177–180
Powell, Thomas 73–4
Prendergast, William 125–7
Preston 108–9, 110
Preston, Battle of 104
Privy Council 29, 31, 33, 38

Quakers (Society of Friends) 34, 64–5, 81, 96, 185
Queen Anne 91
Quigley/O'Coigly, James 217–18
Ramsay, David 177, 181–3
Rawdon, Lord Francis 182
Reeves, John 80
Regulators 125
Rhode Island 29, 36, 69, 139, 206
Richter, John 201
Riot Act (1715) 11
Roatán ('Rattan') 213
Roberts, James 96
Rochford, Earl of 134
Rush, Benjamin 44

Russell, William 6, 58
Ruthven, Lord (of Freeland) 10
Ryder, Sir Dudley (Attorney-General) 8–9, 71

Sabatini, Rafael 94
Sacheverell, Dr Henry 89
Sandwich, Earl of 134
Sankey, Margaret 109
Saratoga 15
Sayre, Stephen 147, 151–2
Schmitt, Carl 10
Scotland Presbyterian Covenanters 91–2
Sedgemoor, Battle of 93–4
sedition 47–52; numbers of English cases 81–2, 186–8
Sedley, Sir Charles 61
servants 20
Seton, Sir Bruce Gordon 115–16
Shropshire 82
Sidney, Algernon 6, 60, 87
Siebert, Wilbur 185
Simsbury Mine (Connecticut) 190
slave rebellions 207–12
slaves 15, 20
Somerset 96–7
South Carolina 40, 42–3, 73–4, 111–12
South Carolina Gazette 73
Spindell, Donna J. 66–7
Spotswood, Alexander 39
St. Eustatius 166–9
St. Lucia 199, 212–13
St. Vincent 208, 212
Stamp Act 127
Star Chamber 54, 57, 59–60, 66, 77
Steffen, Lisa 10, 24, 199
Stirling 104
Stroh, Silke 101
Szechi, Daniel 111

Taunton 94, 96
Test Acts (United States, 1776) 182–5
Thelwall, John 201
Thompson, E.P. 128, 147
Todd, Anthony (Postmaster General) 178–9
Tomkies, Charles 170
Tone, Theobald Wolf 216
Tooke, John Horne 201
Tories (American) 177, 185
Tower of London 172

Transportation 111, 210–11
Treason, 'constructive' 207
Treason, Petit (Petty) 19–21
Trumbull, John 119, 162–5
Truxes, Thomas S. 41
Tryon, Governor William (North Carolina) 128
Turnbull, Gordon 211
Tutchin, John 70, 93
Tyler, Amanda 160

Ulster 216
United Irishmen 216
US Laws Alien and Sedition Acts 90

Van Tyne, Claude H. 180, 186, 195
Vanderlyn, John 15
Vattel, Emer de (see *De Vattel*)
Virginia 7, 8, 27, 35, 41–2, 64–5, 66–7, 72–3, 86, 112, 139, 149, 170–1, 212–13,
Virginia Gazette 135

Wade, General 102
Wadsworth, Captain Joseph 72
Wales 82
Wanton, Joseph (Governor, Rhode Island) 141
War, Austrian Succession (1743–8) 13

War, Seven Years' (1756–63) 23
Ward, Francis 80
Ward, Harry 181, 186
Wardle, Thomas 201
Warner, Jessica 146
Warren, Winslow 165–6
Wells 96, 98
Weston Zoyland 94
Wexford 216–17
Whigs (American) 177
Whiteboys 122–33
Wigan 108, 110
Wilkes, John 51, 147, 158
William III (William of Orange) 99
Williams, Colin 181
Wilmington (North Carolina) 187
Wilson, James 194
Winthrop, Hannah 142
Witherspoon, John 169–70
Wood, Gordon 130
Woodfall, John 77

Yammasee (Native Americans) 112
York 117
Yorkshire, North/North Riding 82

Zenger, John Peter 51, 62, 75–6

www.ingramcontent.com/pod-product-compliance
Lightning Source LLC
Chambersburg PA
CBHW072140290426
44111CB00012B/1930